Colonial American History

BLACKWELL READERS IN AMERICAN SOCIAL AND CULTURAL HISTORY

Series Editor: Jacqueline Jones, Brandeis University

The *Blackwell Readers in American Social and Cultural History* series introduces students to well-defined topics in American history from a socio-cultural perspective. Using primary and secondary sources, the volumes present the most important works available on a particular topic in a succinct and accessible format designed to fit easily into courses offered in American history or American studies.

Colonial American History

Edited by

Kirsten Fischer and Eric Hinderaker

Copyright © Blackwell Publishers Ltd 2002; editorial matter and organization copyright
© Kirsten Fischer and Eric Hinderaker 2002

First published 2002

2 4 6 8 10 9 7 5 3 1

Blackwell Publishers Inc.
350 Main Street
Malden, Massachusetts 02148
USA

Blackwell Publishers Ltd
108 Cowley Road
Oxford OX4 1JF
UK

All rights reserved. Except for the quotation of short passages for the purposes of criticism
and review, no part of this publication may be reproduced, stored in a retrieval system, or
transmitted, in any form or by any means, electronic, mechanical, photocopying,
recording, or otherwise, without the prior permission of the publisher.

Except in the United States of America, this book is sold subject to the condition that it
shall not, by way of trade or otherwise, be lent, resold, hired out, or otherwise circulated
without the publisher's prior consent in any form of binding or cover other than that in
which it is published and without a similar condition including this condition being
imposed on the subsequent purchaser.

Library of Congress Cataloging-in-Publication Data has been applied for.

0-631-21853-X (hardback); 0-631-21854-8 (paperback)

British Library Cataloguing in Publication Data
A CIP catalogue record for this book is available from the British Library.

Typeset in 10/12 Plantin
by Kolam Information Services Private Ltd., Pondicherry, India
Printed in Great Britain by TJ International, Padstow, Cornwall

This book is printed on acid-free paper.

To our nieces and nephews:
Nikolas and Monique Fischer
David, Eric, Laura, Alison, Kathryn, Andrew,
and Mark Hinderaker

Contents

Series Editor's Preface

The purpose of the Blackwell Readers in American Social and Cultural History is to introduce students to cutting-edge historical scholarship that draws upon a variety of disciplines, and to encourage students to "do" history themselves by examining some of the primary texts upon which that scholarship is based.

Each of us lives life with a wholeness that is at odds with the way scholars often dissect the human experience. Anthropologists, psychologists, literary critics, and political scientists (to name just a few) study only discrete parts of our existence. The result is a rather arbitrary collection of disciplinary boundaries enshrined not only in specialized publications but also in university academic departments and in professional organizations.

As a scholarly enterprise, the study of history necessarily crosses these boundaries of knowledge in order to provide a comprehensive view of the past. Over the last few years, social and cultural historians have reached across the disciplines to understand the history of the British North American colonies and the United States in all its fullness. Unfortunately, much of that scholarship, published in specialized monographs and journals, remains inaccessible to undergraduates. Consequently, instructors often face choices that are not very appealing – to ignore the recent scholarship altogether, assign bulky readers that are too detailed for an undergraduate audience, or cobble together packages of recent articles that lack an overall contextual framework. The individual volumes of this series each focus on a significant topic in American history, and bring new, exciting scholarship to students in a compact, accessible format.

The series is designed to complement textbooks and other general readings assigned in undergraduate courses. Each editor has culled particularly innovative and provocative scholarly essays from widely scattered books and journals, and provided an introduction summarizing the major themes of the essays and documents that follow. The essays reproduced here were chosen because of the authors' innovative (and often interdisciplinary) methodology and their ability to reconceptualize historical issues in fresh and insightful ways. Thus students can appreciate the rich complexity of an historical topic and the way that scholars have explored the topic from different perspectives, and in the process transcend the highly artificial disciplinary boundaries that have served to compartmentalize knowledge about the past in the United States.

Also included in each volume are primary texts, at least some of which have been drawn from the essays themselves. By linking primary and secondary material, the editors are able to introduce students to the historian's craft, allowing them to explore this material in depth, and draw additional insights – or interpretations contrary to those of the scholars under discussion – from it. Additional teaching tools, including study questions and suggestions for further reading, offer depth to the analysis.

Jacqueline Jones
Brandeis University

Notes on Contributors

Virginia DeJohn Anderson is Associate Professor of History at the University of Colorado at Boulder. She is the author of *New England's Generation: The Great Immigration and the Formation of Society and Culture in the Seventeenth Century* (1991).

Bernard Bailyn is Adams University Professor, emeritus, and director of the International Seminar on the History of the Atlantic World at Harvard University. He is the author of many works, including *The Ideological Origins of the American Revolution* (1967) and *Voyagers to the West: A Passage in the Peopling of America on the Eve of the Revolution* (1986).

Ira Berlin is Distinguished University Professor at the University of Maryland at College Park. His publications include *Slaves without Masters: The Free Negro in the Antebellum South* (1974) and *Many Thousands Gone: The First Two Centuries of Slavery in North America* (1998).

Kathleen M. Brown is Associate Professor of History at the University of Pennsylvania. She is the author of *Good Wives, Nasty Wenches, and Anxious Patriarchs: Gender, Race, and Power in Colonial Virginia* (1996).

Richard Bushman is Gouverneur Morris Professor of History at Columbia University. His books include *From Puritan to Yankee: Character and the Social Order in Connecticut, 1690–1765* (1967) and *The Refinement of America: Persons, Houses, Cities* (1992).

Colin Calloway is Professor of History and Native American Studies and John Sloan Dickey Third Century Professor in the Social Sciences at Dartmouth College. His books include *The American Revolution in Indian Country: Crisis and Diversity in Native American Communities* (1995) and *New Worlds for All: Indians, Europeans, and the Remaking of Early America* (1997).

David D. Hall is Professor of American Religious History on the Bartlett and Emerson Funds and Chair of the Program in the Study of Religion at Harvard University. His publications include *The Faithful Shepherd: A History of the New England Ministry in the Seventeenth Century* (1972) and *Worlds of Wonder, Days of Judgment: Popular Religious Belief in Early New England* (1989).

Frank Lambert is Professor of History at Purdue University. He is the author of *"Pedlar in Divinity": George Whitefield and the Transatlantic Revivals, 1737–1770* (1994) and *Inventing the "Great Awakening"* (1999).

Acknowledgments

Virginia DeJohn Anderson, "King Philip's Herds: Indians, Colonists, and the Problem of Livestock in Early New England," *The William and Mary Quarterly*, 3rd Series, vol. 51, no. 4, October 1994. Reprinted with permission.

David D. Hall, "A World of Wonders," in *Worlds of Wonder, Days of Judgment: Popular Religious Belief in Early New England* (Cambridge, MA: Harvard University Press, 1989), pp. 71–116. Reprinted with permission.

Kathleen M. Brown, "From 'Foul Crimes' to 'Spurious Issue': Sexual Regulation and the Social Construction of Race," from *Good Wives, Nasty Wenches, and Anxious Patriarchs: Gender, Race, and Power in Colonial Virginia*, by Kathleen M. Brown. Copyright © 1996 by the University of North Carolina Press. Used by permission of the publisher.

Ira Berlin, "Time, Space, and the Evolution of Afro-American Society on British Mainland North America," *American Historical Review*, vol. 85, no. 1, February 1980, pp. 44–78. Reprinted with permission.

Bernard Bailyn, "Worlds in Motion," in *The Peopling of British North America: An Introduction* (New York: Alfred A. Knopf, 1986), pp. 3–43, 135–48. Reprinted with permission.

Frank Lambert, " 'Pedlar in Divinity': George Whitefield and the Great Awakening, 1737–1745," *Journal of American History*, vol. 77, no. 3, December 1990, pp. 812–37. Reprinted with permission.

Richard Bushman, "Bodies and Minds," in *The Refinement of America: Persons, Houses, Cities* (New York: Alfred A. Knopf, 1992), pp. 61–99. Reprinted with permission.

Colin Calloway, "New Worlds for All: Indian America by 1775," prologue to *The American Revolution in Indian Country: Crisis and Diversity in Native American Communities* (New York: Cambridge University Press, 1995), pp. 1–25. Reprinted with the permission of Cambridge University Press.

A Note on the Texts

The essays appear here in shortened form; in particular, many of the original footnotes appear here in an abbreviated form. The interested reader should consult the originals for the complete versions.

To make some of the documents more accessible to readers, archaic spelling, punctuation, and capitalization have been modernized. Some of the colonial sources come from nineteenth- and early twentieth-century publications in which the material already appeared in modernized form.

Introduction

This volume, by its nature, cannot be comprehensive in its coverage. It treats only British America, not the colonies of France or Spain, and it concentrates on the mainland, despite the importance of Barbados and Jamaica among Britain's overseas possessions. The rich diversity of the colonial period defies summary in a single brief collection. What we have chosen to present instead is a series of texts that focus on three important, interrelated themes in the social and cultural history of mainland British North America: *community*, *authority*, and *identity*. Each of these themes is developed through essays by historians and texts from the period in linked chapters that build upon one another to provide a layered portrait of colonial society and culture.

While the pursuit of community, authority, and identity are distinct in theory, they often overlapped in practice. Colonization unsettled old patterns and practices and forced everyone involved – colonists, Native Americans, and African slaves – to reconsider and reestablish the most basic elements of their lives. For colonists, the hard work of community-building was not simply a matter of clearing ground, building houses, and cutting paths through the forests. It also meant that leading men had to assert their authority in new environments or be eclipsed by others who were more capable of doing so. It meant that colonists had to negotiate boundaries with Native American neighbors – boundaries that were as much cultural as geographical. And it meant that colonists, Indians, and Africans who found themselves in new and profoundly unfamiliar circumstances had to consider anew who they were and what their lives meant. Colonization truly created new worlds for everyone involved.

Historians' perspectives on colonization have shifted dramatically during the past generation. In an earlier time, it was common to view colonization as a process that Europeans undertook on their own. All the significant actors, events, and outcomes in that history had Europeans and Euro-Americans as their points of reference. Scholars paid little attention to Native Americans; they did not consider them an important part of the colonial story, except when they violently obstructed its progress. Nor did they regard Africans as integral to early American history. Their story of bondage and degradation made an appearance only as an unfortunate exception to the main trajectory of American history. That trajectory followed the experience of brave bands of English men and women who crossed the Atlantic, established tiny outposts of civilization in the American wilderness against all odds, and gradually, through determination and hard work, built societies that could one day stand up to their mother country in a principled defense of human liberty and self-government.

This story has a powerful and enduring appeal, and it is not entirely wrong. But it leaves out much of the complexity, tragedy, and ambiguity that make the colonial era of American history so compelling. Scholars now recognize that contact and interaction with Native Americans were central to the colonial experience. That interaction shaped the way that colonists understood themselves, their communities, and their surroundings, and it led to dramatic adjustments in colonial societies and cultures. Simultaneously, contact with Europeans unleashed disease and violence in Indian communities on an unprecedented scale, and many groups struggled simply to survive in the face of such pressures and crises. But the persistence and dramatic reorganization of Indian communities is itself a significant and profoundly moving dimension of the colonial story. Any account of early America that fails to take stock of Indians' experiences is as impoverished as it is incomplete.

Nor can the American experience of millions of Africans be treated as a minor sidebar or an unfortunate exception to the colonial story. Most of Britain's colonies struggled to acquire enough laborers to survive. In the places where labor was hardest and living conditions were worst, the mass importation of African slaves allowed the colonies to expand and the British American economy to grow. Though slavery did not take root in Britain's colonies until the third generation of settlement, it exploded after 1680. The heaviest concentration of slaves in British territory was in the West Indian sugar islands of Barbados and Jamaica, but slavery dominated the production of tobacco in Virginia and Maryland and of rice and indigo in South Carolina and Georgia as well.

By the end of the colonial period, nearly three times as many blacks as whites had migrated to British territories on the North American mainland and in the West Indies – 2,339,000 Africans to 815,000 Europeans. Their survival rates told a much different story, however: the white population of the colonies in 1780 was about two and a quarter million; the surviving population of Africans was just over a million.[1] This dramatic difference between immigration and survival highlights the central fact of African history in colonial America: the prosperity of Britain's colonies was built on the backs of an exploited population that suffered tremendous losses. Even in colonies like Massachusetts Bay that had relatively few blacks (though by the end of the colonial period, three-fourths of the wealthiest households in Boston owned at least one slave), the economy depended on slave production. Boston merchants shipped tobacco, sugar, and molasses in large quantities, while Massachusetts farmers sold much of their surplus grain and livestock to the sugar islands. Slavery was the engine of economic growth in Britain's American colonies.

Even the history and background of Europeans in colonial British America are much more complicated than many students realize. While the earliest migrants to the colonies came mostly from England and Wales, the reach of the colonies steadily expanded with the passage of time. More and more immigrants came to British America from Ireland, Scotland, and central Europe (the area that is now Germany). A smaller number of Dutch, French, and Swedish colonists were incorporated into British colonies. These non-English colonists made up almost 30 percent of the population of Britain's mainland colonies by the end of the colonial period. Another 20 percent of the colonies' peoples were African, which meant that English men and women comprised only about half the colonial population by the time of the Revolution.

The British colonies, then, were not isolated outposts where old, familiar patterns of English life were easily recreated. They brought together alien peoples in unfamiliar, challenging circumstances. Under these conditions, the basic elements of community, authority, and identity remained uncertain. Throughout the colonial period, these essential elements of society and culture were subject to negotiation and redefinition. One historian has called the story of early America a "collision of histories."[2] This volume seeks to introduce students to some of the outcomes of that collision. We hope students and instructors alike will find that it enhances their exploration of a fascinating and complex era in American history.

Notes

1   Philip D. Morgan, "British Encounters with Africans and African-Americans,
    circa 1600–1780," table 1: Population of and Emigration to British America,
    1630–1780, in Bernard Bailyn and Philip D. Morgan, eds, *Strangers Within the
    Realm: Cultural Margins of the First British Empire* (Chapel Hill, 1991), 162.
2   Edward Countryman, *Americans: A Collision of Histories* (New York, 1996).

1

First Encounters

Introduction

Markedly different conceptions of property ownership and systems of land use collided in the encounter between Puritans and Native Americans in early New England. The English understood private property as clearly bounded land that an individual possessed by virtue of a deed or title of ownership. The land could be sold or given away as the deed-holder saw fit, although the custom of primogeniture commonly ensured that land passed in its entirety from one male owner to his oldest son, keeping the property intact from one generation to the next. Native Americans, by contrast, believed that people held claim to the land based on the uses they made of it (these were known as usufruct rights), and they often arranged for different groups to share the same terrain by allocating distinct activities to each – hunting, fishing, and agriculture, for example. Indians did not believe that an individual could own a bounded piece of land in any absolute sense; instead, a person's claim to the land ended with the regular use of it.

As Indians and English each asserted their own social arrangements as normative, diverging concepts and customs of land use clashed in early New England. The essay by Virginia Anderson explores how the presence of livestock imported from Europe – the swine, cattle, sheep, and horses that settlers found indispensable – contributed to these Anglo–Indian conflicts. She demonstrates how apparently small irritations such as the trampling of a row of corn or the marking of a sow's ear manifested larger socio-economic differences that eventually proved irreconcilable and fueled the terrible war of 1675. What kinds of intercultural borrowing occurred and who benefited from them? How did the presence of livestock help shift the balance of power in the region? How did English conceptions of property rights impact Indian sovereignty?

Many English observers found Native American customs of land use primitive and "savage." Only English-style "improvements" of land, by which colonists meant the enclosure of land with fences to demarcate property lines and keep livestock from trampling crops, signaled a legitimate claim to an area. The essay by John Winthrop, "Reasons to Be Considered for...the Intended Plantation in New England" (document 1), provides an example of English views of Indian land use. Winthrop, who was governor of Massachusetts Bay Colony for thirteen years and became one of the wealthiest landholders in the colony, wrote this essay even before he migrated to the New World. How did Winthrop describe Native Americans' relationship to the land and how did he justify English expropriation of that territory? What would the Indians presumably receive in return? How did particular kinds of land use serve to consolidate a cultural identity in early America?

As colonists continued to spread out, acquiring land through purchase, trade, or by force, Indians began to change the way they responded to these incursions. In 1727, several bands of Abenaki Indians at Casco Bay (in what is now Maine) made a treaty with the English (document 2). Loron Sauguaarum, a Penobscot who took part in the negotiations, feared that the final English version would misrepresent the proceedings and the treaty's agreements. He therefore wrote his own account, in his own language, of the exchange (document 3). How does each document describe the events that led to the treaty? How does Sauguaarum's account differ from the treaty in substance and in tone? What can you infer about past interactions and current relations of power between these groups?

King Philip's Herds: Indians, Colonists, and the Problem of Livestock in Early New England

Virginia DeJohn Anderson

On a late spring day in 1669, the ambitious younger son of a prominent Rhode Island family received a letter from the town clerk of Portsmouth. Like many of his neighbors, the young man raised livestock and followed the common practice of placing his pigs on a nearby island where they could forage safe from predators. But that was what brought him to the attention of Portsmouth's inhabitants, who ordered the clerk to reprimand him for "intrudeinge on" the town's rights when he ferried his beasts to "hog-Island." The townsmen insisted that he remove "Such Swine or other Catle" as he had put there, on pain of legal action. They took the unusual step of instructing the clerk to make two copies of the letter and retain the duplicate – in effect preparing their legal case even before the recipient contested their action.[1]

It was by no means unusual for seventeenth-century New Englanders to find themselves in trouble with local officials, particularly when their search for gain conflicted with the rights of the community. But this case was different. We can only wonder what Metacom, whom the English called King Philip, made of the peremptory directive from the Portsmouth town clerk – for indeed it was to him, son of Massasoit and now sachem of the Wampanoags himself, that the letter was addressed. Because the records (which directed no comparable order to any English swine owner) do not mention the outcome of the dispute, we may suppose that Philip complied with the town's demand. The episode was thus brief, but it was no less important for that, because it involved the man whose name would soon be associated with what was, in proportion to the populations involved, the most destructive war, in American history.[2]

For three centuries, historians have depicted Philip in many ways – as a savage chieftain, an implacable foe of innocent Christian settlers, and a doomed victim of European aggressors – but never as a keeper of swine. Although the Hog Island episode may seem unrelated to the subsequent horrors of King Philip's War, the two events were in fact linked. Philip resorted to violence in 1675 because of mounting frustrations with colonists, and no problem vexed relations between settlers and Indians more frequently in the years before the war than the control of livestock. English colonists imported thousands of cattle, swine, sheep, and horses (none of which is native to North America) because they considered livestock essential to their survival, never supposing that the beasts would become objectionable to the Indians. But the animals exacerbated a host of problems related to subsistence practices, land use, property rights and, ultimately, political authority. Throughout the 1660s, Philip found himself caught in the middle, trying to defend Indian rights even as he adapted to the English presence. The snub delivered by Portsmouth's inhabitants showed him the limits of English flexibility, indicating that the colonists ultimately valued their livestock more than good relations with his people. When Philip recognized that fact, he took a critical step on the path that led him from livestock keeper to war leader.

Successful colonization of New England depended heavily on domestic animals. Nowhere is this better seen than in the early history of Plymouth Colony. Not until 1624 – four years after the *Mayflower*'s arrival – did Edward Winslow bring from England "three heifers and a bull, the first beginning of any cattle of that kind in the land." This date, not coincidentally, marked the end of the Pilgrims' "starving times" as dairy products and meat began to supplement their diet. By 1627, natural increase and further importations brought the Plymouth herd to at least fifteen animals, whose muscle power increased agricultural productivity.[3] The leaders of Massachusetts Bay Colony, perhaps learning from Plymouth's experience, brought animals from the start. John Winthrop regularly noted the arrival of settlers and livestock during the 1630s, often recording levels of shipboard mortality among animals as well as people. Edward Johnson estimated that participants in the Great Migration spent £12,000 to transport livestock across the ocean, not counting the original cost of the animals.[4]

Early descriptions often focused on the land's ability to support livestock. John Smith noted that in New England there was "grasse plenty, though very long and thicke stalked, which being neither mowne nor eaten, is very ranke, yet all their cattell like and prosper well therewith."

Francis Higginson informed English friends that the "fertility of the soil is to be admired at, as appeareth in the abundance of grass that groweth everywhere." "It is scarce to be believed," he added, "how our kine and goats, horses, and hogs do thrive and prosper here and like well of this country." Colonists preferred to settle in areas with ample natural forage. Salt marshes attracted settlers to Hampton, New Hampshire, and Sudbury's founders valued their town's riverside fresh meadow. Haverhill's settlers negotiated with the colony government for a large tract for their town in order to satisfy their "over-weaning desire . . . after Medow land." Most inland clearings bore mute witness to recent habitation by Indians, whose periodic burnings kept the areas from reverting to forest.[5]

The size of a town's herds soon became an important measure of its prosperity. As early as 1634, William Wood noted that Dorchester, Roxbury, and Cambridge were particularly "well stored" with cattle. Other commentators added to the list of towns with burgeoning herds. In 1651, Edward Johnson tallied the human and livestock populations for several communities as a measure of divine favor. His enumeration revealed that towns with three or four dozen families also contained several hundred head of livestock.[6] Like Old Testament patriarchs, New England farmers counted their blessings as they surveyed their herds.

Their interest in livestock grew in part from their English experience. Many settlers came from England's wood-pasture region, where they had engaged in a mixed husbandry of cattle and grain. In New England, the balance in that agrarian equation tipped toward livestock because the region's chronic labor shortage made raising cattle a particularly efficient use of resources. Selectmen usually hired one or two town herdsmen, freeing other livestock owners to clear fields, till crops, and construct buildings and fences. Until settlers managed to plant English hay, livestock foraged on the abundant, though less nutritious, native grasses, converting otherwise worthless herbage into milk and meat for consumption and sale. Livestock were so important to survival that New Englanders reversed the usual English fencing practices. English law required farmers to protect their crops by confining livestock within fenced or hedged pastures, but New England farmers were enjoined to construct and maintain sufficiently sturdy fences around cornfields to keep their peripatetic beasts out.

Raising livestock had cultural as well as economic ramifications. For colonists, the absence of indigenous domestic animals underscored the region's essential wildness. "The country is yet raw," wrote Robert Cushman in 1621, "the land untilled; the cities not builded; the cattle not settled." The English saw a disturbing symmetry between the savagery of the land and its human and animal inhabitants. America, noted Cushman, "is spacious and void," and the Indians "do but run over the grass, as do also the foxes and wild beasts."[7] Such evaluations ultimately fueled colonists' own claims to the land. The "savage people," argued John Winthrop, held no legitimate title "for they inclose no ground, neither have they cattell to maintayne it, but remove their dwellings as they have occasion." Winthrop's objection to the Indians' seminomadic habits stemmed from a cultural assumption that equated civilization with sedentarism, a way of life that he linked to the keeping of domesticated animals. Drawing on biblical history, Winthrop argued that a "civil" right to the earth resulted when, "as men and cattell increased, they appropriated some parcells of ground by enclosing and peculiar manurance." Subduing – indeed, domesticating – the wilderness with English people and English beasts thus became a cultural imperative. New England could become a new Canaan, a land of milk and honey, only if, Thomas Morton wryly observed, "the Milke came by the industry" of its civilizing immigrants and their imported livestock.[8]

Accordingly, only those Indians who submitted to "domestication" could live in the New England Canaan. They had to accept Christianity, of course; in addition, colonists insisted that they adopt English ways entirely, including the keeping of domestic animals. Roger Williams urged natives to move "from Barbarism to Civilitie, in forsaking their filthy nakednes, in keeping some kind of Cattell." John Eliot offered livestock, among other material incentives, to entice Indians to become civilized. He admonished one native audience: "if you were more wise to know God, and obey his Commands, you would work more then [sic] you do." Labor six days a week, as God commanded and the English did, and, Eliot promised, "you should have cloths, houses, cattle, riches as they have, God would give you them."[9]

To assist Indians in making this transformation, Puritan officials established fourteen "praying towns" where they could proceed toward conversion as they earned the material rewards Providence would bestow. The inhabitants of these communities not only would learn to worship God as the English did but also would wear English clothes, live in English framed houses, and farm with English animals. Among the goods sent from England to support this civilizing program were seven bells for oxen, to be distributed to Indian farmers who exchanged their traditional hoe agriculture for the plow. Soon the increase in livestock became as much a hallmark of the success of the praying towns as it was of English communities. Daniel Gookin reported in 1674 that the praying town of Hassanamesitt (Grafton) was "an apt place for keeping of cattle and swine; in which respect this people are the best stored of any Indian town of their size." He went on to observe, however, that though these natives "do as well, or rather better, than any other Indians" in raising crops and animals, they "are very far short of the English both in diligence and providence."[10]

Praying Indians raised livestock as participants in what may be called an experiment in acculturation. By moving to places such as Natick or Hassanamesitt, they announced their intention to follow English ways – including animal husbandry – in hopes of finding favor with the Christian God. But the praying towns never contained more than a tiny minority of the native population; most Indians rejected the invitation to exchange their ways for English ones. For the vast majority, the cattle and swine that served as emblems of the praying Indians' transformation had a very different meaning. They became instead a source of friction, revealing profound differences between Indians and colonists.

As Indians encountered these unfamiliar animals, they had to decide what to call them. Williams reported that the Narragansetts first looked for similarities in appearance and behavior between an indigenous animal and one of the new beasts and simply used the name of the known beast for both animals. Thus *ockqutchaun-nug*, the name of a "wild beast of a reddish haire about the bignesse of a Pig, and rooting like a Pig," was used for English swine. Finding no suitable parallels for most domestic animals, however, the Narragansetts resorted to neologisms such as "cowsnuck," "goatesuck," and eventually "hogsuck" or "pigsuck." The "termination *suck*, is common in their language," Williams explained, "and therefore they adde it to our English Cattell, not else knowing what names to give them."[11]

Giving these animals Indian names in no way implied that most Indians wanted to own livestock. In fact, contact with domestic animals initially produced the opposite reaction, because livestock husbandry did not fit easily with native practices. Indians could hardly undertake winter hunting expeditions accompanied by herds of cattle that required shelter and fodder to survive the cold weather. Swine would compete with their owners for nuts, berries, and roots, and the presence of livestock of any kind tended to drive away deer. Moreover, the Indians, for whom most beasts were literally fair game, struggled with the very notion of property in animals. They assumed that one could own only dead animals, which hunters shared with their families.[12]

Further, the adoption of livestock would alter women's lives in crucial ways by affecting the traditional gender-based division of labor. Would women, who were mainly responsible for agricultural production, assume new duties of animal husbandry? If not, how would men's involvement with livestock rearing alter women's powerful role as the primary suppliers of food? Who would protect women's crops from the animals? How would the very different temporal cycle of livestock reproduction and care be reconciled with an Indian calendar that identified the months according to stages in the planting cycle?

Animal husbandry also challenged native spiritual beliefs and practices. Because their mental universe assumed no rigid distinction between human and animal beings, the Indians' hunting rituals aimed to appease the spirits of creatures that were not so much inferior to, as different from, their human killers. Such beliefs helped to make sense of a world in which animals were deemed equally rightful occupants of the forest and whose killing required an intimate knowledge of their habits. Would Indians be able to apply these ideas about animals as *manitous*, or other-than-human persons, to domestic beasts as well? Or would those beasts' English provenance and dependence on human owners prohibit their incorporation into the spiritual world with bears, deer, and beaver?

Finally, a decision to keep livestock ran counter to a powerful hostility toward domestic animals that dated from the earliest years of English settlement. Because colonists often established towns on the sites of former Indian villages depopulated by the epidemics that preceded their arrival, no line of demarcation separated English from Indian habitation. Native villages and colonial towns could be quite close together, and the accident of propinquity made for tense relations. At least at first, friction between these unlikely neighbors grew less from the very different ideas that informed Indian and English concepts of property than from the behavior of livestock. Let loose to forage in the woods, the animals wandered away from English towns into Indian cornfields, ate their fill, and moved on.

Indians, who had never had to build fences to protect their fields, were unprepared for the onslaught. Even their underground storage pits proved vulnerable, as swine "found a way to unhinge their barn doors and rob their garners," prompting native women to "implore their husbands' help to roll the bodies of trees" over the pits to prevent further damage.[13] Hogs attacked another important food source when they "watch[ed] the low water (as the Indian women do)" along the shoreline and rooted for clams, making themselves "most hatefull to all Natives," who called them "filthy cut throats, & c."[14] In Plymouth Colony, settlers in Rehoboth and their Indian neighbors engaged in a long-running dispute over damages from trespassing animals. At first, in 1653, the colonists claimed to "know nothing of" the Indian complaints. By 1656, settlers had erected a fence along the town boundary, but because a stream – across which livestock were "apte to swime" – also separated English and native lands, the animals still made their way into Indian cornfields. Four years later, Philip's older brother Wamsutta, known to the English as Alexander, was still bringing the Indians' complaints to the attention of Plymouth authorities.[15]

English livestock also proved to be a nuisance as they roamed through the woods. Cattle and swine walked into deer traps, and the English held the Indians liable for any injuries they sustained. Similarly, in 1638, when William Hathorne of Salem found one of his cows stuck with an arrow, he insisted on restitution. Salem officials demanded the exorbitant sum of £100 from local Indians at a time when a cow was generally valued at about £20. Roger Williams pleaded the natives' case with John Winthrop, explaining that the colonists had charged the wrong Indians and that the sachems were outraged because the English held them personally responsible for the fine levied for their subjects' purported offense. "Nor doe they believe that the English Magistrates doe so practice," Williams reported, "and therefore they hope that what is Righteous amongst our Selves we will accept of from them."[16]

Williams went on to observe that "the Busines is ravelld and needes a patient and gentle hand to rectifie Misunderstanding of Each other and misprisions." He foresaw that endless recriminations would flow from colonists' attempts to raise livestock in the same space where Indians hunted. Native leaders, finding Williams a sympathetic listener, informed him of the "feares of their Men in hunting or travelling," for they had reason to believe they would be held responsible for every domestic animal found hurt or dead in the woods. Williams urged Winthrop to work with the Indians to contrive an equitable procedure to be followed in similar cases so that Indian hunters would not feel so much at risk from the rigors of a judicial system that appeared biased against them.[17]

Instead of recognizing the fundamental incompatibility of English and Indian subsistence regimes, colonial authorities repeatedly permitted joint use of land. In so doing, they assumed that Indians would agree that the colonists' livestock had, in effect, use rights to the woods and fields too. Indians could hunt on lands claimed by the English only if they accepted certain restrictions on their activities. Indians who set traps within the town of Barnstable, for instance, had "fully and dilligenttly" to visit their traps daily to check for ensnared livestock and, if any were found, "thaye shall speedyli lett them out."[18] The Connecticut government imposed stricter limits on Indian hunters when the town of Pequot was founded in 1649. Uncas, the Mohegan sachem, was instructed "that no trapps [should] bee sett by him or any of his men" within the town, although colonial officials saw no reason completely "to prohibitt and restraine Uncus and his men from hunting and fishing" unless they did so on the Sabbath. Connecticut authorities acquired meadow land from the Tunxis Indians in 1650 and similarly recognized native rights of hunting, fishing, and fowling on the property so long as such activities "be not dun to the breach of any orders in the country to hurt cattle."[19] As late as 1676, in the aftermath of King Philip's War, Connecticut officials allowed "friendly" Indians "to hunt in the conquered lands in the Narrogancett Country, provided they sett not traps to prejudice English cattell."[20]

Joint use was doomed to failure, not by Indian unwillingness to comply with English conditions, but by the insurmountable problems that arose from grazing livestock on hunting lands. Accidental injuries were bound to occur and to disturb colonists, while Indians resented the damage done by domestic animals wandering out of the woods and into their cornfields. The behavior of livestock – creatures as indispensable to the English as they were obnoxious to the Indians – undermined the efforts of each group to get along with the other. Attempts to resolve disputes stemming from trespassing livestock led only to mutual frustration.

The Indians were doubtless the first to recognize the difficulties inherent in the joint use of land and the unrestricted foraging of colonists' animals. One Connecticut sachem actually attempted to restrict the *settlers'* use of land that he was willing to grant them outright. When Pyamikee, who lived near Stamford, negotiated with town officials, he tried to make the English agree not to put their livestock on the tract, for he knew that "the English hoggs would be ready to spoyle their [the Indians'] corne" in an adjacent field, "and that the cattell, in case they came over the said five mile river," would do likewise. But the colonists would only assure Pyamikee that livestock would always travel under the supervision of a keeper.[21]

In another case, in 1648 in Rhode Island, an unfortunate Shawomet Indian spent five days chasing swine from his cornfields, only to be confronted by an Englishman, armed with a cudgel, who "asked the Indian in a rage whie he drove out the Swine." When he replied, "because they dide eate the Corne," the Englishman "ran upon the Indian," and a melee ensued among the disputants' companions. An attempt to adjudicate the case led to further complications, for the Englishmen involved were Rhode Islanders whereas the land where the incident occurred was claimed by Plymouth. Skeptical of his chances for a fair hearing in the Plymouth court, Pumham, a Shawomet sachem acting on behalf of the aggrieved Indians, asked to have the case tried in Massachusetts.[22]

It might seem remarkable that Pumham trusted the English judicial system at all. Yet like Pumham, many Indians used colonial courts to seek redress for damage caused by trespassing livestock. English authorities, in turn, often recognized the legitimacy of such complaints and granted restitution, as in 1632 when the Massachusetts General Court ordered Sir Richard Saltonstall to "give Saggamore John a hogshead of corne for the hurt his cattell did him in his corne."[23] Trespass complaints were so frequent, however, that colonial governments instructed individual towns to establish procedures for local arbitration lest the courts be overwhelmed. In Plymouth Colony, the task of reviewing such cases fell either to town selectmen or to *ad hoc* committees. If the livestock owner ignored their orders to pay damages, the aggrieved Indian could "repaire to some Majestrate for a warrant to recover such award by distraint." Massachusetts and Connecticut adopted similar measures.[24]

But the colonists were less accommodating than they seemed. They insisted that Indians resort to an English court system that was foreign to them, the proceedings of which were conducted in an incomprehensible language necessitating the use of not-always reliable translators. (In the case described above, one of Pumham's objections to using the Plymouth court was his mistrust of the court interpreters.) Moreover, the English soon required Indians to fence their cornfields before they could seek reparations. As early as 1632, Sagamore John, who received the award of damages from Saltonstall, had to promise "against the next yeare, & soe ever after" to fence his fields.[25] In 1640 Massachusetts law required settlers to help their Indian neighbors "in felling of Trees, Ryving & sharpning railes, and holing of posts" for fences, but this friendly gesture was coupled with stern provisos. Any Indian who refused to fence his fields after such help was offered forfeited his right to sue for damages. In addition, Indian complainants had to identify which beasts had trampled their corn – an impossible task if the animals had come and gone before the damage was discovered.[26] Beginning in the 1650s, Plymouth magistrates allowed Indians to impound offending beasts, but this meant either that they had to drive the animals to the nearest English pound or construct one on their own land and walk to the nearest town to give "speedy notice" of any animals so confined.[27]

Even if they complied with English conditions, Indians could not depend on the equitable enforcement of animal trespass laws. The coercive power of colonial governments was limited – magistrates could hardly march off to view every downed fence and ruined field – and reliance on local adjudication meant that townsmen had to police themselves. New England colonists were notoriously litigious, but it was one thing to defend against the charges of an English neighbor and quite another to judge impartially an Indian's accusations of trespass. When problems arose near the centers of colonial government, Indians could generally get a fair hearing, as did Sagamore John near Boston. But the enforcement of animal trespass laws became more haphazard toward the edges of settlement. Indians in the praying town of Okommakamesit (Marlborough) – thirty miles from Boston – abandoned a 150-acre tract with an apple orchard for "it brings little or no profit to them, nor is ever like to do; because the Englishmen's cattle, &c. devour all in it, because it lies open and unfenced," and they clearly expected no redress.[28] Along the disputed border between Rhode Island and Plymouth, settlers could scarcely agree among themselves who was in charge. Under such circumstances, as Pumham and his fellow Shawomets discovered, cudgel-wielding Englishmen all too easily took the law into their own hands. Farther away – in Maine, for example – even the pretense of due process could vanish. In 1636, Saco commissioners empowered one of their number to "excecut any Indians that ar proved to have killed any swyne of the Inglishe" and ordered all settlers summarily to "apprehend, execut or kill any Indian that hath binne known to murder any English, kill ther Cattell or any waie spoyle ther goods or doe them violence."[29]

Given the deficiencies of the colonial legal system, it is not surprising that many Indians dealt with intrusive livestock according to their own notions of justice. Indians who stole or killed livestock probably committed such deeds less as acts of wanton mischief, as the English assumed, than in retribution for damages suffered. In their loosely knit village bands, Indians placed a premium on loyalty to kin rather than to the larger social group. The strength of these kinship bonds at once limited the authority of sachems (a point lost on the magistrates who had ordered sachems to pay for Hathorne's cow) and sanctioned acts of violence undertaken in revenge for wrongs done to family members. English authorities did not bother to inquire into Indian motives for theft and violence toward animals. But when, for instance, Pumham and other Shawomets – who had previously encountered irascible colonists and ineffective courts – were later charged with "killing cattle, and forceable entry" on settlers' lands, it takes little imagination to suspect that they were exacting their own retributive justice.[30]

Once they took matters into their own hands, Indians could be charged with theft and destruction of property with the full force of English law turned against them. The penalties for such offenses further corroded relations between the groups. Unable to pay the requisite fines – often levied in English money – Indians found themselves imprisoned or sentenced to corporal punishment. Thus their options shrank even as livestock populations grew. Retaliation against the animals brought severe sanctions from the English, while efforts to accommodate the beasts on English terms required unacceptable alterations in Indian agriculture and the virtual abandonment of hunting. By the middle of the seventeenth century it was clear to the Indians that the English and their troublesome animals would not go away. The English, for their part, assumed that the solution was for Indians to abandon their ways and become livestock keepers themselves.

Some Indians – most notably King Philip – adopted livestock husbandry, though not in capitulation to English example and exhortation. Their adaptation was not a step, either intentional or inadvertent, toward acculturation, for they refused to make the complete transformation advocated by Englishmen who linked animal husbandry to the acquisition of civilized ways. The natives' decision instead fit into a broader pattern of intercultural borrowing that formed an important theme in Anglo–Indian relations during the first decades of contact. Much as settlers incorporated native crops and farming techniques into their agricultural system, Indians selected from an array of English manufactures such items as guns, cloth, and iron pots that were more efficient substitutes for bows and arrows, animal skins, and earthenware. Neither group forfeited its cultural identity in so doing, and when some Indians began to raise livestock – again largely for practical considerations – they deliberately selected the English beast that would least disrupt their accustomed routines.

Indians who raised livestock overwhelmingly preferred hogs. More than any other imported creatures, swine resembled dogs, the one domesticated animal that Indians already had. Both species scavenged for food and ate scraps from their owners' meals. Although hogs also competed with humans for wild plants and shellfish and could damage native cornfields, these disadvantages were offset by the meat they supplied and the fact that Indians could deal with their own swine however they wished. Like dogs, swine aggressively fended off predators, such as wolves. Roger Williams recorded an instance of "two English Swine, big with Pig," driving a wolf from a freshly killed deer and devouring the prey themselves. Hogs could also be trained like dogs to come when called, a useful trait in an animal that foraged for itself in the woods.[31]

Swine keeping required relatively few adjustments to native subsistence routines – far fewer than cattle rearing would have involved. It made minimal demands on labor, rendering moot the issue of who – men or women – would bear primary responsibility for their care. Keeping cattle would have either dramatically increased women's work loads or involved men in new types of labor tying them more closely to the village site. Cattle needed nightly feeding, and cows had to be milked daily. Most male calves would have had to be castrated, and the few bulls required careful handling. Since cattle needed fodder and shelter during the winter, Indians would have had to gather and dry hay and build and clean barns – activities that infringed on their mobility during the hunting season. Some members of each village would have had to become herdsmen. Losing a cow in the woods was a more serious matter than losing a pig, for pigs had a far higher rate of reproduction.

In return for a limited investment in labor, native hog keepers acquired a year-round supply of protein that replaced the meat they could no longer get from a dwindling deer population. These Indians may in fact have enjoyed an improved diet, avoiding the seasonal malnutrition resulting from their former dependence on corn and game. Swine also provided products that replaced items formerly obtained from wild animals. Gookin noted in 1674 that Indians "used to oil their skins and hair with bear's grease heretofore, but now with swine's fat." And in at least one instance Indians fashioned moccasins from "green hogs skinns" in place of deerskin. Settlers, in contrast, valued cattle for reasons that had little appeal for Indians. They plowed with oxen, but Indians who farmed with hoes did not need them. Colonists also prized the meat and dairy products supplied by their herds; although Indians would eat beef, most native adults were physiologically unable to digest lactose except in tiny amounts and would have learned to avoid milk products.[32]

Settlers raised hogs and ate pork, but they did not share the Indians preference for swine over cattle. Cattle were docile and, to the English mind, superior beasts. Swine, on the contrary, were slovenly creatures that wallowed in mud, gobbled up garbage, and were rumored to kill unwary children. Colonists named their cows Brindle and Sparke and Velvet; no one named pigs. The English kept swine as if on sufferance, tolerating their obnoxious behavior in order to eat salt pork, ham, and bacon. Most of all swine keeping did not promote hard work and regular habits so well as cattle rearing did. Writers who extolled the civilizing benefits of livestock husbandry doubtless envisioned sedentary Indian farmers peacefully gathering hay and tending herds of cattle alongside their English neighbors, but the reality was hardly so bucolic.

Settlers instead encountered Indians who lived much as they always had, but who now had swine wandering across their lands – and occasionally into English cornfields. The colonists recognized only grudgingly the Indians' property in animals and usually assumed that the natives' hogs were stolen. In 1672, Bay Colony officials insisted that Indians pilfered swine although they acknowledged that "it be very difficult to proove" that they had done so. Other explanations – that the Indians had captured feral animals or had purchased hogs from settlers – were seldom advanced. The fact that "the English, especially in the inland plantations, . . . loose many swine" and that Indians had hogs invited suspicion.[33]

To discourage the theft of animals among themselves and to identify strays, settlers used earmarks. Each owner had a distinctive mark that was entered in the town records, to be checked when an animal was reported stolen or a stray was found. The proliferation of town and colony orders requiring earmarks, as well as the increasing intricacy of the marks themselves – a mixture of crops, slits, "forks," "half-pennies," and so on – provides as good a measure as any of the growing livestock population. The earmark itself became a form of property handed down from one generation to the next. Instead of assigning earmarks to native owners, however, magistrates ordered that "no Indians shall give any ear mark to their Swine, upon the penalty of the forfeiture" of the animal. An Indian who wished to sell a hog had to bring it with its ears intact; if he sold pork, he had to produce the unmarked ears from the carcass. This practice made native purchases of English hogs problematic, for the animals would already have marked ears. Should the Indian subsequently desire to sell such an animal, he could be required to "bring good Testimonies that he honestly obtained such Swine so marked, of some English." Moreover, Indian owners were at the mercy of unscrupulous settlers who might steal their animals and mark them as their own. Colonists did not prohibit Indian ownership of swine, but they denied Indians the acknowledged symbol of legitimate possession.[34]

The Indians' selective involvement with animal husbandry scarcely improved relations between natives and colonists. To the previous list of problems new and equally vexing issues were added, including trespasses by Indian animals, theft, and difficulties with proving ownership of animal property. For settlers, probably the least welcome change appeared when enterprising Indians started selling swine and pork in competition with English producers of the same commodities. Many orders pertaining to earmarks begin with a preamble that assumes that native competition went hand in hand with native dishonesty. In the Bay Colony, there was "ground to suspect that some of the Indians doe steale & sell the English mens swine;" in Plymouth, settlers complained "of Indians stealing of live Hogs from the English, and selling them." Thus magistrates urged colonists to mark their animals to protect their property from native thieves. In fact, the charges of theft were not substantiated; the real problem was commercial, not criminal. Earmark regulations aimed at least as much to make Indian sales difficult as to make Indians honest.[35]

Competition with Indians was more than colonists had bargained for. In 1669 – just six years before the start of King Philip's War – the Plymouth General Court proposed to license certain colonists "to trade powder, shott, guns, and mony (now under prohibition) with the Indians" as a means of discouraging the local Indians' pork trade. The magistrates complained that "a greate parte of the porke that is now carryed by the Indians to Boston" was "sold there at an under rate," hurting Plymouth pork sellers. The court felt no need to make explicit connections between its proposal to sell arms and its complaint about competition, but the likeliest explanation is that Plymouth Indians were using the proceeds of their Boston pork sales to purchase guns from licensed Bay Colony sellers, tapping into an arms trade that the Massachusetts General Court had established in the previous year. If the Indians could obtain arms from Plymouth suppliers, they presumably would cede the Boston pork trade to Old Colony producers. The court expressed no particular interest in helping out Boston consumers who spurned the wares of their fellow Englishmen in order to buy cheaper meat; its explicit aim was to ensure that the pork trade would "fall into the hands of some of our people, and soe the prise may be kept up."[36]

The Plymouth government's concern in this instance testifies to a remarkable set of native adaptations. If the Indians indeed brought pork and not live animals to the Bay Colony, they had learned to preserve meat in a way that appealed to English consumers. Some colonists, noting native ignorance of salting techniques, had assumed that Indians did not know how to preserve food. We do not know whether Plymouth Indians had learned to salt as well as to sell pork, but there is no doubt that they had identified Boston as New England's most lucrative food market. Almost from the start, Boston merchants and shopkeepers vied with farmers over the relatively scarce amount of land on the small peninsula occupied by the town. As early as 1636, officials prohibited families from grazing more than two cows on the peninsula itself, and in 1647, the town herd was fixed at seventy beasts. By 1658, swine had become such a public nuisance that Boston officials required owners to keep them "in their owne ground," effectively limiting the number of hogs each family could maintain.[37] Given these restrictions, many Bostonians apparently gave up raising animals and bought meat from livestock producers in nearby towns, who were also raising stock for the West Indies market. Did the Plymouth Indians know this when they went to Boston? Their business acumen should not be underestimated. Although he did not refer specifically to the meat trade, Williams noticed that Indian traders "will beate all markets and try all places, and runne twenty thirty, yea forty mile, and more, and lodge in the Woods, to save six pence." Ironically, native enterprise met with suspicion rather than approbation from colonists who liked the Indians less the more like the English they became.[38]

The extent of native livestock husbandry is difficult to measure because colonial records mainly preserve instances in which animals became a source of conflict. The evidence does suggest that Indians residing near English settlements had a greater tendency to raise domestic animals than did those farther away. The Wampanoags, living in the Mount Hope area between Plymouth Colony and Rhode Island, apparently began to raise hogs by the middle of the seventeenth century, after some thirty years of contact with English settlers. The location and timing of their adaptation were scarcely accidental.

The Wampanoags had close contact with settlers and, accordingly, a greater need for livestock than did native peoples living elsewhere. The ecological changes caused by English settlers steadily converting woodland into fenced fields and open meadows around Mount Hope reduced the deer population on which the Wampanoags depended; their swine keeping substituted one form of protein for another. Their trade in hogs and pork may also have been intended to offer a new commodity to settlers as other trade items disappeared or diminished in value. By the 1660s, the New England fur trade had ended with the virtual extinction of beaver. At the same time, English demand for wampum sharply declined as an improving overseas trade brought in more hard currency and colonies ceased accepting wampum as legal tender. But hogs and pork failed as substitutes for furs and wampum. Most colonists owned swine themselves and – as the response of the Plymouth magistrates in 1669 suggests – evidently preferred to limit the market in animals to English producers.

Wampanoag swine keeping also contributed to growing tensions with colonists over land, creating disputes that were even harder to resolve than those concerning trade. Land that diminished in usefulness to Indians as it ceased to support familiar subsistence activities regained value for raising hogs; indeed, such places as offshore islands held a special attraction to keepers of swine. The Wampanoags' desire to retain their land awakened precisely when settlers evinced an interest in acquiring it. By the 1660s, a younger generation of settlers had reached maturity and needed farms. In Plymouth Colony, bounded on the north by the more powerful Bay Colony and on the west by an obstreperous Rhode Island, aggressive settlers eyed the lands of their Wampanoag neighbors. During the 1660s, new villages were formed at Dartmouth, Swansea, and Middleborough, while established towns such as Rehoboth and Taunton enlarged their holdings – and in effect blockaded the Wampanoags on Mount Hope peninsula.

No man was harder pressed by these developments than King Philip. As sachem of the Wampanoags since 1662, he had tried to protect his people and preserve their independence in the face of English intrusion. Over time, his tasks became far more difficult. The number of occasions when the interests of Indians and settlers came into conflict grew as his ability to mediate diminished. Since Wampanoag land bordered on Massachusetts, Rhode Island, and Plymouth, Philip had to contend at various times with three, often competing, colonial governments. Even more problematic were his relations with neighboring towns, whose inhabitants pursued their economic advantage with little fear of intervention from any colony government and no regard for how their actions would affect Indian welfare.

Philip confronted the implications of New England localism most directly in cases of trespass. Colonial governments ordered towns to address Indian grievances but could not or would not enforce compliance. For six years, beginning in the mid-1650s, Rehoboth's inhabitants virtually ignored complaints from nearby Indians about damage from livestock, despite orders from the Plymouth court to solve the problem. In 1664, more than a decade after the issue first arose, Philip himself appeared at court – this time to complain about Rehoboth men trespassing on Wampanoag land to cut timber – and even then he may have hoped for a favorable outcome. But if he did, the court soon compounded his problems by deciding to refer trespass cases to the selectmen of the towns involved. From then on, Philip and his people would have to seek justice at the hands of the very people who might well own the offending beasts.

The Wampanoag leader's problems in dealing with townsmen whose attitudes ranged from unsympathetic to hostile worsened after the colony government declared its hands-off policy on trespass and reached a low point in 1671, when Plymouth officials charged Philip with stockpiling arms and conspiring with other Indian groups to attack the colonists. He denied the charges and appealed to Bay Colony magistrates to confirm his innocence. But Plymouth threatened coercion if he did not submit to its authority, and Philip signed a compact that further eroded his ability to safeguard Wampanoag interests. This agreement compelled him to seek Plymouth's approval before he disposed of any native territory, but colony officials were not similarly constrained by the need for Philip's permission before they approached Indians to purchase land. He also agreed that differences between natives and settlers would be referred to the colony government for resolution, although the magistrates' record in dealing even with straightforward cases of trespass gave little cause for optimism.

The Plymouth court intended to subvert Philip's authority over his people in order to facilitate the acquisition of Wampanoag land by a new generation of colonists who would, in turn, raise new generations of livestock. As early as 1632, William Bradford recognized that settlers who owned animals required a lot of land to support their beasts. He complained when families abandoned Plymouth to form new towns where meadow was available, but he could not stop them. Instead, he could only lament that "no man now thought he could live except he had cattle and a great deal of ground to keep them."[39] Expansion accelerated during the 1660s and early 1670s, once again fueled by a burgeoning livestock population. During the two decades before King Philip's War, Plymouth officials approached local Indians at least twenty-three times to purchase land, often mentioning a specific need for pasture. Sometimes they only wanted "some small parcells"; on other occasions they desired "all such lands as the Indians can well spare."[40]

The need to sustain their herds drove the English to seek Indian land, and their expansionary moves collided with an urgent Wampanoag need to preserve what remained of their territory. Joint use of land, although fraught with problems, at least recognized mutual subsistence needs; by the 1660s, however, the practice had greatly diminished. Now the English not only wanted more land but demanded exclusive use of it. They asserted their property rights even in situations when accommodating Indian interests would have presented little threat. Allowing Philip to put his swine on Hog Island probably would not have harmed Portsmouth's inhabitants and might have improved relations between Indians and settlers. But what was Philip to think of the townsmen's summary refusal to share land, even when he proposed to use it for precisely the same purpose as they did? In that spring of 1669, Philip personally experienced the same English intransigence that he encountered as the representative of his people. After the Hog Island episode, and even more after his forced submission to Plymouth in 1671, he could not fail to see that while the colonists insisted that he yield to them, they would not yield in any way to him.

In an atmosphere of increasing tension, trespass assumed new significance. As colonists moved closer to native villages, the chances that livestock would stray onto Indian lands multiplied. With both groups competing for a limited supply of land, colonists did not restrain their animals from grazing wherever they could, while Indians grew ever more sensitive to such intrusions. Whenever livestock were concerned, the English ignored the Indians' property rights, while demanding that the natives recognize English rights. Indians resented encroachment by beasts that usually presaged the approach of Englishmen requesting formal ownership of land that their animals had already informally appropriated. Faced with the manifest inability – or unwillingness – of New England towns to solve the problem of trespass, and discouraged from seeking help from colony governments, Indians often resorted to their own means of animal control; they killed the offending beasts. This response would once have landed Indians in court, but by 1671 they faced far more serious consequences.

In that year, a group of angry colonists living near Natick very nearly attacked the Wampanoags of Mount Hope for killing livestock that had trespassed on Indian land. Interceding on behalf of the Indians, the Bay Colony's Indian commissioner, Daniel Gookin, begged for forbearance from the settlers, arguing that it was not worth *"fighting with Indians about horses and hogs,"* as matters too low to shed blood." He urged the settlers to keep their animals on their own land; if any strayed into native territory and were killed, the owners should make a record of the fact, presumably to facilitate legal recovery.[41] War was averted, but this incident nonetheless showed that tension over livestock had reached dangerously high levels.

Both sides now understood that disputes over trespassing animals epitomized differences so profound as to defy peaceful solution. Whenever Indians killed livestock that had damaged their cornfields, colonists denounced such acts as willful violations of English property rights – rights that some settlers wanted to defend by force of arms. For Indians, trespassing animals constituted an intolerable violation of *their* sovereign rights over their land. The problem intensified by the early 1670s, for the English were determined to deprive Philip of all means of ensuring the integrity of the shrinking tracts of Wampanoag land, even as they refused effectively to control their beasts. The issue of trespassing livestock generated such tension precisely because it could not be separated from fundamental questions of property rights and authority.

When war broke out in 1675, the Indians attacked first, but the underlying causes resembled those that had provoked English belligerence four years earlier. John Easton, a Rhode Island Quaker, sought out Philip early in the conflict to ask why he fought the colonists; Philip's response indicated that intermingled concerns about sovereignty, land, and animals had made war inevitable. He supplied Easton with a litany of grievances that recalled past confrontations with the English and particularly stressed intractable problems over land and animals. He complained that when Indian leaders agreed to sell land, "the English wold say it was more than thay agred to and a writing must be prove [proof] against all them." If any sachem opposed such sales, the English would "make a nother king that wold give or seell them there land, that now thay had no hopes left to kepe ani land." Even after they sold land, Indians suffered from English encroachments, for "the English Catell and horses still increased that when thay removed 30 mill from wher English had anithing to do" – impossible for the native inhabitants of Mount Hope – "thay Could not kepe ther coren from being spoyled." The Indians had expected that "when the English boft [bought] land of them that thay wold have kept ther Catell upone ther owne land."[42]

Because livestock had come to symbolize the relentless advance of English settlement, the animals were special targets of native enmity during the war. Colonel Benjamin Church, who led colonial forces in several campaigns, reported that Indians "began their hostilities with plundering and destroying cattle."[43] In an attack near Brookfield, Indians burned dwellings and "made great spoyle of the cattel belonging to the inhabitants." At Rehoboth "they drove away many cattell & h[ors]es"; at Providence they "killed neer an hundred cattell"; in the Narragansett country they took away "at the least a thousand horses & it is like two thousan Cattell And many Sheep."[44] As the human toll also mounted in the summer of 1675, English forces failed to stop Philip from slipping away from Mount Hope and only managed to capture "six, eight, or ten young Pigs of King Philip's Herds."[45]

The livestock on which colonists depended exposed them to ambush. Early in the war, Indians attacked "five Men coming from Road-Island, to look up their Cattel upon Pocasset Neck." Settlers sought refuge in garrison houses and secured their cattle in palisaded yards but could not provide enough hay to sustain them for long. Sooner or later they had to drive the creatures out to pasture or bring in more hay. Philip and his forces – who had a keen understanding of the voraciousness of English livestock – would be waiting. Near Groton in March 1676 "a Parcel of Indians . . . laid an Ambush for two Carts, which went from the Garison to fetch in some Hay." At about the same time at Concord, "two men going for Hay, one of them was killed." Settlers counted themselves lucky when they escaped, even if their animals fell victim. When Hatfield inhabitants let their livestock out to graze in May 1676, they lost the entire herd of seventy cattle and horses to Indians who had anticipated the move.[46]

The Indians seized and killed cattle mainly to deprive the colonists of food, but some of their depredations also suggest an intense animosity toward the animals themselves. One contemporary reported that "what cattle they took they seldom killed outright: or if they did, would eat but little of the flesh, but rather cut their bellies, and letting them go several days, trailing their guts after them, putting out their eyes, or cutting off one leg, &c."[47] Increase Mather described an incident near Chelmsford when Indians "took a Cow, knocked off one of her horns, cut out her tongue, and so left the poor creature in great misery."[48] Such mutilations recalled the tortures more often inflicted on human victims and perhaps similarly served a ritual purpose. Certainly when Indians – who found a use for nearly every scrap of dead game animals – killed cattle "& let them ly & did neither eat them nor carry them away," they did so deliberately to send a message of terror to their enemies.[49]

Symbolic expressions of enmity, however, were a luxury that the Indians generally could not afford. As the war progressed, with corn-fields ruined and hunting interrupted, Indians often needed captured livestock for food. When Church and his troops came upon an abandoned

Indian encampment in an orchard, they found the apples gone and evidence of "the flesh of swine, which they had killed that day." At another site, colonial forces "found some of the English Beef boiling" in Indian kettles. In Maine, where fighting dragged on for months after Philip's death in August 1676, the "English took much Plunder from the Indians, about a thousand Weight of dried Beef, with other Things."[50] Edward Randolph, sent by the crown to investigate New England affairs in the summer of 1676, reported to the Council of Trade on the devastation caused by the war. He estimated that the settlers had lost "eight thousand head of Cattle great and small" – a tremendous reduction in the livestock population but not enough to starve the colonists into defeat or sustain the Indians to victory.[51]

The presence of livestock in New England was not the sole cause of the deterioration in relations between Indians and settlers. But because of their ubiquity and steady increase, domestic animals played a critical role in the larger, tragic human drama. The settlers had never been able to live without livestock, but as the animal population grew, Indians found it increasingly difficult to live with them. Both sides threatened violence over the issue of livestock – the English in 1671 and the Indians, who made good on the threat, in 1675. The cultural divide separating Indians and colonists would have existed without the importation to America of domestic animals. But the presence of livestock brought differences into focus, created innumerable occasions for friction, tested the limits of cooperation – and led, in the end, to war.

Notes

1 Clarence S. Brigham, ed., *The Early Records of the Town of Portsmouth* (Providence, RI, 1901), 149–50.

2 For a detailed account of the impact of the war on one town see Richard I. Melvoin, *New England Outpost: War and Society in Colonial Deerfield* (New York, 1989), 92–128.

3 William Bradford, *Of Plymouth Plantation, 1620–1647*, ed. Samuel Eliot Morison (New York, 1952), 141; Nathaniel Shurtleff and David Pulsifer, eds., *Records of the Colony of New Plymouth in New England*, 12 vols. (Boston, 1855–1861), XII, 9–13.

4 John Winthrop, *The History of New England from 1630 to 1649*, ed. James Savage, 2 vols. (Boston, 1825–1826), I, passim; Edward Johnson, *Johnson's Wonder-Working Providence, 1628–1651*, ed. J. Franklin Jameson, Original Narratives of Early American History (New York, 1910), 54.

5 John Smith, "Advertisements for the unexperienced Planters of New-England, or any where..." (1631), in Massachusetts Historical Society,

Collections, 3rd Scr., III (1833), 37; Higginson to His Friends at Leicester, September 1629, in Everett Emerson, ed., *Letters from New England: The Massachusetts Bay Colony, 1629–1638* (Amherst, MA, 1976), 31; *Johnson's Wonder-Working Providence*, ed. Jameson, 188–9, 195–6, quotations on 234–5. See also William Wood, *New England's Prospect*, ed. Alden T. Vaughan (Amherst, MA, 1977; orig. pub. 1634), 33–4. For the choice of Indian clearings for English settlement, see Howard S. Russell, *A Long, Deep Furrow: Three Centuries of Farming in New England* (Hanover, NH, 1976), 22.

6   Wood, *New England's Prospect*, ed. Vaughan, 58–60; Samuel Maverick, *A Briefe Discription of New England and the Severall Townes Therein Together with the Present Government Thereof* (1660), (Boston, 1885), 8–15; Paul J. Lindholdt, ed., *John Josselyn, Colonial Traveler: A Critical Edition of "Two Voyages to New-England"* (Hanover, NH, 1988), 110–19, 138–41; *Johnson's Wonder-Working Providence*, ed. Jameson, 68–9, 72, 110, 188–9, 195–7.

7   Cushman, "Reasons and Considerations Touching the Lawfulness of Removing Out of England into the Parts of America" and "Of the State of the Colony, and the Need of Public Spirit in the Colonists," in Alexander Young, ed., *Chronicles of the Pilgrim Fathers of the Colony of Plymouth, From 1602 to 1625*, 2nd ed. (Boston, 1844), 265, 243.

8   Allyn B. Forbes et al., eds., *Winthrop Papers, 1498–1654*, 6 vols. (Boston, 1929–1992), II, 120; Thomas Morton, *New English Canaan or New Canaan . . .* (1637), ed. Charles Francis Adams, Jr., *Publications of the Prince Society*, XIV (Boston, 1883), 230.

9   Glenn W. LaFantasie, ed., *The Correspondence of Roger Williams*, 2 vols. (Hanover, NH, and London, 1988), II, 413; letter from Eliot in Thomas Shepard, "The Clear Sun-shine of the Gospel Breaking Forth upon the Indians in New-England . . ." (1648), Massachusetts Historical Society, *Collections*, 3rd Ser., IV (1834), 57–8.

10 Gookin, "Historical Collections of the Indians in New England" (1674), MHS, *Colls.*, 1st Ser., I (1792), 185; see also 184, 189, and Lindholdt, ed., *John Josselyn, Colonial Traveler*, 105.

11 Williams, *A Key into the Language of America*, ed. John J. Teunissen and Evelyn J. Hinz (Detroit, MI, 1973), 173–5. An *"ockqutchaun"* was a woodchuck; I am grateful to James Baker of Plimoth Plantation for this information.

12 Williams Cronon, *Changes in the Land: Indians, Colonists, and the Ecology of New England* (New York, 1983), 101, 108, 129–30.

13 Nathaniel B. Shurtleff, ed., *Records of the Governor and Company of the Massachusetts Bay in New England*, 5 vols. (Boston, 1853–1854), I, 102, 121, 133; John Noble, ed., *Records of the Court of Assistants of the Colony of the Massachusetts Bay, 1630–1692*, 3 vols. (Boston, 1901–1928), II, 46, 49; quotation from Wood, *New England's Prospect*, ed. Vaughan, 113.

14 Williams, *Key into the Language of America*, ed. Teunissen and Hinz, 182.

15 Shurtleff and Pulsifer, eds., *Plym. Col. Recs.*, III, 21, 106, 119–20, 167, 192.

16 LaFantasie, ed., *Correspondence of Williams*, I, 192.

17 Ibid., I, 193, quotations on 192.

18 Shurtleff and Pulsifer, eds., *Plym. Col. Recs.*, II, 130–1.

19   Quotation in Kenneth L. Feder, "'The Avaricious Humour of Designing Englishmen': The Ethnohistory of Land Transactions in the Farmington Valley," *Bulletin of the Archaeological Society of Connecticut*, no. 45 (1982), 36.

20   J. Hammond Trumbull et al., eds., *The Public Records of the Colony of Connecticut . . .* , 15 vols. (Hartford, CT, 1850–1890), II, 289.

21   Charles J. Hoadly, ed., *Records of the Colony and Plantation of New Haven*, 2 vols. (Hartford, CT, 1857–1858), II, 104–7.

22   Forbes et al., eds., *Winthrop Papers*, V, 246–7. Pumham had established connections with the Bay Colony 6 years earlier, when he sold land to settlers from Massachusetts; Neal Salisbury, *Manitou and Providence: Indians, Europeans and the Making of New England, 1500–1643* (New York, 1982), 230.

23   Shurtleff, ed., *Mass. Bay Recs.*, I, 102.

24   Shurtleff and Pulsifer, eds., *Plym. Col. Recs.*, V, 62; IX, 143 (quotation), 219; Shurtleff, ed., *Mass. Bay Recs.*, I, 293–4; Trumbull et al., eds., *Public Recs. of Conn.*, III, 42–3.

25   Shurtleff, ed., *Mass. Bay Recs.*, I, 99.

26   William H. Whitmore, ed., *The Colonial Laws of Massachusetts, Reprinted from the Edition of 1660, with the supplements to 1672, Containing Also, the Body of Liberties of 1641* (Boston, 1889), 162.

27   Trumbull et al., eds, *Public Recs. of Conn.*, III, 42–3; Shurtleff and Pulsifer, eds., *Plym. Col. Recs.*, III, 106, 192, XI, 123, 137–8.

28   Gookin, "Historical Collections of the Indians in New England," 220.

29   Charles Thornton Libby et al., eds., *Province and Court Records of Maine*, 5 vols. (Portland, ME, 1928–1960), I, 2–4.

30   John Russell Bartlett, ed., *Records of the Colony of Rhode Island and Providence Plantations in New England*, 10 vols. (New York, 1968; orig. pub. 1856–1865), I, 391.

31   Williams, *Key into the Language of America*, ed. Teunissen and Hinz, 226.

32   Gookin, "Historical Collections of the Indians in New England," 153; Shurtleff, ed., *Mass. Bay Recs.*, IV, pt 2, 360.

33   Shurtleff, ed., *Mass. Bay Recs.*, IV, pt 2, 512.

34   John D. Cushing, ed., *The Laws of the Pilgrims: A Facsimile Edition of "The Book of the General Laws of the Inhabitants of the Jurisdiction of New-Plimouth, 1672 & 1685"* (Wilmington, DE, 1977), 44; see also Shurtleff, ed., *Mass. Bay Recs.*, IV, pt 2, 512–3.

35   Shurtleff, ed., *Mass. Bay Recs.*, IV, pt 2, 512; Cushing, ed., *Laws of the Pilgrims*, 44.

36   Shurtleff and Pulsifer, eds., *Plym. Col. Recs.*, V, 11–12.

37   City of Boston, *Second Report of the Record Commissioners*, (Boston, 1877), 145.

38   Williams, *Key into the Language of America*, ed. Teunissen and Hinz, 218.

39   Bradford, *Of Plymouth Plantation*, ed. Morison, 253.

40   Shurtleff and Pulsifer, eds., *Plym. Col. Recs.*, III, 84, 104, 123, 142, 216–17, IV, 18, 20, 45, 70, 82, 97, 109, 167, V, 20, 24, 24–5, 95, 96, 97–8, 98–9, 109, 126, 151.

41   Gookin's comments were paraphrased in a letter to him from Gov. Thomas Prince of Plymouth. Gookin had heard a rumor that he was accused of

inciting Philip to fight against the English; Prince's letter aimed to reassure him that that was not the case, see MHS, *Colls.*, 1st Ser., VI (1799; repr. 1846), 200–1.

42 "A Relacion of the Indyan Warre, by John Easton, 1675," in Charles H. Lincoln, ed., *Narratives of the Indian Wars, 1675–1699*, Original Narratives of Early American History (New York, 1913), 11.

43 Church, *Diary of King Philip's War, 1675–1676*, ed. Alan and Mary Simpson (Chester, CT, 1975), 75.

44 "Capt. Thomas Wheeler's Narrative of an Expedition with Capt. Edward Hutchinson into the Nipmuck Country, and to Quaboag, now Brookfield, Mass., first published 1675," *Collections of the New-Hampshire Historical Society*, II (1827), 21; Douglas Edward Leach, ed., *A Rhode Islander Reports on King Philip's War: The Second William Harris Letter of August, 1676* (Providence, RI, 1963), 44, 46, 58.

45 Samuel G. Drake, *The Old Indian Chronicle; Being a Collection of Exceeding Rare Tracts, Written and Published in the Time of King Philip's War* ... (Boston, 1836), 10.

46 Quotations from William Hubbard, *History of the Indian Wars in New England from the First Settlement to the Termination of the War with King Philip*, ed. Samuel G. Drake (New York, 1969; org. pub. 1865), 83, 195–6, 222.

47 Quotation from an anonymous narrative of the war reprinted in Drake, *Old Indian Chronicle*, 102.

48 Increase Mather, *A Brief History of the War with the Indians in New-England* ... (1676), ed. Samuel G. Drake (Boston, 1862), 132.

49 Leach, ed., *A Rhode Islander Reports on King Philip's War*, 46.

50 Church, *Diary of King Philip's War*, ed. Simpson and Simpson, 133; Hubbard, *History of the Indian Wars*, 276, pt 2, 223.

51 Randolph's report is in Nathaniel Bouton et al., eds., *Provincial Papers: Documents and Records Relating to the Province of New-Hampshire*, vol. 1 (Concord, NH, 1867), 344.

Reasons to Be Considered for Justifying the Undertakers of the Intended Plantation in New England and for Encouraging Such whose Hearts God shall Move to Join with Them in it (1629)

John Winthrop

First, it will be a service to the church of great consequence to carry the gospel into those parts of the world, to help on the coming in of fullness of the Gentiles, and to raise a bulwark against the kingdom of anti-Christ which the Jesuits labor to rear up in those parts.

2.   All other churches of Europe are brought to desolation, and our sins, for which the Lord begins already to frown upon us, do threaten us fearfully, and who knows but that God hath provided this place to be a refuge for many whom he means to save out of the general calamity. And seeing the church hath no place left to fly into but the wilderness, what better work can there be than to go before and provide tabernacles and food for her, against she cometh thither?

3.   This land grows weary of her inhabitants, so as man who is the most precious of all creatures is here more vile and base than the earth we tread upon, and of less price among us than a horse or a sheep; masters are forced by authority to entertain servants, parents to maintain their own children. All towns complain of the burthen of their poor, though we have taken up many unnecessary, yea unlawful, trades to maintain them. And we use the authority of the law to hinder the increase of people, as urging the execution of the state against cottages and inmates, and thus it is come to pass that children, servants, and neighbors (especially if the[y] be poor) are counted the greatest burthen, which if things were right it would be the chiefest earthly blessing.

4.   The whole earth is the Lord's garden, and He hath given it to the sons of men with a general condition, Gen. 1:28, "Increase and multiply, replenish the earth and subdue it," which was again renewed to Noah. The end is double moral and natural that man might enjoy the fruits of the earth, and God might have his due glory from the creature. Why then should we stand here striving for places of habitation (many men spending as much labor and cost to recover or keep sometimes an acre or two of land as would procure them many hundred as good or better in an other country) and in the meantime suffer a whole continent as fruitful and convenient for the use of man to lie waste without any improvement? . . .

Divers objections which have been made against this plantation with their answers and resolutions.

Objection 1: We have no warrant to enter upon that land which hath been so long possessed by others.

Answer 1: That which lies common and hath never been replenished or subdued is free to any that will possess and improve it, for God hath given to the sons of men a double right to the earth; there is a natural right and a civil right. The first right was natural when men held the earth in common, every man sowing and feeding where he pleased, and then as men and the cattle increased they appropriated certain parcels of ground by enclosing, and peculiar manurance, and this in time gave them a civil right. Such was the right which Ephron the Hittite had in the field of Machpelah, wherein Abraham could not bury a dead corpse without leave, though for the out parts of the country which lay common he dwelt upon them and took the fruit of them at his pleasure. The like did Jacob, which fed his cattle as bold in Hamor's land (for he is said to be the lord of the country) and other places where he came as the native inhabitants themselves. And that in those times and places men accounted nothing their own but that which they had appropriated by their own industry appears plainly by this: that Abimelech's servants in their own country, when they oft contended with Isaac's servants about wells which they had digged, yet never strove for the land wherein they were. So likewise between Jacob and Laban: he would not take a kid of Laban's without his special contract, but he makes no bargain with him for the land where they feed, and it is very probable if the country had not been as free for Jacob as for Laban, that covetous wretch would have made his advantage of it and have upbraided Jacob with it, as he did with his cattle. And for the natives in New England, they enclose no land, neither have any settled habitation, nor any tame cattle to improve the land by, and so have no other but a natural right to those countries. So as if we leave them sufficient for their use, we may lawfully take the rest, there being more than enough for them and us.

Secondly, we shall come in with the good leave of the Natives, who find benefit already by our neighborhood and learn of us to improve part to more use than before they could do the whole. And by this means we come in by valuable purchase, for they have of us that which will yield them more benefit than all the land which we have from them.

Thirdly, God hath consumed the Natives with a great plague in those parts so as there be few inhabitants left. . . .

Treaty between the Abenaki Indians and the English at Casco Bay (1727)

The Submission and Agreement of the Delegates of the Eastern Indians

Whereas the several Tribes of the Eastern Indians Viz. The Penobscot, Nerridgawock, St. Johns, Cape Sables, and other Tribes Inhabiting within His Majesties Territories of *New England* and *Nova*

Scotia, who have been engaged in the present War, from whom we, Saguaarum alias Loron, Arexis, Francois Xavier, & Meganumbee, are Delegated and fully Impowered to enter into Articles of Pacification with His Majesties Governments of the *Massachusetts-Bay*, *New-Hampshire* and *Nova Scotia*, have contrary to the several Treaties they have Solemnly entred into with the said Governments, made an Open Rupture, and have continued some Years in Acts of Hostility against the Subjects of His Majesty King GEORGE within the said Governments.

They being now sensible of the Miseries and Troubles they have involved themselves in, and being desirous to be restored to His Majesties Grace and Favour, and to Live in Peace with all His Majesties Subjects of the said Three Governments, and the Province of *New York* and Colonies of *Connecticut* and *Rhode Island* and that all former Acts of Injury be forgotten, have Concluded to make, and we do by these Presents in the Name and Behalf of the said Tribes, make Our Submission unto His most Excellent Majesty GEORGE by the Grace of GOD of *Great Britain, France* and *Ireland*, KING Defender of the Faith, &c. in as Full and Ample Manner, as any of our Predecessors have heretofore done.

And we do hereby promise and engage with the Honourable WILLIAM DUMMER Esq; as he is Lieutenant Governour and Commander in Chief of His Majesties Province of the *Massachusetts Bay* and with the Governours or Commanders in Chief of the said Province for the Time being, *That is to say.*

We the said Delegates for and in behalf of the several Tribes abovesaid, Do Promise and Engage, that at all times for Ever, from and after the Date of these Presents, We and They will Cease and Forbear all Acts of Hostility, Injuries and Discords towards all the Subjects of the Crown of *Great Britain*, and not offer the least Hurt, Violence or Molestation to them or any of them in their Persons or Estates, But will hence forward hold and maintain a firm and constant Amity and Friendship with all the English, and will never confederate or combine with any other Nation to their Prejudice.

That all the Captives taken in this present War, shall at or before, the Time of the further Ratification of this Treaty be restored without any Ransom or Payment to be made by them or any of them.

That His Majesty's Subjects the English shall and may peaceably and quietly enter upon, improve and for ever enjoy all and singular their Rights of Land and former Settlements, Properties and Possessions within the Eastern parts of the said Province of the *Massachusetts Bay*, together with all Islands, Isletts, Shoars, Beaches and Fishery within the same, without any Molestation or Claims by us or any other Indians, and be in no ways Molested, Interrupted or Disturbed therein. Saving unto the *Penobscot, Nerridgawock*, and other Tribes within His Majesties Province aforesaid, and their Natural Decendants respectively, all their Lands, Liberties and Properties not by them conveyed or Sold to or Possessed by any of the English Subjects as aforesaid, as also the Priviledge of Fishing, Hunting, and Fowling as formerly.

That all Trade and Commerce which hereafter may be Allowed betwixt the English and Indians, shall be under such Management and Regulation as the Government of the *Massachusetts* Province shall Direct.

If any Controversie or Difference at any time hereafter happen to arise between any of the English and Indians for any real or supposed Wrong or Injury done on either side, no Private Revenge shall be taken for the same but proper Application shall be made to His Majesties Government upon the place for Remedy or Redress thereof in a due course of Justice.

We Submitting Our selves to be Ruled and Governed by His Majesty's Laws, and desiring to have the Benefit of the same.

We also the said Delegates, in Behalf of the Tribes of Indians, inhabiting within the French Territories, who have Assisted us in this War, for whom we are fully Impowered to Act in this present Treaty, DO hereby Promise and Engage, that they and every of them shall henceforth Cease and Forbear all Acts of Hostility Force and Violence towards all and every the Subjects of His Majesty the King of Great Britain.

We do further in Behalf of the Tribe of the *Penobscot* Indians, promise and engage, that if any of the other Tribes intended to be Included in this Treaty, shall notwithstanding refuse to Confirm and Ratifie this present Treaty entred into on their Behalf and continue or Renew Acts of Hostility against the English, in such case the said *Penobscot* Tribe shall joine their Young Men with the English in reducing them to Reason.

In the next place we the aforenamed Delegates Do promise and engage with the Honourable John Wentworth Esq; as He is Lieut. Governour and Commander in Chief of His Majesties Province of *New Hampshire*, and with the Governours and Commader in Chief of the said Province for the time being, that we and the Tribes we are deputed from will henceforth cease and forbear all Acts of Hostility, Injuries & Discords towards all the Subjects of His Majesty King GEORGE within the said Province. And we do understand and take it that the said Government of *New Hampshire* is also included and comprehended in all and every the Articles aforegoing excepting that respecting the regulating the Trade with us.

And further we the aforenamed Delegates do Promise and Engage with the Honourable Lawrance Armstrong Esq; Lieutenant Governour and Commander in Chief of His Majesties Province of *Nova Scotia* or *L'Acadie* to live in peace with His Majesties Good Subjects and their Dependants in that Government according to the Articles agreed on with Major Paul Mascarene commissioned for that purpose, and further to be Ratified as mentioned in the said Articles.

That this present Treaty shall be Accepted Ratified and Confirmed in a Publick and Solemn manner by the Chiefs of the several Eastern Tribes of Indians included therein at *Falmouth* in *Casco Bay* some time in the Month of *May* next. *In Testimony* whereof we have Signed these Presents, and Affixed Our Seals. Dated at the Council Chamber in *Boston* in *New England*, this Fifteenth Day of December, Anno Domini, One Thousand Seven Hundred and Twenty- five, Annoque Regni Regis GEORGIJ, Magnae Britanniae, &c. Duodecimo.

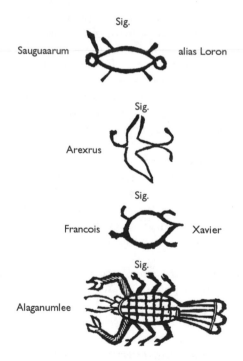

Sauguaarum   Sig.   alias Loron

Arexrus   Sig.

Francois   Sig.   Xavier

Alaganumlee   Sig.

Done in the presence of the Great and General Court or Assembly of the Province of the *Massachusetts Bay* aforesaid, being first Read distinctly, and Interpreted by Capt *John Gyles*, Capt *Samuel Jordan*, and Capt *Joseph Bane*, Sworn Interpreters.

Attest J. Willard, Secr.

Indian Explanation of the Treaty of Casco Bay (1727)

Loron Sauguaarum

I, Panaouamskeyen, do inform ye – Ye who are scattered all over the earth take notice – of what has passed between me and the English in negotiating the peace that I have just concluded with them. It is from the bottom of my heart that I inform you; and, as a proof that I tell you nothing but the truth, I wish to speak to you in my own tongue.

My reason for informing you, myself, is the diversity and contrariety of the interpretations I receive of the English writing in which the articles of Peace are drawn up that we have just mutually agreed to. These writings appear to contain things that are not, so that the Englishman himself disavows them in my presence, when he reads and interprets them to me himself.

I begin then by informing you; and shall speak to you only of the principal and most important matter.

First, that I did not commence the negotiation for a peace, or settlement, but he, it was, who first spoke to me on the subject, and I did not give him any answer until he addressed me a third time. I first went to Fort St. George to hear his propositions, and afterwards to Boston, whither he invited me on the same business.

We were two that went Boston: I, Laurance Sagouarrab, and John Ehennekouit. On arriving there I did indeed salute him in the usual mode at the first interview, but I was not the first to speak to him. I only answered what he said to me, and such was the course I observed throughout the whole of our interview.

He began by asking me, what brought me hither? I did not give him for answer – I am come to ask your pardon; nor, I come to acknowledge you as my conqueror; nor, I come to make my submission to you; nor, I come to receive your commands. All the answer I made was that I was come on his invitation to me to hear the propositions for a settlement that he wished to submit to me.

Wherefore do we kill one another? he again asked me. 'Tis true that, in reply, I said to him – You are right. But I did not say to him, I acknowledge myself the cause of it, nor I condemn myself for having made war on him.

He next said to me – Propose what must be done to make us friends. 'Tis true that thereupon I answered him – It is rather for you to do that.

And my reason for giving him that answer is, that having himself spoken to me of an arrangement, I did not doubt but he would make me some advantageous proposals. But I did not tell him that I would submit in every respect to his orders.

Thereupon, he said to me – Let us observe the treaties concluded by our Fathers, and renew the ancient friendship which existed between us. I made him no answer thereunto; much less, I repeat, did I, become his subject, or give him my land, or acknowledge his King as my King. This I never did, and he never proposed it to me. I say, he never said to me – Give thyself and thy land to me, nor acknowledge my King for thy King, as thy ancestors formerly did.

He again said to me – But do you not recognize the King of England as King over all his states? To which I answered – Yes, I recognize him King of all his lands; but I rejoined, do not hence infer that I acknowledge thy King as my King, and King of my lands. Here lies my distinction – my Indian distinction. God hath willed that I have no King, and that I be master of my lands in common.

He again asked me – Do you not admit that I am at least master of the lands I have purchased? I answered him thereupon, that I admit nothing, and that I knew not what he had reference to.

He again said to me – If, hereafter, any one desire to disturb the negotiation of the peace we are at present engaged about, we will join together to arrest him. I again consented to that. But I did not say to him, and do not understand that he said to me, that we should go in company to attack such person, or that we should form a joint league, offensive and defensive, or that I should unite my Brethren to his. I said to him only, and I understand him to say to me, that if any one wished to disturb our negotiation of Peace, we would both endeavor to pacify him by fair words, and to that end would direct all our efforts.

He again said to me – In order that the peace we would negotiate be permanent, should any private quarrel arise hereafter between Indians and Englishmen, they must not take justice into their own hands, nor do any thing, the one to the other. It shall be the business of us Chiefs to decide. I again agreed with him on that article, but I did not understand that he alone should be judge. I understood only that he should judge his people, and that I would judge mine.

Finally he said to me – There's our peace concluded; we have regulated every thing.

I replied that nothing had been yet concluded, and that it was necessary that our acts should be approved in a general assembly. For the present, an armistice is sufficient. I again said to him – I now go to inform all my relatives of what has passed between us, and will afterwards come and report to you what they'll say to me. Then he agreed in opinion with me.

Such was my negotiation on my first visit to Boston.

As for any act of grace, or amnesty, accorded to me by the Englishman, on the part of his King, it is what I have no knowledge of, and what the Englishman never spoke to me about, and what I never asked him for.

On my second visit to Boston we were four: I, Laurence Sagourrab, Alexis, François Xavier and Migounambé. I went there merely to tell the English that all my nation approved the cessation of hostilities, and the negotiation of peace, and even then we agreed on the time and place of meeting to discuss it. That place was Caskebay, and the time after Corpus Christi.

Two conferences were held at Caskebay. Nothing was done at these two conferences except to read the articles above reported. Every thing I agreed to was approved and ratified, and on these conditions was the peace concluded.

One point only did I regulate at Caskebay. This was to permit the Englishman to keep a store at St. Georges; but a store only, and not to build any other house, nor erect a fort there, and I did not give him the land.

These are the principal matters that I wished to communicate to you who are spread all over the earth. What I tell you now is the truth. If, then, any one should produce any writing that makes me speak otherwise, pay no attention to it, for I know not what I am made to say in another language, but I know well what I say in my own. And in testimony that I say things as they are, I have signed the present Minute which I wish to be authentic and to remain for ever.

Further Reading

Cronon, William, *Changes in the Land: Indians, Colonists, and the Ecology of New England.* New York: Hill and Wang, 1983.

Crosby, Alfred, *Ecological Imperialism: The Biological Expansion of Europe, 900–1900.* New York: Cambridge University Press, 1986.

Gleach, Frederic W., *Powhatan's World and Colonial Virginia: A Conflict of Cultures.* Lincoln: University of Nebraska Press, 1997.

Jennings, Francis, *The Invasion of America: Indians, Colonialism, and the Cant of Conquest.* New York: W. W. Norton, 1976.

Kupperman, Karen, *Indians and English: Facing Off in Early America.* Ithaca: Cornell University Press, 2000.

Mancall, Peter C. and James Merrell (eds.), *American Encounters: Natives and Newcomers from European Contact to Indian Removal, 1500–1850.* New York: Routledge, 2000.

Oberg, Michael Leroy, *Dominion and Civility: English Imperialism and Native America, 1585–1685*. Ithaca: Cornell University Press, 1999.

O'Brien, Jean M., *Dispossession by Degrees: Indian Land and Identity in Natick, Massachusetts, 1650–1790*. New York: Cambridge University Press, 1997.

Plane, Ann Marie, *Colonial Intimacies: Indian Marriage in Early New England*. Ithaca: Cornell University Press, 2000.

Richter, Daniel K., *The Ordeal of the Longhouse: The Peoples of the Iroquois League in the Era of European Colonization*. Chapel Hill: University of North Carolina Press, 1992.

Salisbury, Neal, *Manitou and Providence: Indians, Europeans, and the Making of New England, 1500–1643*. New York: Oxford University Press, 1982.

2

Puritan Culture

Introduction

New Englanders, like their European counterparts, witnessed wonders, saw strange apparitions, and believed that portents had supernatural causes. Theirs was a world suffused with mystery and magic. As David Hall explains, the uncanny and incomprehensible was, in a sense, commonplace, and the difficulty lay not in distinguishing between "real" and "false" visions, but rather in knowing whether the source of any given wonder was evil or divine. Hall's essay on the eclectic and synthetic beliefs of Puritan New Englanders shows how ordinary men and women as well as their ministers looked to omens and wonders as signposts for the direction they should take as a corporate entity. Since the success of their community depended on the piety of each and every member, their godly experiment was threatened from within as well as from outside forces. They believed that mysterious signs could be interpreted to help them uncover the sources of social disorder and distress. How did Puritans make sense of tensions in their midst? How did belief in the supernatural help them define who was included and who was excluded from their community of believers?

The Puritans who sailed to Massachusetts in 1630 sought to establish a new kind of community, one based on the tenets of Calvinism and committed to becoming the perfect exemplar of God's will. Puritans believed that human frailty could only be redeemed by God's grace, and that – although most people were too worldly, fickle, and vain to be saved – true believers could, with vigilant introspection and constant defiance of temptation, hope to find within themselves evidence that they were among the small group of the "elect" who were saved. (As Calvinists they believed in predestination, i.e. that God had already and irrevocably chosen their individual fates.) While this outlook may seem rather bleak today, Puritans were devoted to establishing a community of mutual responsibility and love to which all members would contribute meaningfully and with dignity. They would cast aside all arrogance and greed and infuse every moment with the intent to live as they believed God wanted them to. Puritans hoped this community would serve as a stellar example to those back in England, and that members of the Anglican Church would be inspired to reform their corrupt practices and purify their beliefs. This new and pure community would be closely bound together by their shared faith and by their solemn and binding agreement with God (which they called a covenant) to create a just, harmonious, and god-fearing society. Such was the dream, and before the first Puritan settlers had even anchored the *Arbella*, John Winthrop gave a speech that outlined this ideal community. Called a "Model of Christian Charity" (document 1, below), this speech served as a blueprint for the future colony. How does Winthrop describe this model community? What are the prescribed relations between the people in this commonwealth? What social customs will the Puritans keep and what arrangements will they change? According to Winthrop, why is this experiment so important, and what will happen if it fails?

The vision of a beloved community was an ideal, and social tension and conflict beset the Massachusetts Bay Colony from the start. Shared responsibility for the outcome of this utopian experiment led Puritans to insist upon religious and social conformity, and when dissenters like Roger Williams and Anne Hutchinson expressed their criticism of orthodox Puritan ministers in the 1630s, they were expelled from the community. Hutchinson's regular meetings, in which she preached to men and women alike and criticized the Puritan clergy, represented an especially egregious transgression, since women were meant to be submissive and obedient helpmeets to men and to defer to male authority in the household. Women less visionary than Hutchinson could also present a challenge to Puritan gender norms. Brought to court to explain themselves, they showed varying degrees of repentance for unruly behavior and speech. Mrs. Lucy Brewster was one such woman; her irreverent talk landed her in the courtroom of New Haven colony in 1646. What, exactly, had her neighbors found objectionable? What can we infer about Brewster's social position in the community and how were local relations acted out in contests over words? How were social and religious mores intertwined? Brewster was eventually fined for her misconduct. What does her court case tell us about tensions within the Puritan community?

In Salem in 1692, fears of sorcery fell on fertile ground, resulting in a flurry of accusations and the eventual hanging of 19 women. The transcript of the trial of Susanna Martin (document 3) shows what kind of behavior could lead to an accusation of witchcraft. She pleaded not guilty but was hanged on July 19, 1692. What evidence was brought against Martin? What kinds of speech was she accused of and how might prescriptions of female subservience have made such speech especially intolerable? How did men in the community reestablish their authority over "wayward" women?

A World of Wonders

David D. Hall

The people of seventeenth-century New England lived in an enchanted universe. Theirs was a world of wonders. Ghosts came to people in the night, and trumpets blared, though no one saw the trumpeters. Nor could people see the lines of force that made a "long staff dance up and

down in the chimney" of William Morse's house in Newbury. In this
enchanted world, the sky on a "clear day" could fill with "many companies of armed men in the air, clothed in light-colored garments, and
the commander in sad [somber]." The townsfolk of New Haven saw a
phantom ship sail regally into the harbor. An old man in Lynn espied

> a strange black cloud in which after some space he saw a man in arms
> complete standing with his legs straddling and having a pike in his hands
> which he held across his breast . . . After a while the man vanished in whose
> room appeared a spacious ship seeming under sail though she kept the
> same station.

Voices spoke from heaven and children from their cradles.[1]

All of these events were "wonders" to the colonists, events betokening
the presence of the supernatural. Some wonders were like miracles in
being demonstrations of God's power to suspend or interrupt the laws of
nature. The providence of God was "wonder-working" in making manifest the reach of his sovereignty; such acts of "special providence"
represented God's clearer and more explicit than usual intervention
into the affairs of man. But he was not alone in having supernatural
power. The events that Cotton Mather described in *Wonders of the
Invisible World* were the handiwork of Satan and his minions. A wonder
was also any event people perceived as disrupting the normal order of
things – a deformity of nature such as a "monster" birth, a storm or
devastating fire. Always, wonders evidenced the will of God.[2]

Many of the colonists experienced such wonders. Many also read
about or were told stories of them. There was nothing odd about this
practice. Everywhere in Europe people were observing the same kinds of
portents and telling the same kinds of stories. Everywhere these stories
drew upon a lore of wonders rooted in the Bible and antiquity. Chaucer
used this lore in *The Canterbury Tales*, as did the fourteenth-century
author of *The Golden Legend*, a collection of saints' lives. Whenever the
colonists spoke or wrote of wonders, they relied on an old tradition;
theirs was a borrowed language.

The transmitters of this language were the London printers and booksellers, who churned out tales of wonders in abundance. Portents and
prodigies were the stuff of scores of English printed broadsides. "Strange
news from Brotherton," announced a broadside ballad of 1648 that told
of wheat that rained down from the sky. "A wonder of wonders" of 1663
concerned an invisible drummer boy who banged his drum about the
streets of Tidworth. In "Strange and true news from Westmoreland," a
tale of murder ended with the Devil pointing out the guilty person.
Newssheets, which began appearing with some regularity in the 1620s,

carried tales of other marvels. Pamphlets contained reports of children speaking preternaturally and offered *Strange and wonderful News . . . of certain dreadfull Apparitions*. The yearly almanacs weighed in with their accounts of mystic forces emanating from the stars and planets.[3]

The same events occur repeatedly. Tales of witchcraft and the Devil, of comets, hailstorms, monster births, and apparitions – these were some of the most commonplace. "Murder will out," as supernatural forces intervened to indicate the guilty. The earth could open up and swallow persons who told lies. "Many are the wonders which have lately happened," declared the man who compiled *A Miracle, of Miracles*,

> as of sodaine and strange death upon perjured persons, strange sights in the Ayre, strange births on the Earth, Earthquakes, Commets, and fierie Impressions, with the execution of God himselfe from his holy fire in heaven, on the wretched man and his wife, at Holnhurst. . . .

A single ballad spoke of blazing stars, monstrous births, a rainstorm of blood, lightning, rainbows, and the sound of great guns. Others told of dreams and prophecies that bore upon the future of kings and countries. Almanacs and other astrological compendia reported similar events: comets, eclipses, joined fetuses, infants speaking.[4]

All of these were inexpensive forms of print. Hawked by peddlers and hung up in stalls for everyone to see and gape at, they reached people who were barely literate as well as readers of more means and schooling. The stories they contained turn up as well in books that ran to several hundred pages. Big books, perhaps in the grand format of the folio, were costly and had authors who announced themselves as of the learned. But these differences in form and audience did not extend to the contents. The lore of portents and prodigies appeared in such massive books as Thomas Beard's *The Theatre of Gods Judgements* as in the cheapest pamphlet.

Thomas Beard was a graduate of Cambridge. Schoolteacher and ordained minister, late in the reign of Queen Elizabeth he published *The Theatre of Gods Judgements* (1597). Three more editions followed, the last of these in 1648. That same year Samuel Clarke, like Beard a Cambridge graduate and a minister turned nonconformist after 1662, brought out *A Mirrour or Looking Glasse both for Saints, and Sinners, Held forth in about two thousand Examples: Wherein is presented, as Gods Wonderful Mercies to the one, so his severe Judgments against the other*. Clarke's *Examples* (to call it by the title the colonists would use) went through five editions, the final one appearing in 1671. The sequel to his book was William Turner's folio *Compleat History of the Most Remarkable Providences, both of Judgement and Mercy, which have hapned in this Present Age*

(1697). To this series should be added another Elizabethan work, Stephen Batman's *The Doome warning all men to Judgmente: Wherein are contayned for the most parte all the straunge Prodigies hapned in the Worlde* (1581).

As in the ballads and the chapbooks, so in these folios nature offered up innumerable signs of supernatural intervention:

> Now according to the variety and diversity of mens offences, the Lord in his most just and admirable judgement, useth diversity of punishments: ... sometimes correcting them ... by stormes and tempests, both by sea and land; other times by lightning, haile, and deluge of waters ... and not seldome by remedilesse and sudden fires, heaven and earth, and all the elements being armed with an invincible force, to take vengeance upon such as are traytors and rebels against God.

Earthquakes, multiple suns, strange lights in the sky, rainbows, sudden deaths, monstrous births – these were other frequent signs or signals.[5]

Like the ballad writers, Beard and Batman reported events that often ran to violence: rats that ate a man, a crow whose dung struck someone dead, the agonies of martyrs. In one or another of these books, we learn of dreams and prophecies, of crimes detected by some form of sympathetic magic, of thieves who rot away, of armed men in the sky.[6] Much too was made of Satan. He offered compacts to young men in need of money, though also serving as God's agent for inflicting vengeance. Many tales revolved around the curse "The Devil take you," and its surprising consequences:

> Not long since a Cavalier in Salisbury in the middest of his health-drinking and carrousing in a Tavern, drank a health to the Devil, saying, That if the devil would not come, and pledge him, he would not believe that there was either God or devil: whereupon his companions strucken with horror, hastened out of the room, and presently after hearing a hideous noise, and smelling a stinking savour, the Vintner ran up into the Chamber: and coming in, he missed his guest, and found the window broken, the Iron barre in it bowed, and all bloody, but the man was never heard of afterwards.

The Devil wore a range of guises. Black bears, a favorite of the ballad writers, turn up again in stories told by Beard and Batman, as do black dogs.[7]

In telling of these wonders, the men who organized the great collections borrowed from the broadside and the chapbook; thus, a ballad tale of someone swallowed up into the ground appeared in Clarke's *Examples* and again in Turner's *Compleat History*.[8] This flow of stories meant that "learned" men accorded credibility to wonders as readily as any of the ballad writers. The one format was employed by the learned, the other by commercial printers and their literary hacks. But each participated in a common culture, a lore that linked small books and great, the reader of the ballad and the reader of the folio.

This was a lore that other Europeans were collecting and reporting in the sixteenth and seventeenth centuries, ... Many of these continental stories were retold in England. Certain ballads were translated or adapted from a foreign source. Thomas Beard described *The Theatre of Gods Judgements* as "translated from the French." Batman's *Doome* was a translation of Conrad Lycosthenes's *De prodigiis liber* (1552), itself a new edition of a second-century text, Julius Obsequens's *Prodigiorum liber*. Whatever the specific source, the English writers culled most of their materials from printed books that subsumed the sweep of western culture.[9] The classical and early Christian sources included Virgil, Pliny, Plutarch, Seneca, Cicero, Josephus (a favorite), Gildas, Eusebius, and Bede. The Middle Ages yielded chronicles and compilations of exempla. The sixteenth and seventeenth centuries supplied a fresh group of chronicles and encyclopedias: the *Magdeburg Centuries*, the *Chronicles* of Hollingshead, and collections (some more critical than others) by such writers as Polydore Vergil, Sleiden, Camden, and Heylin. No work was more important to the English than John Foxe's *Acts and Monuments*, itself a résumé of narratives and chronicles extending back to Eusebius. A final source was that great wonder book the Bible. Its narratives of visions, voices, witches, and strange deaths lent credence to such stories of a later date.[10]

All of this borrowing enriched the lore of wonders with the debris of much older systems of ideas. To be sure, Beard, Batman, and their successors made modest efforts to be critical. As Protestants they followed Foxe's lead in dropping from their histories the visions, cures, and other miracles found in legends of the saints. As Christians, they rejected divination and believed that God had ceased to issue revelations. But otherwise the English writers were willing to retell the stories that descended to them from the Middle Ages and antiquity. No one questioned the accuracy of Pliny's *Natural History* and its kin, to which, in fact, these men conceded an unusual authority. The parting of the ways between the "ancients" and the "moderns" was yet to occur. Ancient and modern, Christian and non-Christian, Catholic and Protestant, high and low – these great lines of cleavage had but little impact on the lore of wonders. In conceding so much to their sources, whether classical or of the early Church or even of the Middle Ages, Beard and Clarke admitted to their pages a strange mixture of ideas and themes. This was a mixture that requires closer scrutiny, for the stories in these books were charged with several meanings.

Much of this great mass of materials was compounded out of four main systems of ideas – apocalypticism, astrology, natural history, and the meteorology of the Greeks. Each of these systems was in decay or disrepute by the middle of the seventeenth century, under challenge either from an alternative, more up-to-date science or from a growing disenchantment with prophetic visionaries. But even in decay these systems continued to give meaning to the wonder tales.

The most widely used of these traditions was the meteorology of the Greeks and Romans. In Aristotle's physics, meteorology referred to everything occurring in the region between the earth and moon, a region that encompassed blazing stars, comets (deemed to circle earth below the moon), rainbows, lightning, and thunder as well as fanciful or misinterpreted phenomena like apparitions in the sky. After Aristotle, the key student of this science was Pliny, whose *Natural History* "embellished Aristotle's rational theory with many elements of wonder and even superstition." Pliny was available in English translation by the 1560s, and most other major Roman writers who spoke of meteors – Seneca, Plutarch, Virgil – had been Englished by the early seventeenth century. But English readers learned of blazing stars and comets chiefly from translations of medieval and Renaissance encyclopedias, or from a widely selling English version of Du Bartas's *La Sepmaine*.[11]

No less commonplace to most Elizabethans was astrology, the science of celestial bodies. Elizabethans learned their astrology from a medley of medieval and Renaissance handbooks. These books taught a Christian version of the science, affirming that the stars and planets had no independent power but depended on the will of God. The key vehicle (as we have seen already) was the almanacs and their "prognostications." Predictions of the weather were another means of spreading astrological ideas and images.[12]

A third intellectual tradition was apocalyptic prophecy. Several different strands converged to form this tradition. The Bible offered up a vision of the end in the Apocalypse. The Old and New Testaments told of persons who had prophesied the future on the basis of a vision, or perhaps by hearing voices: "If there be a prophet among you, I the Lord will make myself known unto him in a vision, and will speak to him in a dream" (Numbers 12: 6). The legends of the saints were rich in visions, as were the lives of martyrs in Eusebius.[13] A story circulated in the late thirteenth century of a monk who saw a hand writing out the message of the gathering of a new crusade to free Jerusalem. A Lutheran printer saw enough of value in this prophecy to publish it in Germany in 1532, the same year that Martin Luther, though repudiating this specific story, affirmed the general principle that God revealed his will in episodes of this nature.[14] In general, apocalyptic prophecy gained new vigor with the coming of the Reformation, for the feeling was pervasive that contemporary history manifested the great struggle between Christ and Antichrist. In an influential explication of Revelation, a seventeenth-century English Protestant much read in New England, Joseph Mede, reaffirmed the apocalyptic significance of voices, thunder, lightning, hail, eclipses, blazing stars, and the rise and fall of kings. Mede regarded all the seals and trumpets in Revelation as figures tied to real events, and in working out the parallels he made it seem that Judgment lay not far ahead. Meanwhile certain printers were reviving legendary prophecies from the past, like those of Merlin and "Mother Shipton," or even of obscure Germans whose manuscript predictions were somehow being rediscovered.[15]

A fourth tradition was natural history. The men in mid-seventeenth-century England who pursued "natural philosophy" and who founded the Royal Society in 1662 were generously inclusive in their curiosity. They wished to collect and catalogue "all the phaenomena of nature hitherto observed, and all experiments made and recorded." By "all" they meant the "curious things of nature" as much as what was normal or routine. For them the "natural" extended to the "unnatural" in the sense of prodigies and wonders, phenomena that loomed as above or beyond the merely natural. As far back as Aristotle, the men who described nature had been intrigued by abnormalities. Why were some animals born deformed, and why some humans? The answer was that "monster births" were signs from heaven of some sinful act or perhaps apocalyptic warnings of disaster. Batman took this view, as did his sources, Lycostenes and Obsequens. The ballad writers reveled in the theme, some holding that a mother's mental state could alter the fetus. The members of the Royal Society were interested, too, in spiritual and occult phenomena, like the invisible drummer boy of Tidworth.[16]

The meaning of the wonder owed much to these four structures of ideas. But the most crucial framework was the doctrine of God's providence. That doctrine antedated Luther and Calvin. Chaucer's Knight had spoken of "Destiny, that Minister General / Who executed on earth and over all / That Providence which God has long foreseen," and the Psalmist sang of a God who stretched out his protection to the ends of the earth. Nonetheless, the doctrine gained fresh importance in the sixteenth century. Calvin gave providence a position of prominence in the *Institutes*, contrasting it with Stoic fatalism and mere chance. In the wake of Calvin, Thomas Beard assured his readers that God was immediately and actively present in the world, the ultimate force behind everything that happened: "Is there any substance in this world that hath no cause of his subsisting? . . . Doth not every thunderclap constraine you to tremble at the blast of his voyce?" Nothing in the world occurred according to contingency or "blind chance." The "all-surpassing power of God's will" was manifested in a regularity that Beard thought of as "marvellous," though never to be counted on completely since God retained the power to interrupt the laws of nature. The providence of God was as manifest in the unexpected or surprising as in the "constant" order of the world.[17]

And Providence revealed an angry God. Portents and prodigies arose within a world besmirched with sin, a world of men and women who failed to heed his laws. The murderer, the mocking cavalier, the liar, the sabbath-breaker – all these and many others could expect that someday, somehow, their violation of the moral order would provoke awful warnings or more awful judgments. Behind the logic of this theory lay a long tradition, far older than the Reformation, of foreseeing order collapse into chaos or peace give way to violence.[18] Strife and violence abound in the wonder tales, whether caused by man, the Devil, or an avenging God.

These several themes gave meaning to the wonder in any of its many forms. Take comets, for example. Among Beard and his contemporaries, comets were remarked on more frequently than any other heavenly phenomenon described in ancient science. According to convention, comets signaled drastic change, if not disaster – "drought, the pestilence, hunger, battels, the alteration of kingdomes, and common weales, and the traditions of men. Also windes, earthquakes, dearth, landflouds, and great heate to follow." Du Bartas summed up this wisdom in *La Sepmaine*:

> There, with long bloody Hair, a Blazing Star
> Threatens the World with Famine, Plague & War:
> To Princes, death; to Kingdomes many crosses:
> To all Estates, Inevitable Losses. . . .

This motif came straight from Pliny, who, in viewing comets as "a very terrible portent," had noted their appearance "during the civil disorder in the counsulship of Octavius, and again during the war between Pompey and Caesar." Another classical source was Seneca. Readers of the Bible could add Matthew 24, where Jesus described to his disciples the signs of the last days, including what seem like eclipses of the sun and moon, and the phenomenon of stars that "fall from heaven."[19]

Thunder and lightning were other portents that drew on ancient sources. In Scripture, these events were construed as the instruments of an avenging God: "Cast forth lightning, and scatter them: Shoot out thine arrows, and destroy them" (Psalms 144: 6). The prophecies of St John in Revelation foresaw the "voice" of God in thunder, lightning, and earthquakes (8: 5; 10: 4). Pliny had viewed thunderbolts as "direful and accursed," associating them with other wonders such as prophecy. To writers of the Renaissance, lightning seemed especially to betoken destructive violence. Prophecy and violence were linked in plays like Marlowe's *Tamburlaine*, where the hero saw himself as the scourge of "a God full of revenging wrath, / From whom the thunder and the lightning breaks."[20]

Apparitions in the sky were yet another phenomenon that portended defeat or disaster. They were credible as signs according to both Pliny and the Bible. Among Beard, Clarke, and their contemporaries, a much-repeated apparition story concerned the fall of Jerusalem. Recounting the destruction of that city, the Jewish historian Josephus had described at length "the strange signes and tokens" that appeared before the city's fall. "One while there was a comet in form of a fiery sword, which for a year together did hang over the city." There were voices, and someone who cried out, "Wo, wo unto Jerusalem." Iron chariots flew through the air, and an army became visible in the clouds. All this seemed true not only to Elizabethans, but to Englishmen plunged into civil war, when armies in the sky were frequently perceived. Some saw ships, as when a "person of credit" watched a cloud form "into the likeness of a compleat Ship, with Masts and Sails. . . . He discerned also in the Ship, the likeness of the upper parts of Men; and at the Head of the Ship he saw many Men with Pikes on their shoulders as perfectly (according to his own Relation) as ever he saw them painted."[21]

Here as in the broadside ballads and the great collections, the wonder signified God's providence. Yet most portent stories drew on several overlapping frames of meaning. An important source of meaning and motifs was astrology, which taught men to regard the heavens as infused with order. Another source, the meteorology of Aristotle and Pliny, assumed the existence of fixed laws, as did the natural philosophy of mid-seventeenth-century scientists. However old or up-to-date, science remained allied with religion in the sense of affirming a coherence that depended on the will of God.[22] But science also taught that disruption and disorder were endemic. The conjunction of two planets could send shock waves through the universe. Stars could wander out of their ordained paths, and storms arise as nature fell into imbalance. The world as pictured by astrologers and scientists was prone to violent eruptions. This sense of things was echoed in apocalyptic prophecy, and writers who described the coming of Christ's kingdom referred to comets and eclipses as presaging the Apocalypse. Meanwhile Satan raged incessantly against God's kingdom, leading many into sin and tormenting godly seekers after truth. Sin, injustice, persecution – these disorders of the moral order were mirrored in the physical disorder of monster births. An angry God was the supreme agent of disruption.

Astrologers, the Hebrew prophets, the oracles of Greece and Rome, the Englishmen at war in 1645 – all spoke alike of doom portended in the turmoil of the heavens and the earth. A teleological universe yielded incessant signs of God's providential plan and his actual or impending judgments.

A further set of themes, all circulating widely in Elizabethan England, affected the significance of wonders. Portents never seemed to hint at progress or improvement but at degeneration. Dissolution or decay, the notion that the world was running down and soon would be exhausted, prevailed as a concept.[23] Another theme was *De casibus*, or the fall from wealth and power of great men. In Beard as in books like the *Mirrour of Magistrates*, Elizabethans read of kings and princes who seemed driven to destruction.[24] A third theme concerned evil as a power operating almost on its own. Evil was not distant or abstract but something always present in the flow of daily life. A book like Beard's, with its grand metaphor of "theatre," made good and evil the main actors in the drama of existence.[25] Yet another motif was fortune, its symbol a great wheel that swept some people up and others down.[26]

The wonder books incorporated all these themes without fear of contradiction. No one viewed them as in conflict, though fortune and providence were competing, if not antithetical, interpretations of the world. Yet the wonder books retained their tolerance. They made room for decayed systems of belief; in their pages the pagan coexisted with the Christian, the science of the Greeks with the apocalypticism of Scripture and the providential worldview of John Calvin. Moreover, these books reached out to folklore for stories of the Devil as black dog or bear, for legends of the saints and their "white magic," for tales of fairies, ghosts, and apparitions, of "murder will out," of curses and their consequences. In their tolerance, the great collections ended up without a unifying order. Clarke verged off into sensationalism and into citing "wonders" that were merely curiosities, like the rhinoceros that was taken to the King of Portugal. Certain of the learned may have preferred more discrimination. But in the first half of the seventeenth century, the lore of wonders remained generously eclectic in its themes and audience, with writers such as Shakespeare and Milton using the same motifs as the ballad writers. Conventional, familiar, tolerant, and open-ended, the lore of wonders was a language that almost everyone could speak and understand.[27]

I

But were the colonists this tolerant, or did they order and discriminate in keeping with their Puritanism?

The same wonder tales that circulated in seventeenth-century England turn up in the colonies, often via books imported from the London book trade. As a student at Harvard in the 1670s, Edward Taylor had access to a copy of Samuel Clarke's *Examples*, out of which he copied "An account of ante-mortem visions of Mr. John Holland." In sermons of the 1670s, Increase Mather quoted frequently from Clarke and Beard.[28] Imported or reprinted broadsides made some of Beard's stories familiar to New England readers; John Foster, the founder of the Boston press, published in 1679 his version of a London broadside, *Divine Examples of Gods Severe Judgments against Sabbath-Breakers*, a set of illustrated warning tales drawn mostly from *The Theatre of Gods Judgements*. Booksellers were importing copies of English wonder books in the 1680s.[29] Many more such books and broadsides reached New England in the seventeenth century, though leaving no specific trace of their existence.

What passed in general from England to New England was a language or mentality. Early on, New England almanacs reiterated references and formulas derived from English counterparts. The almanac for 1649 offered its readers a lengthy "prognostication" that played on the theme of earthquakes as a portent of impending catastrophe:

> Great Earth-quakes frequently (as one relates)
> Forerun strange plagues, dearths, wars & change of states,
> Earths shaking fits by venemous vapours here,
> How is it that they hurt not, as elsewhere!

In keeping with the genre, local almanacs contained cryptic prophecies:

> The morning Kings may next ensuing year,
> With mighty Armies in the aire appear,
> By one mans means there shall be hither sent
> The Army, Citty, King and Parliament...
> A child but newly born, shall then foretell
> Great changes in a Winding-sheet; Farewell.

The almanac for 1648 tucked portents and prodigies into a "Chronologicall Table" that successive books updated:

Mr. Stoughton and all the souldiers returned home, none being slain. Mrs. Dier brought forth her horned-foure-talented monster. The great and general Earth-quake.[30]

Soon the colonists were issuing commentaries of their own on comets, Samuel Danforth describing the comet of 1664 in a brief pamphlet,

Ichabod Wiswell the comet of 1680 in *A judicious observation of that dreadful comet. . . . Wherein is shewed the manifold judgments that are like to attend upon most parts of the world,* and Increase Mather the same comet and one of 1682 in longer books.[31] Mather also undertook a more ambitious project, a collection of New England portents somewhat on the lines of Clarke's *Examples.* Mather's *Essay for the Recording of Illustrious Providences* (1684), which received a London printing, summed up the lore accumulated after half a century of settlement.

Soon too, public groups and ordinary men and women were collecting and retelling wonder tales. Certain organizations, like the churches in Dorchester and Roxbury and the town of Newbury, incorporated references to "remarkable providences" – fires, storms, eclipses, victories, sudden deaths – into their records. Three lay members of the immigrant generation, Edward Johnson, William Bradford, and John Winthrop, wrote works of history that were richly providential in telling how the colonists had overcome adversity and conflict. This public record-keeping was paralleled in private journals and interleaved almanacs – the Reverend Joshua Moodey had "kept 30. years' Almanacks together with fayr paper between every year, setting down remarkable Providences" – that functioned as individual "memorials" of notable events. People retold such stories in their letters and passed them on by word of mouth.[32]

This trade in stories is strikingly revealed in several documents. Lawrence Hammond, a merchant in Charlestown, made notes on wonder stories in his diary. The source for one was the minister of Billerica; two others he may have learned from books. John Hull, a Boston merchant, kept an extensive diary that was largely given over to the lore of portents. His entry for 1666, a year with rich prophetic overtones, reveals a wide curiosity about events in New England:

> At New Haven was distinctly and plainly heard the noise of guns, two, three, five at a time, a great part of the day, being only such noises in the air. The same day, at evening, a house at Northampton [was] fired by lightning; a part of the timber split; a man in it killed. . . . At Narriganset, in Mr. Edward Hutchinson's flock of sheep, were several monsters. In July were very many noises heard by several towns on Long Island, from the sea, distinctly, of great guns and small, and drums.

The diary of Hull's son-in-law, Samuel-Sewall, was even more extensive in searching out coincidences.[33]

A college classmate of Sewall's, Edward Taylor, was on the receiving end of several stories. In a notebook kept while he was at Harvard, Taylor recorded a story of "magical performances by a juggler." He heard the story from Jonathan Mitchel, the young minister in Cambridge, who learned it as a student ("during recitation") from Henry Dunster, then the president of Harvard. Dunster had it from the Reverend John Wilson of Boston – and here the chain comes to an end. In his notebook Taylor wrote down the essence of another story passed on by word of mouth. A minister and Harvard president, Urian Oakes, had done the telling:

> A child that was born at Norich last Bartholomew-Day... being in the nurses arms last Easterday... being about 30 weeks old spake these words (This is an hard world): the nurse when she had recovered herselfe a little from her trembling, & amazement at the Extrardinariness of the thing, said Why deare Child! thou hast not known it: the Child after a pause, replied, But it will be an hard world & you shall know it.

To this same notebook Taylor added his extracts out of Clarke's *Examples,* and, from some other printed source, the prophetic scaffold speech of an Englishman executed in 1651. Here too he noted an event of his first night in Cambridge rooming in the house of Charles Chauncy, the Harvard president. As Taylor and one of Chauncy's sons were "going to bed . . . there came a white peckled Dove Pidgeon & flew against the Casement of o[u]r Chamber window." The two boys opened the window and took in the dove, which "run from us & cooed & brissled at us." Setting it free in the morning, they told the president of the event, who "said he would not (of any good) he should be hurt: ffor one should not heare of the like: it was omenous surely."[34]

Such traffic in wonder stories was crucial to the making of Increase Mather's *Essay for the Recording of Illustrious Providences.* In the early 1680s, Mather solicited his fellow ministers for contributions to his impending book. John Higginson of Salem, an older man who came to Boston as a student in the 1630s, responded to this call for stories by sending word of Moodey's annotated almanacs, "so that I doubt not but besides those [stories] he hath sent you, you may have many more from him. For instance, – he speaks of 26 men therabouts, dying or cast away in their drunkennes, which calls to mind some such cases here." The following year, having learned from Mather that he did not "confine" himself "to things done in NE.," Higginson wrote out and dispatched two wonder stories attributed to "persons credible," and of events "I believe . . . to be certain." Both concerned the Devil, the one a story of a book that acted strangely on its readers, the other of a man who covenanted with the Devil to insinuate "that there was neither God nor Devil, nor Heaven nor Hell." The informant who told Higginson of the magical book, a man no longer living, had been a ruling elder of the church in Salem. Long after having the experience (it happened back in England) he remembered that

> as he read in it, he was seized on by a strange kind [of] Horror, both of Body & minde, the hair of his head standing up, &c. Finding these effects severall times, he acquainted his master with it, who observing the same effects, they concluding it was a Conjuring Book, resolved to burn it, which they did. He that brought it, in the shape of a man, never coming to call for it, they concluded it was the Devil.

The other story Higginson had collected in his days as minister at Guilford "from a godly old man yet living."[35]

As Higginson predicted, Joshua Moodey had stories to pass on. One was of a house inhabited by evil spirits as told by William Morse, the man who lived there. All was relatively quiet at the time of Moodey's writing; "the last sight I have heard of was the carrying away of severall Axes in the night, notwithstanding they were laied up, yea, lockt up very safe." From a "sober woman" Moodey also had received a story of a "monstrous birth" that he described at length, concluding with an offer "to goe up & discourse with the midwife" if Mather wanted more details.[36]

Informants from Connecticut supplied further stories. The minister in Stamford, John Bishop, had written him some years before to answer inquiries about "the noise of a great gun in the air." In his new letter, Bishop poured out a string of tales:

> We have had of late, great stormes of rain & wind, & somtimes of thunder & lightning, whereby some execution hath been done by the Lord's holy Hand, though with sparing mercy to mankind. Mr. Jones his house at N[ew] H[aven] broken into, & strange work made in one room thereof especially, wherein one of his daughters had been a little before; & no hurt to any of the family, but the house only. . . . A little after which, at Norwalk, there were nine working oxen smitten dead in the woods, in a few rods space of ground, & after that, at Greenwich . . . there were seven swine & a dog smitten all dead, & so found the next morning, very near the dwelling house, where a family of children were alone (their parents not then at home) & no hurt to any of them, more then amazing fear.[37]

More such stories came to Mather from other hands – a narrative of a Hartford woman's bewitchment, together with the story of a man who drank too much and died, accounts of providential rainstorms and remarkable deliverances, and of "two terrible strokes by thunder and lightning" that struck Marshfield in Plymouth Colony.[38]

From his brother, finally, came a letter reminding him of stories he had not included. Nathaniel Mather had moved to England in the early

1650s. Yet he still remembered the stories he had listened to while growing up in Dorchester and as a Harvard student:

> Mrs. Hibbons witchcrafts, & the discovery thereof, as also of H. Lake's wife, of Dorchester, whom, as I have heard, the devill drew in by appearing to her in the likenes, & acting the part of a child of hers then lately dead, on whom her heart was much set: as also another of a girl in Connecticut who was judged to dye a reall convert, tho shee dyed for the same crimes Storyes, as I heard them, as remarkable for some circumstances as most I have read. Mrs. Dyer's & Mrs. Hutchinson's monstrous births, & the remarkable death of the latter, with Mr. Wilson's prediction or threatning thereof, which, I remember, I heard of in New England.

Flowing from the memories of a man who long since had left New England, this résumé of stories is revealing both of how such stories were transmitted (Mather "heard" these tales) and of the buildup of a native stock of wonders.[39]

Most of this local lore had counterparts in stories told by Clarke, Beard, or ballad writers. Many of these older stories passed among the colonists as well, enriching and legitimizing their own testimonies of the supernatural. The man in Lynn who saw phantoms in the sky could almost have been quoting from an English tract of 1662 that described similar phenomena. So it went for others: experience coincided with the narrative tradition. We may also infer the existence of a lore of wonders that approached being common knowledge. The circulation of this lore was not limited to print, as Mather's correspondence with his friends and fellow ministers so clearly indicates. Nor was it something only the rude multitude and not the learned could appreciate. When presidents of Harvard told wonder tales in class, when ministers delighted in recalling tales of "magical" books and freakish bolts of lightning, we can be sure that we are dealing with a culture shared, with few exceptions, by all the colonists. . . .

The repertory in general use among the colonists was closely akin to the repertory amassed in Beard and Clarke, from which, indeed, these people gained instruction. Prophecy, prodigy, providence – these were the stuff of everyday experience. When William Hibbins stood up in Boston church in 1642 and asked his fellow members to take note of "sea-deliverances" – "what desperate dangers they were delivered from upon the seas, such as the eldest seamen were amazed" – he was expressing a popular awareness of wonders that Increase Mather would reiterate.[40]

This attentiveness to prodigies and portents bespoke deep feelings about communal danger and security. The men who interlaced the

Dorchester and Roxbury church records with providential events were consciously performing a public function. So were Winthrop and Bradford in their journal histories, and Edward Johnson in *The Wonder-Working Providence of Sions Saviour*. To chronicle the wonder was to chart the zones of danger through which a community must pass. In early modern Europe, every community had its good times and its bad. The good times were when rain came at the right moment and the harvest was abundant, when neighbors lived in peace and landlords were not greedy, when servants obeyed their masters. The hard times were when food ran low and famine threatened, when disease was epidemic, or when peace gave way to conflict. In many European villages, a craving for protection was satisfied by "miracles" or extraordinary events that promised the return of peace, health, and prosperity. Thus, when epidemics threatened, villagers in late-medieval Spain – young girls, shepherds, old men – had visions of the Virgin Mary in which she demanded that the village build a chapel or renew its vows of faith. In thirteenth-century Burgundy, women washed newborn or ailing infants in water from a well associated with a miracle.[41]

Women were still bringing infants to the well of St. Guinefort in Burgundy when the colonists departed for New England. In the towns from which these people came, many of the customs that once addressed the dangers of everyday life had lapsed into disuse. Once past their own "starving time," these people found themselves becoming prosperous – owners of their land, blessed with healthy children, reaping ample harvests. Yet all of the first generation had risked the dangers of the sea in coming to New England. Then as well as later, the wilderness that lay around them contained hostile Indians and their Catholic allies from French Canada. Back in England, the government (except when Puritans had reigned) regarded them with disfavor. And, as they discovered, there were enemies within – those who lied, cursed, or profaned the Sabbath, old women who allied themselves with Satan, children who grew up rebellious, neighbors who disputed each stray pig and cow, and, increasingly, merchants who lived ostentatiously. Danger pressed as much upon the godly in their new home as in England.

Responding to these dangers, the colonists employed an old language of interpretation in which the key words were "sin" and "judgment." That language reached them via Beard and the ballad writers, and also via poems like *Pestilence* (1625), a narrative of epidemic illness that painted it as God's response to man's indifference. What enriched and made this language relevant was the colonists' assumption that they lived in covenant with God. For them the covenant transformed the body social into a moral order, a "Theocratie" erected on the basis of the laws of God. It was the wonder that made visible this fusion of the social and the moral, at once manifesting God's protection and – more frequently – warning of God's anger at their carelessness.

John Winthrop kept his journal not out of private curiosity but in order to record the flow of "providences" betokening the situation of a covenanted people. "It is useful to observe, as we go along," Winthrop wrote in 1635, "such especial providences of God as were manifested for the good of these plantations." What he meant by "good" was the safety of the whole, and the general welfare. Anyone who put self-interest ahead of the welfare of the whole was likely to become an example of God's judgments – to drown in a shipwreck, die in an explosion ("wherein the judgment of God appeared, for the master and company were many of them profane scoffers at us"), lose some of his property. Perhaps because he sacrificed so much of his own estate, Winthrop was especially attracted to cases of the rich and covetous becoming poor. "Divers homes were burnt this year," he noted in 1642, "by drying flax. Among others, one Briscoe, of Watertown, a rich man, a tanner, who had refused to let his neighbor have leather for corn, saying he had corn enough...." Servants and sea captains who were suddenly enriched at the expense of others often suffered bad dreams or psychological distress, or simply lost their money as rapidly as it had been acquired. Winthrop's conception of the general good extended to those standbys of the Puritan program, Sabbatarianism and temperance. He told of drunkards who drowned and of people who died after having worked on the Sabbath – in one case, after carting dung. He was much relieved when murderers and thieves were detected by special acts of providence; reporting two examples, he summed up their meaning as "show[ing] the presence and power of God in his ordinances, and his blessing upon his people, while they endeavor to walk before him with uprightness."[42] Always portents reaffirmed the rightness of a moral order.

Meanwhile there were constant "plots" spawned by the Devil to "disturb our peace, and to raise up instruments one after another." The "old serpent" tried his hand at "sowing jealousies and differences between us and our friends at Connecticut." But God sent tokens to reveal that he stood by the colonists. Perhaps the most impressive of these tokens for the men and women who came in the 1630s was their safe passage of the ocean. A folklore emerged from the fact that every ship but one (the *Angel Gabriel*) had reached New England safely: "wherein" (as William Hibbins told the Boston congregation in 1642) "it was very observable what care the Lord had of them." Citing Hibbins in the journal, Winthrop added that "indeed such preservations and deliverances have been so frequent, to such ships as have carried those of the Lord's family between the two Englands, as would fill a perfect volume to report them all."[43] A more confusing token was the snake that crawled into Cambridge meetinghouse while a synod of the ministers was listening to a sermon. There was panic before "Mr. Thomson, one of the elders of Braintree, (a man of much faith) trode upon the head of it." Interpretation followed, the ministers agreeing that the snake was Satan attempting "their disturbance and dissolution": "This being so remarkable, and nothing falling out but by divine providence, it is out of doubt, the Lord discovered somewhat of his mind in it." Mixed in with events Winthrop knew how to interpret were others that remained mysterious. It was not clear why "one James Everell...saw a great light in the night at Muddy River," or why "a voice was heard upon the water between Boston and Dorchester, calling out in a most dreadful manner, boy, boy, come away, come away," or why at Ipswich in 1646 "there was a calf brought forth with one head, and three mouths, three noses, and six eyes": "What these prodigies portended the Lord only knows, which in his due time he will manifest."[44]

As chronicle of prodigies and portents demonstrating God's protection of the colonists, Winthrop's journal history had its parallel in Nathaniel Morton's *New-Englands Memoriall*. Basing much of what he wrote on William Bradford's then unpublished journal history, Morton celebrated the "simplicity" of life in those early decades when no one had been covetous or proud. Another of his themes was the success of the "weak" and "lowly" Pilgrims in overcoming stronger enemies. Thus the menace of the Indians, who far outnumbered the few people who survived their first winter in New England, was removed by a sickness God had sent among them. "Ancient Indians" told him that not long before the English first arrived, "they saw a Blazing Star or Comet, which was a fore-runner of this sad Mortality...." Reversal struck the proud merchant Thomas Weston. The men he sent to Plymouth mocked the Pilgrims, but then fell short of food and turned to begging. "A strange alteration there was" in Weston himself, after he arrived and was betrayed by the Indians. Likewise the defeat of the Pequots – so "Proud and Blasphemous an Enemy" – was the doing of the Lord. But if God struck some with judgments, he gave godly people strength to persevere against their enemies. The overriding theme of Morton's narrative was deliverance: how the weak, because they rested on God's mercy, came to triumph over every adverse circumstance.[45]

These public texts taught the importance of the Protestant community. So did the record-keeping in such churches as Dorchester and Roxbury. John Eliot, the minister in Roxbury, noted the drowning of two "ungodly" servants who went out at night to gather oysters: "a dreadful example of God's displeasure against obstinate servants." But God protected those in covenant, as in the providential healing of the deacon's daughter from a head wound that exposed her brains, and another of a man so badly hurt blood gushed from his ear; yet "thro' Gods mercy he recovered his senses ... to the wonder of all men."[46] Similarly, private diaries detailed portents that signified protection of a family or a household. People told the story of their lives in this same fashion, as when John Dane of Ipswich composed "A Declaration of Remarkabell Proudenses in the Corse of My Lyfe," to which he added a long poem that celebrated his prosperity as one of the godly. Always in such texts the private and the public – self, household, church, community – were not differentiated, but conjoined. And always they provided reassurance. Even after learning of a new defeat in King Philip's War, a layman voiced the wisdom that "It is a day of the wicked's tryumph, but the sure word of God tells us his tryumphing is *brief*." The lore of wonders held the lesson that the godly, should they live up to their values, would pass safely through all trial and tribulation.[47]

At a still deeper level, the wonder story embodied confusing lessons about danger and security. The people of New England viewed the world about them as demonstrating pattern. This was the order of God's providence, the order of a theocentric universe. It was also teleological, its structure the grand scheme laid out in the Apocalypse, the war of Antichrist against the godly. Evil was a force of great strength and cunning, so much so, indeed, that the providential order could seem to be "overthrowne and turned upside downe, men speak[ing] evil of good, and good of evill, accounting darknesse light, and light darknesse."[48] Disorder was profound in other ways, as Winthrop half perceived in struggling to make sense of the array of portents. The world was rife with violence – of neighbors angered by stray animals or slander, of death that came to children without apparent cause, of Indians on the rampage, of great storms and terrifying earthquakes.

The people of New England acted out their fear of what such wonders revealed at moments like the earthquake of 1638, which "shook the earth ... in a very violent manner to our great amazement and wonder" (as the residents of Newbury recorded in the town records) and caused

> divers men (that had never knowne an Earthquake before) being at worke in the Fields, to cast downe their working tooles, and run with gastly terrified lookes, to the next company they could meet withall.

On Cape Ann in 1692, phantoms roused men into frenzied firing of their guns. A servant girl in Boston, awakened by a fire near the water, saw its "Light ... reflecting from a Black Cloud, and came crying to [her master] under Consternation; supposing the last Conflagration had begun." People felt uneasy when the sun passed into the darkness of an eclipse, and the officers of Harvard College postponed commencement in 1684 because it fell too close to one of these events.[49] Witches too were terrifying in their power to disrupt community.

Each kind of violence was attuned to every other, as were the forms of order. Certainly the order of the universe often seemed to be hidden or difficult to decipher. If there was purpose and plan, there was also mystery at the heart of things.

> One providence seems to look this way, another providence seems to look that way, quite contrary one to another. Hence these works are marveilous. Yea, and that which adds to the wonderment, is, in that the works of God sometimes seem to run counter with his word: so that there is dark and amazing intricacie in the ways of providence.

Death could strike at any moment, the Devil could mislead, the earth begin to tremble. In dramatizing all these possibilities, the wonder tale evoked the radical contingency of a world so thoroughly infused with invisible forces. It came down to this, that nothing was secure, that no appearance of security could hide the mystery beneath.[50]

II

I have spoken of the wonder stories as embodying a mentality that united the learned and the unlearned. Being so pervasive, and so widely credited as real, these stories readily became, as well, weapons in a complex game of politics. When consensus lapsed, competing groups used purported wonders to discredit their opponents. One axis of this conflict in New England placed Baptists and Quakers in opposition to the Orthodoxy. Another set the ministers against the "cunning folk" who offered to help people know the future. A third revolved around "declension," or the perceived decline of community, and whom or what to blame for it. One major result of this politicization was to make the interpretation of wonders generally uncertain. Moreover, embedded in the very books and broadsides that conveyed this lore was a definite skepticism about portents. Was astrology a science? Were dreams and voices mere delusions? Learned culture, Scripture, even popular tradition, warned against false prophets and misleading signals. The many layered meanings of a portent thus included the possibility of its having no significance at all or of its being overly politicized.

In using portents to discredit others and, at the same time, to legitimize their own position, the colonists were playing an old game. The oracle at Delphi, the Sibyllines in Rome, the texts attributed to Merlin in the thirteenth century, all were preludes to the uses of wonders in the

Reformation. Martin Luther helped revive the story of a deformed monster fished out of the Tiber, which he construed as condemnation of the Catholic clergy. . . . When fire devastated Tiverton, Puritans read it as a warning to observe the Sabbath. The same people liked to tell of blows inflicted on the Catholics. A much-favored story described the collapse of a gallery in Blackfrairs Hall, London, where a clandestine Catholic service was being conducted. . . . The politics of portent-watching intensified as Royalists and Parliamentarians maneuvered for support. On the eve of civil war, each side hired astrologers to issue respectively sympathetic readings of the stars and planets. Even when the game was up and Charles II restored to the throne, opponents issued propaganda in the form of portent lore. A frenzy of such portent-mongering occurred as opposition parties worked to exclude James II from the throne.[51]

Well versed in these campaigns before leaving for New England, the colonists discovered in the 1630s that a prophetess was in their midst, a charismatic woman who claimed God had given her the gift of prophecy. Anne Hutchinson arrived in Boston in 1634. She brought with her a reputation as a prophetess. Two specific prophecies or "revelations" survive in the records of her life, one forecasting that her ship would need three more weeks to reach New England, the other a prediction that "a young man in the ship should be saved, but he must walk in the ways" she specified. We may infer that her voyage did last three more weeks, for this prophecy (and doubtless others we know nothing of) was cited by admirers who went on to speak "of rare Revelations of things to come from the spirit." Edward Johnson, a hostile witness, remembered someone saying to a newcomer, "Come along with me . . . i'le bring you to a Woman . . . who hath had many Revelations of things to come, and for my part, saith hee, I had rather hear such a one . . . then any of your learned Scollers. . . ." Questioned by the General Court in 1637 as it acted to suppress the movement known as Antinomianism, Mrs. Hutchinson described herself as bearing "immediate" revelations and cited a key text of Scripture: "And it shall come to pass afterward, / That I will pour out my Spirit upon all flesh; / And your sons and your daughters shall prophesy, / Your old men shall dream dreams, / Your young men shall see visions" (Joel 28–9; the passage goes on to speak of wonders and deliverance). At this session of the court, one of the deputies reported that in London she had told him she "was very inquisitive after revelations and said that she never had any great thing done about her but it was revealed to her beforehand." He remembered too that "when she came within sight of Boston" for the first time, "and looking upon the meanness of the place . . . she uttered these words, if she had not a sure word that England should be destroyed her heart would shake."[52]

Without claiming the same status, her two allies in the ministry, John Cotton and John Wheelwright, both voiced apocalyptic views. At Wheelwright's fast-day sermon in Boston meetinghouse in January 1637, he linked the growing dispute over doctrine to the "combate" between Christ and Antichrist. "The day shall come," the "terrible day" foreseen in Scripture, when all the enemies of Christ would be "consumed" by fire. An audience well versed in apocalyptic speculation understood his meaning when Wheelwright asked rhetorically, "Why should we not further this fire, who knoweth not how soone those Jewes may be converted?"[53]

Statements such as these had an altogether different meaning from the dreams and visions of a Mercy Lewis or a Winthrop. Here, the role of prophetess was turned against the men in power, the ministers Anne Hutchinson denounced for preaching "works." She may have known of Eleanor Davis, an Englishwoman who, in 1625, declared she "heard early in the morning a Voice from Heaven, speaking as through a trumpet these words: 'There is nineteen years and a half to the Judgment Day.' " Davis was able to have some of her sayings printed, but she also was imprisoned for predicting the downfall of Charles I. Or the story may have reached Anne Hutchinson of Jane Hawkins, a visionary who in 1629 foretold "the downfall of the bishops and the Anglican Church." In the years when Anne was learning to respect the voices that she heard as sent from God, still other men and women arose to proclaim the downfall of the state and church and their own mission as inspired prophets. One died at the stake for heresy, and others were imprisoned.[54] When she found herself in danger from the magistrates and ministers, she warned them that, like Daniel in the lion's den, she would be "delivered" by a miracle from the grasp of persecutors: "and if you go on in this course you begin you will bring a curse upon you and your posterity, and the mouth of the Lord hath spoken it." A fuller report has her telling the court that in England "the Lord did reveale himselfe to me, sitting upon a Throne of Justice, and all the world appearing before him, and though I must come to New England, yet I must not feare nor be dismaied," and insisting to the ministers that "I feare none but the great Jehovah, which hath foretold me of these things, and I doe verily believe that he will deliver me out of [y]our hands."[55]

In her footsteps followed other prophetlike outsiders who denounced the doctrines of the ministers and rejected their authority. A standard theme among the Quakers, who picked up where she left off, was to declare that all persecutors of the saints would suffer from God's anger. Like Anne Hutchinson, moreover, the Quakers used the fearful weapon of the curse against the magistrates and ministers. From prison Humphrey Norton accused Thomas Prence, the governor of Plymouth, of transgressing "the laws and waics of God," and warned him that he must expect "the vengeance of God."

> The day of thy wailing will bee like unto that of a woman that murthers the fruite of her wombe; the anguish and peine that will enter upon thy reignes will be like knawing worms lodging betwixt thy hart and liver: When these things come upon thee, and thy backe bowed down with pain, in that day and houre thou shalt know to thy griefe, that prophetts of the Lord God wee are, and the God of vengeance is our God.

John Hull recorded in his diary in 1661 that "The Quakers have given out such speeches as gave cause to think they intended mischief unto our magistrates and ministers, and threatened fire and sword to be our speedy portion...."[56] When King Philip's War broke out in 1675, Samuel Groom declared that God was making an example of the colonists for their extreme cruelty: "... and therefore thou must drink of the Cup of terrible Amazement and Astonishment, poured out by a Just Hand, as from God upon thy Inhabitants Oh New-England!" It was also in these troubled years that a Quaker "marcht" through Boston, "crying, 'Repent, & c.,'" and that Quaker women stripped themselves of all their clothes, rubbed their faces "black," and rushed into meetinghouses to proclaim the coming judgment. The entry of such a woman (partly dressed) into Boston Third Church "occasioned the greatest and most amazing uproar that" one eyewitness "ever saw."[57]

This "amazing uproar" lasted through the 1690s. George Keith, who came to Massachusetts to debate the ministers in 1690, defended Quakers for believing that the saints received new revelations and illuminations from the Holy Spirit. "I say it with Sorrow," Keith declared in taking up the classic pose of prophet, "if ye were not blind, ye might see some of the Judgments of the Lord begun to be executed upon you...." Thomas Maule, a Salem Quaker, invoked the Salem witchcraft executions as evidence of "Gods Judgments upon...the chief persecuting Priests and Rulers." Citing Foxe, he argued that the ministers belonged in the tradition of false teachers that included Rome, and placed victims like himself in the context of the *Book of Martyrs*. In these years a small group of men and women gathered around a merchant of New London, John Rogers, who claimed to be inspired. Imprisoned, whipped, and fined, the Rogerenes persisted by appropriating the myth of "God's Children" suffering at the hands of their worldly "Persecutors."[58]

From Hutchinson to Keith and Rogers, these radicals relied on Scripture in defending their right to interpret God's commands. More, they drew on motifs which the orthodox themselves articulated – the expectation of the coming kingdom, the role of certain men as prophets. The social memory of the radicals was little different from the memory of the men who punished them; both groups cited Foxe, both were fascinated with the Book of Revelation. Crossing and recrossing a line that was difficult to fix, the radicals played on ambiguities intrinsic to the role of prophet.

A different group of men and women, those who served as fortune-tellers, healers, and magicians, exploited other ambiguities. We learn of fortune-telling from court records, and especially those involving accusations of witchcraft. A servant girl accused of stealing responded with the threat to "burn" one of the girls who had testified against her; according to a witness, "She said shee had a book in which she could read and call the divill to kill Sarah." John Broadstreet of Rowley, "presented" to the Essex County Court in 1652 "for having familiarity with the devil," told someone "he read in a book of magic, and that he heard a voice asking him what work he had for him." He was not persuasive, for the court dismissed him with a fine for lying. Yet others had substantial credibility as healers and fortune-tellers. Margaret Jones of Charlestown, convicted of being a witch and executed in 1648, practiced healing and prophecy. She was critical of the doctors with whom she competed, warning "such as would not make use of her physic, that they would never be healed, and accordingly their diseases and hurts continued, with relapse against the ordinary course, and beyond the apprehension of all physicians and surgeons." John Brown of New Haven, a young man already known for drinking and disorderly behavior, boasted to his friends in 1665 that he could make the Devil appear at his bidding; before their eyes he drew circles and "strange figures which he called the lords of the second, third, tenth and twelfth house," and adduced "the aid of the seven stars and the planets" – though all in vain, apparently. A New Haven woman, Elizabeth Goodman, was accused of witchcraft because she seemed to know beforehand of events or see what was hidden. Mercy Goodwin was empowered by the demon spirit that possessed her to detect where stolen goods were hidden. At the witchcraft trial of Katherine Harrison of Wethersfield, a former servant testified that Katherine "told fortunes." According to this witness, she also boasted "of her great familiarity with Mr. Lilley, one that told fortunes and foretold many matters that in future times were to be accomplished." "Mr. Lilley" was a practicing astrologer who took the side of Parliament in the portent propaganda of the 1640s. His books or others like them may have reached Caleb Powell, who told William Morse, the man whose house was beset by spirits in 1679, that "he had understanding in Astrology and Astronomy and knew the working of spirits." Though Powell escaped charges of witchcraft, Dorcas Hoar of Beverly did not. The owner of a "book of fortune telling," she read palms and told fortunes.

Alice Parker was sought out by persons who wanted to know if their sons or husbands were safe at sea. Samuel Wardwell was consulted for advice on lovers and children; he informed one woman that she would have five girls before a son, "which thing is come to pase." Among some of her neighbors, Elizabeth Morse was perceived as a "cunning woman" who had healing powers.[59]

Fortune-telling veered over into remedies and sayings that had roots in folklore. Rebecca Johnson told the Salem court in 1692 that, wanting to know if her son "was alive or dead," she had her daughter perform "the turneing of the sieve... and that if the sieve turned he was dead, and so the sieve did turn." To make this device work she used word magic, repeating the phrase "By Saint Peter & Saint Paul, if [the person] be dead let this sieve turn round." Sarah Cole of Lynn "owned" to the same court "that she & some others toyed w'th a Venus glase & an Egg what trade their sweet harts should be of." (John Hale, the minister of Beverly, heard that "there came up a Coffin, that is, a Spectre in likeness of a Coffin.") Drawing on an old folklore, people nailed up horseshoes to protect themselves or struck back by tricks that broke the power of witchcraft – baking a cake made out of a suspected person's urine mixed with flour or else boiling or baking bits of hair.[60]

Prophecy and magic were alike in helping people to become em-powered, prophecy because it overturned the authority of mediating clergy and magic because it gave access to the realm of occult force. It may be that some of those who practiced magic and/or witchcraft were explicitly rebellious. One or two at times articulated a worldview that was clearly blasphemous – William Barker at Salem in 1692, and a woman in Connecticut in 1663 who a witness testified had come to her and said that "god was naught, god was naught, it was very good to be a witch," while adding that "she should not ned far going to hell, for she shold not burne in the fire." Perhaps this taint of blasphemy is why many of the colonists confused prophecy and fortune-telling with witch-craft, as though prophets could cause death or sickness. When William Graves of Stamford came to his daughter's house not long before she went into labor, he "suddenly began to counsail" her, "sayeing Abigall fitt thyselfe to meet the Lord." Were his words a curse that caused her death? Was he acting out of love or malice, as witch or caring father? Dozens of such questions arose in the flow of everyday experience, questions springing from the doubleness of prophecy and healing.[61]

Such acts were open to interpretation as white magic – or as black. It was in the interests of the clergy to resolve this situation by declaring *all* magic unlawful. Yet the hostility of elite magistrates and ministers was shared by many of the colonists, who came to see the cunning folk as threatening. In denouncing them at Salem or in other trials for witchcraft, lay men and women resolved their suspicion that the witch who healed was not far removed from the witch who harmed their children. Nor was it clear that prophets and fortune-tellers were depending on the Holy Spirit rather than the Devil.

Hence the fascination in 1637 and 1638 with two medical disasters that were open to interpretation as judgmental portents. In October 1637, Anne Hutchinson's close friend and supporter, Mary Dyer, gave birth to a stillborn and premature fetus, "so monstrous and misshapen, as the like hath scarce been heard of." Winthrop, who promptly ordered the fetus exhumed once he learned of its existence, worked telling clues into his description of the object – a midwife who was "notorious for familiarity with the devill," a sudden illness that struck most of the women who were helping with the birth, a violent rocking of the mother's bed at the moment when the fetus died, the coincidence of hearing of the monster "that very day Mistris Hutchinson was cast out of the Church for her monstrous errours, and notorious falsehood." Not long thereafter, Anne Hutchinson herself gave birth to a deformed fetus that, gruesomely described in Winthrop's journal, was summed up in Thomas Weld's report of the whole controversy as "30. monstrous births" corresponding to the "about 30 [misshapen] opinions" she had expressed. Weld, who was then in England, estimated that these were "such monstrous births as no Chronicle (I thinke) hardly ever recorded the like."[62]

Here was one form of response to the "fearful uproar" of prophesying: describe would-be prophets as deluded liars, and link them with Satan. So the ministers in 1638 informed Anne Hutchinson herself that her revelations were from "Satan."[63] Anyone in later years who prophesied against the orthodox ran the greater risk of being accused of witchcraft. So did those who practiced fortune-telling. Included in the nineteen persons executed in 1692 were Parker, Hoar, and Wardwell. Mary Hawkins, the midwife who assisted Mary Dyer in 1637, had previously been executed as a witch. Though not executed on this charge, Quaker women were stripped and their bodies searched for certain growths that, according to the lore of witchcraft, were unique to witches.[64]

Hundreds of the colonists participated in witch-hunting – and did so with such a vengeance as, from time to time, dismayed the magistrates and ministers. The special contribution of the ministers was twofold. First, it was they who made much of the Devil, portraying him as the grand conspirator ever plotting to subvert the godly and install the "Kingdom of Darkness."[65] Their second contribution was to proscribe certain beliefs as *too* magical, and not suited to a godly people. In *An Essay for the Recording of Illustrious Providences*, Increase Mather denounced several practices and artifacts – "herbs and plants to preserve from witchcrafts," "characters, words, or spells, to charm away witches, devils, or diseases," drawing "blood from those whom they suspect for witches," putting "urine into a bottle," nailing horseshoes "at their door, or the like, in the hope of recovering health thereby" – as "unlawful" customs that drew their force (and Mather said they sometimes worked) from the Devil. He went on to criticize the water trial for witches, "divination by sieves," and the "foolish sorcery of those women that put the white of an egg into a glass of water, that so they may be able to divine of what occupation their future husbands shall be." He labeled all such matters "superstitious," and denounced the people involved in them as "implicitly" in compact with the Devil. . . . [66]

Mather . . . drew on the reasoning of learned men in Europe in decrying certain beliefs as mere superstitions. There was much else in the learned tradition to deploy against practices like prophecy. For one, the ministers insisted on the point that revelations ceased with Christ and the apostles. For another, they evoked the natural world of medicine with its descriptions of the diseases of melancholy and lunacy. For a third, they drew on a critique of dreams that originated with the Greeks. These lines of criticism converged in a book that Marmaduke Johnson, the Cambridge printer, published in 1668, an English translation of a sixteenth-century attack on the Anabaptists. Its main theme was the unreliability of visions, dreams, prophecy, and portents as manifested in the troubled history of Thomas Muntzer and his fellow Anabaptists. Equating dreams with "Satanical illusions," the French author described Muntzer as an opportunist who "preached dreams" in order to "cheat and deceive the poor ignorant people." Deception, not truth, "madness," not sanity, "rage," not peace – such were the qualities or consequences of this way of acting. Nor had Muntzer told the truth in citing portents like a rainbow to encourage his troops. As narrated by this critic, in another city Anabaptists went out into public "quite naked . . . crying after a horrible manner, Wo, wo, wo, Divine vengeance, Divine vengeance." Madmen all in their behavior, the Anabaptists were an object lesson in the danger of uncontrolled interpretation. The New England clergy pointed out this danger time and time again in justifying their repression of "enthusiasm" like Anne Hutchinson's.[67]

But the best defense of all was to take the offense and match prophecy for prophecy, portent for portent. The politicizing of Mary Dyer's "monster" was part of such a campaign, one in which a London printer happily cooperated by issuing *Newes from New England of A most strange and prodigious Birth* in 1642. Down through the years the story lived on – cited in the almanac of 1648, remembered by Nathaniel Mather, remarked on by English writers, retold by Nathaniel Morton in *New-Englands Memoriall*, disputed by Quakers anxious to defend a woman who became an early convert.[68]

Another spate of portent-mongering occurred around the Robert Child affair of 1646, occasioned by a visitor from England, Dr. Robert Child, who protested certain policies of the Massachusetts government. What made his protest dangerous was Child's threat to inform authorities in England that the colonists did not concede the authority of Parliament. Child and his associates made matters worse by revising the official version of God's providence. Instead of falling in with the idea that God "meanes to carry his Gospel westward, in these latter times of the world," they enumerated numerous "afflictions" – not the acts of special providence! – "which God hath pleased to exercise" the colonists "with, and that to the worst appearance." Child made much of events like the death of Edward Winslow's horse "as he came riding to Boston," and an accidental killing in Winslow's brother's family. According to his reading of these events, they signaled God's disfavor toward an "evil" Massachusetts government.

The magistrates and ministers responded in kind. Believing as they did in portents, and aware of their effect on public thinking, the defenders of the government hastened to adduce contrary evidence – an ally of Child's who became lame and others who lost property, including a stray horse. Help came from John Cotton, who told his Boston congregation that God had surely "manifested his gratious presence" to the colonists. Cotton prophesied God's vengeance on the group of malcontents: "speak[ing] as a poore prophet of the Lord according to the word of Grace in my text," he declared that the God who had brought the immigrants safely to New England would make sure that their "enemies shall not prosper... but shall bee taken every one of them in the snares they lay for it." He warned, too, that if any of Child's group remained hostile to New England, the Lord would treat them when they left by ship as he did Jonah: "That if any shall carry any Writings, Complaints against the people of GOD in that Country, it would be as Jonas in the ship."[69]

What happened thereafter was an extraordinary demonstration of God's providence. According to the chief propagandist for the colonists, the ship would experience "the terriblest passage that ever I heard on for extremitie of weather." The storm led certain passengers, remembering Cotton's sermon, to demand if anyone on board was carrying Child's petition to the English government. When a paper was produced, they threw it into the sea, whereupon the storm abated. Later in the voyage, the ship struck a sandbar, but by a "miracle" and a "deliverance" worked its way to safety.[70] Edward Winslow published this interpretation of the voyage to counter a quite different version of events offered by Robert Child's brother. What the frightened passengers threw over-board was only a "copy" of the petition; the original and other copies remained on board. No cause-and-effect relationship existed between the "great and wonderful deliverance from shipwreck" and "the throw-ing of that Writing over-board; for that was thrown over long before, at least 14 dayes."[71]

The humor of this exchange was completely lost on Winslow. Nor did any of the magistrates and ministers regard lightly the task of determin-ing New England's providential situation. Early on, many English (and some of the colonists) were shocked by the harshness of the weather and hard times economically into speculating that it had been a mistake to leave England. In the 1640s, the triumph of the Puritans in England produced similar misgivings.[72] In later years, the effort to elaborate a "myth" of "errand" ran into difficulties as the colonists divided over issues like the halfway covenant and whether to allow Baptists and Quakers some degree of toleration. The struggle between friends and foes of the halfway covenant achieved focus in the much-disputed founding of Boston Third Church (pro-covenant) in 1669. The next spring, the Massachusetts General Court received a petition from many of the townspeople of Hadley in which they affirmed that portents like a recent comet were signs of God's disfavor with Third Church.[73] The ministers fought back with the aid of allies like Nathaniel Morton. But it was the outbreak of King Philip's War in the spring of 1675 that intensi-fied this politics. What kind of judgment was the war? For Quakers, now achieving some small measure of accommodation, the war was punish-ment on those who made them suffer.[74] For ministers like Increase Mather, the war served as a warning to overcome "declension" and resume a pure way of life. So it went for episodes like Salem witchcraft, the dissolution of the charter government, and further wars against the Indians: always there were clergy quick to read the meaning of these events, yet always someone proposed an alternative interpretation.

No other writer plunged into this politics more intensively than In-crease Mather. In book after book, as in scores of letters and unpub-lished sermons, he addressed the meaning of the wonder for his times. What he wrote and said illuminates the politicizing of this lore. More-over, his efforts at interpretation make manifest new tensions between learned uses of the wonder and the popular tradition.

Mather used portents to enhance the message of reform. When two young boys fell through the ice on Fresh Pond in Cambridge and drowned while skating on a Sunday, he was quick to note the moral: God punished Sabbath-breakers. Thomas Beard had filled a long section of *The Theatre of Gods Judgements* with similar stories, some of which turned up anew on a broadside (originally English, but reprinted in Boston) that vividly portrayed four "divine judgments" on people who in one way or another broke the moral law. Such warnings of "declension" were endemic in the sermons Mather preached and wrote. Thus he represented King Philip's War as a warning sign from God, and in *Wo to Drunkards* told story after story of the consequences of this "sin," citing in addition to the judgments exercised by (or on) Turks, Indians, rain, and fires, "a Drunkard, that when he was drinking there hapned to be a Spider in the Pot, which he not observing, was poisoned, and died immediately." Always, portents served him as a means of promoting "Reformation," though Mather defined reformation to encompass problems Thomas Beard had never known, like the presence of the Quakers.[75]

Similarly, Mather used the lore of portents to sustain the special meaning of New England. After 1660, with Royalists again controlling England, it was harder to affirm the role that some in his father's generation had imagined for New England and the "Congregational Way." History, ever rich in clues as to God's intentions, seemed to signify the triumph of a wholly different party, the despised Anglicans, who even managed to set up a church in Boston! Yet, like his fellow ministers, Mather continued to insist that prodigies and portents revealed God's favoring of New England. When news reached Boston of "a great Persecution . . . against the Protestants in France," the government proclaimed a fast day for which Mather preached a sermon in which, citing Foxe and Clarke repeatedly, he insisted that the very success of the Catholics was a "token" that "destruction . . . [was] hastening upon" them. Another of his themes was the well-worn plea that godly people "are alwayes the subjects of great persecution: being much hated in the world. . . ." His efforts at collecting portents in the early 1680s served, he hoped, to place beyond all doubt the meaning of New England.[76]

Yet the contradictions increased with each passing year. The Baptists and the Quakers rejected his interpretation of events. "Contention" became more intense as churches split on issues like the halfway covenant, as merchants lobbied for acceptance of a royal government, as towns ran short of land. Even as he pleaded for reform, a few fellow ministers were suggesting an alternative interpretation of King Philip's War, one less keyed to special providences.[77] Lay men and women had reasons of their own for discounting Mather's prophecy-cum-moral exhortation, disliking, as some did, his harsh criticism of contemporary morals and resenting what he had to say about the Baptists and the Quakers. In the midst of war he received "reviling" letters; in 1676 two men came up to him after he had read aloud the General Court's new laws requiring moral reformation and told him "that when ministers did lay a solemn charge upon the people, it might take in the ignorant, but no rational men would regard what was said the more for it."[78] This incident, the foot-dragging of the magistrates on moral legislation (the laws they passed went largely unenforced), the criticism he received from Baptists and Quakers, the unchecked process of "declension," the report of an older colleague who, having read aloud the new laws (including all the fines and whippings prescribed as the punishments), found that the experience "seems to expose us to the reproach & contempt of ill minded people, and to give them occasion to say this & that against the ministers" – all these suggest that ordinary people were becoming more selective in their response to a lore of wonders that had become openly political.[79]

As consensus slowly dissolved in these decades, learned men like Mather had reasons of their own for becoming more selective. An avid reader of imported books, he was learning in the 1680s that scientists in Europe were questioning the physics of the Greeks and Romans. Comets were a case in point; a new understanding of their regularity was making it impossible to view them as providential warnings of impending judgment.[80] Another was the monster, which now seemed a freak of nature unrelated to the workings of the supernatural.[81] A wholly different reason for this disenchantment with the supernatural was the response within learned culture to the outbursts of "enthusiasm" that occurred in England in the midst of civil war. The excitement of those years stirred prophets by the score to declaim that God entrusted them with supernatural inspiration. Afterward, in the cool mood of Restoration England, Anglicans and scientists renounced visions, dreams, and other unseen wonders, like the drummer boy of Tidworth, as tricks of the imagination.[82] A medical interpretation of "enthusiasm" came to prevail, an interpretation tracing it to merely natural factors. Some, like Thomas Hobbes, extended this critique to witchcraft, adding to old doubts that it was being practiced by the women swept up in a witch-hunt.[83] Mather did not know of Hobbes directly. But close to home, in nearby Charlestown, lived Charles Morton, a minister-turned-academic who emigrated to Massachusetts in 1686. Harvard students were soon learning science from a textbook Morton had prepared in England, a far more up-to-date survey in which he denied comets and eclipses any role as portents, offered natural causes for thunder, lightning, and rainbows, and in general liberated nature from the lore of wonders.[84] . . .

Reports continued to arrive from Europe of episodes of fraud, as when someone claimed to see an apparition. Mather was inclined to believe what he read about the Huguenots in Savoy, France, who heard voices singing to them. But as he rummaged through the books he had on hand, he began to realize that the sources he once took for granted

should be treated with a grain of skepticism. He emerged from a reread-
ing of the sources and rethinking of the issues with two statements:
angels did exist, as did witchcraft and the Devil (to believe otherwise
was "Atheism"); yet many of the events that, in popular tradition, were
interpreted as supernatural interventions in the world were better understood as "delusions" that had natural causes or were signs of "Satanicall
Possession." All in all, the witchcraft episode capped a reappraisal that
ended with his questioning the testimony of Eusebius, proposing that
appearances of angels have "in a great measure ceased," and doubting
most reports of apparitions, dreams, and voices. By the middle of the
1690s, when he published *Angelographia*, he had also more or less
conceded much of medicine and nature to the naturalists, agreeing
with them that the source of certain spiritual phenomena was not the
Holy Spirit but "enthusiasm."[85]

In thus voicing his mistrust of the lore of wonders, Mather fell in step
with a broader movement that a historian has aptly named the "reform
of popular culture."[86] Here, the meaning of this term was that certain
clergy redefined the line between religion and mere superstition –
redefined it in such a way that some of what had once been shared in
common by lay people and the clergy now was being designated as
improper or mistaken. There was nothing new about this effort; Protestants had first redefined this line in breaking with the church of Rome,
and redefined it once again in response to the Anabaptists. Increase
Mather surely knew of what was said against the Anabaptists and their
visions. He knew of Anne Hutchinson, and how a synod which included
both his father and stepfather had declared that revelation ended with
the apostles. He knew all the reasons why astrologers should not attri-
bute binding power to the stars and planets. In the last two decades of
the century, he extended the critique of superstition to include biblio-
mancy and the healing practices of cunning folk. He agreed with William
Perkins and Richard Bernard that the methods of detecting witches must
be sharply limited to confession and the testimony of two witnesses;
scornful of the test of throwing suspects into water to see if they would
drown or float, he had allies in the clergy of Connecticut, who ruled in
1692 (when consulted by the magistrates) against the water trial. In all
likelihood, the reluctance of the magistrates to enforce jury verdicts – a
reluctance manifested as early as the 1660s – paralleled his growing
doubts about what was put in evidence by ordinary people.[87]

By the 1690s, therefore, Increase Mather and his fellow clergy[88] were
participating in the dissolution of the lore of wonders that Anglicans and
rationalists initiated in the middle of the century. Ahead lay publications
like Thomas Robie's anonymous *Letter To a Certain Gentleman*, in which
Robie, a Harvard graduate, ridiculed the thinking of the common

people, who, as he advised his "gentleman," regarded as "amazing" a meteor that Robie knew had "Natural" causes. He went on to dismiss a whole way of thinking:

> As to Prognostications from [meteors] I utterly abhor and detest 'em all, and look upon these to be but the Effect of Ignorance and Fancy; for I have not so learned Philosophy or Divinity, as to be dismayed at the Signs of Heaven. . . .

Via such remarks, Robie manifested a self-consciousness of separation from the culture of the people; he rejected what had once prevailed, a common culture of the lore of wonders.[89] What also emerged in the early decades of the eighteenth century was a more generalized perception of God's providence, an interpretation that emphasized its regularities and not the interruptions that so fascinated Beard and Clarke.[90]

Yet Increase Mather did not fully overthrow the tradition he invoked so often in his sermons before 1692. The reality of witches was an article of faith, as was the presence of a Devil who enticed men and women into covenant. He continued to accept as true some stories of the supernatural, and in speaking of God's providence, he lingered on its mystery.[91] His son Cotton, who shared with him the recognition that the Devil had deceived witch-hunters, filled the *Magnalia Christi Americana* with scores of events he interpreted as wonders. Condemned in the case of Anabaptists, dreams returned to center stage in the pages of the *Magnalia* as authentic promptings from the supernatural. So did prophesying. Thus he dared report that John Cotton and John Wilson learned in dreams who would be selected by the Boston church to succeed them. Prophetic dreams had come to James Noyes, the minister of Newbury; his son recorded, "I have heard him tell . . . that the great changes of his life had been signified to him before-hand by *dreams*." John Eliot, the great preacher to the Indians, "often had strange *forebodings* of things that were to come." And Mather here added his own affirmation that "I have been astonished at some of his predictions, that . . . were followed with exact accomplishments."

But of all these men the most astonishing was John Wilson, the minister who had once shared dream lore with John Winthrop. Wilson, so we learn from Mather, used prayer to affect events; as chaplain of the expedition sent out to subdue the Pequots he had saved someone from death by impromptu prayers that deflected an arrow from its target. He had dreams that worked as prophecy, and his "blessings" healed the sick.

Yet Mather could not wholly endorse such proceedings. Though he went on to affirm the truth of witchcraft (including some events that involved magic), he also noted that John Wilson preached a sermon criticizing the claims of "opinionists" that God spoke to them in dreams. After writing of John Eliot he reaffirmed the doctrine that true prophecy must coincide with what the Scripture declares, a principle that worked (he said) against the Quakers. Like his father in *An Essay*, Cotton criticized the "little sorceries" of people who "would... cure hurts with spells" and use horseshoes to ward off the Devil. Responsive though he was to arguments against the long tradition of prophetic dreams and portents, Mather nonetheless gave far more weight to that tradition than to its alternative.[92] ...

... It is clear that [Mather] regarded ministers in general as gifted with extraordinary powers, along with certain individual laymen. But in lavishing attention on a man like Wilson whom the Quakers had denounced (and Anne Hutchinson, before them), Mather was defending the authority of everyone in office in New England. In effect, he invested his position with a strange two-sidedness: the power both to bless and to wreak destruction. Thus he told a classic wonder story of how someone rebuked by a minister for working on a fast day, and who "made him an obstinate and malapert answer... came home... [and] found one of his children suddenly dead; upon this he could have no rest in his mind, until he came to this 'reprover in the gate,' with humble and many tokens of repentance." Thus too he revealed the doubleness of blessings by John Eliot: "If he said of any affair, 'I cannot bless it!', it was a worse omen to it...." All this was like magic, albeit godly magic.[93]

The many levels of these texts forbid any simple separation of elite belief from popular. True, the lore of wonders was falling out of favor within learned culture. Yet tradition remained strong, and clergy like the Mathers, anxious to enhance their role, continued to invoke the wonder. But in doing so they had to face the fact that ordinary people sometimes disagreed with them. In effect, the clergy and the people were rethinking the relationship between the lore of wonders and the message of God's judgment. Even in the sixteenth century some lay people had resisted this connection, as when England's Queen Elizabeth rejected the advice of certain of her bishops that an earthquake was a portent of her death.[94] Anglicans, in general, shrugged off Puritan manipulations of the wonder to support a cause like reform of the Sabbath, just as, in the 1650s, moderates among the Puritans fought off would-be prophets who denounced a "hireling" ministry. How lay men and women in New England acted to select among competing versions of the wonder is not easy to discern. What is certain is that they held at arm's distance the specifics of the preachers' message about taverns, drinking, and the like.[95] Interpretation, always openended, had become less clear thanks to excess special pleading and to growing doubts about the meaning of God's providence. ...

IV

Even though ... partisans of different causes shamelessly politicized the process of interpretation, people never stopped believing that God signaled his intentions through extraordinary events like a fire or an earthquake. The colonists who kept diaries or wrote letters repeatedly referred to prodigies and portents as having real significance; in these private statements, as in public, they perceived the wonder as betokening God's judgments.

When Michael Wigglesworth, a Harvard tutor, learned of a "great fire" that destroyed part of Boston, he wrote in his diary that

> my heart was much affected and dejected within me upon deep thoughts of these things and what I have heard god speak to me in his word, (for he met with sundry of my sins and gave dreadful examples of gods judgments that should have warned me from them)....

Writing of the battles they were fighting in King Philip's War, other men consistently referred to victories and defeats as providential. Still others manifested a mentality of fearfulness by the way they behaved when they thought the Day of Judgment had arrived – the maid who fled to her master when she saw reflected in the clouds another Boston fire, Samuel Sewall's children when an earthquake shook their home.[96] The same kinds of people demonstrated time and time again their belief that dreams, strange sounds, and accidents had occult or prophetic meaning. Not always, but often, people traced misfortune to the powers of a witch. Those who became Quakers believed that they could prophesy. So did others who were orthodox; the sense of having special knowledge of the future – or of serving as the voice of God – was endemic in this culture.

A world so full of wonders, of supernatural forces that seeped into daily life, was a world that many different kinds of people essayed to interpret. The process of interpretation remained open-ended. In part this happened because stories circulated in bewildering confusion, and by routes that no one could control – conversations, rumor, letters, and public demonstrations, and in such forms of print as broadsides and cheap pamphlets. Printers played a crucial role in keeping older lore afloat, and in adding to the stock of stories. Surprisingly, the same role suited learned men like Beard and Clarke. Never, in New England, did the learned culture impose systematic order on the meaning of the wonder. Nor could the clergy silence or suppress the prophesying that lay people or outsiders like the Quakers practiced. It was in the very nature of the wonder that it be "surprising," that it run against the grain of routine expectations. In a culture that empowered every layman to interpret Scripture, the wonder was as meaningful to ordinary men and women – and as open to quotation or retelling – as the Book of Psalms. Bewildered though they often were by prodigies and portents, lay people in New England were free to accept or reject the meanings for these events that the clergy might propose.

Yet the clergy also taught them to prefer a certain set of meanings. One of these concerned God's providential guidance of New England and, more generally, of Protestants. Here the clergy more or less reiterated attitudes that lay writers also voiced, and that had their great original in Foxe's *Book of Martyrs*. A more distinctive meaning, though not solely voiced by clergy, had to do with morals and the good society. A long line of clergy, from Thomas Beard to Cotton Mather, insisted that the lesson of the wonder was that people must give up "Sabbath-breaking" and behave in keeping with a moral code. John Winthrop voiced a broader vision of what portents signified for daily life, an ethic of community or fellowship.

Out of all these uses emerged the most common meaning that the clergy offered for the wonder, that it signified impending judgment. In one sense there was nothing new in this interpretation; the motif of judgment (or disaster) was prefigured in the Bible, the lore descended from antiquity, and the message of exempla in the Middle Ages. The story line of judgment was in every sense a cliché of the times, a convention that hack writers used as freely as the preachers. Yet what made this theme distinctive as employed by the clergy was its kinship to their message about sin. For them a world of wonders was a world of fallen sinners who must learn to plead for forgiveness from a sovereign, judging God. The wonder served this end by instructing people in the doctrine of God's providence and its corollary, the message of man's weakness in God's presence.

> But we should consider that the Most High God doth sometimes deal with men in a way of Absolute Soveraignty. . . . If he does destroy the perfect with the wicked, and Laugh at the Trial of the innocent . . . who shall enter into his Counsels! who has given Him a Charge over the Earth! or who had disposed the whole world! Men are not able to give an account of his ordinary Works, much less of his secret Counsels, and the Dark Dispensations of his Providence.[97]

This evocation of a sovereign God and his "Dark Dispensations" may have been designed to impress laymen who ignored the lesson of the wonder. It was in the preachers' interest to emphasize the insecurity of sinners, to paint the course of life as prone to abrupt interruption.

Hence the many references to sudden death. It exemplified the quickness – the terrifying quickness – by which God could render judgment:

> ... the voice of the Lord in this Providence [is] Calling upon all that hear of it and, saying Prepare for Death! Prepare for Death! Prepare for Death! ... The best man in this Congregation, yea upon the face of the earth, may for ought that any one can say, be (as Moses was) suddenly taken out of the world.

Writing to console a mourning widow, a New England minister invoked the long-persisting echoes of the wheel of fortune, reminding her (and readers of his sermon) of how "the late and present rouling posture of the wheels of Providence" had overturned great emperors and caused them to tremble when they saw the king of terrors approach.[98] If death loomed as fearful, and if preachers played upon these fears in order to impose a system of repentance on the people, the lore of wonders was in part their means of doing so. ...

Notes

1 Paul Boyer and Stephen Nissenbaum, eds., *The Salem Witchcraft Papers: Verbatim Transcripts of the Legal Documents of the Salem Witchcraft Outbreak of 1692*, 3 vols. (New York, 1997) 1: 246 (cited hereafter as *SWP*); John Hale, *A Modest Enquiry into the Nature of Witchcraft* (Boston, 1708), 34; Increase Mather, *An Essay for the Recording of Illustrious Providences* (1684); repr. London, 1856), 101 (cited hereafter as *Essay*); "The Diaries of John Hull," American Antiquarian Society, *Transactions and Collections* 3 (1857), 218; *John Winthrop's Journal "History of New England,"* 2 vols., ed. James K. Hosmer, Original Narratives of Early American History (1910; repr., New York, 1953) 2: 346; "The Diary of Noadiah Russell," *New England Historical and Genealogical Register* 7 (1853), 53–4 (cited hereafter as *NEHGR*); Nathaniel Morton, *New-Englands Memoriall* (Cambridge, MA, 1669), 52; M. Halsey Thomas, ed., *The Diary of Samuel Sewall*, 2 vols. (New York, 1973), 1: 281 (cited hereafter as *Sewall Diary*).
2 Edward Johnson, *The Wonder-Working Providence of Sions Saviour* (1654), ed. J. Franklin Jameson, Original Narratives of Early American History (1910; repr., New York, 1959) (cited hereafter as Johnson, *WWP*); John Sherman, "To the Reader," in Cotton Mather, *Wonders of the Invisible World* (Boston, 1693 [1692]); Kitty Scoular, *Natural Magic: Studies in the Presentation of Nature in English Poetry from Spenser to Marvell* (Oxford, 1965), 5; Increase Mather, *The Latter Sign Discoursed of*, bound with *Kometographia* (Boston, 1683), third pagination, 7–11. Strictly speaking, a "wonder" was distinct from a "miracle," though in everyday discourse, and even among the ministry, the two words became interchangeable. Cf. John Preston,

The Breast-Plate of Faith and Love (London, 1630), pt 2, 176–7. See also Samuel Willard, *The Fiery Tryal no strange thing* (Boston, 1682), 4–7, for an explication of "strange" events.

3   Hyder Rollins, ed., *The Pack of Autolycus or Strange and Terrible News of Ghosts, Apparitions . . . as told in Broadside Ballads of the Years 1624–1693* (Cambridge, MA, 1927), 36–43, 117–21, 162–7, and passim; Joseph Frank, *The Beginnings of the English Newspaper, 1620–1660* (Cambridge, MA, 1961), 17; Bernard Capp, *English Almanacs 1500–1800* (Ithaca, NY, 1979), ch. 6; *Strange and wonderful News from Chipingnorton . . . Of certain dreadful Apparitions* ([London, 1679]); Matthias A. Shaaber, *Some Forerunners of the Newspaper in England 1476–1622* (Philadelphia, 1928).

4   Rollins, ed., *Pack of Autolycus*, 62, 139, 82, 23; [John Trundle], *A Miracle, of Miracles* ([London, 1614]), 5; John Gadbury, *Natura Prodigiorum or, A Discourse touching the nature of Prodigies* (London, 1660).

5   Thomas Beard, *The Theatre of Gods Judgements* (London, 1648), 409; Stephen Batman, *The Doome warning all men to the Iudgmente* (London, 1581), 317, 379, 390, 397.

6   Beard, *Theatre of Gods Judgements*, 37, 48, 195; Batman, *Doome warning all men to the Iudgemente*, 403; [R. B.], *Admirable Curiosities, Rarities, & Wonders in England* (London, 1682), passim. Here as elsewhere in this chapter, the possible references run into the hundreds.

7   Samuel Clarke, *A Mirrour or Looking Glasse both for Saints, and Sinners*, 2nd edn (London, 1654), 92–3 (hereafter cited as Clarke, *Examples*); Beard, *Theatre of Gods Judgements*, bk. 1, ch. 30; Rollins, ed., *Pack of Autolycus*, 75, 222.

8   Rollins, ed., *Pack of Autolycus*, 62.

9   Rollins, ed., *Pack of Autolycus*, 81. Philip Stubbes incorporated numerous continental stories into *The Anatomie of Abuses* some of which he learned from Dutch publications: *The Anatomie of Abuses*, 3rd edn (London, 1585), 121. John R. McNair, in his introduction to Batman's *Doome warning all men* (1581; repr. in facsimile, Delmar, NY, 1984), describes sources and precedents.

10 A book of great practical utility, as my citations from it indicate, is S. K. Heninger, Jr., *A Handbook of Renaissance Meteorology* (Durham, NC, 1960), which opens with an important survey of the encyclopedias that codified and transmitted so much of the wonder lore. No less important is Kester Svendsen, *Milton and Science* (New York, 1969), with its superb discussion (ch. 1) of "The Compendious Method of Natural Philosophy: Milton and the Encyclopedia Tradition." The notes and cross-references in Hyder Rollins's *Pack of Autolycus* remain the best guide to the print culture that I describe briefly. An exhaustive survey is Lynn Thorndike, *A History of Magic and Experimental Science*, 8 vols (New York, 1923–58), esp. vols 4–7.

11 Heninger, *Handbook of Renaissance Meteorology*, 12, and chs 2–3.

12 Ibid., 30–2; Don Cameron Allen, *The Star-Crossed Renaissance: The Quarrel About Astrology and Its Influence in England* (1941; New York, 1966), ch. 5; Capp, *English Almanacs*, ch. 5.

13 Eusebius, *The Ancient ecclesiastical histories* (London, 1619), 64, 80; *Bede's Ecclesiastical History of the English People*, ed. Bertram Colgrave and R. A. B.

Mynors (Oxford, 1960), 141, 361–3; G. R. Owst, *Literature and Pulpit in Medieval England* (Cambridge, 1938), 129–30.

14 Robert E. Lerner, *The Powers of Prophecy: The Cedar of Lebanon Vision from the Mongol Onslaught to the Dawn of the Enlightenment* (Berkeley and Los Angeles, 1983), passim, and 164 (Luther). See also J. S. P. Tatlock, *The Legendary History of Britain* (Berkeley and Los Angeles, 1950); and Rupert Taylor, *The Political Prophecy in England* (New York, 1911).

15 R. W. Scribner, *For the Sake of Simple Folk: Popular Propaganda for the German Reformation* (Cambridge, 1981), 116–17, 140–7, 184; Katharine R. Firth, *The Apocalyptic Tradition in Reformation Britain, 1530–1645* (Oxford, 1979); Joseph Mede, *The Key of the Revelation, searched and demonstrated out of the Naturall and proper Characters of the Visions* (London, 1643), pt 1, 84, 88, 94; Keith Thomas, *Religion and the Decline of Magic* (London, 1971), ch. 13.

16 Katharine Park and Lorraine J. Daston, "Unnatural Conceptions: The Study of Monsters in Sixteenth- and Seventeenth-Century France and England," *Past and Present* 92 (1981), 20–54; T. K. Hoppe, "The Nature of the Early Royal Society," *British Journal for the History of Science* 9 (1976), 1–24, 243–7.

17 Geoffrey Chaucer, *The Canterbury Tales*, tr. Neville Coghill (Baltimore, 1952), 70; John Calvin, *Institutes of the Christian Religion*, ed. John T. McNeill, tr. Ford Lewis Battles, 2 vols. (Philadelphia, 1960), bk 1, ch. 16; Beard, *Theatre of Gods Judgements*, 88–93; Peter Lake, *Moderate Puritans and the Elizabethan Church* (Cambridge, 1982), 119–20.

18 Cf. Victor Harris, *All Coherence Gone* (Chicago, 1949).

19 Heninger, *Handbook of Renaissance Meteorology*, 87–91; Du Bartas, *La Sepmaine*, quoted on the reverse of title page, Samuel Danforth, *An Astronomical Description of the late Comet or Blazing Star* (Cambridge, MA, 1665); Pliny, *Natural History*, tr. H. Rackham, 10 vols. (Cambridge, MA, 1949), 1: 235 (bk II.xxiii); C. Doris Hellman, *The Comet of 1577: Its Place in the History of Astronomy* (New York, 1944), 252–8.

20 Pliny, *Natural History*, 1: 275 (bk II.liii); Heninger, *Handbook of Renaissance Meteorology*, 72–87.

21 *The Famous and Memorable Workes of Josephus . . . Faithfully Translated . . . by Thomas Lodge* (London, 1620), 738; Heninger, *Handbook of Renaissance Meteorology*, 91–4; Rollins, ed., *Pack of Autolycus*, 38; *Mirabilis Annus Secundus; Or, The Second Year of Prodigies. Being A true and impartial Collection of many strange Signes and Apparitions . . .* ([London], 1662), 2–3.

22 Paul H. Kocher, *Science and Religion in Elizabethan England* (New York, 1969).

23 Capp, *English Almanacs*, 165; Hershel Baker, *The Race of Time* (Toronto, 1967), 57–63; Joseph J. Morgan, Jr, *Chaucer and the Theme of Mutability* (The Hague, 1961); Harris, *All Coherence Gone*, chs 4–5.

24 Willard Farnham, *The Medieval Heritage of Elizabethan Tragedy* (Berkeley, 1936), ch. 7; Scribner, *For the Sake of Simple Folk*, 117; Beard, *Theatre of Gods Judgements*, 80.

25 Michael MacDonald, *Mystical Bedlam: Madness, Anxiety, and Healing in Seventeenth-Century England* (Cambridge, 1981), 175, 202.

26 Howard R. Patch, *The Goddess Fortuna in Medieval Literature* (Cambridge, MA, 1927); J. G. A. Pocock, *The Machiavellian Moment: Florentine Political Thought and the Atlantic Republican Tradition* (Princeton, NJ, 1975), 349–50.

27 Katharine M. Briggs, *The Anatomy of Puck: An Examination of Fairy Beliefs Among Shakespeare's Contemporaries and Successors* (London, 1959); C. Grant Loomis, *White Magic: An Introduction to the Folklore of Christian Legend* (Cambridge, MA, 1948); Kittredge, *Old Farmer and His Almanac*, ch. 6; Clarke, *Examples*, bks 69–71. As Sydney Anglo observes in "Evident Authority and Authoritative Evidence: The *Malleus Maleficarum*," in Anglo, ed., *The Damned Art: Essays in the Literature of Witchcraft* (London, 1977), 6: "Throughout the Middle Ages and the Renaissance, arguments in virtually every field of human enquiry proceeded upon the basis of accumulated authority." Hence (p. 10) the Puritan William Perkins cited Homer as an "unimpeachable source" for an understanding of witchcraft!

28 William P. Upham, "Remarks," Massachusetts Historical Society, *Proceedings* (hereafter *MHS Proc.*), 2nd ser., 13 (1900), 126–7; Increase Mather, *Wo to Drunkards* (Cambridge, MA, 1673), 28; "The Diary of Increase Mather," *MHS Proc.*, 2nd ser., 13 (1900), 345.

29 Worthington C. Ford, *The Boston Book Market, 1679–1700* (Boston, 1917), 149.

30 Kenneth B. Murdoch, ed., *Handkerchiefs from Paul being Pious and Consolatory Verses of Puritan Massachusetts* (Cambridge, MA, 1927), 109–11; [Samuel Danforth], *An Almanacke for the Year of Our Lord 1648* (Cambridge, MA, 1648).

31 Samuel Danforth, *An Astronomical Description of the late Comet or Blazing Star* (Cambridge, MA, 1665); Wiswell, *A judicious observation* (London, 1683); Mather, *Heavens Alarm to the World* (Boston, 1682); the same, *The Latter Sign Discoursed of* (Boston, 1682); and *Kometographia*.

32 *Records of the First Church at Dorchester in New England 1636–1734* (Boston, 1891); *Roxbury Land and Church Records, [Sixth] Report of the Record Commissioners of the City of Boston* (Boston, 1884), 187–212; *Mather Papers*, Massachussetts Historical Society, *Collections* (hereafter *MHS Coll*), 4th ser., 8 (1868), 282 (hereafter cited as *Mather Papers*); John Langdon Sibley, *Biographical Sketches of Graduates of Harvard University in Cambridge, Massachusetts*, 3 vols. (Cambridge, MA, 1873–85), 1: 508, for reference to John Cotton of Plymouth's "diary of remarkables."

33 "Diary of Lawrence Hammond," *MHS Proc.*, 2nd ser., 7 (1892), 147–9; "The Diaries of John Hull," 217–18.

34 Upham, "Remarks," 127–8; John H. Lockwood, *Westfield and Its Historic Influences, 1669–1919*, 2 vols. (Springfield, MA, 1922), 1: 132. In Arthur Dent's *The Plain Mans Pathway to Heaven* (London, 1610), one of the characters says, "For it is an hard world, and goods are not easie to come by" (p. 91).

35 *Mather Papers*, 282–7.

36 Ibid., 360–2.

37 Ibid., 306–10.

38   Ibid., 466–81. The Marshfield episode, told in a letter from the Reverend
     Samuel Arnold, was later published by N. B. Shurtleff as *Thunder &*
     Lightning; and Deaths at Marshfield in 1658 & 1666 (Boston, 1850). For a
     previous effort by Mather to collect stories, cf. Thomas Cobbett, "A Narra-
     tive of New England's Deliverance," *NEHGR* 7 (1853), 209–19.

39   *Mather Papers*, 58–9.

40   *Winthrop Journal*, 2: 71.

41   William Christian, Jr., *Apparitions in Late Medieval and Renaissance Spain*
     (Princeton, NJ, 1981); J.-C. Schmitt, *Le Saint Levrier: Guinefort, guérisseur*
     d'enfants depuis le xiii siècle (Paris, 1979).

42   *Winthrop Journal*, 1: 163, 176; 2: 9; 1: 195; 2: 97; 88; 1: 115; 2: 44; 1: 322,
     195.

43   Ibid., 1: 285, 287, 308; 2: 71. Citing the safe voyages of so many of the
     colonists became common practice. Cf. *Wyllys Papers*, Connecticut Histor-
     ical Society, *Collections* 21 (1924), 68; Mather, *Essay*, ch. 1 ("Of Remark-
     able Sea Deliverances"); and Donald P. Wharton, "Providence and the
     Colonial American Sea-Deliverance Tradition," *Essex Institute Historical*
     Collections 119 (1983), 42–8.

44   *Winthrop Journal*, 2: 347–8; 1: 294; 2: 156, 264.

45   Morton, *New-Englands Memoriall*, 84, 1, 23, 44, 97.

46   *Roxbury Land and Church Records*, 188, 78.

47   Charles F. Adams, Jr, "Abstract of [John] Marshall's Diary, *MHS Proc.*,
     2nd ser., 1 (1884–5), 148–64, and its continuation, Samuel A. Green,
     "Remarks," ibid., 2nd ser., 14 (1900–1), 13–34; "John Dane's Narrative,
     1682," *NEHGR* 8 (1854), 149–156; "Diary of Lawrence Hammond,"
     147–8; Samuel Deane, *History of Scituate, Massachusetts* (Boston, 1831),
     123.

48   Beard, *Theatre of Gods Judgements*, 2.

49   Joshua Coffin, *A Sketch of the History of Newbury* (Boston, 1845), 26;
     Johnson, *WWP*, 185; Marshall Swan, "The Bedevilment of Cape Ann,
     1692," *Essex Institute Historical Collections*, 117 (1981), 153–77; *Sewall Diary*,
     1: 603; Robert W. Lovett, ed., *Documents From the Harvard University*
     Archives, 1638–1750, CSM Pub., 49 (Boston, 1975), 150.

50   Increase Mather, *The Doctrine of Divine Providence Opened and Applyed*
     (Boston, 1684), 43, 30–2, 34, 81, 133; and for the figure of the wheel and
     the rise and fall of kings, cf. 9, 16–17. The image of the wheel derives from
     Ezekiel 1: 15–16 et seq.

51   The best brief treatment of this subject is Thomas, *Religion and the Decline of*
     Magic, ch. 5 and pp. 342–4.

52   David D. Hall, *The Antinomian Controversy, 1636–1638: A Documentary*
     History (Middletown, CT, 1968), 268, 337–9 (hereafter *AC*); Johnson,
     WWP, 129, 127.

53   *AC*, 165.

54   Thomas, *Religion and the Decline of Magic*, 137–8, 135. See also Phyllis
     Mack, "Women as Prophets During the English Civil War," *Feminist Studies*
     8, 1 (Spring 1982), 19–45. I hazard the opinion that separatist Puritans
     (and Anne Hutchinson was like a separatist in questioning the legitimacy of

the English church) were prone to prophesying the destruction of England; for one example, see Edward Arber, ed., *The Story of the Pilgrim Fathers* (London, 1897), 246.

55 *AC*, 337–8, 272–3.
56 Isaac Backus, *A History of New-England, with special reference to the Baptists*, 2 vols. (1771; repr., Newton, MA, 1871), 1: 322.
57 "Diaries of John Hull," 202; [Thomas Maule], *New-England Persecutors Mauld With their own Weapons* [New York, 1697], 32; S[amuel] G[room], *A Glasse for the People of New England* ([London], 1676), 15; *Sewall Diary*, 1: 44, 18.
58 George Keith, *The Pretended Antidote Proved Poyson* (Philadelphia, 1690), 204; [Maule], *New-England Persecutors*, sig. A2 recto, 19; John Rogers, *A Brief Account of some of the late Suffering of several Baptists* ([New York, 1726]), 13.
59 *Essex Court Recs.*, 7: 46; 1: 265; *Winthrop Journal*, 2: 344; R. G. Tomlinson, *Witchcraft Trials of Connecticut* (Hartford, CO, 1978), 41–3, 14; Cotton Mather, *Memorable Providences, Relating to Witchcrafts and Possessions* (Boston, 1689), 20; Coffin, *History of Newbury*, 123; John Taylor, *The Witch-craft Delusion in Colonial Connecticut, 1647–1697* (New York, 1908), 56; *Essex Court Recs.*, 7: 357; *SWP*, 2: 397–9, 626; 3: 787–8; Samuel G. Drake, *Annals of Witchcraft in New England* (Boston, 1869), 287, 281. For other episodes, cf. Thomas Gage, *The History of Rowley* (Boston, 1840), 72; "Memoir of the Rev. William Adams," *MHS Coll.*, 4th ser., 1 (1852), 17–18.
60 *SWP*, 2: 507; 1: 228, 308; Hale, *A Modest Enquiry*, 133; Drake, *Annals*, 275.
61 Ronald Marcus, *"Elizabeth Clawson... Thou Deseruest to Dye: An Account* (Stamford, CT, 1976) [pamphlet at the Connecticut Historical Society]; Hoadley transcripts, Connecticut Historical Society, testimony of Samuel Debell (1667).
62 *Winthrop Journal*, 1: 266–8, 277; 280–2, 214.
63 *AC*, 273. John Cotton was interested in exploring whether Mrs. Hutchinson meant by "miracle" a "work above nature or... some wonderful providence for that is called a miracle often in the psalms"; Mrs. Hutchinson did indeed revert to the word "providence," but by this time the magistrates were ready to convict her. Ibid., 340–2.
64 [Maule], *New-England Persecutors*, 8.
65 Mather, *Wonders of the Invisible World*, 13–15.
66 Mather, *Essay*, ch. 8.
67 Alice L. Brown, "Religious Dreams and Their Interpretation in Some Thinkers of the Seventeenth Century" (PhD thesis, University of London, 1975), traces dream theory forward from the Greeks (I am grateful to the late D. P. Walker for this reference); Guy de Brez, *The Rise, Spring and Foundation of the Anabaptists, Or ReBaptized of our Time*, tr. J. S. (Cambridge, MA, 1668), 47, 1, 12–13, 20–1, 7; *AC* 342–3.
68 Clarke, *Examples*, 221–2; Morton, *New-Englands Memoriall*, 108; G[roome], *A Glasse For the People of New-England*, 11.
69 *Winthrop Journal*, 2: 317; 321–2; Edward Winslow, *New-Englands Salaman-der, Discovered by an Irreligious and Scornfull Pamphlet* (1647); repr., *MHS*

Coll., 3rd ser., 2 (1830), 128–9; John Child, *New-Englands Jonas Cast up at London* (1647); repr., *MHS Coll.*, 2nd ser., 4 (1816), 114–16. The charges made against the Child group included "They lay open the afflictions, which God hath pleased to exercise us with, and that to the worst appearance, and impute it to the evil of our government." *Winthrop Journal*, 2: 297.

70 Winslow, *New-Englands Salamander*, 130–3. This story lived on in oral and written tradition, to be cited by John Allin to his son in 1668: "... letters written against the country to great ones in England, divers violent storms, to the apparent danger of ship & lives, forced the mesanger to produce them (as Jonas once himself) which being viewed and thrown overboard they had after it an happy and prosperous voyage, which accident is the 6th time that letters against the country hath from time to time miscarried." Sibley, *Biographical Sketches*, 1: 297.

71 Child, *New-Englands Jonas* , 115–16.

72 *Winthrop Papers*, 5: 126; Sidney Perley, *The History of Boxford* (Boxford, MA, 1880), 62 n. Cf. Andrew Delbanco, "The Puritan Errand Reviewed," *Journal of American Studies* 18 (1984), 343–60.

73 Sylvester Judd, *History of Hadley* (Springfield, MA, 1905), 77.

74 Samuel Willard, *Ne Sutor Ultra Crepidam* (Boston, 1681), 24, refers to Baptist celebrations of a war hero as one of their own.

75 Increase Mather, *A Discourse Concerning the Uncertainty of the Times of Men* (Boston, 1697); Mather, *Wo to Drunkards*, 12, 20–4. For more in this vein, cf. Increase Mather, *Meditations On the Sanctification of the Lord's Day* (Boston, 1712). It is worth repeating that Mather followed English literary models, e.g, Samuel Ward, *Wo to Drunkards* (London, 1622). Though this way of preaching was disappearing in the early eighteenth century, some ministers continued to employ it; cf. John Barnard, *The Nature and Danger of Sinful Mirth, Exhibited in a Plain Discourse* (Boston, 1728).

76 Increase Mather, *A Sermon Wherein is shewed that the Church of God is sometimes a Subject of Great Persecution* (Boston, 1682), 16, 7, sig. A3 recto.

77 For example, William Hubbard, *A Narrative of the Troubles with the Indians in New-England* (Boston, 1677).

78 "Diary of Increase Mather," *MHS Proc.*, 2nd ser., 13 (1900), 347, 359–60.

79 *Mather Papers*, 279. For a good example of futility, cf. *Essex Court Recs.*, 7: 71.

80 Robert Middlekauff, *The Mathers: Three Generations of Puritan Intellectuals* (New York, 1971), 139–43.

81 Park and Daston, "Unnatural Conceptions," 51–4.

82 John Aubrey, *Three Prose Works*, ed. John Buchanan-Brown (Fontwell, 1972), 427–8. Cf. Moody E. Prior, "Joseph Glanvill, Witchcraft, and Seventeenth-Century Science," *Modern Philology* 30 (1932 3), 167–94.

83 Ronald A. Knox, *Enthusiasm: A Chapter in the History of Religion* (1950; repr., New York, 1961), ch. 15; Thomas Hobbes, *Leviathan*, ed. Michael Oakeshott (Oxford, 1957), pt IV.

84 Charles Morton, *Compendium Physicae, CSM Pub.*, 33 (Boston, 1940), 35, 93, 87, 111–12.

85 Increase Mather, *Angelographia, or A Discourse Concerning the Nature and Power of the Holy Angels* (Boston, 1696), sig. B2 recto, verso, 63; the same, *A Disquisition Concerning Angelical Apparitions, In Answer to a Case of Conscience* (Boston, 1696), 5–6, 12, 17–22, 26–8.

86 Peter Burke, *Popular Culture in Early Modern Europe* (New York, 1978), ch. 8, and 241.

87 Mather, *Disquisition Concerning Angelical Apparitions*, 31; Mather, *Essay*, 198–203; Middlekauff, *The Mathers*, 155–7; Taylor, *Witchcraft in Connecticut*, 75–6.

88 Notably, John Hale, Samuel Willard, and Thomas Brattle. See, e.g., Samuel Willard, *The Checkered State of the Gospel Church* (Boston, 1701), 36, for the effort to differentiate Scripture predictions from prognostications, which Willard defined as mostly mistakes made by persons who pretend to possess the spirit of prophecy.

89 [Thomas Robie], *A Letter To a Certain Gentleman, &c* (Boston, 1719), 1–2, 8.

90 See, e.g., Nathan Fiske, *Remarkable Providences to be gratefully recollected, religiously improved, and carefully transmitted to Posterity* (Boston, 1776).

91 As Middlekauff points out, Mather did not really listen to the critics. *The Mathers*, 157–9.

92 *Magnalia*, 1: 295, 486, 544, 307–14, 312, 544, 205.

93 *Magnalia*, 2: 61–2; 1: 544.

94 L. M. Buell, "Elizabethan Portents: Superstition or Doctrine," in *Essays Critical and Historical Dedicated to Lily B. Campbell* (Berkeley and Los Angeles, 1950), 33.

95 Cf. *Essex Court Recs.*, 7: 71. When Richard Brown preached a fast-day sermon in Newbury in 1700 and "concluded . . . to lay open in peticular the sins that most openly abounded and to press them home," his audience was "highly offended, as taking all to themselves. . . . Great was their rage against me, they threatened me to my face, But more Behind my Back" – to the point of open violence. Lilly Eaton, *Genealogical History of the Town of Reading* (Boston, 1874), 54.

96 Edmund S. Morgan, ed., *The Diary of Michael Wigglesworth 1653–1657: The Conscience of a Puritan* (1946; repr., New York, 1965), 8–9; Thomas Waters, *Ipswich in the Massachusetts-Bay Colony*, 2 vols. (Ipswich, 1905), 1: 172, 178, 183; Deane, *History of Scituate*, 122; "Letter from Benj. Corbyn to Thomas Fuller," *NEHGR* 22 (1968), 296.

97 I. Mather, *Cases of Conscience Concerning evil Spirits Personating Men* (Boston, 1693); 16; Mather, *Doctrine of Divine Providence*, 77–8.

98 Mather, *The Times of Men*, 20; Leonard Hoar, *The Sting of Death and Death Unstung* (Boston, 1680), sig. A2 recto, 6–8.

A Model of Christian Charity (1630)

John Winthrop

Christian Charity: A Model Hereof

God Almighty, in his most holy and wise providence, hath so disposed of the condition of mankind, as in all times some must be rich, some poor, some high and eminent in power and dignity, others mean and in subjection.

The Reason Hereof

First, to hold conformity with the rest of his works. Being delighted to show forth the glory of his wisdom in the variety and difference of the creatures; and the glory of his power, in ordering all these differences for the preservation and good of the whole; and the glory of his greatness, that as it is the glory of princes to have many officers, so this great king will have many stewards, counting himself more honored in dispensing his gifts to man by man, than if he did it by his own immediate hands.

Secondly, that he might have the more occasion to manifest the work of his Spirit. First, upon the wicked, in moderating and restraining them: so that the rich and mighty should not eat up the poor, nor the poor and despised rise up against their superiors and shake off their yoke. Secondly, in the regenerate, in exercising his graces in them: as in the great ones, their love, mercy, gentleness, temperance, etc.; in the poor and inferior sort, their faith, patience, obedience, etc.

Thirdly, that every man might have need of other, and from hence they might be all knit more nearly together in the bond of brotherly affection. From hence it appears plainly that no man is made more honorable than another or more wealthy, etc., out of any particular and singular respect to himself, but for the glory of his creator and the common good of the creature, man. Therefore God still reserves the property of these gifts to himself, as [in] Ezekiel, 16: 17. He there calls wealth his gold and his silver. [In] Proverbs, 3: 9 he claims their service as his due: honor the Lord with thy riches, etc. All men being thus (by divine providence) ranked into two sorts, rich and poor, under the first are comprehended all such as are able to live comfortably by their own means duly improved; and all others are poor, according to the former distribution. . . .

Question: What rule must we observe in lending?

Answer: Thou must observe whether thy brother hath present or probable or possible means of repaying thee; if there be none of these, thou must give him according to his necessity, rather than lend him as he requires. If he hath present means of repaying thee, thou art to look at him, not as an act of mercy, but by way of commerce, wherein thou art to walk by the rule of Justice. But if his means of repaying thee be only probable or possible, then is he an object of thy mercy – thou must lend him, though there be danger of losing it, Deuteronomy, 15: 7. If any of thy brethren be poor, etc., thou shalt lend him sufficient. That men might not shift off this duty by the apparent hazard, he tells them that, though the Year of Jubilee were at hand (when he must remit it, if he were not able to repay it before), yet he must lend him, and that cheerfully: It may not grieve thee to give him (saith he). And because some might object why so I should soon impoverish myself and my family, he adds, with all thy work, etc., for our Saviour. Matthew, *5: 42:* "From him that would borrow of thee, turn not away."

Question: What rule must we observe in forgiving?

Answer: Whether thou didst lend by way of commerce or in mercy, if he have nothing to pay thee [thou] must forgive him (except in case where thou hast a surety or a lawful pledge), Deuteronomy, 15: 2: Every seventh year the creditor was to quit that which he lent to his brother if he were poor, as appears verse [4], save when there shall be no poor with thee. In all these and like cases, Christ was a general rule, Matthew, [7: 12]. Whatsoever ye would that men should do to you, do ye the same to them also. . . .

The definition which the scripture gives us of love is this: "Love is the bond of perfection." First, it is a bond, or ligament. Secondly, it makes the work perfect. There is no body but consists of parts, and that which knits these parts together, gives the body its perfection, because it makes each part so contiguous to others as thereby they do mutually participate with each other, both in strength and infirmity, in pleasure and pain. To instance in the most perfect of all bodies, Christ and his church make one body: the several parts of this body considered apart, before they were united, were as disproportionate and as much disordering as so many contrary qualities or elements; but when Christ comes and by his spirit and love knits all these parts to himself and each to other, it is become the most perfect and best proportioned body in the world, Ephesians, 4: 16: "Christ, by whom all the body being knit together, by every joint for the furniture thereof, according to the effectual power which is in the measure of every perfection of parts," "a glorious body, without spot or wrinkle," the ligaments hereof being Christ, or his love, for Christ is love, (I John 4: 8). So this definition is right: "Love is the bond of perfection."

From hence we may frame these conclusions. First, all true Christians are of one body in Christ, I Corinthians, 12: 27: "Ye are the body of Christ and members of [your?] part." Secondly, the ligaments of this body which knit together are love. Thirdly, no body can be perfect which wants its proper ligaments. Fourthly, all the parts of this body, being thus united, are made so contiguous in a special relation as they must needs partake of each other's strength and infirmity, joy and sorrow, weal and woe, I Corinthians, 12: 26: "If one member suffers, all suffer with it, if one be in honor, all rejoice with it." Fifthly, this sensibleness and sympathy of each other's conditions will necessarily infuse into each part a native desire and endeavor to strengthen, defend, preserve and comfort the other. . . .

Thus stands the cause between God and us. We are entered into covenant with him for this work, we have taken out a commission, the Lord hath given us leave to draw our own articles, we have professed to enterprise these actions upon these and those ends, we have hereupon besought him of favor and blessing. Now if the Lord shall please to hear us, and bring us in peace to the place we desire, then hath he ratified this covenant and sealed our commission, [and] will expect a strict performance of the articles contained in it. But if we shall neglect the observation of these articles which are the ends we have propounded, and, dissembling with our God, shall fall to embrace this present world and prosecute our carnal intentions, seeking great things for ourselves and our posterity, the Lord will surely break out in wrath against us, be revenged of such a perjured people and make us know the price of the breach of such a covenant.

Now the only way to avoid this shipwreck and to provide for our posterity is to follow the counsel of Micah: to do justly, to love mercy, to walk humbly with our God. For this end, we must be knit together in this work as one man, we must entertain each other in brotherly affection, we must be willing to abridge ourselves of our superfluities, for the supply of others' necessities, we must uphold a familiar commerce together in all meekness, gentleness, patience and liberality, we must delight in each other, make others' conditions our own, rejoice together, mourn together, labor and suffer together, always having before our eyes our commission and community in the work, our community as members of the same body. So shall we keep the unity of the spirit in the bond of peace. The Lord will be our God and delight to dwell among us as his own people and will command a blessing upon us in all our ways, so that we shall see much more of his wisdom, power, goodness and truth, than formerly we have been acquainted with. We shall find that the God of Israel is among us, when ten of us shall be able to resist a thousand of our enemies, when he shall make us a praise and glory, that men shall say of succeeding plantations: "the Lord make it like that of New England." For we must consider that we shall be as a city upon a hill: the eyes of all people are upon us, so that if we shall deal falsely with our God in this work we have undertaken, and so cause him to withdraw his present help from us, we shall be made a story and a by-word through the world: we shall open the mouths of enemies to speak evil of the ways of God and all professors for God's sake. We shall shame the faces of many of God's worthy servants, and cause their prayers to be turned into curses upon us till we be consumed out of the good land whither we are going.

And to shut up this discourse with that exhortation of Moses, that faithful servant of the Lord, in his last farewell to Israel. Deuteronomy, 30: Beloved, there is now set before us life and good, death and evil, in that we are commanded this day to love the Lord our God, and to love one another, to walk in his ways and to keep his commandments and his ordinance and his laws, and the articles of our covenant with him, that we may live and be multiplied, and that the Lord our God may bless us in the land whither we go to possess it. But if our hearts shall turn away, so that we will not obey, but shall be seduced and worship other Gods – our pleasures and profits – and serve them, it is propounded unto us this day, we shall surely perish out of the good land whither we pass over the vast sea to possess it;

> Therefore let us choose life,
> that we and our seed may live
> by obeying His voice and cleaving to Him,
> for He is our life and our prosperity.

Trial of Mrs Lucy Brewster at a Court Held at Newhaven (1646)

Mrs. Brewster, Mrs. Moore & Mrs. Leach being warned about several miscarriages of a public nature, appeared and were charged severally as follows,

Elizabeth Smith late servant to Mrs. Leach, says that hearing Mrs. Brewster loud in conference with Mrs. Eaton, Mrs. Moore & her Mrs. as she sat at work in the next room, she called Job Hall, her fellow servant to hear also, who could better remember the particulars of such a conference then herself.

Imprimis [firstly], Job & Elizabeth both affirm that Mrs. Brewster repeating something of Mr. Davenport's prayer to this purpose, Lord add to the church such as shall be saved & build up to perfection those whom thou hast added; and speaking of his sermon said, Mr. Davenport makes the people believe that to come into the church is as much as the receiving of Christ. Job said she added, Mr. Davenport carries it as if they could not have salvation without coming into the church. . . .

Mrs. Brewster as before the Governor & Mr. Goodyeare formerly, so now in court denied the charge.

2dly. Job & Elizabeth affirm that Mrs. Brewster speaking of something Mr. Davenport had delivered upon Ephes. 4, 12, concerning personal faith, that if a man lived where he might join to the church & did not, it would prove a delusion to him. Job affirms that Mrs. Brewster said, when she heard it her stomach wombled as when she bred child, & spoke it twice or thrice if not oftener in reference to the sermon. Elizabeth said, that twice or thrice she spoke to that purpose, that she was sermon sick, & that proceeding in conference she presently said that when she came home she bade her son make waste paper of it, which she the said Elizabeth conceives was spoken in reference to the notes of Mr. Davenport's sermon.

Mrs. Brewster denied these words, sermon sick, or that it was in reference to the sermon, & those words of making waste paper &c. but confesses she said her stomach wrought, smelling an ill savor in the seat, wherein she gave no satisfaction to the court. . . .

4^{thly}. Job & Elizabeth affirm that Mrs. Brewster speaking of the contributions said, it was as going to mass or going up to the high altar, & being asked by Mrs. Moore why she then went to them, she answered, because her husband had commanded her.

Mrs. Brewster denies that ever she spoke of mass, or high altar in reference to the contributions, the first time she heard of the word altar, applied that way, was in the seat, Mrs. Lamberton speaking of that text, when thou bringest thy gift to the altar, but she said Mrs. Moore asked what rule there was for going to the high altar in the contributions, but Mrs. Eaton defended the practice of the church. . . .

6^{thly}. Job affirms that Mrs. Brewster asked Mrs. Leach whether she had any mind to join with the church, Mrs. Leach answered, no, Mrs. Brewster asked whether she had not formerly had a mind, Mrs. Leach answered, yes. Mrs. Brewster replied, your mother is a woman of wisdom, this she doubled, your mother is a woman of wisdom, adding she can teach you well enough at home. Elizabeth remembers the question put to Mrs. Leach with her answer as before, & that Mrs. Brewster replied, her mother could teach her, or tutor her well enough at home, or words to that purpose.

Mrs. Brewster said she told Mrs. Leach she had heard she was about to join with the church but now declined it. Mrs. Leach answered, (as formerly to Mrs. Wackman or some other of the church,) it was because she found so many untruths among them, but Mrs. Brewster denies that she said her mother was a woman of wisdom & could teach her at home.

7^{thly}. Elizabeth says that Mrs. Brewster being asked by Mrs. Moore whether she saw the persons whipped for their unnatural filthiness about a month since, she answered no, but they were cruelly whipped & that her son said he had rather fall into the hands of Turks, & had rather be hanged then fall into their hands.

Mrs. Brewster denies that ever she spoke of cruelty in their punishment, she rather thought they deserved more, & that the censure was merciful, nor ever did she hear her son speak of falling into the hands of Turks, though he spoke something pertaining them that were first corrected & that if he were fit for death, he would rather be hanged then so whipped.

8^{thly}. Elizabeth says that on the fourth day of the week, before William Preston was cast out of the church, Mrs. Brewster met with some sister of the church betwixt her own house & Mr. Leach's, & seeing her look sad, Mrs. Brewster asked her what was the cause. The sister told her some passages of William Preston's miscarriages for which the church was like to proceed against him, Elizabeth said Mrs. Brewster related this to Mrs. Moore in a scoffing manner, adding in her speech to Mrs. Moore, I looked pitifully when I spoke with the sister, as if I had been one of them, which Elizabeth conceives she did, to draw from the sister what she could.

Mrs. Brewster confesses she met with Goody Charles & spoke with her, to the purpose the charge, (in the first part,) imports, but denies the latter part, concerning scoffing & looking pitifully, as if she had been one of them. . . .

10^{thly}. Job says, that the last day of the week, being May the 9th, he was called up before Mrs. Brewster, Mrs. Moore & Mrs. Leach, at Mr. Leach's house. Mrs. Brewster told him she had been where she had justified herself against a great many of his lies & added, she would have him & his slut, you & your harlot, to the whipping post. Elizabeth said that she being below in the house at this time, heard the former words.

Mrs. Brewster spoke them so loud that, (as she conceives,) they might be heard into the midst of the street.

Mrs. Brewster denied those words, you & your slut, you & your harlot, to the whipping post, in reference to Job Hall. Mrs. Moore & Mrs. Leach being questioned about them, acknowledged such words were spoken, but conceive, your slut, your harlot, were not referred to Job Hall, but to them the said Mrs. Moore & Mrs. Leach, Elizabeth standing in relation to Mrs. Leach as her servant.

The court thought it scarce probable, the whole speech being continued to Job Hall, that your slut, your harlot should be referred to others, nor is it likely that Mrs. Brewster should cast any appearance of blame upon Mrs. Moore and Mrs. Leach for Elizabeth's miscarriages, as your slut, your harlot seem to import.

11^{thly}. Elizabeth says that on the same day, May the ninth, Mrs. Brewster told her that she went about carrying lies, to curry favor to keep her whore's back from whipping, adding, she would call her nothing but whore and harlot until she had been whipped and was married, then she must call her so no more, & if the fellow did not come home he must take his money if he can get it, or else he must take it out in whipping. Mrs. Brewster further said that Elizabeth told half truths & half lies. Elizabeth answered, her half truths will prove whole truths. Mrs. Brewster replied, will they so, you brazen faced whore. Elizabeth answered she was grieved for her sin, & desired to be so all her days. Mrs. Brewster said, she had gotten a few of the fine words.

Mrs. Brewster denied the word whore, she said she called her only harlot, she was told such railing language was uncomely & sinful, Michael the Archangel durst not carry it so with the Devil, though he had matter enough against him. . . .

Mrs. Brewster being asked what further she had to say either for herself or against the witnesses, she was full of speech, offered to take hold of the witnesses & to draw them to her, as if she would have overruled their testimony; she was told meekness & modesty would better become her in such a place. In anything she doubted or denied, the court would take no evidence but upon oath, she seemed to charge the court as if she could not be heard, but being reproved for such boldness contrary to truth, she felt to justify herself that she approved Mr. Davenport's ministry. If some one time he had not expressed himself so clearly and fully as at others she propounded questions for his information, and at last, going to Mr. Davenport's, she was fully satisfied. She denied that ever she used the words sermon sick, or mass, or high altar, in reference to the contributions. She confessed she had rather have given twice as much in a private way to pastor or teacher, she went because her husband commanded her, yet afterwards she expressly denied that her husband had commanded her. . . .

Then she laded the witnesses with reproach that she might disable their testimony, all of them were liars, Job by his lying had been the death of Mrs. Leach her child, which, (she not being able to prove,) was accounted a rash or false charge.

Which being duly considered, the magistrates & deputies severally expressed themselves that Mrs. Brewster had proved nothing to disable any of the witnesses, they were therefore to give in evidence severally upon oath, that the cause might come to a due issue.

Tryal of Susanna Martin in Salem, June 29, 1692

1. Susanna Martin, pleading *Not Guilty* to the Indictment of *Witchcraft*, brought in against her, there were produced the Evidences of many Persons very sensibly and grievously Bewitched; who all complained of the Prisoner at the Bar, as the Person whom they believed the cause of their Miseries. And now, as well as in the other Trials, there was an extraordinary Endeavour by *Witchcrafts*, with Cruel and frequent Fits, to hinder the poor Sufferers from giving in their Complaints, which the Court was forced with much Patience to obtain, by much waiting and watching for it . . .

IV. *John Atkinson* testifi'd, That he exchanged a Cow with a Son of *Susanna Martin's*, whereat she muttered, and was unwilling he should have it. Going to receive this Cow, tho he Hamstring'd her, and Halter'd her, she, of a Tame Creature, grew so mad, that they could scarce get her along. She broke all the Ropes that were fastned unto her, and though she were ty'd fast unto a Tree, yet she made her escape, and gave them such further trouble, as they could ascribe to no cause but Witchcraft.

V. *Bernard Peache* testifi'd, That being in Bed, on the Lord's-day Night, he heard a scrabbling at the Window, whereat he then saw *Susanna Martin* come in, and jump down upon the Floor. She took hold of this Deponent's Feet, and drawing his Body up into an Heap, she lay upon him near Two Hours; in all which time he could neither speak nor stir. At length, when he could begin to move, he laid hold on her Hand, and pulling it up to his Mouth, he bit three of her Fingers, as he judged, unto the Bone. Whereupon she went from the Chamber, down the Stairs, out at the Door. This Deponent thereupon called unto the People of the House, to advise them of what passed; and he himself did follow her. The People saw her not; but there being a Bucket at the Left-hand of the Door, there was a drop of Blood found upon it; and several more drops of Blood upon the Snow newly fallen abroad: There was likewise the print of her 2 Feet just without the Threshold; but no more sign of any Footing further off. . . .

VI. *Robert Downer* testified, That this Prisoner being some Years ago prosecuted at Court for a Witch, he then said unto her, *He believed she was a Witch*. Whereat she being dissatisfied, said, *That some She-Devil would shortly fetch him away!* Which words were heard by others, as well as himself. The Night following, as he lay in his Bed, there came in at the Window, the likeness of a *Cat*, which flew upon him, took fast hold of his Throat, lay on him a considerable while, and almost killed him. At length he remembred what *Susanna Martin* had threatned the Day before; and with much striving he cried out, *Avoid, thou She-Devil! In the Name of God the Father, the Son, and the Holy Ghost, Avoid!* Whereupon it left him, leap'd on the Floor, and flew out at the Window.

And there also came in several Testimonies, that before ever *Downer* spoke a word of this Accident, *Susanna Martin* and her Family had related, *How this* Downer *had been handled!* . . .

VIII. *William Brown* testifi'd, That Heaven having blessed him with a most Pious and Prudent Wife, this Wife of his, one day met with *Susanna Martin*; but when she approach'd just unto her, *Martin* vanished out of sight, and left her extreamly affrighted. After which time, the said *Martin* often appear'd unto her, giving her no little trouble; and when she did come, she was visited with Birds, that sorely peck'd and prick'd her; and sometimes, a Bunch, like a Pullet's Egg, would rise in her Throat, ready to choak her, till she cry'd out, *Witch, you shan't choak me!* While this good Woman was in this extremity, the Church appointed a Day of Prayer, on her behalf; whereupon her Trouble ceas'd; she saw not *Martin* as formerly; and the Church, instead of their Fast, gave Thanks for her Deliverance. But a considerable while after, she being Summoned to give in some Evidence at the Court, against this *Martin*, quickly thereupon, this *Martin* came behind her, while she was milking her Cow, and said unto her, *For thy defaming her at Court, I'll make thee the miserablest Creature in the World*. Soon after which, she fell into a strange kind of distemper, and became horribly frantick, and uncapable of any reasonable Action; the Physicians declaring, that her Distemper was preternatural, and that some Devil had certainly bewitched her; and in that condition she now remained.

IX. *Sarah Atkinson* testify'd, That *Susanna Martin* came from *Amesbury* to their House at *Newbury*, in an extraordinary Season, when it was not fit for any to Travel. She came (as she said, unto *Atkinson*) all that long way on Foot. She brag'd and shew'd how dry she was; nor could it be perceived that so much as the Soles of her Shoes were wet. *Atkinson* was amazed at it; and professed, that she should her self have been wet up to the knees, if she had then came so far; but *Martin* reply'd, *She scorn'd to be Drabbled!* It was noted, that this Testimony upon her Trial, cast her in a very singular Confusion.

X. *John Pressy* testify'd, That being one Evening very unaccountably Bewildred, near a Field of *Martins*, and several times, as one under an Enchantment, returning to the place he had left, at length he saw a marvellous Light, about the bigness of an Half-bushel, near two Rod, out of the way. He went, and struck at it with a Stick, and laid it on with all his might. He gave it near forty blows; and felt it a palpable substance. But going from it, his Heels were struck up, and he was laid with his Back on the Ground, sliding, as he thought, into a Pit; from whence he recover'd by taking hold on the Bush; altho' afterwards he could find no such Pit in the place. Having, after his Recovery, gone five or six Rod, he saw *Susanna Martin* standing on his Left-hand, as the Light had done before; but they changed no words with one another. He could scarce find his House in his Return; but at length he got home extreamly affrighted. The next day, it was upon Enquiry understood, that *Martin* was in a miserable condition by pains and hurts that were upon her.

It was further testify'd by this Deponent, That after he had given in some Evidence against *Susanna Martin*, many years ago, she gave him foul words about it; and said, *He should never prosper more*; particularly, *That he should never have more than two Cows; that tho' he was never so likely to have more, yet he should never have them.* And that from that very day to this, namely for twenty years together, he could never exceed that number; but some strange thing or other still prevented his having any more.

XI. *Jervis Ring* testify'd, That about seven years ago, he was oftentimes and grievously oppressed in the Night, but saw not who troubled him; until at last he Lying perfectly Awake, plainly saw *Susanna Martin* approach him. She came to him, and forceably bit him by the Finger; so that the Print of the bite is now, so long after, to be seen upon him.

XII. But besides all of these Evidences, there was a most wonderful Account of one *Joseph Ring*, produced on this occasion.

This Man has been strangely carried about by *Daemons*, from one *Witch-meeting* to another, for near two years together; and for one quarter of this time, they have made him, and keep him Dumb, tho' he is now again able to speak. There was one *T. H.* who having, as 'tis judged, a design of engaging this *Joseph Ring* in a snare of Devillism, contrived a while, to bring this *Ring* two Shillings in Debt unto him.

Afterwards, this poor Man would be visited with unknown shapes, and this *T. H.* sometimes among them; which would force him away with them, unto unknown Places, where he saw Meetings, Feastings, Dancings; and after his return, wherein they hurried him along through the Air, he gave Demonstrations to the Neighbours, that he had indeed been so transported. When he was brought unto these hellish Meetings, one of the first Things they still did unto him, was to give him a knock on the Back, whereupon he was ever as if bound with Chains, uncapable of stirring out of the place, till they should release him. He related, that there often came to him a Man, who presented him a *Book*, whereto he would have him set his Hand; promising to him, that he should then have even what he would; and presenting him with all the delectable Things, Persons, and Places, that he could imagin. But he refusing to subscribe, the business would end with dreadful Shapes, Noises and Screeches, which almost scared him out of his Wits. Once with the Book, there was a Pen offered him, and an Ink-horn with Liquor in it, that seemed like Blood: But he never toucht it.

This Man did now affirm, That he saw the Prisoner at several of those hellish Randezvouzes.

Note, this Woman was one of the most impudent, scurrilous, wicked Creatures in the World; and she did now throughout her whole Tryal, discover her self to be such an one. Yet when she was asked, what she had to say for her self? Her chief Plea was, *That she had lead a most virtuous and holy Life.*

Further Reading

Anderson, Virginia, *New England's Generation: The Great Migration and the Formation of Society and Culture in the Seventeenth Century.* New York: Cambridge University Press, 1991.

Cressy, David, *Coming Over: Migration and Communication Between England and New England in the Seventeenth Century.* New York: Cambridge University Press, 1987.

Dayton, Cornelia Hughes, *Women before the Bar: Gender, Law, and Society in Connecticut, 1639–1789.* Chapel Hill: University of North Carolina Press, 1995.

Foster, Stephen, *The Long Argument: English Puritanism and the Shaping of New England Culture, 1570–1700.* Chapel Hill: University of North Carolina Press, 1991.

Gura, Philip F., *A Glimpse of Sion's Glory: Puritan Radicalism in New England, 1620–1660.* Middletown, CT: Wesleyan University Press, 1984.

Hambrick-Stowe, Charles, *The Practice of Piety: Puritan Devotional Disciplines in Seventeenth-century New England*. Chapel Hill: University of North Carolina Press, 1982.

Innes, Stephen, *Creating the Commonwealth: The Economic Culture of Puritan New England*. New York: W. W. Norton, 1995.

Kamensky, Jane, *Governing the Tongue: The Politics of Speech in Early New England*. New York: Oxford University Press, 1997.

Karlsen, Carol, *The Devil in the Shape of a Woman: Witchcraft in Colonial New England*. New York: Vintage Books, 1989.

Martin, John Frederick, *Profits in the Wilderness: Entrepreneurship and the Founding of New England Towns in the Seventeenth Century*. Chapel Hill: University of North Carolina Press, 1991.

Norton, Mary Beth, *Founding Mothers and Fathers: Gendered Power and the Forming of American Society*. New York: Vintage Books, 1996.

Peterson, Mark, *The Price of Redemption: The Spiritual Economy of Puritan New England*. Stanford, CA: Stanford University Press, 1997.

Reis, Elizabeth, *Damned Women: Sinners and Witches in Puritan New England*. Ithaca, NY: Cornell University Press, 1997.

3

Making Race

Introduction

In 1675–6, the Virginia colony experienced a rebellion made up largely of discontented and land-hungry white farmers and former indentured servants who were hindered by Governor William Berkeley from engaging in raids against neighboring Indians. Called Bacon's Rebellion (after the young and recently arrived aristocrat Nathaniel Bacon who led the uprising against the Governor, his distant relative), the attack on Williamsburg led wealthier landowners to view landless lower-class whites as a source of social unrest. The rebellion subsided when Bacon died of dysentery, but the elite had reason to wonder whether in the future servants who completed their terms of service and failed to acquire land in the tightening real estate market of Virginia might team up with one another again and cause further disorder.

Bacon's Rebellion occurred just as the supply of servants available for migration from England was beginning to dry up and wealthy planters were turning increasingly to enslaved Africans to cultivate the tobacco that made some men so rich. The shift toward slavery was aided by the monopolies that the crown granted British companies in the booming trade in African slaves. The move toward slavery as the main form of labor in the Southern colonies had multiple causes, including demographic trends, shifts in international trade, and the economics of staple crops like tobacco and rice. But accommodation on a social level was also required in order for slavery to work: whites had to believe that Africans were inherently suited for grueling labor and that their permanent enslavement (and not just a finite term of service of the kind allotted to white servants) was somehow appropriate. The development of an ideology of racial difference, one that allowed English colonists to justify the permanent enslavement of forcefully imported African people, was not a foregone conclusion and it took time. Racialist thinking in the late seventeenth century had to be reconfigured to explain the permanent degradation of a new population of workers. As the essay by Kathleen Brown demonstrates, much of the definition of race occurred in legislation about sex and marriage that defined blacks and whites differently and sought to control their interactions. Brown focuses especially on the regulation of white women's sexuality and the legal arrangements made for interracial children born to white mothers. The laws banned interracial sex and marriage, but they generally punished only white women and not white men who had sex with black women. How did the laws help to define racial difference in late seventeenth-century Virginia? Why were women central to this process of defining racial differences? What is the relationship between morality and the law, and how did women respond to changes in both?

Initially, living and working conditions in Virginia were very harsh. The discovery that tobacco sold in London for enormous profits led landowners to insist that servants cultivate that labor-intensive crop rather than grow food or try to improve living conditions in the colony. Richard Frethorne wrote to his parents from Virginia in 1623, lamenting the trials he endured there (document 1). How did Frethorne describe life in early Virginia and how did he hope his parents would respond?

Gradually, as conditions in Virginia stabilized, the social hierarchy also hardened. Servants began to survive their terms of service in greater numbers, eventually joining the growing ranks of freeholders in the colony. The Virginia Slave Codes (document 2) are evocative documents that can tell us much about real and ideal social relations in a growing slave society. How do these laws create distinctions between servants and slaves? How do the laws attempt to conflate race with status? How is slavery made permanent and hereditary? How do the laws make slaves fear for their lives? What do the laws reveal about the extent to which they are obeyed?

Colonial laws created racial categories, but they could not ensure that all people defined as "black" would be slaves. The petition of Ruth Tillett from North Carolina (document 3) shows how one woman fought tenaciously for her freedom. What strategies did Tillett employ in her decades-long odyssey? What does her story reveal about race relations in the second half of the eighteenth century?

From "Foul Crimes" to "Spurious Issue": Sexual Regulation and the Social Construction of Race

Kathleen M. Brown

After Bacon's Rebellion, white planters seeking new ways to reduce the rebellious potential of servants and slaves turned increasingly to African labor. Although enslaved men suffered disproportionately from many of the postrebellion restrictions upon economic activity and geographic mobility, lawmakers also made new use of existing restrictions on white women's sexuality to refine the legal meanings and practical consequences of racial difference. Fornication between white women and black men threatened not only to compromise the utility of female servants – a perennial problem no matter what the race of the male offender – but to blur racial distinctions and increase the free black population. Previous legislation making slavery heritable through the mother had made it possible for white women to disconnect slavery from race by bearing children of African descent. By putting the traditional sexual regulations of white servant women to the service of patrolling racial boundaries, lawmakers created new legal meanings for race.

The sexualization of race occurred within the context of changing legal practices and new relationships between courtrooms and daily life during the last quarter of the seventeenth century. Three legal developments paved the way for the growing interdependence of definitions of racial difference and illicit sexuality. First, county courts narrowed the range of their prosecutions of sexual misdemeanors to focus on bastardy, punishing it with fines and whippings and abandoning ecclesiastical-style punishments such as penance. Second, reflecting the growing sophistication of justices and the decline of women's influence over public spaces like courtrooms, the county courts also began to enforce more rigorous standards for proof of wrongdoing, giving less credence to hearsay evidence and the "common fame." The formality and uniformity of these legal standards eroded the influence of female speech and local customs over the judicial process, widening the distance between the legal identities produced by lawmakers and courtrooms and those that evolved through community negotiations and interactions. Third, in the context of these changes in legal practice, the colonial legislature refined its definition of whiteness to exclude individuals of African and Indian descent from Anglo-Virginian constructions of marriage and legitimacy.

Control over labor, white and black, provided a powerful motive for these legal shifts, as did the traditional concern to protect the masters of servant women from loss. But with the colonial legislature's exclusion of slaves from white definitions of marriage and legitimacy came new imperatives to maintain racial distinctions beyond the immediate needs of the labor system. What began with legal initiatives to defend the boundaries of slavery expanded to incorporate protections for legal concepts of race. Some of these legal constructs of racial identity filtered into popular attitudes toward racial difference and illicit sexual behavior. In most communities, however, some individuals continued, at the pleasure of their neighbors, to exercise privileges denied to them by law.

Having avoided some of the worst aspects of slavery through a combination of luck and perseverance, free Afro-Virginians were not completely excluded from white-centered definitions of marital sexuality before Bacon's Rebellion. But, at the end of the seventeenth century, they, too, were beginning to be distinguished from whites sexually. By the early eighteenth century, sexual and racial regulation had become interwoven components of social relations in the colony. The concern with the "foul crime" of white fornication had been replaced with attempts to punish bastardy, especially the "spurious issue" of interracial unions.

From Sin to Crime

In the spring of 1661, a churchwarden from York County presented Thomas Heyricke and servant woman Rebecca Noble to the local court for crimes of "Adultery and fornication." Heyricke requested time to gather evidence to clear himself of the sexual offense that had resulted in Noble's pregnancy. When the court met again in August, Heyricke claimed that "hee never had any Carnall Copulacon" with Noble and further argued that Noble herself had named another man as the father of her child while in the pains of labor. He also denied the charge that he "had made an agreem[en]t with the said Noble to bury the misdemean[o]rs in oblivion . . . [so that they] should not be determined by Law."[1]

Most damning for Noble was Heyricke's charge that "shee kept company with a Negro man of Col[one]l Mathewes" and was to have married a "Negro of Col[one]l Reads." Heyricke sealed his case by reminding the court that Noble was, "by the Common fame," a "woman of a very evill life and conversation." Convinced by his evidence, the court cleared Heyricke of all wrongdoing and ordered the sheriff to take Noble into custody. As punishment for her sexual offense, Noble was sentenced to ten lashes upon her bare back and the performance of penance in York County's Poquoson parish by "standing in a white sheet and asking open forgiveness on hir knees of God Almighty for hir said offence before the whole congregation."[2]

Rebecca Noble's case took place at the juncture of changing attitudes toward sexual offenses and their punishment. During the first fifty years of settlement in Virginia, justices heard cases such as Noble's in a dual capacity. As arbiters of secular suits involving money damages, they functioned much as English secular judges by prescribing fines, corporal punishment, and extended terms of service to offenders. But, because the colony lacked church courts, justices also occasionally incorporated ecclesiastical sanctions, such as penance, into their repertoire of punishments when the sin in question would have been remedied by a church tribunal had it taken place in England. From 1630 until 1662, the year in which post-Restoration legal reforms changed the practices of local courts in Virginia, servant women like Noble who violated sexual mores might receive one or both types of punishment (see table 3.1).[3]

When the Virginia courts sentenced an offender such as Noble to perform penance, they required a formal, public apology that functioned as a ritual purification. Dressed in a white sheet and carrying a white wand, the sinner would be forced to confess her or his fault several times in front of the congregated parish. Such a punishment was

Table 3.1 Punishments for bastardy by white female servants, Norfolk, Lancaster, and York Counties

Penalty	Cases specifying penalty	% of known cases punished
1643–62		
Whipping	12	60.0
Penance	4	20.0
Extra time	4	20.0
Fine	3	15.0
Other		
1663–99		
Whipping	33	26.4
Penance	0	
Extra time	102	81.6
Fine	32	25.6
Other	8	6.4

Note: For 1643–62, data are based on 20 cases where punishment is known of 37 cases overall. For 1663–99, data are based on 125 cases where punishment is known of 148 overall. Punishments are not mutually exclusive, therefore percentage totals do not necessarily equal 100%.

Sources: Norfolk Deed Book A, 1637–1646, Book B, 1646–1652, Wills and Deeds C, 1651–1656, Wills and Deeds D, 1656–1666, Wills and Deeds E, 1666–1675, Orders, 1675–1686, Deed Book 5, 1686–1695; Lancaster Deeds 1, 1652–1654, Orders, 1656–1666, 1666–1680, Orders 2, 1680–1686, Orders 3, 1686–1696, Orders 4, 1696–1702; York Orders, 1646–1648, DOW 2, 1645–1657, DOW 3, 1657–1662, DOW 4, 1665–1672, DOW 5, 1672–1676, DOW 6, 1677–1684, DOW 7, 1685–1687, DOW 8, 1687–1691, DOW 9, 1687–1694, DOW 10, 1694–1698, DOW 11, 1698–1702.

intended both to shame the offender and formally to readmit her or him into the community of the God-fearing.[4]

Sexual activity became illicit when it occurred outside marriage, the institution that safeguarded private property and ensured the dependence of women and children on male providers through patrilineal systems of inheritance. Those couples who began sexual activity or cohabited without the prerequisite licenses and public announcements might be prosecuted for prenuptial fornication, bridal pregnancy, or clandestine unions, depending upon local inclination. Bastardy represented an even more serious and universal problem for Virginia's parishes. Throughout the seventeenth century, the colony's unusual demography and lack of traditional restraints on sexual behavior produced bastardy rates for female servants two and sometimes three times higher than those in England and New England.

Although all counties prosecuted bastardy, precise boundaries between licit and illicit sexual activity varied from community to community, reflecting local budget constraints and the zeal of local officials and neighbors. Justices, parish vestrymen, and grand jurors depended upon fellow residents to report wrongdoing and provide testimony in court. Each householder ultimately bore some share of the financial burden when an individual committed a sexual offense. When parish budgets were overburdened and householders struggled to meet their tax obligations, such as during the 1670s, it was in their best interest to discourage behavior that might result in expense for the county by diligently enforcing prohibitions on prenuptial sexual activities. The moral transgression and economic damage to the community were readily apparent in cases of bastardy but less so in cases of fornication, where the evidence and nature of the offense were highly susceptible to community interpretation.

Virginia county courts abandoned the use of penance rituals after Restoration church courts in England failed to regain jurisdiction over sexual offenses. The colony's local courts relied instead upon secular punishments, particularly extra service, which offered compensation to masters. Rebecca Noble was nearly the last person to appear in the penitent's white robes in York County; both Norfolk and Lancaster Counties appear to have dropped the purification rituals several years earlier. After 1662, most female servant offenders would have received a punishment similar to that ordered for Elizabeth Stratford in 1666. Norfolk justices required Stratford to serve her master for two years after her term of indenture expired as compensation for the loss of labor and costs of the delivery of her infant. In addition, they sentenced her to receive twenty lashes.[5]

The shift in punishments accompanied the county courts' increasing emphasis upon bastardy, the sexual offense most costly to parishes and counties. After the 1660s, courts focused more exclusively on the monetary damages owed to masters by female servants and their lovers rather than on the moral nature of the sexual transgression. They thus abandoned the practice of prosecuting married couples for the moral violation involved in the birth of "premature" infants, a trend that distinguished them from their peers in New England.

The court's focus on bastardy coincided with and may have been partially a consequence of new standards of proof for criminal activity. A few shards of evidence suggest that following the mid-seventeenth-century influx of well-heeled royalist migrants, Virginia's justices may have been more inclined to literal interpretations of the common law and to consulting texts like Dalton's *Justice of the Peace*. Although the "common fame" or the "clamour of the community" continued to play an important role in bringing wrongdoers to the attention of the grand jury and churchwardens, its influence over the official workings of the court had waned by the last quarter of the century. Unlike other sexual offenses in which convictions depended upon word-of-mouth accounts of illicit unions and reputations, bastardy provided incontrovertible proof that an illicit act had taken place and had not been remedied by marriage. Courts that focused their attention on illegitimate births rather than on rumors of lewd conduct had less need for the testimony of community informers.

Justices pursued several social goals in their punishments of bastardy: to identify fathers and make them financially responsible for bastards, to punish unwed mothers, to create a mechanism for absorbing the costs of children who lacked identifiable fathers, and to suppress the sexual activity of servants. Identifying the father and extracting support for the illegitimate child, in particular, appear to have been important priorities of the Virginia courts for most of the century. From 1640 to 1700, the three county courts in this study identified fathers in more than half of the bastardy cases they heard. Courts usually tried to gain accurate information about the father of a bastard child with the help of a cooperative midwife, although even this process was vulnerable to the manipulations of masters.[6]

Although sexual offenses never completely shed the taint of sin that came from the long history of their classification as transgressions within the jurisdiction of church courts, the Virginia courts treated them almost exclusively as criminal after 1662 and applied only secular punishments. Indeed, the shift from sin to crime can be seen most revealingly in the failure of James Blair's 1690 plan to introduce ecclesiastical courts to Virginia for the prosecution of moral offenses. Despite periodic legislative outbursts calling for more stringent prosecution of all moral offenses, Virginia justices had largely abandoned the project of prosecuting couples for the sinful dimension of premarital and extramarital fornication. They also resorted increasingly to evidence of sexual wrongdoing other than the reports and rumors that circulated in community gossip networks. Instead, they focused upon the criminal component of bastardy and other sexual offenses, seeking remedies in years of service, pounds of tobacco, and lashes of the whip rather than in penitent words.

Regulating Servants

County courts began to focus on the crime of bastardy to the exclusion of other sexual offenses during the same decade in which the supply of

English male servants began to dwindle and other populations, including those of English and Irish women, may have become relatively more important to the labor force. The 1662 statute calling for masters to pay tithes on all female servants . . . also may have been a manifestation of this trend. Although bastardy became relatively more significant among prosecuted sexual offenses, in part as a result of changes in the judicial process, it also may have become a priority for county courts because it threatened the productivity of a growing population of female laborers. Prescriptions of celibacy during servitude, fears that female sexuality was dangerous to the social order, and well-established English traditions for controlling the sexuality of the poor all influenced the treatment of servant women during the second half of the seventeenth century.

The control of white women's sexual behavior was crucial to the security of labor arrangements in the colony, much as it was in other early modern agricultural societies. Servitude in Virginia, as in England, took place in a presumably celibate context in which servants were construed as unmarried dependent laborers. The separation of servile celibacy and marital sexuality was based upon two assumptions: first, that marriage defined licit sexuality, rendering all prenuptial sexual activity "illicit," and, second, that successful labor arrangements required the authority of the master not to conflict with the authority of a husband.

Although cases of servant women and men's marrying during their terms of service were not unheard of, they generally occurred early in the century and almost always complicated master–servant relations. Husbands of servant women finishing their terms of service occasionally appeared in court to sue for missing freedom dues or to bring an end to masters' claims on their wives' labor. Richard Beck of Norfolk, for instance, sued John Feringhaugh in 1649 for the remaining corn and clothes due his wife Elizabeth for her service to Feringhaugh and his wife. Twenty years later, John Cole complained that he and his wife had not received their freedom clothes from Major John West of York County. By the last quarter of the seventeenth century, apprentice contracts often specified that a servant neither engage in fornication nor enter into matrimony during his or her term of service. The mother of Elizabeth Bartlett of York County made such a promise on behalf of her four-year-old daughter in 1701, agreeing that, as the apprentice of Adduston Rogers, Elizabeth would "not fornicate in his house."[7]

Reflecting English traditions for controlling the sexuality of the poor, Virginia's county courts treated crimes such as bastardy as consensual sexual acts, even if the father of an illegitimate child was known to be the woman's master. Until 1662, the courts did not acknowledge that master–servant bastardy cases could occur within a context of unequal power relations. With the passage in December 1662 of a law punishing "dissolute" masters who impregnated their servants, English female servants received a modicum of protection. The courts still did not treat the woman herself as a victim of her circumstances, however; in addition to completing the remainder of her original term, she had to serve an additional two years to a new master for her sexual offense. Motivated to protect the property of masters and predisposed to believe women were lusty creatures, barely capable of controlling their own bodily urges, the courts were little inclined to view servant women as the victims of coercion.

Beliefs in the potence of female sexuality also made rape convictions nearly impossible. As a felony, rape would have been tried at the General Court, the records of which have largely been destroyed. In several counties, however, rape accusations were denounced as the trumped-up charges of devious servants or slandering women and never reached the superior court. The Norfolk court's dismissal of three rape charges in a single session and its punishment of two of the three female plaintiffs for making false accusations (a set of cases discussed later in this chapter) is a vivid example of the legal response to rape allegations. In one of the few known sexual assault convictions, a case of child molestation early in the century, the General Court refused to assign all the blame to the male offender but ordered the seven-year-old female victim to be "corected by her mother for that her fault and for that there appeareth in her a signe of more grace and greife for her offence."[8]

Beliefs in the existence of powerful female sexual desires along with long-standing traditions of regulating the sexuality of poor women underscored the colony's growing concern with servant bastardy. Servant women accounted for the majority of bastardy cases appearing before the county courts of Lancaster, York, and Norfolk Counties between 1640 and 1710. During the fifty-year period between 1650 and 1700, moreover, servant women constituted nearly all such cases (see figure 3.1). Owing to their growing numbers and their potential to undermine the fragile authority of masters, white servant women became the central focus of the colony's efforts to regulate sexuality after mid-century. Their sexual activity became even more significant after Bacon's Rebellion, as planters increasingly sought to accentuate racial differences among their laborers.

Sexualizing Race

The presence of increasing numbers of enslaved Africans in Virginia's tobacco fields during the last quarter of the seventeenth century challenged the ideal of celibate servitude and forced new legal definitions

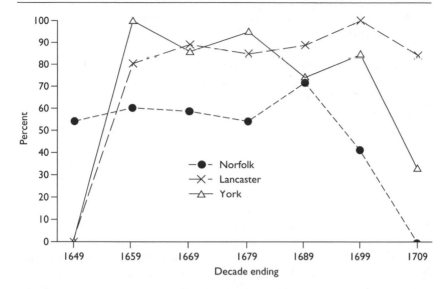

Figure 3.1 Bastardy cases attributed to white servant women by decade, Norfolk, Lancaster, and York Counties.

of illicit sexual activity. Prosecutions of female slaves for bastardy were meaningless, for example, if paternity and the usual relationship between male provider and female economic dependent were irrelevant for enslaved fathers and mothers. Questions about the applicability of English constructions of sexuality arose most urgently in cases involving mixed-race couples and free black people. As Virginia lawmakers began to delineate one sexual standard for its white population and another for its enslaved population, they seemed unsure of how to handle the anomalies of interracial and free black unions.

Before 1662, incidents of interracial fornication were treated criminally in much the same way as all fornication cases, although they may have been regarded as more sinful. The General Court's denunciation of Hugh Davis's fornication in 1630, for example, contained stronger language than that normally used to describe the sexual offense of two English people. Davis was accused of "abusing himself to the dishonr of God and shame of Christianity by defiling his body in lying with a negro." The main difference between the treatment of Davis's case and that of other fornication cases was the description of his sin as defiling, a term justices would not have used to describe the sexual interaction of two English people. Despite this difference, however, interracial activity received roughly the same legal treatment as illicit unions between white people.[9]

Much of the evenhanded treatment of interracial fornication before 1662 resulted from the lack of precise legal identities for enslaved Africans and from the important role of communities in determining the allocation of privileges to individuals in their locales. Significantly, before that date, interracial couples remained legally capable of marrying if each individual was a free person, an option that undoubtedly influenced the courts' egalitarian treatment of fornicating couples who crossed racial lines. The tiny enclave of free African men marrying white wives in Northampton County is perhaps the best example of the moderate degree of social integration that these couples enjoyed. Isolated instances of interracial matches in other counties also appear to have been tolerated.

The colonial government first treated interracial sexual intimacy, race relations, and regulation of the labor force as related concerns in 1662. By that date, many planters were already anxious over recent servant uprisings and evidence of cooperation among servant and slave runaways. They also may have been alarmed by the growing problem of controlling the sexual activity of female servants. The Assembly passed two measures in that year that addressed the issues of slave children's status and interracial sexual activity and redefined slave motherhood and paternity. The first . . . declared that the children of enslaved women should follow the condition of their mother. This act redefined slave motherhood and vitiated the legal foundation of slave paternity, thereby making distinctions between legitimacy and illegitimacy legally irrelevant for enslaved people.[10]

The second clause of the 1662 statute emphasized distinctions of race rather than of status. Attempting to distinguish between "christian[s]" and "negroe[s]," the law differentiated between the illicit sexual acts of two white people and those of an interracial couple: "*And* that if any christian shall committ fornication with a negro man or woman, hee or shee soe offending shall pay double the fines imposed by the former act."[11]

The doubled fines mandated by the second clause of the 1662 law for cases of "christian"–"negro" fornication had three main legal consequences. First, and most obviously, the law intensified the criminality of transgressing racial boundaries in its attempt to discourage potential white offenders from seeking sexual unions with women and men of African descent. Second, the law specifically targeted the white partner of an interracial couple and did not mention any new punishments for the black partner, perhaps under the assumption that the African people in question usually would be enslaved and incapable of paying fines or serving extra time. Third, and most significantly, not all white people were equally affected by this law. Irrelevant slave paternity and the growing emphasis on bastardy, in which the birth of a child constituted "proof" of sexual misconduct, meant that white women bearing mixed-race children were the most easily prosecuted under this legislation.

With this measure, Virginia lawmakers created and incorporated into their legal definitions of racial difference a concept of black sexuality that was implicitly most dangerous to the social order when embodied by black men and directed toward white women. Excluding slaves from English constructs of licit and illicit sexuality and designating heavy fines or whippings for white people whose sexual partners were of African descent, lawmakers left little doubt that they viewed white unions with black people as threatening to patriarchal authority, property, and the security of labor. By failing to make special provisions to enforce the prohibition on white male unions with enslaved women, however, the law effectively left only white women vulnerable to prosecution. As long as enslaved women's illegitimate children were of little concern to masters, white men were likely to escape penalties for interracial fornication.

In the years after Bacon's Rebellion, sexual regulations became an increasingly important means of consolidating white patriarchal authority and defining racial difference. With the importation of large numbers of African slaves during the 1680s and 1690s, planter attention shifted from a concern with the laboring population in general to a specific interest in controlling black laborers. Between 1680 and 1699, ... lawmakers passed new legislation aimed at subordinating potentially rebellious slaves. This legislation did not always apply to enslaved men and women equally, however, nor did it set uniform rules governing slave interactions with white men and women. Rather, several of the new laws targeted enslaved men and white female servants, distinguishing among slaves on the basis of sex and among white women on the basis of class and marital status. Codifying intervention in the lives of these potentially disruptive women and men, these laws fortified the rough alliance of white men along the lines of race and patriarchal privilege that had emerged after the rebellion.

The first wave of post-rebellion prosecutions of white women for sexual offenses with black men appeared in Norfolk County during the late 1680s and early 1690s. From 1681 to 1691, Norfolk justices punished seventeen women for bastardy, all of whom were white. Of these offenders, four were accused of bearing children fathered by black men who appear to have been slaves. Like the majority of their bastard-bearing predecessors, the four female offenders were servants and therefore probably poor and single. Kathren Mathews, a servant belonging to Simon Holstead, for example, appeared before the court holding a child fathered "by a negro who is now out of the county." When the court

ordered her to be whipped and fined, her master agreed to pay the sum
for her, leading the court to remit her punishment.[12] In York County,
isolated interracial offenses surfaced in 1662 and 1683, with more
appearing during the 1690s. In Lancaster County, these cases came to
court mainly after 1700.

In 1691, legislators explicitly addressed the problem presented by
these relationships by refashioning older traditions for regulating servant
sexuality to fit newer concerns with race. Expressing their anxieties
about the sexual activities of white women in a preamble to the new
statute, lawmakers noted the danger presented by the "abominable
mixture and spurious issue which heareafter may encrease in this dominion, as well by negroes, mulattoes, and Indians intermarrying with
English, or other white women." Provoked by the threat of a growing
population of racially indeterminate people, Virginia's planters took
radical steps to enforce racial difference:

> Whatsoever English or other white man or woman being free shall inter-
> marry with a negroe, mulatto, or Indian man or woman bond or free shall
> within three months after such marriage be banished and removed from
> this dominion forever.

The act further specified severe punishments for English women, free or
servant, who bore illegitimate children by black or mulatto men. Even
the children of these unions received the stigma of punishment. They
were ordered to serve extended terms of indenture until age thirty, a
measure that set them apart from other illegitimates who served only
until age twenty-four.[13]

The statute of 1691 made *all* interracial sexual acts illicit, criminaliz-
ing relationships that might previously have been eligible for the protection of marriage. Sexual relationships between white people and Indians,
moreover, became as subject to censure as those between white people
and individuals of African descent. Despite the law's seeming concern to
prevent all "spurious issue," however, its preamble revealed the special
place that unions between white women and black men occupied in the
thinking of Virginia lawmakers. Sexual activity that resulted in the birth
of mixed race children to *white women* had sparked the concern that led
to the law's passage. Perhaps most significantly, the legal attempt to
separate Anglo-Virginians sexually from Indians and people of African
descent marked the first use of the term "white" in the Virginia statutes.
"Englishmen" and "Christians" had become white in the context of a
law that redefined the nature of illicit sexuality.

In their efforts to enforce the racial exclusivity of white women's sexual
relationships, lawmakers also revealed the growing overlap between

patriarchal privilege and racial domination. The 1691 law distinguished between the rights of black and white men, solidifying the patriarchal stake of all white men in a slave system that offered the greatest benefits to large planters. By elevating the authority of land- and status-poor white men, planters secured their consent to and cooperation with the local arm of the colonial government. With their access to white women sanctioned by law and protected from the dual threat of white female sexual autonomy and black male encroachments, moreover, white men could rest easy knowing that their authority over male slaves had been confirmed legally. By 1691, patriarchal authority had officially become a privilege of race as well as of sex.

Removing any doubts that the children of interracial unions were illegitimate, the 1691 law struck at their access to patrilineal systems of inheritance and naming. If their parents could not marry legally and remain within the colony, mixed-race children technically could not inherit property. The convergence of mixed parentage with legal definitions of illegitimacy after 1691 also may account in part for the similarity between free black naming patterns and those used by courts in England to designate illegitimacy. Free people of color in Virginia, many of whom had white mothers and black fathers, often appeared in the court records with two surnames, the second of which was labeled an alias.

The 1691 law had an immediate impact upon the prosecution of sexual offenses in the colony. Between 1691 and 1721 in the counties of Lancaster, York, and Norfolk, white servant women punished for interracial sexual acts became a more significant proportion of the servant women prosecuted. Representing less than 10 percent of the cases of servant bastardy in the decade of the 1680s, white servant women bearing children by black men constituted more than 17 percent of those cases during the 1690s and nearly 30 percent by the 1700s (see table 3.2). The presentment of servant Catherine McCollins is typical of how this statute was enforced. In 1705, McCollins's master informed the court that she had "a mulatto child born of her body begotten by a negro man." After McCollins confessed the truth of this allegation, the court ordered her to be sold for five years, with the proceeds being divided between the parish, the informant (her master), and the crown.[14]

The new legal attention to interracial cases was dispersed unevenly, with white servant women and their children bearing most of the expense and punishment. During the thirty years between 1680 and 1710, white servant women constituted at least 81 percent and possibly as much as 100 percent of all interracial prosecutions. The contrast to the treatment of other known interracial offenders is striking. Very few white men were prosecuted for interracial sexual misconduct during this

Table 3.2 Interracial bastardy offenses by white servant women, 1660–1729, Norfolk, Lancaster, and York Counties

	Total servant cases	Interracial cases
1660–69	34	1 (3.0%)
1670–79	44	1 (2.2%)
1680–89	46	3 (6.5%)
1690–99	35	6 (17.1%)
1700–09	38	11 (29.0%)
1710–19	23	3 (13.0%)
1720–29	17	1 (5.8%)
Overall	237	26 (10.9%)

Sources: Norfolk Wills and Deeds D, 1656–66; Wills and Deeds E, 1666–75; Orders, 1675–86; Orders, 1719–22; Orders, 1724–34; Deed Book 5, 1686–95; Deed Book 7, 1703–06; Deed Book 8, 1708–10; Deed Book 9, 1710–17. Lancaster Orders, 1656–66; Orders, 1666–80; Orders 2, 1680–86; Orders 3, 1686–96; Orders 4, 1696–1702; Orders 5, 1702–13; Orders 6, 1713–21; Orders 7, 1721–29. York DOW 3, 1657–62; DOW 4, 1665–72; DOW 5, 1672–76; DOW 6, 1677–84; DOW 7, 1685–87; DOW 8, 1687–91; DOW 9, 1687–94; DOW 10, 1694–98; DOW 11, 1698–1702; DOW 12, 1702–08; DOW 13, 1708–10; DOW 14, 1710–16; DOW 15, 1716–20; DOW 16, 1720–29.

period, and none was punished. The closest calls may have been the Norfolk justices' warnings to two men during the 1710s – a decade during which white residents of the county were particularly worried about rebellious slaves – to desist from relationships with women of African descent. Justices admonished William Powell in 1711 for suspected intimacies with a "mulatto" woman he claimed worked for him. When Powell convinced the court that the woman had left his house, his case was dismissed without punishment. In 1718, the Norfolk grand jury presented another man, John Young, for cohabiting with a black woman, but the court did not pursue the complaint.[15] The courts also made no effort to discover the paternity of more than twenty illegitimate children born between 1680 and 1750 to free Afro-Virginian and Indian mothers, revealing a consistent disinterest in determining whether these children were the products of interracial unions. Each woman absorbed the penalty herself in whippings, fines, and extra service while the fathers went unpunished.

Black fathers were often as successful as their white counterparts in escaping punishment for interracial sexual crimes, but for distinctly different reasons. An enslaved man could not legally make restitution or provide for his child. In most cases, the court simply ignored his participation in the offense, casually mentioning that the father of the illegitimate child was "a negro." The notable instances in which black fathers were punished illuminate the courts' fears of public assertions of black male sexuality. In Norfolk County in 1681, the court insisted on punishing a slave named William who had committed fornication with Mary Williamson, an English woman whom he claimed as his wife. Charging that William "hath veary arrogantly behaved himself in Linhaven Church in face of the Congregation," the court sentenced him to be whipped even though he had a master who could have assumed responsibility for punishing his sexual transgression. William's arrogant behavior compounded his sexual wrongdoing in the eyes of the court, making it appear to be part of a pattern of self-assertion and trespass upon white male privilege. In York County, a free black man named Joseph Water similarly came to the court's attention for "keepin company with an English woman and constantly lying with her." Water's masterless condition might have provoked the grand jury to present him. The court's interest in punishing him, moreover, was especially striking in light of its practice of allowing financially solvent white men to avoid paternal responsibilities when their sexual partners were free Afro-Virginians.[16]

The relative legal immunity of white men from prosecution for interracial sexual acts was in actuality part of a larger legal trend toward more lenient investigations of paternity, no matter what the race of the offending woman. After 1700, occasions in which the fathers of illegitimate children were named in court dwindled to a small percentage of the cases. During the late seventeenth century, it had been common for fathers' names to appear in the court record at least half the time. After 1700, fathers frequently disappeared from the county or made private settlements with the mothers of illegitimate children. On average, local courts listed fathers' names in only 12 percent of the cases between 1700 and 1750, a far cry from the 57 percent average of the preceding half-century.

By the last decade of the seventeenth century, legal definitions of racial difference and the sexual regulation of white women had become intertwined bases of patriarchal power. Laws banning interracial unions defined white participation as the transgression, imparting to black sexuality the power to taint. Perceived by the courts as the population most likely to blur racial boundaries and incur expenses for masters, white servant women bore the brunt of many of the new regulations. White men, meanwhile, avoided prosecution for interracial sexual misconduct and, increasingly, all sexual misconduct, creating a distinctly skewed grid of prosecution for interracial sexual activity.

Racial and Sexual Margins

By the last quarter of the seventeenth century, county courts' increasingly formal and consistent legal standards had narrowed the distance between legal practices in different counties. Yet individuals still managed to fashion social identities somewhat autonomously from the laws regulating race relations and sexual behavior. Although the laws of the late seventeenth century clearly had an impact upon how communities defined illicit sexuality and racial identity, reputations and social networks also determined whether a community would strictly follow the letter of the law regarding interracial sexual unions.

Eleven years after the 1691 law forbade interracial unions and prescribed harsh punishments, officials in Lancaster County were still unfamiliar with the law. The first case of interracial fornication to reach the justices in July 1702 found them ill prepared. Catherine Cassity, the offending white servant, was ordered to come to a subsequent court because "the act relating thereto" could not be found, leaving justices unsure of how to proceed. Between court sessions, the clerk of the court was ordered to "serch for the s[ai]d Act soe that the s[ai]d Cathr[ine] may be condemned accordingly" for her crime of bearing a child by a black man.[17] Although Lancaster justices subsequently proved to be as conformist as officials in neighboring counties, the law had little direct impact on the county for nearly a decade after its passage.

Hardly the passive recipients of the General Assembly's dicta, county residents sometimes pressured the Assembly to enact more stringent measures for prosecuting bastardy. In 1696, Colonel Lawrence Smith of Gloucester County complained before the House of Burgesses that the charge to taxpayers for maintaining the bastards of servant women was excessive and required more severe punishments to provide some fiscal relief. Apparently deciding that existing laws were tough enough, the House reenacted previous statutes against fornication and bastardy in subsequent sessions. Many years later, two Lancaster County church-wardens became activists for harsher regulations. Implicitly blaming the problem of bastardy on female convicts, Thomas Edwards and William Stepto also sought to make the "reputed Fathers" of bastard children financially responsible for their progeny if they were freemen. Their proposal reached the Council in 1740 in the significantly altered form of an Act "to oblige the owners of convict Women Servants having Bastards to give security to indempnifie the Parish." The plan of Edwards and Stepto to make fathers pay had been reconfigured as an additional burden to masters. After reading the bill twice, the Council rejected it.[18]

Some planters openly disapproved of the new prohibitions upon inter-racial sexual unions. In 1696, George Ivie, descendant of a prominent Norfolk family, submitted a petition to the Governor's Council protest-ing against the law that prevented "English people's marrying with Negroes Indians and Mullattoes." Ivie's petition, which was signed by several other people, suggests that the new sexual regulations of race had not emerged without dissent. For some white people, the law might have represented a loss of social contacts and an inexplicable separation of men and women.[19]

By narrowing the pool of eligible marriage partners, the 1691 law also created new grounds for parental disapproval, altering the dynamics of parent–child conflicts over marriage decisions in some families. In one such case, familial intervention into an allegedly interracial match sub-jected both the couple and the disapproving relative to the scrutiny of the local court. Grand jury men in Norfolk County presented George Isle-wood and Elizabeth Dunkley in 1714 for cohabiting unlawfully. In his defense, Islewood informed the justices that he and Dunkley had tried to marry but were wrongly prevented from doing so by the 1691 law prohibiting interracial matches. After the banns of marriage were an-nounced for the first time, Islewood reported, Dunkley's uncle George Mathews forbade the union, claiming that his niece's intended was a mulatto. Concerned both to avoid illegitimacy and to prevent an illegal interracial marriage from taking place, the court ordered Islewood to prove his white parentage. When he brought evidence to show that his grandfather was a Spaniard and his grandmother and father were white, the justices dismissed Mathews's petition and allowed the banns to be announced.[20] In this instance, a man's objection to a kinswoman's marriage choice was overruled when its pretended racial grounds could not be proven in court.

Amid changing legal standards, harsher punishments for interracial offenses, and an increased chance that white men might never be pun-ished for sexual offenses or forced to marry their pregnant lovers, white female servants participated in illicit sexual liaisons at great risk by the final decade of the seventeenth century. Bearing the full burden of local attempts to extract compensation for supporting illegitimate children, many servant women became semipermanent residents of the social margins. Their contacts might include both enslaved Africans and free Afro-Virginians, the latter often themselves the offspring of interracial unions.

Servant women's reports of the sites of their illicit acts, most of which date to the middle of the seventeenth century, suggest that a significant degree of physical intimacy may have been tolerated by neighbors and housemates. Once a woman became pregnant, however, her behavior was construed as illicit. Servant Mary Gunnell, for example, declared that Stephen Torlington "had to do with hir severall time by day and also by night in hir Masters hall and alsoe in other places." Anne Collins revealed a similarly wide range of opportunities for trysts, reporting that her erstwhile lover Robert Peirce "would take a bout with mee at the fireside and sometimes in the tobaccoe house[,] milke house[,] and orchard at spring sometimes 8 or 9 times a day." Other servant women mentioned having sexual intercourse in their master's hall, "in a bedd in a little roome" in the house, "under an Appletree in the orchard," "by the spring where ordinarily we fetch water," "behind the house," and in a thicket of bushes.[21]

It is difficult to believe that, within the cramped and communal atmosphere of most Virginia households, indications of pregnancy were the first gleanings of a particular couple's activities. More likely, neighbors and members of households disapproved of such goings-on but tolerated intimacies short of open fornication. As long as the couple avoided outright detection of their dalliance, communities could safely ignore their behavior until a pregnancy occurred. The increasing local concern with punishing white female servants who did give birth out of wedlock is thus consistent with traditions of relaxed community stand-ards for couples' behavior before an offense had taken place. Yet such latitude, when considered in the context of the trend in punishments, suggests that servant women who participated in premarital sexual ac-tivities, perhaps believing they were part of courtship, did so at great risk and with little protection from their communities.

Servant women who found themselves pregnant used several different methods to avoid detection. Running away during late pregnancy to deliver the child in another county was one means of avoiding the midwife's interrogation. In 1693, Isaac Jessop successfully petitioned the court for extra service from his servant Joane Terrell, who had run away and borne two illegitimate children. Disappearing at the time of a court presentment was also effective in the short term. If a woman could not be found for several meetings of the justices, the case might be dropped altogether. Running away proved to be a somewhat more effective tactic for pregnant single women during the eighteenth century than it had been previously because larger settlements and populations made it easier for a woman to fabricate an account of her past. Some of the advantage might have been lost, however, by increasingly efficient local bureaucracies and incentives for the capture and return of runaway servants. In most county courts after 1700, claims for rewards for servants returned to masters ten to fifteen miles away bespoke the existence of an increasingly vigilant population eager to receive monetary compensation for policing the laborers of other individuals.[22]

When a woman could not arrange to escape to relatives or friends in another county while she delivered her child, she might resort to abortion or infanticide. The courts were generally uninterested in prosecuting women for abortion, however, unless it occurred late in the pregnancy. In cases where a miscarriage suspiciously resembled abortion, justices might ask housemates and neighbors whether the woman in question "ever took any thing to make her miscarry." Individuals offering testimony in such cases seemed aware that herbal means of terminating pregnancies existed, even if they were not party to the secret remedies.[23]

Although abortion might have been easier to conceal than infanticide, it was often less effective, leaving pregnant women's dilemmas unresolved. For women such as Ann Jacobson, who tried to avoid stigma and prosecution by killing and "privily Burrying" her bastard child, infanticide was the answer. Elizabeth Lewis, a single woman who resided in the Norfolk home of Henry Walston, also sought such a remedy in 1688. Lewis delivered her child alone, "noe one being by her and that she called noe body to assist her." Claiming that the infant was stillborn, Lewis told the court that she buried it in a thicket, concealing the knowledge of the birth from everyone. Like many other single women in similar situations, Lewis found that her efforts to conceal the birth incriminated her in the death of her child. Ann Tandy, the daughter of a York County resident, was similarly indicted for being an accessory to the death of her male infant in 1701.[24]

In the effort to prevent this method of escaping detection and to gain better control over the mothers of illegitimate children, the Governor's Council called for a law in 1710 to prevent the murder of bastard children. Legislators eventually adapted a century-old English statute to punish infanticide. The law specified that any free woman caught concealing the death of her bastard child would be executed for murder whether or not murder could actually be proved. Subsequent laws set severe punishments for householders who secretly allowed unmarried women to bear children in their homes. Striking at the social networks that allowed single women to avoid punishment for violating the legal prohibitions on sexual intimacy, these statutes implicitly recognized the ways in which communities provided dynamic reinterpretations of the law and played vital roles in enforcing morality.

Harsh punishments did not deter some women from repeating sexual offenses. The lopsided emphasis on punishing women rather than men after 1700, moreover, also did nothing to protect women from being victimized a second or third time. Although never widespread, recidivism became more significant during the early eighteenth century than it had been previously. Between 1710 and 1740, second, third, and fourth offenses constituted between 8 and 12 percent of all bastardy cases. As one might expect, many but not all of these women were servants. Elizabeth Morris, a white woman from York County, is a striking exception. In 1738, she bore the first of four illegitimate children by Jones Irwin, a white man. Irwin had separated from his wife Ann and apparently lived with Morris. Each time the grand jury presented Morris for bastardy, Irwin paid her fine and acted as her security. This illicit behavior ultimately cost Morris her paternal inheritance; when her father died in 1739, just a year after the birth of her first illegitimate child, he excluded Morris from the will, leaving bequests to her four sisters and her mother.[25]

Generational patterns of sexual misconduct provide vivid evidence of the power of laws to conjoin racial and sexual stigmas in community life, leaving the illegitimate daughters of white mothers and black fathers more vulnerable than their white peers to out-of-wedlock pregnancy. Mandating thirty-year terms of service for the offspring of interracial unions, legislators placed these young women in servitude, where they remained accessible to unscrupulous masters and likely to form their own illicit relationships with enslaved men. Elizabeth Banks, a white servant from York County, provides a good example of this pattern. While still a servant to Major James Goodwin, Banks bore an illegitimate daughter, Mary, by a male slave in 1683. A second daughter may have been born a few years later. Twenty years later, an adult Mary Banks was serving the Goodwin family. In 1704, she agreed that her illegitimate daughter Elizabeth would serve Martin Goodwin "untill she be free according to law and custome of the country for all mollatto bastards." Mary Banks had previously given birth to a daughter named Hannah, whom the court also described as a mulatto. An Ann Banks, quite possibly the granddaughter of the first Elizabeth Banks, subsequently faced bastardy charges in 1731. By mid-century, there were six free women representing three generations of the Banks family, all of whom appear to have been descended from Elizabeth Banks and her daughter by an unknown enslaved father.[26]

The legal association of interracial sex with illegitimacy effectively Africanized the social margins of each county, connecting white mothers to larger networks of marginalized white, free black, and enslaved peoples. Yet the individuals who composed these families could hardly be described as the passive victims of exploitation at the hands of the county's great men. Theft, Sabbath violations, drunkenness, swearing, and trading with other people's servants checkered the legal histories of these families, testifying to their lack of deference and their persistent activities outside the bounds of the major county institutions of court and parish. The white Biggs family of Norfolk County was one such family. Possibly the descendants of the persecuted seventeenth-century dissident sheriff, the Biggs were charged with failing to maintain roadways, neglecting to attend church, abusing servants, and bearing illegitimate children.[27]

By the mid-eighteenth century, the small population of free people of color inhabited enclaves created by recurring generational patterns of illegitimacy and interracial networks. The three local courts in this study charged sixteen Afro-Virginian women with bastardy after the passage of the 1691 law; three of these women committed second offenses, and eight of the offenders were related to at least one other offending woman. The courts do not appear to have inquired into the possible interracial nature of these incidents, perhaps as a consequence of their studied indifference to the sexual activities of white men. Rather, illicit behavior by free black women was treated as ordinary sexual misconduct. Free people of color, such as members of the Afro-Virginian Roberts or Banks families, thus appeared before the court charged with many of the same offenses as the Anglo-Virginian Biggs family and, indeed, stood a good chance of being their partners in crime.

When local courts did prosecute free black women for bearing illegitimate children, nearly one-fifth of the time the accused were identified as servants. At least three of the sixteen Afro-Virginian women charged with bastardy after 1691 came to court at the behest of masters who gained extra labor by prosecuting them. In one such case in Norfolk in 1712, the courts ignored the sexual misconduct of Moll until she petitioned for her freedom at the end of her term. When presented with the choice of a fine, whipping, or a year's service to whoever paid her penalty, Moll agreed to additional service instead of beginning her life as a free woman.[28]

The General Assembly soon perceived the danger of allowing a generation of "mulatto" servant women – who had themselves paid part of the penalty for their white mothers' interracial crimes – to beget illegitimate children. In 1723, the Assembly prescribed additional punishments for these women and their offspring, a measure that effectively prolonged their dependence and increased the possibility that their daughters would also produce children out of wedlock. Concern over the interracial sexual misconduct of white servant women between 1680 and 1700 thus resurfaced in a new form during the 1720s, as the daughters of the original offenders came of age.

Legal initiatives designed to put sexual regulations to the service of race relations did not meet with full or automatic compliance. Nor did harsh punishments for interracial offenders expunge the behavior as legislators had hoped. Men and women continued to cross racial lines, testifying to the permeability and fragility of definitions of racial difference.

For poorer Virginians, perhaps more than for other groups of people, the combination of sexual and racial regulations ironically brought men and women together, conjoining traditional acts of sexual misconduct with new transgressions of racial boundaries. Although the laws did not exert hegemonic influence over people's lives, legal changes did transform some patterns of sexual deviance, Africanizing the sexual and social margins of colonial society.

Racializing Sex

Post-rebellion laws knit together traditional measures for regulating the sexuality of poor people and servants with newer efforts to establish legal meanings for racial difference. Prohibitions on interracial marriages safeguarded white male access to white women, providing assurance that white female domesticity and sexuality would remain the preserve of white men. Harsh punishments greeted white servant women who threatened this arrangement by enjoying illicit pleasures with black men. Together, these legal measures racialized legal constructs of patriarchal privilege and female honor, creating a codependence between the two that excluded black men and women. But did these legal identities seep into everyday life to affect the way ordinary people understood honor and racial difference? In community responses to rape and acts of racial slander after 1691, it appears that legal constructs of sexualized race did change the way individuals engaged in conflict, even as people continued to circumvent the letter of the law in their daily interactions.

The differences between popular attitudes toward black and white women appeared most obviously in the incidence and legal treatment of rape. Conceived legally as a crime against property embodied by a white man's wife, daughter, or servant woman, rape was also an illicit sexual act forced upon an unwilling woman. The property and sexual connotations of rape, however, were not distinct. A husband's claims to his wife's labor included rights to the fruits of her reproductive work: her bearing, feeding, clothing and raising of children. All of these factors may have influenced Eliza Farrell and her husband to press charges against Thomas Seawell in 1689. Seawell claimed to have met up with a "swinishly Drunk" Eliza Farrell at a party in that year. When the "weary" Farrell stumbled to the upper chamber of the house to lie down, Seawell followed her, sexually assaulting her with an ox horn and a lit candle. He brought the incident to Farrell's husband's attention by waving some of Eliza's singed pubic hair in front of his face. Brian and Eliza Farrell did not simply claim damages for the sexual assault or physical injury committed against her, nor was Brian simply interested in defending his violated sense of honor. Rather, the claim of damages against Seawell cited the then-pregnant Eliza's miscarriage as the couple's loss.[29]

If a female litigant was a particularly unlikely victim of rape or if her alleged attacker seemed incapable of overpowering her, she might find her claims received with incredulity. Such was the case with Elizabeth Hansford Burt, daughter of an executed Baconian rebel, who claimed to have been raped in 1692. Several witnesses reported their conversations with Burt about her encounter with John Eaton on the way home from a tavern in York County. One witness, Captain Charles Hansford, who happened to be Burt's uncle, refused to swear out a warrant against John Eaton for rape when Burt first reported the incident. Hansford explained his doubts about his niece's account:

> She spoke to that purpose that Eaton would have lane w[ith] her a coming from C[our]t. y[ou]r dep[onent] s[ai]d what then it may be he did not intend it, though he profered itt, shee replyed indeed he did doe it and I will take my oath of it, I am not of a man's strength and he did force me and did it whether I would or noe.

Burt's insistence that she was "not of a man's strength" was ultimately not sufficient to convince Hansford. Refusing to accept Burt's gender claim to weakness, Hansford

> tould her hee thought such a thing could not possibly be for she was near as strong as Eaton and that he could not doe it except shee was willing[.] shee then s[ai]d he did doe itt ag[ains]t her will.[30]

Hansford's questions may have been based upon his personal knowledge of his niece and her reputation for physical strength. Just a month before she claimed to have been raped, the court found her guilty of beating a pregnant woman so severely that the victim miscarried. Her claims that John Eaton physically overpowered and raped her may have been received with skepticism because she had so brutally proven her strength and aggression in a case with another woman. Apparently, Eaton believed that Burt's reputation would protect him, for he responded to her accusation by initiating a defamation suit. He lost his case, however, after he confessed to putting his hands underneath Burt's petticoats. Yet Burt's husband did not press charges against Eaton for rape. Perhaps he sensed that community sentiments were not running in his wife's favor.

Throughout the seventeenth and eighteenth centuries, women like Elizabeth Burt found it nearly impossible to convince their communities to treat accusations of rape seriously. During the seventeenth century, although several white women accused white men of rape, none succeeded in bringing her case to the General Court. After being charged with raping two of his servants in 1670, Henry Smith of Accomack was not only acquitted but awarded extra time from the women as their punishment for accusing him. The court judged the public scandal about a master's reputation to be more damaging than the possible injury to his female servants.[31]

Fourteen years later, a spate of rape accusations reached a single session of the Norfolk court, suggesting that the women in question may have acted collectively after sharing stories of mistreatment. Complaining that her master Dennis Ashly had "Ravished her," Mary Buck was unable to convince a jury of matrons that "any man had lately made use of her body." The examining women were not sworn to this, however, and the court ordered Ashly and Buck to return to a future session. Their failure to appear suggests that Buck may have dropped her suit. At the very same court session in which Buck introduced her suit, two other servant women brought charges of rape against their masters. Jane Williams lost her case when she confessed "that she did nott Cry out nor resist him because her master told her he would not hurt her." The Norfolk justices viewed Williams's charge as a scandalous ploy "to gett her freedome" and ordered the sheriff to give her twenty lashes. Ann Perry fared no better at the same court. Her claim that John Prescott had ravished her was dismissed by the justices, who found no evidence to support her claim other than what she had alleged three years earlier. Perry received fourteen lashes for being a malicious informer.[32]

A Lancaster County rape case in 1743 had similar consequences. Elizabeth Ben, described by the court as "a single woman," charged laborer Robert Horton with rape but failed to produce material evidence that would convince the court. Not only was Horton discharged, but Martha Flint, one of Ben's witnesses, was censured by the justices for having "unnecessarily and maliciously fomented and procured the accusation" against him.[33]

The fragmentary extant evidence from the county court records suggests that very few white women successfully convicted white men of rape. One notable exception was Alccy (or Anccy) Butt, who seems to have had unusual good fortune in her suit against Peter Gully. Charged with attempting to ravish Butt, Gully was convicted and bound "in the county goale [jail]" until he produced bond. In this singular instance, a white woman successfully brought a white man to trial but only on the lesser charge of attempted rape.[34]

When a white woman accused a black man of rape, her chances of conviction appear to have been much higher. Of eighteen such cases to appear in Virginia's local and General Courts between 1670 and 1767, only two are known to have been dismissed. At least twelve of the nineteen accused black men were executed for their crimes, a far cry from the treatment of alleged white rapists. Ironically, the formal and informal mechanisms of racial subordination that supported Virginia's slave system afforded white women less protection from the men most likely to exploit them – white men – targeting instead the men who were themselves the victims of slavery's destructive power.

As the trial of Harry reveals, part of the reason for the discrepancy between judgments of white and black offenders can be traced to the type of court in which slave felonies were tried. Accused of raping a servant named Janet Young, Harry, an enslaved man, appeared in Lancaster's court of oyer and terminer in February 1724. Courts of oyer and terminer provided speedy local tribunals that circumvented expensive and lengthy hearings at the General Court. In Harry's case, the court moved surely and swiftly. Janet Young testified that Harry "did by force Ravish her" on the night of December 15, 1723. Thomas Thornton, a slaveowner, served as a second witness against Harry while Toney, his slave, presented additional testimony supporting Young's claims. Despite Harry's protests of innocence, the court found him guilty and ordered him to be hanged by the neck at the courthouse. From the date of the alleged rape to Harry's execution, the entire procedure took just over two months. A similar fate befell the slave Toney in Northumberland County and Tom of Elizabeth City County in 1767.[35]

As long as the alleged rapist was a white man, the court's assumptions of female consent and the procedural complications of a superior court trial made it difficult to gather sufficient evidence to convict. When the accused was a male slave, however, the swift justice of the court of oyer and terminer and presumptions of white female resistance combined to make convictions relatively easy.

No rape cases were ever brought by or on behalf of black women until late in the eighteenth century. Rape violated a man's legal rights over an economic dependant. The obvious difficulty, then, in acknowledging the rape of an enslaved woman was that no man was recognized as being injured by the offense. The only man with legal claims to a female slave's labor and reproductive capacity was her master. Rape did not jeopardize his investment. If Elizabeth Burt's case is instructive of popular attitudes linking the credibility of rape accusations to beliefs in female weakness, moreover, then black women, who were legally defined as tithable field laborers, bore an extra burden of proof. Excluded from the constructs of white female sexual honor and often unprotected by the claims of a husband or father, most black women lacked the legal grounds for a suit in cases of rape. After the laws of 1723 made it easier for masters to recoup losses from pregnant black servants, free women of color also may have experienced increasing vulnerability to rape.

The legislation of 1691 outlawing interracial unions also appears to have had an impact upon popular attitudes toward illicit sexuality and racial difference as expressed in slander. Soon after that date, the first slanderous remarks by white people containing references to race, interracial sexual behavior, or kinship connection to Africans came to the county courts. The slander charges brought by Jane Hide and her husband against Joanna Deloney provide one such example. Three years after the "spurious issue" statute spelled out severe punishments for white women engaging in interracial sexual activity, Hide brought witnesses to court who testified that Deloney had hurled numerous insults at her, including a remark to a black boy that "Mrs Hide was such a whore that she would lye with a negro."[36] Convinced that Hide was trying to steal her husband, Deloney apparently hoped to publicize Hide's diminished sexual credit. Her comment about Hide's longing for a black lover reinforced other allegations of sexual deviance, including incest and attempted abortion, forming a triumvirate of dishonorable and taboo white female behavior. That Deloney chose a racial slander to shame Hide suggests changes in popular concepts of female honor and reputation in the years after laws banned interracial unions.

In eighteenth-century Northampton County, historian Douglas Deal has found similar examples of racially tinged slanderous remarks in which white people traded insults by alleging sexual intimacy or family relationships with black people. Ann Batson, for example, successfully defended herself against another woman's claim, "You are a Negro whore and a Negros strumpet and you would have Jumpt over nine hedges to have had a Negroe." The insult in this case was the disgrace brought by a white woman's sexual desire for a black man. Most intriguing was John Cobb's response to Henry Stott's public charge that he was a mulatto. Cobb denied Stott's allegation, insisting that his history of collecting debts and giving evidence in cases involving white people "proved" that he was a white person.[37] In both of these cases, the denial of legal privileges to black people and the prohibitions on interracial sexuality created new opportunities for slanderous speech, transforming the repertoire of remarks capable of damaging reputations.

The seriousness with which racial slanders were treated and the new interdependence between definitions of illicit sexuality and racial difference are most visible in a case in which an enslaved black man verbally violated the boundaries that were supposed to separate black male and white female sexual activity. In 1705, a slave named Tom belonging to Mrs Dinah Thorowgood received thirty-nine lashes for insisting that he had "Layn" with a white woman named Mary Hoskins at "Divers places and Divers times with abundance of other very gross and scandalized abuses and terms." No attempt was ever made to prove that Tom committed any illegal sexual behavior; rather, his crime was his persistent refusal to maintain verbally the sanctity of white female sexuality.[38]

The 1691 law was part of a long process of changes in definitions and prosecutions of sexual offenses and in the social construction of racial difference. Alarmed by the potential of sexual unions between white servant women and enslaved black men to undermine the still-tentative racial distinctions among laborers, the colonial legislature appropriated sexual regulations to redefine and reinforce racial boundaries. By the eighteenth century, the legal foundations of race, class, and gender relations in the colony had become interdependent. Although the new legal constructions impinged upon local autonomy, communities continued to exercise discretion in matters of race and sexuality. Racialized patriarchy and sexualized concepts of race created new ways for white men to consolidate their power in a slave society but did not suppress individual negotiations of behavior and identity.

Notes

1 York County Deeds, Orders, Wills, Colonial Williamsburg Foundation, Williamsburg, Virginia (hereafter York DOW), 3, August 15, 1661, 120, 125, 129.
2 Ibid., 130.
3 When punishments of female servants are compared to those of male offenders, women appear to have been whipped more often than men. Men were more frequently fined but equally likely to be sentenced for penance. This pattern probably reflects the status (servant or free) rather than the sex of the individual punished, although status in the colony was in part a function of gendered privileges of property ownership and the gendered pattern of migration. Servants represented 37 of 49 cases of women charged with bastardy. Although it is more difficult to compile figures for men, it appears that a smaller proportion of male offenders were servants. These conclusions are based on court records from Norfolk, Lancaster, and York Counties, 1637–62.
4 A similar penance ritual was used in England and New England.
5 Norfolk Wills and Deeds E, May 12, 1666, 1, 5.
6 Many of these measures for controlling sexuality originated with English poor laws. See Keith Wrightson and David Levine, "The Social Context of Illegitimacy in Early Modern England," in Peter Laslett, Karla Oosterveen, and Richard M. Smith, eds., *Bastardy and Its Comparative History: Studies in the History of Illegitimacy and Marital Non conformism in Britain, France, Germany, Sweden, North America, Jamaica, and Japan* (London, 1980), 172.

7 Norfolk Book B, February 1, 1649, fol. 106; York DOW 4, April 10, 1668, 177; York DOW 11, October 24, 1701, 528.

8 See Norfolk Orders, 1675–1686, August 18, 1684, 249–50; *MCGC*, 149.

9 "Conway Robinson's Notes," in H. R. McIlwaine, ed., *Minutes of the Council and General Court of Colonial Virginia*, 2nd edn (Richmond, VA, 1979), 477, 479 (hereafter *MCGC*).

10 William Waller Henning, ed., *The Statutes at Large; Being a Collection of All the Laws of Virginia, from the first Session of the Legislature*, 13 vols. (1823; facsimile reprint, Charlottesville, VA, 1969) (hereafter *SAL*) December 23, 1662, II, 170.

11 *SAL*, December 23, 1662, II, 170.

12 Norfolk Deed Book 5, June 2, 1686, 315; July 14, 1686, 320; September 15, 1690, 190; March 16, 1691, 214.

13 *SAL*, April 16, 1691, III, 86–8.

14 Lancaster Orders 5, September 12, 1705, 127.

15 Norfolk Deed Book 9, August 17, 1711, 16; September 21, 1711, 17; October 19, 1711, 20; Norfolk Deed Book 10, June 20, 1718, 11.

16 Norfolk Orders, 1675–1686, March 16, 1681, 136; April 4, 1681, 139; York DOW 10, February 25, 1695, 106–7.

17 Lancaster Orders 5, July 8, 1702, 172.

18 *Minutes of the House of Burgesses*, September 28, 1696, cited in Philip Alexander Bruce, *Institutional History of Virginia in the Seventeenth Century*, 2 vols. (1910; repr., Gloucester, MA, 1964), I, 50; Lancaster Order Book 8, May 16, 1740, 275.

19 H. R. McIlwaine, ed., *Legislative Journals of the Council of Colonial Virginia*, 2nd edn (Richmond, VA, 1979), I, 262.

20 Norfolk Deed Book 9, January 15, 1714, 76.

21 York DOW 3, September 11, 1660, 92; January 25, 1662, 149; October 24, 1659, 68; June 24, 1662, 170; October 24, 1662, 176.

22 Lancaster Orders 3, February 14, 1694, 280.

23 Lancaster Orders 6, September 9, 1714, 75, 76.

24 See Princess Anne County Orders, VSL microfilm, January 8, 1707, 456; Norfolk Deed Book 5, May 15, 1688, 133; York DOW 9, October 24, 1701, 518; York DOW 13, January 24, 1709, 187.

25 For evidence of the Morris–Irwin relationship, see York County Orders, Wills, Inventories, Colonial Williamsburg Foundation, Williamsburg, Virginia, 18, May 15, 1738, 414; September 14, 1739, 562; May 19, 1740, 597–8; York County Orders, Wills, 19, May 19, 1746, 426; York County Judgments, Orders, 1, May 16, 1748, 80; York Wills and Inventories 20, June 20, 1748, 108.

26 See York DOW 6, June 25, 1683, 498; York DOW 12, February 24, 1704, 188; York DOW 17, December 20, 1731, 248.

27 Norfolk Deed Book 5, September 17, 1688, 106.

28 Norfolk Deed Book 9, March 20, 1713, 51.

29 See "Colonial Papers," VSL microfilm, reels 609–12, petition to the General Court and testimony, folder 6, nos 16, 18, 1689.

30 York DOW 9, September 26, 1692, 174–6.

31 *MCGC*, 212.
32 Norfolk Orders, 1675–1686, August 18, 1684, 249–50.
33 Lancaster Orders 8, August 24, 1743, 393.
34 Norfolk Deed Book 8, May 16, 1709, 63.
35 Lancaster Orders 7, February 12, 1723, 136–7; Edward H. Bonekemper, "Negroes' Freedom of Contract in Antebellum Virginia, 1620–1860" (Master's thesis, Old Dominion University, 1971), ch. 4; Elizabeth City County Orders, VSL microfilm, September 19, 1767, 493.
36 York DOW 10, June 25, 1694, 12–13.
37 Deal, "A Constricted World," in Lois Green Carr, Philip D. Morgan, and Jean B. Russo, eds, *Colonial Chesapeake Society* (Chapel Hill, NC, 1988), 279–80.
38 Princess Anne Order Book 1, VSL microfilm, September 7, 1705, 419.

Richard Frethorne's Letter to his Parents (1623)

Loving and kind father and mother:

My most humble duty remembered to you, hoping in God of your good health, as I myself am at the making hereof. This is to let you understand that I your child am in a most heavy case by reason of the nature of the country, [which] is such that it causeth much sickness, as the scurvy and the bloody flux and diverse other diseases, which maketh the body very poor and weak. And when we are sick there is nothing to comfort us; for since I came out of the ship I never ate anything but peas, and loblollie (that is water gruel). As for deer or venison I never saw any since I came into this land. There is indeed some fowl, but we are not allowed to go and get it, but must work hard both early and late for a mess of water gruel and a mouthful of bread and beef. A mouthful of bread for a penny loaf must serve for four men which is most pitiful. If you did know as much as I, when people cry out day and night – Oh! that they were in England without their limbs and would not care to lose any limb to be in England again, yea, though they beg from door to door. For we live in fear of the enemy every hour, yet we have had a combat with them on the Sunday before Shrovetide, and we took two alive and made slaves of them. But it was by policy, for we are in great danger; for our plantation is very weak by reason of the death and sickness of our company. For we came but twenty for the merchants, and they are half dead just; and we look every hour when two more should go. Yet there came some four other men yet to live with us, of which there is but one alive; and our Lieutenant is dead, and his father and his brother. And there was some five or six of the last year's twenty, of which there is but three left, so that we are fain to get other men to plant with us; and yet we are but 32 to fight against 3000 if they should come, and the nighest help that we have is ten miles of us, and when the rogues overcame this place last [time] they slew 80 persons. How then shall we do, for we lie even in their teeth. They may easily take us, but [for the fact] that God is merciful and can save with few as well as with many, as he showed to Gilead. And like Gilead's soldiers, if they lapped water, we drink water which is but weak.

And I have nothing to comfort me, nor is there nothing to be gotten here but sickness and death, except [in the event] that one had money to lay out in some things for profit. But I have nothing at all – no, not a shirt to my back but two rags (2), nor no clothes but one poor suit, nor but one pair of shoes, but one pair of stockings, but one cap, but two bands. My cloak is stolen by one of my own fellows, and to his dying hour [he] would not tell me what he did with it but some of my fellows saw him have butter and beef out of a ship, which my cloak, I doubt [not], paid for. So that I have not a penny, nor a penny worth, to help me to either spice or sugar or strong waters, without the which one cannot live here. For as strong beer in England doth fatten and strengthen them, so water here doth wash and weaken these here [and] only keeps life and soule together. But I am not half a quarter so strong as I was in England, and all is for want of victuals, for I do protest unto you that I have eaten more in [one] day at home than I have allowed me here for a week. You have given more than my day's allowance to a beggar at the door; and if Mr. Jackson had not relieved me, I should be in a poor case. But he like a father and she like a loving mother doth still help me.

For when we go up to Jamestown (that is 10 miles of us) there lie all the ships that come to land, and there they must deliver their goods. And when we went up to town, as it may be, on Monday at noon, and come there by night, then load the next day by noon, and go home in the afternoon, and unload, and then away again in the night, and be up about midnight. Then if it rained or blowed never so hard, we must lie in the boat on the water and have nothing but a little bread. For when we go into the boat we have a loaf allowed to two men, and it is all [we would get] if we stayed there two days, which is hard; and [we] must lie all that while in the boat. But that Goodman Jackson pitied me and made me a cabin to lie in always when I come up, and he would give me some poor jacks [to take] home with me, which comforted me more than peas or water gruel. Oh, they be very godly folks, and love me very well, and will do anything for me. And he much marvelled that you would send me a servant to the Company; he saith I had been better knocked on the head. And indeed so I find it now, to my great grief and misery; and [I] saith that if you love me you will redeem me suddenly, for which I do entreat and beg. And if you cannot get the merchants to redeem me for some little money, then for God's sake get a gathering or entreat some good folks to lay out some little sum of money in meal and cheese and butter and beef. Any eating meat will yield great profit. Oil and vinegar is very good; but, father, there is great loss in leaking. But for God's sake send beef and cheese and butter, or the more of one sort and none of another. But if you send cheese, it must be very old cheese; and at the cheesemonger's you may buy very good cheese for twopence farthing or halfpenny, that will be liked very well. But if you send cheese, you must have a care how you pack it in barrels; and you must put cooper's chips between every cheese, or else the heat of the hold will rot them. And look whatsoever you send me – be it never so much – look, what[ever] I make of it, I will deal truly with you. I will send it over and beg the profit to redeem me; and if I die before it come, I have entreated Goodman Jackson to send you the worth of it, who hath promised he will. If you send, you must direct your letters to Goodman Jackson, at Jamestown, a gunsmith. (You must set down his freight, because there be more of his name there.) Good father, do not forget me, but have mercy and pity my miserable case. I know if you did but see me, you would weep to see me; for I have but one suit, but it is a strange one, it is very well guarded. Wherefore, for God's sake, pity me. I pray you to remember my love to all my friends and kindred. I hope all my brothers and sisters are in good health, and as for my part I have set down my resolution that certainly will be; that is, that the answer of this letter will be life or death to me. Therefore, good father, send as soon as you can, and if you send me any thing let this be the mark.

    ROT

Richard Frethorne,
Martin's Hundred

The names of them that be dead of the company [that] came over with us to serve under our Lieutenants:

John Flower	George Goulding
John Thomas	Jos. Johnson
Thos. Howes	our lieutenant, his father and brother
John Butcher	Thos. Giblin
John Sanderford	George Banum
Rich. Smith	a little Dutchman
John Olive	one woman
Thos. Peirsman	one maid
William Cerrell	one child

Virginia Slave Codes (1661–1705)

William Waller Hening

1   March, 1660/61. Act XXII: English running away with negroes.

Bee itt enacted that in case any English servant shall run away in company with any negroes who are incapable of making satisfaction by addition of time, *Bee itt enacted* that the English so running away in company with them shall serve for the time of the said negroes absence as they are to do for their owne by a former act.

2   March 1661/62. Act CII: Run-aways.

Whereas there are diverse loytering runaways in this country who very often absent themselves from their masters service and sometimes in a long time cannot be found, that losse of the time and the charge in the seeking them often exceeding the value of their labour: *Bee itt therefore enacted* that all runaways that shall absent themselves from their said masters service, shalbe lyable to make satisfaction by service after the times by custome or indenture is expired (vizt.) double their times of service soe neglected, and if the time of their running away was in the crop or the charge of recovering them extraordinary the court shall lymitt a longer time of service proportionable to the damage the master shall make appeare he hath susteyned . . .; and in case any English servant shall run away in company of any negroes who are incapable of making satisfaction by addition of a time, *it is enacted* that the English soe running away in the company with them shall at the time of service to their owne masters expired, serve the masters of the said negroes for their absence soe long as they should have done by this act if they had not beene slaves, every christian in company serving his proportion; and if the negroes be lost or dye in such time of their being run away, the christian servants in company with them shall by proportion among them, either pay fower thousand five hundred pounds of tobacco and caske or fower yeares service for every negroe so lost or dead.

3   December, 1662. Act VI: Women servants gott with child by their masters after their time expired to be sold by the Churchwardens for two yeares for the good of the parish.

Whereas by act of Assembly every woman servant haveing a bastard is to serve two yeares, and late experiente shew that some dissolute masters have gotten their maides with child, and yet claime the benefitt of their service, and on the contrary if a woman gott with child by her master should be freed from that service it might probably induce such loose persons to lay all their bastards to their masters; *it is therefore thought fitt and accordingly enacted and be it enacted henceforward* that each woman servant gott with child by her master shall after her time by indenture or custome is expired be by the churchwardens of the parish where she lived when she was brought to bed of such a bastard, sold for two years, and the tobacco to be imployed by the vestry for the use of the parish.

4   December, 1662. Act XII: Negro womens children to serve according to the condition of the mother.

Whereas some doubts have arrisen whether children got by any Englishman upon a negro woman should be slave or free, *Be it therefore enacted and declared by this present grand assembly,* that all children borne in this country shalbe held bond or free only according to the condition of the mother, *And* that if any christian shall committ ffornication with a negro man or woman, hee or shee so offending shall pay double the ffines imposed by the former act.

5   September, 1667. Act III: An act declaring that baptisme of slaves doth not exempt them from bondage.

Whereas some doubts have risen whether children that are slaves by birth, and by the charity and piety of their owners made pertakers of the blessed sacrament of baptisme, should by vertue of their baptisme be made ffree; *It is enacted and declared by this grand assembly, and the authority thereof,* that the conferring of baptisme doth not alter the condition of the person as to his bondage or ffreedome; that diverse masters, ffreed from this doubt, may more carefully endeavour the propagation of christianity by permitting children, though slaves, or those of greater growth if capable to be admitted to the sacrament.

6   October, 1669. Act I: An act about the casual killing of slaves.

Whereas the only law in force for the punishment of refractory servants resisting their master, mistris or overseer cannot be inflicted upon negroes, nor the obstinancy of many of them by other than violent meanes supprest, *Be it enacted and declared by this grand assembly,* if any slave resist his master (or others by his masters order correcting him) and by the extremity of the correction should chance to die, that his death shall not be accompted ffelony, but the master (or that other person appointed by the master to punish him) be acquit from molestation, since it cannot be presumed that prepensed malice (which alone makes murther ffelony) should induce any man to destroy his own estate.

7   June, 1680. Act X: An act for preventing Negroes Insurrections.

Whereas the frequent meeting of considerable numbers of negroe slaves under pretence of feasts and burialls is judged of dangerous consequence; for prevention whereof for the future, *Bee it enacted by the kings most excellent majestie by and with the consent of the general assembly* . . . that from and after the publication of this law, it shall not be lawfull for any negroe or other slave to carry or arme himselfe with any club, staffe, gunn, sword or any other weapon of defence or offence, nor to go or depart from of his masters ground without a certificate from his master, mistris, or overseer, and such permission not to be granted but upon perticular and necessary occasions; and every negroe or slave soe offending not haveing a certificate as aforesaid shalbe sent to the next constable, who is hereby enjoyned and required to give the said negroe twenty lashes on his bare back well layd on, and soe sent home to his said master, mistris or overseer. *And it is further enacted by the authority aforesaid* that if any negroe or other slave shall presume to lift up his hand in opposition against any christian, shall for every such offence, upon due proof made thereof by the oath of the party before a magistrate, have and receive thirty lashes on his bare back well laid on. *And it is hereby further enacted by the authority aforesaid* that if any negroe or other slave shall absent himself from his masters service and lye hid and lurking in obscure places, comitting injuries to the inhabitants, and shall resist any person or persons that shalby any lawful authority be imployed to apprehend and take the said negroe, that then in case of such resistance, it shalbe lawful for such person or persons to kill the said negroe or slave so lying out and resisting, and that this law be once every six months published at the respective county courts and parish churches within this colony. [Editor's note: In November 1682 this act was amended because it "hath not had its intended effect for want of due notice thereof being taken." The law was now to be read aloud in church twice a year, and masters were fined 200 pounds of tobacco if they let other masters' slaves stay on their plantation longer than 4 hours without the owner's permission.]

8   April, 1691. Act XVI: An act for suppressing outlying slaves.

Whereas many times negroes, mulattoes, and other slaves unlawfully absent themselves from their masters and mistresses service, and lie hid and lurk in obscure places killing hoggs and committing other injuries to the inhabitants of this dominion, for remedy whereof for the future, *Be it enacted by their majesties lieutenant governour, councell, and burgesses of this present generall assembly, and the authoritie thereof, and it is hereby enacted,* that in all such cases upon intelligence of any such negroes, mulattoes, or other slaves lying out, two of their majesties justices of the peace of that country... shall be impowered and commanded [to issue warrants to the sheriff to summon as many men as he needs to arrest the runaways] and in case any negroes, mulattoes or other slave or slaves lying out as aforesaid shall resist, runaway, or refuse to deliver and surrender him or themselves... in such cases it shall and may be lawfull... to kill and destroy such negroes, mulattoes, and other slave or slaves by gunn or any otherwaise whatsoever.

Provided that where any negroe or mulattoe slave shall be killed in pursuance of this act, the owner or owners of such negro or mulatto slave shall be paid for such negro or mulatto slave four thousand pounds of tobacco by the publique. And for the prevention of that abominable mixture and spurious issue which hereafter may encrease in this dominion, as well as by negroes, mulattoes, and Indians intermarrying with English, or other white women, as by their unlawfull accompanying with one another, *Be it enacted by the authoritie aforesaid, and it is hereby enacted,* that for the time to come, whatsoever English or other white man or woman being free shall intermarry with a negroe, mulatto, or Indian man or woman bond or free shall within three months after such marriage be banished and removed from this dominion forever. *And be it further enacted*... That if any English woman being free shall have a bastard child by any negro or mulatto, she pay the sume of fifteen pounds sterling, within one month after such bastard child shall be born, to the Church wardens of the parish where she shall be delivered of such a child, and in default of such payment she shall be taken into the possession of the said Church wardens and disposed of for five years, and the said fine of fifteen pounds, or whatever the woman shall be disposed of for, shall be paid, one third part to their majesties for and towards the support of the government and the contingent charges thereof, and one other third part to the use of the parish where the offense is committed, and the other third part to the informer, and that such bastard child be bound out as a servant by the said Church wardens until he or she shall attaine the age of thirty yeares, and in case such English woman that shall have such a bastard child be a servant, she shall be sold by the said church wardens, (after her time is expired that she ought by law to serve her master) for five yeares, and the money she shall be sold for divided as is before appointed, and the child to serve as aforesaid.

And foreasmuch as great inconveniences may happen to this country by the setting of negroes and mulattoes free, by their either entertaining negroe slaves from their masters service, or receiving stolen goods, or being grown old bring a charge upon the country; for prevention thereof, *Be it enacted by the authority aforesaid, and it is hereby enacted,* That no negro or mulattoe be after the end of this present session of assembly set free by any person or persons whatsoever, unless such person or persons, their heires, executors or administrators pay for the transportation of such negro or negroes out of the countrey within six months after such setting them free, upon penalty of paying tenn pounds sterling to the Church wardens of the parish where such person shall dwell with, which money, or so much thereof as shall be necessary, the said Church wardens are to cause the said negro or mulatto to be transported out of the countrey, and the remainder of the said money to imploy to the use of the poor of the parish.

9   1705. An act concerning servants and slaves.

I.   *Be it enacted, by the governor, council, and burgesses, of this present general assembly, and it is hereby enacted, by the authority of the same,* That all servants brought into this country without indenture, if the said servants be christians, and of christian parentage, and above nineteen years of age, shall serve but five years; and if under nineteen years of age, 'till they shall become twenty-four years of age, and no longer. ...

IV.   *And also be it enacted, by the authority aforesaid, and it is hereby enacted,* That all servants imported and brought into this country, by sea or land, who were not christians in their native country, (except Turks and Moors in amity with her majesty, and others that can make due proof of their being free in England, or any other christian country, before they were shipped, in order to transportation hither) shall be accounted and be slaves, and as such be here bought and sold notwithstanding a conversion to christianity afterwards. ...

VII.   *And also be it enacted, by the authority aforesaid, and it is hereby enacted,* That all masters and owners of servants, shall find and provide for their servants, wholesome and competent diet, clothing, and lodging, by the discretion of the county court; and shall not, at any time, give immoderate correction; neither shall, at any time, whip a christian white servant naked, without an order from a justice of the peace: And if any, notwithstanding this act, shall presume to whip a christian white servant naked, without such order, the person so offending, shall forfeit and pay for the same, forty shillings sterling, to the party injured. ...

XI.   And for a further christian care and usage of all christian servants, *Be it also enacted, by the authority aforesaid, and it is hereby enacted,* That no negros, mullatos, or Indians, although christians, or Jews, Moors, Mahometans, or other infidels, shall, at any time, purchase any christian servant, nor any other, except of their own complexion, or such as are declared slaves by this act: And if any negro, mulatto, or Indian, Jew, Moor, Mahometan, or other infidel, or such as are declared slaves by this act, shall, notwithstanding, purchase any christian white servant, the said servant shall, *ipso facto,* become free and acquit from any service then due, and shall be so held, deemed, and taken: And any person, having such christian servant, shall intermarry with any such negro, mulatto, or Indian, Jew, Moor, Mahometan, or other infidel, every christian white servant of every such person so intermarrying, shall, *ipso facto*, become free and acquit from any service then due to such master or mistress so intermarrying, as aforesaid. . . .

XIII. And whereas there has been a good and laudable custom of allowing servants corn and cloaths for their present support, upon their freedom; but nothing in that nature ever made certain, *Be it also enacted by the authority aforesaid, and it is hereby enacted,* That there shall be paid and allowed to every imported servant, not having yearly wages, at the time of service ended, by the master or owner of such servant, viz: To every male servant, ten bushels of indian corn, thirty shillings in money, or the value thereof, in goods, and one well fixed musket or fuzee, of the value of twenty shillings, at least: and to every woman servant, fifteen bushels of indian corn, and forty shillings in money, or the value thereof, in goods. . . .

XVIII. And if any woman servant shall be delivered of a bastard child within the time of her service aforesaid, *Be it enacted, by the authority aforesaid, and it is hereby enacted,* That in recompense of the loss and trouble occasioned her master or mistress thereby, she shall for every such offence, serve her said master or owner one whole year after her time by indenture, custom, and former order of court, shall be expired; or pay her said master or owner, one thousand pounds of tobacco; and the reputed father, if free, shall give security to the church-wardens of the parish where that child shall be, to maintain the child, and keep the parish indemnified; or be compelled thereto by order of the county court, upon the said church-wardens complaint: But if a servant, he shall make satisfaction to the parish, for keeping the said child, after his time by indenture, custom, or order of court, to his then present master or owner, shall be expired; or be compelled thereto, by order of the county court, upon complaint of the church-wardens of the said parish, for the time being. And if any woman servant shall be got with child by her master, neither the said master, nor his executors, administrators, nor assigns, shall have any claim of service against her, for or by reason of such child; but she shall, when her time due to her said master, by indenture, custom or order of court, shall be expired, be sold by the church-wardens, for the time being, of the parish wherein such child shall be born, for one year, or pay one thousand pounds of tobacco; and the said one thousand pounds of tobacco, or whatever she shall be sold for, shall be emploied, by the vestry, to the use of the said parish. And if any woman servant shall have a bastard child by a negro, or mulatto, over and above the years service due to her master or owner, she shall immediately, upon the expiration of her time to her then present master or owner, pay down to the church-wardens of the parish wherein such child shall be born, for the use of the said parish, fifteen pounds current money of Virginia, or be by them sold for five years, to the use aforesaid: And if a free christian white woman shall have such bastard child, by a negro, or mulatto, for every such offence, she shall, within one month after her delivery of such bastard child, pay to the church-wardens for the time being, of the parish wherein such child shall be born, for the use of the said parish fifteen pounds current money of Virginia, or be by them sold for five years to the use aforesaid: And in both the said cases, the church-wardens shall bind the said child to be a servant, until it shall be of thirty one years of age.

XIX. And for a further prevention of that abominable mixture and spurious issue, which hereafter may increase in this her majesty's colony and dominion, as well by English, and other white men and women intermarrying with negros or mulattos, as by their unlawful coition with them, *Be it enacted, by the authority aforesaid, and it is hereby enacted,* That whatsoever English, or other white man or woman, being free, shall intermarry with a negro or mulatto man or woman, bond or free, shall, by judgment of the county court, be committed to prison, and there remain, during the space of six months, without bail or mainprize; and shall forfeit and pay ten pounds current money of Virginia, to the use of the parish, as aforesaid.

XX. *And be it further enacted,* That no minister of the church of England, or other minister, or person whatsoever, within this colony and dominion, shall hereafter wittingly presume to marry a white man with a negro or mulatto woman; or to marry a white woman with a negro or mulatto man, upon pain of forfeiting and paying, for every such marriage the sum of ten thousand pounds of tobacco; one half to our Sovereign lady the Queen, her heirs and successors, for and towards the support of the government, and the contingent charges thereof; and the other half to the informer. . . .

XXIII. And for encouragement of all persons to take up runaways, *Be it enacted, by the authority aforesaid, and it is hereby enacted,* That for the taking up of every servant, or slave, if ten miles, or above, from the house or quarter where such servant, or slave was kept, there shall be allowed by the public, as a reward to that taker-up, two hundred pounds of tobacco; and if above five miles, and under ten, one hundred pounds of tobacco. . . .

XXV. And further, the said justice of the peace, when such runaway shall be brought before him, shall, by his warrant commit the said runaway to the next constable, and therein also order him to give the said runaway so many lashes as the said justice shall think fit, not exceeding the number of thirty-nine; and then to be conveyed from constable to constable, until the runaway shall be carried home. . . .

XXX. *And also be it enacted, by the authority aforesaid, and it is hereby enacted,* That every runaway servant, upon whose account, either of the rewards aforementioned shall be paid, for taking up, shall for every hundred pounds of tobacco so paid by the master or owner, serve his or her said master or owner, after his or her time by indenture, custom, or former order of court, shall be expired, one calendar month and an half, and moreover, shall serve double the time such servant shall be absent in such running away; and shall also make reparation, by service, to the said master or owner, for all necessary disbursements and charges, in pursuit and recovery of the said runaway; to be adjudged and allowed in the county court, after the rate of one year for eight hundred pounds of tobacco, and so proportionably for a greater or lesser quantity. . . .

XXXII. *And also be it enacted, by the authority aforesaid, and it is hereby enacted,* That no master, mistress, or overseer of a family, shall knowingly permit any slave, not belonging to him or her, to be and remain upon his or her plantation, above four hours at any one time, without the leave of such slave's master, mistress, or overseer, on penalty of one hundred and fifty pounds of tobacco to the informer. . . .

XXXIV. And if any slave resist his master, or owner, or other person, by his or her order, correcting such slave, and shall happen to be killed in such correction, it shall not be accounted felony; but the master, owner, and every such other person so giving correction shall be free and acquit of all punishment and accusation for the same, as if such accident had never happened: And also, if any negro, mulatto, or Indian, bond or free, shall at any time, lift his or her hand, in opposition against any christian, not being negro, mulatto, or Indian, he or she so offending, shall, for every such offence, proved by the oath of the party, receive on his or her bare back, thirty lashes, well laid on.

XXXV. *And also be it enacted, by the authority aforesaid, and it is hereby enacted,* That no slave go armed with gun, sword, club, staff, or other weapon, nor go from off the plantation and seat or land where such slave shall be appointed to live, without a certificate of leave in writing, for so doing, from his or her master, mistress, or overseer: And if any slave shall be found offending herein, it shall be lawful for any person or persons to apprehend and deliver such slave to the next constable or head-borough, who is hereby enjoined and required, without further order or warrant, to give such slave twenty lashes on his or her bare back, well laid on, and so send him or her home: And all horses, cattle, and hogs, now belonging, or that hereafter shall belong to any slave, or of any slaves mark in this her majesty's colony and dominion, shall be seised and sold by the church-wardens of the parish, wherein such horses, cattle, or hogs shall be, and the profit thereof applied to the use of the poor of the said parish: And also, if any damage shall be hereafter committed by any slave living at a quarter where there is no christian overseer, the master or owner of such slave shall be liable to action for the trespass and damage, as if the same had been done by him or herself. . . .

XXXVII.   And whereas, many times, slaves run away and lie out, hid and lurking in swamps, woods, and other obscure places, killing hogs, and committing other injuries to the inhabitants of this her majesty's colony and dominion, *Be it therefore enacted, by the authority aforesaid, and it is hereby enacted,* That in all such cases, upon intelligence given of any slaves lying out, as aforesaid, any two justices of the peace of the county wherein such slave is supposed to lurk or do mischief, shall be and are empowered and required to issue proclamation against all such slaves, reciting their names, and owners names, if they are known, and thereby requiring them, and every of them, forthwith to surrender themselves: and also empowering the sheriff of the said county, to take such power with him, as he shall think fit and necessary, for the effectual apprehending such out-lying slave or slaves, and go in search of them: Which proclamation shall be published on a Sabbath day, at the door of every church and chapel, in the said county, by the parish clerk, or reader, of the church, immediately after divine worship: And in case any slave, against whom proclamation hath been thus issued, and once published at any church or chapel, as aforesaid, stay out, and do not immediately return home, it shall be lawful for any person or persons whatsoever, to kill and destroy such slaves by such ways and means as he, she, or they shall think fit, without accusation or impeachment of any crime for the same: And if any slave, that hath run away and lain out as aforesaid, shall be apprehended by the sheriff, or any other person, upon the application of the owner of the said slave, it shall and may be lawful for the county court, to order such punishment to the said slave, either by dismembering, or any other way, not touching his life, as they in their discretion shall think fit, for the reclaiming any such incorrigible slave, and terrifying others from the like practices.

XXXVIII.   *Provided always, and it is further enacted,* That for every slave killed, in pursuance of this act, or put to death by law, the master or owner of such slave shall be paid by the public:

XXXIX.   And to the end, the true value of every slave killed, or put to death, as aforesaid, may be the better known; and by that means, the assembly the better enabled to make a suitable allowance thereupon, *Be it enacted,* That upon application of the master or owner of any such slave, to the court appointed for proof of public claims, the said court shall value the slave in money, and the clerk of the court shall return a certificate thereof to the assembly, with the rest of the public claims.

XL.   And for the better putting this act an due execution, and that no servants or slaves may have pretense of ignorance hereof, *Be it also enacted,* That the church-wardens of each parish in this her majesty's colony and dominion, at the charge of the parish, shall provide a true copy of this act, and cause entry thereof to be made in the register book of each parish respectively; and that the parish clerk, or reader of each parish, shall, on the first sermon Sundays in September and March, annually, after sermon or divine service is ended, at the door of every church and chapel in their parish, publish the same; and the sheriff of each county shall, at the next court held for the county, after the last day of February, yearly, publish this act, at the door of the court-house. ...

Ruth Tillett's Petition against Zachareah Jordan (1783)

Pasquotank County [North Carolina]

To the Worshipfull the Justices of the Inferior Court of Pleas & Quarter Sessions of the County of Pasquotank County now in Court Sitting. The Humble Petition of Ruth Tillett, a free Born coloured Woman, Humbly sheweth unto your Worships That she was Born of a Free Woman named Ann Tillett, the Daughter of the Wife of one [blank] Tillet of Powels Point in Currituck County, supposed by a Black Man; That your Petitioner's Mother moved from Currituck to a Neighbourhood on Little River and was delivered of your Petitioner at the House of one Timothy Mead, where she remained until the Death of her Mother and the said Timothy, at whose Vendue [?] she was sold to one Blackstock who she verily believes was not ignorant of her Condition and Rights to Liberty, and [who] sold her to a distant Merchant called Barny Coff of Newbern, At which Place she had eight Several Masters each getting rid of her, as soon as they could, on hearing of her Story and Resolution to regain her Liberty. That in the lifetime of her last Master, John Bishop, she made her Escape and came to her Native Country, to which place the said Bishop followed her and sold her to one Zachareah Jordan (and he, as she has been informed, gave no Purchase Money for her, and that the said Bishop injoin'd the said Zachareah Jordan to inquire into her Rights and if true, to let her enjoy them, and if Otherwise, to send him payment, which was like the Common honest Behaviour of his Life) who, she believes, noways ignorant of the Promises, still detains her in Slavery and Distress. Your Petitioner humbly begs to inform your Worships that she has been so happy as to find reputable and honest Evidence alive, although at the Distance of Forty Years, of her Birth and of her Civil and Social Rights. Whereupon your poor and Distressed Petitioner humbly prays (Altho [despite] her complection, which is an Act of the Almighty God, not her Crime) [that] Your Worships will of your Mercy, take her case under your Guidance and Consideration, and to render her such Redress as to your Worships in your Great Wisdom and Justice you shall deem Meet. And your Poor Petitioner as in Duty Bound will ever pray etc.

Ruth Tillet, by Will Cumming her Atty [attorney]

March Court 1783

Judgement of the Court on the examination of the Witnesses that the Allegation of the Petitioner's Petition are supported and true and Ajudge to her Freedom.

Further Reading

Breen, T. H. and Stephen Innes, *"Myne Owne Ground": Race and Freedom on Virginia's Eastern Shore, 1640–1676*. New York: Oxford University Press, 1980.

Brown, Kathleen M., *Good Wives, Nasty Wenches, and Anxious Patriarchs: Gender, Race, and Power in Colonial Virginia*. Chapel Hill, NC: University of North Carolina Press, 1996.

Carr, Lois G., Russell R. Menard, and Lorena S. Walsh, *Robert Cole's World: Agriculture and Society in Early Maryland*. Chapel Hill: University of North Carolina Press, 1991.

Clinton, Catherine and Michele Gillespie (eds), *The Devil's Lane: Sex and Race in the Early South*. New York: Oxford University Press, 1997.

Fischer, Kirsten, *Suspect Relations: Sex, Race, and Resistance in Colonial North Carolina*. Ithaca: Cornell University Press, 2002.

Horn, James, *Adapting to a New World: English Society in the Seventeenth-century Chesapeake*. Chapel Hill: University of North Carolina Press, 1996.

Isaac, Rhys, *The Transformation of Virginia, 1740–1790*. New York: W. W. Norton, 1982.

Jordan, Winthrop D., *White Over Black: American Attitudes Toward the Negro, 1550–1812*. Chapel Hill: University of North Carolina Press, 1968.

Morgan, Edmund, *American Slavery, American Freedom: The Ordeal of Colonial Virginia*. New York: W. W. Norton, 1975.

Sobel, Mechal, *The World They Made Together: Black and White Values in Eighteenth-century Virginia*. Princeton: Princeton University Press, 1987.

Wood, Peter, *Black Majority: Negroes in Colonial South Carolina from 1670 Through the Stono Rebellion*. New York: W. W. Norton, 1974.

4

African Diaspora

Introduction

The trans-Atlantic slave trade began in the late fifteenth century and continued for more than three hundred years. It was the largest forced migration in history. Before the American Revolution, more Africans than Europeans arrived in the New World. Most of the more than 10 million Africans debarked in Brazil and the Caribbean, where they labored in sugar cane fields to produce the immensely profitable staple crop that enriched European investors. (Barbados sugar yielded a far higher and steadier profit than even tobacco from Virginia.) By 1775, approximately 260,000 Africans had been transported to the mainland American colonies, where they labored in a wide variety of ways.

As the essay by Ira Berlin shows, there was no one single slave experience. Location and the local economy, demography, and the interactions of newly imported Africans and second-generation African Americans (or Creoles) shaped slaves' experiences and the cultures that developed. Berlin focuses on three regions to investigate these differences. In the "nonplantation system" of New England and the Middle colonies, he finds that blacks and whites lived and worked in close proximity. African-Americans there developed a distinctive Creole culture, even as they engaged in a wide variety of tasks, often alongside white workers. In the mid-eighteenth century, a sudden rise in the numbers of enslaved workers imported directly from Africa led to a renewal of Creole culture, at the same time that newcomers were integrated into African-American society. By contrast, the arrival of African slaves after 1700 in the low country of Georgia and South Carolina left blacks deeply divided. Skilled urban slaves, many of whom were lighter-skinned African-Americans, lived apart from the large groups of fieldhands recently imported from Africa to grow staple crops of rice and indigo. This plantation-based black majority retained many African customs and remained geographically as well as culturally isolated from whites and urban slaves. In Berlin's third example, the Chesapeake (Virginia and Maryland), slavery developed along yet another trajectory. Increased African importation after 1680 initially led to a split between African and Creole cultures, but over the next century, whites consolidated the racial hierarchy in ways that obscured differences in the African-American community and led to a more unified Creole culture. How much influence did slaveowners exert over African-American culture in these three regions? What aspects remained "autonomous" or beyond the owners' purview, and why?

In 1703, William Bosman, the "Chief Dutch Factor for the Dutch West India Company," published his description of the slave trade on the coast of Guinea (document 1). How, according to Bosman, are slaves handled on Dutch ships? How does he evaluate their treatment by different groups of

Europeans, and why might he make these distinctions? How do the captives resist enslavement?

The Reverend Francis Le Jau, an Anglican missionary on the South Carolina frontier from 1706 until his death in 1717, tried hard to convert African slaves despite their owners' concern that baptism might induce slaves to push harder for the freedom they desired (document 2). How does Le Jau appease owners while trying to gain enslaved converts? What evidence of slaves' resistance does Le Jau relate?

Venture Smith's account of enslavement in the eighteenth century describes how he was captured as a child in Africa and how he responded to the violence endemic to slavery (document 3). How did Smith cope with slavery and how did his acts of resistance change over time? How was his relationship to his master and mistress part of a psychological warfare as well as a physical struggle?

Time, Space, and the Evolution of Afro-American Society on British Mainland North America

Ira Berlin

Time and space are the usual boundaries of historical inquiry. The last generation of slavery studies in the United States has largely ignored these critical dimensions but has, instead, been preoccupied with defining the nature of American slavery, especially as compared with racial bondage elsewhere in the Americas. These studies have been extraordinarily valuable not only in revealing much about slave society but also in telling a good deal about free society. They have been essential to the development of a new understanding of American life centered on social transformation: the emergence of bourgeois society in the North with an upward-striving middle class and an increasingly self-conscious working class and the development of a plantocracy in the South with a segmented social order and ideals of interdependence, stability, and hierarchy. But viewing Southern slavery from the point of maturity, dissecting it into component parts, comparing it to other slave societies, and juxtaposing it to free society have produced an essentially static vision of slave culture. This has been especially evident in the studies of Afro-American life. From Stanley M. Elkins's Sambo to John W. Blassingame's Nat-Sambo-Jack typology, scholars of all persuasions have held time constant and ignored the influence of place. Even the most comprehensive recent interpretation of slave life, Eugene D. Genovese's *Roll, Jordan, Roll,* has been more concerned with explicating the dynamic of the patriarchal ideal in the making of Afro-American culture than in explaining its development in time and space. None of the histories written since World War II has equaled the temporal and spatial specificity of U. B. Phillips's *American Negro Slavery.*[1]

Recent interest in the beginnings of slavery on the mainland of British North America, however, has revealed a striking diversity in Afro-American life. During the seventeenth and eighteenth centuries, three distinct slave systems evolved: a Northern nonplantation system and two Southern plantation systems, one around Chesapeake Bay and the other in the Carolina and Georgia lowcountry. Slavery took shape differently in each with important consequences for the growth of black culture and society. The development of these slave societies depended upon the nature of the slave trade and the demographic configurations of blacks and whites as well as upon the diverse character of colonial economy. Thus, while cultural differences between newly arrived Africans and second and third generation Afro-Americans or creoles[2] everywhere provided the basis for social stratification within black society, African–creole differences emerged at different times with different force and even different meaning in the North, the Chesapeake region, and the lowcountry. A careful examination of the diverse development of Afro-American culture in the colonial era yields important clues for an understanding of the full complexity of black society in the centuries that followed.

The nature of slavery and the demographic balance of whites and blacks during the seventeenth and first decades of the eighteenth centuries tended to incorporate Northern blacks into the emerging Euro-American culture, even as whites denied them a place in Northern society.[3] But changes in the character of the slave trade during the middle third of the eighteenth century gave new impetus to African culture and institutions in the Northern colonies. By the American Revolution, Afro-American culture had been integrated into the larger Euro-American one, but black people remained acutely conscious of their African inheritance and freely drew on it in shaping their lives.

Throughout the colonial years, blacks composed a small fraction of the population of New England and the Middle Colonies. Only in New York and Rhode Island did they reach 15 percent of the population. In most Northern colonies the proportion was considerably smaller. At its height, the black population totaled 8 percent of the population of New Jersey and less than 4 percent in Massachusetts and Connecticut. But these colony-wide enumerations dilute the presence of blacks and underestimate the importance of slave labor. In some of the most productive agricultural regions and in the cities, blacks composed a larger share of the population, sometimes constituting as much as one-third of the whole and perhaps one-half of the work force. Although many Northern whites never saw a black slave, others had daily, intimate contact with them. And, although some blacks found it difficult to join together with their former countrymen, others lived in close contact.

The vast majority of Northern blacks lived and worked in the countryside. A few labored in highly capitalized rural industries – tanneries, salt works, and iron furnaces – where they often composed the bulk of the work force, skilled and unskilled. Iron masters, the largest employers of industrial slaves, also were often the largest slaveholders in the North. Pennsylvania iron masters manifested their dependence on slave labor when, in 1727, they petitioned for a reduction in the tariff on slaves so they might keep their furnaces in operation. Bloomeries and forges in other colonies similarly relied on slave labor. But in an overwhelmingly agrarian society only a small proportion of the slave population engaged in industrial labor.

Like most rural whites, most rural blacks toiled as agricultural workers. In southern New England, on Long Island, and in northern New Jersey, which contained the North's densest black populations, slaves tended stock and raised crops for export to the sugar islands. Farmers engaged in provisioning the West Indies with draft animals and foodstuffs were familiar with slavery and had easy access to slaves. Some, like the Barbadian émigrés in northern New Jersey, had migrated from the sugar islands. Others, particularly those around Narragansett Bay, styled themselves planters in the West Indian manner. They built great houses, bred race horses, and accumulated slaves, sometimes holding twenty or more bondsmen. But, whatever the aspirations of this commercial gentry, the provisioning trade could not support a plantation regime. Most slaves lived on farms (not plantations), worked at a variety of tasks, and never labored in large gangs. No one in the North suggested that agricultural labor could be done only by black people, a common assertion in the sugar islands and the Carolina low-country. In northern New England, the Hudson Valley, and Pennsylvania, the seasonal demands of cereal farming undermined the viability of slavery. For most wheat farmers, as Peter Kalm shrewdly observed, "a Negro or black slave requires too much money at one time," and they relied instead on white indentured servants and free workers to supplement their own labor. Throughout the North's bread basket, even those members of the gentry who could afford the larger capital investment and the concomitant risk that slave ownership entailed generally depended on the labor of indentured servants more than on that of slaves. Fully two-thirds of the bond servants held by the wealthiest

farmers in Lancaster and Chester counties, Pennsylvania, were indentured whites rather than chattel blacks. These farmers tended to view
their slaves more as status symbols than as agricultural workers. While
slaves labored in the fields part of the year, as did nearly everyone, they
also spent a large portion of their time working in and around their
masters' houses as domestic servants, stable keepers, and gardeners.
Significantly, the wills and inventories of Northern slaveholders listed
their slaves with other high status objects like clocks and carriages rather
than with land or agricultural implements.[4]

The distinct demands of Northern agriculture shaped black life in the
countryside. Where the provisioning trade predominated, black men
worked as stock minders and herdsmen while black women labored as
dairy maids as well as domestics of various kinds. The large number of
slaves demanded by the provisioning trade and the ready access to horses
and mules it allowed placed black companionship within easy reach of
most bondsmen. Such was not always true in the cereal region. Living
scattered throughout the countryside on the largest farms and working in
the house as often as in the field, blacks enjoyed neither the mobility nor
the autonomy of slaves employed in the provisioning trade. But, if the
demands of Northern agriculture affected black life in different ways,
almost all rural blacks lived and worked in close proximity to whites.
Slaves quickly learned the rudiments of the English language, the Christian religion, the white man's ways. In the North, few rural blacks
remained untouched by the larger forces of Euro-American life.

Northern slaves were also disproportionately urban. During the eighteenth century, a fifth to a quarter of the blacks in New York lived in New
York City. Portsmouth and Boston contained fully a third of the blacks
in New Hampshire and Massachusetts, and nearly half of Rhode Island's
black population resided in Newport. Ownership of slaves was almost
universal among the urban elite and commonplace among the middling
classes as well. On the eve of the Revolution, nearly three-fourths of
Boston's wealthiest quartile of propertyholders ranked in the slavehold-
ing class. Fragmentary evidence from earlier in the century suggests that
urban slave-ownership had been even more widespread but contracted
with the growth of a free working class. Viewed from the top of colonial
society, the observation of one visitor that there was "not a house in
Boston" that did "not have one or two" slaves might be applied to every
Northern city with but slight exaggeration.[5]

Urban slaves generally worked as house servants – cooking, cleaning,
tending gardens and stables, and running errands. They lived in back
rooms, lofts, closets, and, occasionally, makeshift alley shacks. Under
these cramped conditions, few masters held more than one or two slaves.
However they might cherish a large retinue of retainers, urban slave-

holders rarely had the room to lodge them. Because of the general shortage of space, masters discouraged their slaves from establishing families in the cities. Women with reputations for fecundity found few buyers, and some slaveholders sold their domestics at the first sign of pregnancy. A New York master candidly announced the sale of his cook "because she breeds too fast for her owners to put up with such inconvenience," and others gave away children because they were an unwarranted expense. As a result, black women had few children, and their fertility ratio was generally lower than that of whites. The inability or unwillingness of urban masters to support large households placed a severe strain on black family life.[6] But it also encouraged masters to allow their slaves to live out, hire their own time, and thereby gain a measure of independence and freedom.

Slave hirelings along with those bondsmen owned by merchants, warehouse keepers, and ship chandlers kept Northern cities moving. Working outside their masters' houses, these bondsmen found employment as teamsters, wagoners, and stockmen on the docks and drays and in the warehouses and shops that composed the essential core of the mercantile economy. In addition, many slaves labored in the maritime trades not only as sailors on coasting vessels, but also in the rope walks, shipyards, and sail factories that supported the colonial maritime industry. Generally, the importance of these slaves to the growth of Northern cities increased during the eighteenth century. Urban slavery moved steadily away from the household to the docks, warehouses, and shops, as demonstrated by the growing disproportion of slave men in the urban North. Aside from those skills associated with the maritime trades, however, few slaves entered artisan work. Only a handful could be found in the carriage trades that enjoyed higher status and that offered greater opportunity for an independent livelihood and perhaps the chance to buy freedom.

In the cities as in the countryside, blacks tended to live and work in close proximity to whites. Northern slaves not only gained first-hand knowledge of their masters' world, but they also rubbed elbows with lower-class whites in taverns, cock fights, and fairs where poor people of varying status mingled. If urban life allowed slaves to meet more frequently and enjoy a larger degree of social autonomy than did slavery in the countryside, the cosmopolitan nature of cities speeded the transformation of Africans to Afro-Americans. Acculturation in the cities of the North was a matter of years, not generations.

For many blacks, the process of cultural transformation was well under way before they stepped off the boat. During the first century of American settlement, few blacks arrived in the North directly from Africa. Although American slavers generally originated in the North, few gave priority to Northern ports. The markets to the south were simply too large and too lucrative. Slaves dribbled into the Northern colonies from the West Indies or the mainland South singly, in twos and threes, or by the score but rarely by the boatload. Some came on special order from merchants or farmers with connections to the West Indian trade. Others arrived on consignment, since few Northern merchants specialized in selling slaves. Many of these were the unsalable "refuse" (as traders contemptuously called them) of larger shipments. Northern slaveholders generally disliked these scourings of the transatlantic trade who, the governor of Massachusetts observed, were "usually the worst servants they have"; they feared that the West Indian re-exports had records of recalcitrance and criminality as well as physical defects. In time, some masters may have come to prefer seasoned slaves because of their knowledge of English, familiarity with work routines, or resistance to New World diseases. But, whatever their preference, Northern colonies could not compete with the wealthier staple-producing colonies for prime African field hands. Before the 1740s, Africans appear to have arrived in the North only when a temporary glut made sale impossible in the West Indies and the mainland South. Even then they did not always remain in the North. When conditions in the plantation colonies changed, merchants reexported them for a quick profit. The absence of direct importation during the early years and the slow, random, haphazard entry of West Indian creoles shaped the development of black culture in the Northern colonies.[7] While the nature of the slave trade prevented the survival of tribal or even shipboard ties that figured so prominently in Afro-American life in the West Indies and the Lower South, it better prepared blacks to take advantage of the special circumstances of their captivity.

Newly arrived blacks, most already experienced in the New World and familiar with their proscribed status, turned Northern bondage to their advantage where they could. They quickly established a stable family life and, unlike newly imported Africans elsewhere on the continent, increased their numbers by natural means during the first generation. By 1708, the governor of Rhode Island observed that the colony's slaves were "supplied by the offspring of those they have already, which increase daily. . . ." The transplanted creoles also seized the opportunities provided by the complex Northern economy, the relatively close ties of master and slave, and, for many, the independence afforded by urban life. In New Amsterdam, for example, the diverse needs of the Dutch mercantile economy induced the West India Company, the largest slaveholder in the colony, to allow its slaves to live out and work on their own in return for a stipulated amount of labor and an annual tribute. "Half-freedom," as this system came to be called, enlarged black opportunities and allowed for the development of a strong black community. When the West India Company refused to make these privileges hereditary, "half-free" slaves organized and protested, demanding that they be allowed to pass their rights to their children. Failing that, New Amsterdam slaves pressed their masters in other ways to elevate their children's status. Some, hearing rumors that baptism meant freedom, tried to gain church membership. A Dutch prelate complained that these blacks "wanted nothing else than to deliver their children from bodily slavery, without striving for piety and Christian virtues." Even after the conquering English abolished "half-freedom" and instituted a more rigorous system of racial servitude, blacks continued to use the leverage gained by their prominent role in the city's economy to set standards of treatment well above those in the plantation colonies. Into the eighteenth century, New York slaves informally enjoyed the rights of an earlier era, including the right to hold property of their own. "The Custome of this Country," bristled a frustrated New York master to a West Indian friend, "will not allow us to use our Negroes as you doe in Barbados."[8]

Throughout the North, the same factors that mitigated the harshest features of bondage in New York strengthened the position of slaves in dealing with their masters. Small holdings, close living conditions, and the absence of gang labor drew masters and slaves together. A visitor to Connecticut noted in disgust that slaveowners were "too Indulgent (especially the farmers) to their Slaves, suffering too great a familiarity from them, permitting them to sit at Table and eat with them (as they say to save time) and into the dish goes the black hoof as freely as the white hand." Slaves used knowledge gained at their masters' tables to press for additional privileges: the right to visit friends, live with their families, or hire their own time. One slaveholder reluctantly canceled the sale of his slaves because of "an invariable indulgence here to permit Slaves of any kind of worth or Character who must change Masters, to choose those Masters," and he could not persuade his slaves "to leave their Country (if I may call it so), their acquaintances & friends."[9] Such indulgences originated not only in the ability of slaves to manipulate their masters to their own benefit, but also from the confidence of slaveholders in their own hegemony. Surety of white dominance, derived from white numerical superiority, complemented the blacks' under-standing of how best to bend bondage to their own advantage and to maximize black opportunities within slavery.

During the middle decades of the eighteenth century, the nature of Northern slavery changed dramatically. Growing demand for labor, especially when European wars limited the supply of white indentured servants and when depression sent free workers west in search of new opportunities, increased the importance of slaves in the work force. Between 1732 and 1754, blacks composed fully a third of the immigrants (forced and voluntary) arriving in New York. The new importance of slave labor changed the nature of the slave trade. Merchants who previously took black slaves only on consignment now began to import them directly from Africa, often in large numbers. Before 1741, for example, 70 percent of the slaves arriving in New York originated in the West Indies and other mainland sources and only 30 percent came directly from Africa. After that date, the proportions were reversed. Specializing in the slave trade, African slavers carried many times more slaves than did West Indian traders. Whereas slaves had earlier arrived in small parcels rarely numbering more than a half-dozen, direct shipments from Africa at times now totaled over a hundred and, occasionally, several times that. Slaves increasingly replaced white indentured servants as the chief source of unfree labor not only in the areas that had produced for the provisioning trade, where their preeminence had been established earlier in the century, but in the cities as well. In the 1760s, when slave importation into Pennsylvania peaked, blacks composed more than three-quarters of Philadelphia's servant population.

Northern whites generally viewed this new wave of slaves as substitutes for indentured labor. White indentured servants had come as young men without families, and slaves were now imported in much the same way. "For this market they must be young, the younger the better if not quite children," declared a New York merchant. "Males are best." As a result, the sex ratio of the black population, which earlier in the century had been roughly balanced, suddenly swung heavily in favor of men. In Massachusetts, black men outnumbered black women nearly two to one. Elsewhere sex ratios of 130 or more became commonplace.[10] Such sexual imbalance and the proscription of interracial marriage made it increasingly difficult for blacks to enjoy normal family lives. As the birth rate slipped, mortality rates soared, especially in the cities where newly arrived blacks appeared to be concentrated. Since most slaves came without any previous exposure to New World diseases, the harsh Northern winters took an ever higher toll. Blacks died by the score; the crude death rate of Philadelphia and Boston blacks in the 1750s and 1760s was well over sixty per thousand, almost double that of whites. In its demographic outline, Northern slavery at mid-century often bore a closer resemblance to the horrors of the West Indies during the height of a sugar boom than to the relatively benign bondage of the earlier years.

Whites easily recovered from this demographic disaster by again switching to European indentured servants and then to free labor as supplies became available, and, as the influx of slaves subsided, black life also regained its balance. But the transformation of Northern slavery had a lasting influence on the development of Afro-American culture. Although the Northern black population remained predominantly Afro-American after nearly a century of slow importation from the West Indies and steady natural increase, the direct entry of Africans into Northern society reoriented black culture.

Even before the redirection of the Northern slave trade, those few Africans in the Northern colonies often stood apart from the creole majority. While Afro-American slaves established precedents and customs, which they then drew upon to improve their condition, Africans tended to stake all to recapture the world they had lost. Significantly, Africans, many of whom did not yet speak English and still carried tribal names, composed the majority of the participants in the New York slave insurrection of 1712, even though most of the city's blacks were creoles. The division between Africans and Afro-Americans became more visible as the number of Africans increased after mid-century. Not only did creoles and Africans evince different aspirations, but their life-chances – as reflected in their resistance to disease and their likelihood of establishing a family – also diverged sharply. Greater visibility may have sharpened differences between creoles and Africans, but Africans were too few in number to stand apart for long. Whatever conflicts different life-chances and beliefs created, whites paid such distinctions little heed in incorporating the African minority into their slaveholdings. The propensity of Northern whites to lump blacks together mitigated intraracial differences. Rather than permanently dividing blacks, the entry of Africans into Northern society gave a new direction to Afro-American culture.

Newly arrived Africans reawakened Afro-Americans to their African past by providing direct knowledge of West African society. Creole blacks began to combine their African inheritance into their own evolving culture. In some measure, the easy confidence of Northern whites in their own dominance speeded the syncretization of African and creole culture by allowing blacks to act far more openly than slaves in the plantation colonies. Northern blacks incorporated African culture into their own Afro-American culture not only in the commonplace and unconscious way that generally characterizes the transit of culture but also with a high degree of consciousness and deliberateness. They designated their churches "African," and they called themselves "Sons of Africa." They adopted African forms to maximize their freedom, to choose their leaders, and, in general, to give shape to their lives. This new African influence was manifested most fully in Negro election day, a ritual festival of role reversal common throughout West Africa and celebrated openly by blacks in New England and a scattering of places in the Middle Colonies.

The celebration of Negro election day took a variety of forms, but everywhere it was a day of great merrymaking that drew blacks from all over the countryside. "All the various languages of Africa, mixed with broken and ludicrous English, filled the air, accompanied with the music of the fiddle, tambourine, the banjo, [and] drum," recalled an observer of the festival in Newport. Negro election day culminated with the selection of black kings, governors, and judges. These officials sometimes held symbolic power over the whole community and real power over the black community. While the black governors held court, adjudicating minor disputes, the blacks paraded and partied, dressed in their masters' clothes and mounted on their masters' horses. Such role reversal, like similar status inversions in Africa and elsewhere, confirmed rather than challenged the existing order, but it also gave blacks an opportunity to express themselves more fully than the narrow boundaries of slavery ordinarily allowed. Negro election day permitted a seeming release from bondage, and it also provided a mechanism for blacks to recognize and honor their own notables. Most important, it established a framework for the development of black politics. In the places where Negro election day survived into the nineteenth century, its politics shaped the politics within the black community and merged with partisan divisions of American society. Slaves elsewhere in the New World also celebrated this holiday, but whites in the plantation colonies found the implications of role reversal too frightening to allow even symbolically. Northern whites, on the other hand, not only aided election day materially but sometimes joined in themselves. Still, white cooperation was an important but not the crucial element in the rise of Negro election day. Its origin in the 1740s and 1750s suggests how the entry of Africans reoriented Afro-American culture at a formative point in its development.[11]

African acculturation in the Northern colonies at once incorporated blacks into American society and sharpened the memory of their African past and their desire to preserve it. While small numbers and close proximity to whites forced blacks to conform to the forms of the dominant Euro-American culture, the confidence of whites in their own hegemony allowed black slaves a good measure of autonomy. In this context it is not surprising that a black New England sea captain established the first back-to-Africa movement in mainland North America.[12]

Unlike African acculturation in the Northern colonies, the transformation of Africans into Afro-Americans in the Carolina and Georgia lowcountry was a slow, halting process whose effects resonated differently within black society. While creolization created a unified Afro-American population in the North, it left lowcountry blacks deeply divided. A minority lived and worked in close proximity to whites in the cities that lined the rice coast, fully conversant with the most cosmopolitan sector of lowland society. A portion of this urban elite, increasingly light-skinned, pressed for further incorporation into white society, confident they could compete as equals. The mass of black people, however, remained physically separated and psychologically estranged from the Anglo-American world and culturally closer to Africa than any other blacks on continental North America.

The sharp division was not immediately apparent. At first it seemed that African acculturation in the Lower South would follow the Northern pattern. The first blacks arrived in the lowcountry in small groups from the West Indies. Often they accompanied their owners and, like them, frequently immigrated in small family groups. Many had already spent considerable time on the sugar islands, and some had doubtless been born there. Most spoke English, understood European customs and manners, and, as their language skills and family ties suggest, had made the difficult adjustment to the conditions of black life in the New World.

As in the Northern colonies, whites dominated the population of the pioneer Carolina settlement. Until the end of the seventeenth century, they composed better than two-thirds of the settlers. During this period and into the first years of the eighteenth century, most white slaveholders engaged in mixed farming and stock raising for export to the West Indian islands where they had originated. Generally, they lived on small farms, held few slaves, and worked closely with their bond servants. Even when they hated and feared blacks and yearned for the prerogatives of West Indian slave masters, the demands of the primitive, labor-scarce economy frequently placed master and slave face-to-face on opposite sides of a sawbuck.[13] Such direct, equalitarian confrontations tempered white domination and curbed slavery's harshest features.

White dependence on blacks to defend their valuable lowland beachhead reinforced this "sawbuck equality." The threat of invasion by the Spanish and French to the south and Indians to the west hung ominously over the lowcountry during its formative years. To bolster colonial defenses, officials not only drafted slaves in time of war but also regularly enlisted them into the militia. In 1710 Thomas Nairne, a knowledgeable Carolina Indian agent, observed that "enrolled in our Militia [are] a considerable Number of active, able, Negro Slaves; and Law gives every one of those his freedom, who in Time of an Invasion kills an Enemy." Between the settlement of the Carolinas and the conclusion of the Yamasee War almost fifty years later, black soldiers helped fend off every military threat to the colony. Although only a handful of slaves won their freedom through military service, the continued presence of armed, militarily experienced slaves weighed heavily on whites. During the Yamasee War, when the governor of Virginia demanded one Negro woman in return for each Virginia soldier sent to defend South Carolina, the beleaguered Carolinians rejected the offer, observing that it was "impracticable to Send Negro Women in their Roomes by reason of the Discontent such Usage would have given their husbands to have their wives taken from them which might have occasioned a Revolt."[14]

The unsettled conditions that made the lowcountry vulnerable to external enemies strengthened the slave's hand in other ways. Confronted by an overbearing master or a particularly onerous assignment, many blacks took to the woods. Truancy was an easy alternative in the thinly settled, heavily forested lowcountry. Forest dangers generally sent truant slaves back to their owners, but the possibility of another flight induced slaveholders to accept them with few questions asked. Some bondsmen, however, took advantage of these circumstances to escape permanently. Maroon colonies existed throughout the lowland swamps and into the backcountry. Maroons lived a hard life, perhaps more difficult than slaves, and few blacks chose to join these outlaw bands. But the ease of escape and the existence of a maroon alternative made masters chary about abusing their slaves.

The transplanted African's intimate knowledge of the subtropical lowland environment – especially when compared to the Englishman's dense ignorance – magnified white dependence on blacks and enlarged black opportunities within the slave regime. Since the geography, climate, and topography of the lowcountry more closely resembled the West African than the English countryside, African not European technology and agronomy often guided lowland development. From the first, whites depended on blacks to identify useful flora and fauna and to define the appropriate methods of production. Blacks, adapting African techniques to the circumstances of the Carolina wilderness, shaped the lowland cattle industry and played a central role in the introduction and development of the region's leading staple. In short, transplanted Englishmen learned as much or more from transplanted Africans as did the former Africans from them. While whites eventually appropriated this knowledge and turned it against black people to rivet tighter the bonds of servitude, white dependence on African know-how operated during those first years to place blacks in managerial as well as menial positions and thereby permitted blacks to gain a larger share of the fruits of the new land than whites might otherwise allow. In such circumstances, white domination made itself felt, but both whites and blacks incorporated much of West African culture into their new way of life.

The structure of the fledgling lowland economy and the demands of stock raising, with deerskins as the dominant "crop" during the initial years of settlement, allowed blacks to stretch white military and economic dependence into generous grants of autonomy. On the small farms and isolated cowpens (hardly plantations by even the most latitudinous definition), rude frontier conditions permitted only perfunctory supervision and the most elementary division of labor. Most units were simply too small to employ overseers, single out specialists, or benefit from the economies of gang labor. White, red, and black laborers of varying legal status worked shoulder to shoulder, participating in the dullest drudgery as well as the most sophisticated undertakings. Rather than skilled artisans or prime field hands, most blacks could best be characterized as jacks-of-all-trades. Since cattle roamed freely through the woods until fattened for market, moreover, black cowboys – suggestively called "cattle chasers" – moved with equal freedom through the countryside, gaining full familiarity with the terrain. The autonomy of the isolated cowpen and the freedom of movement stock raising allowed made a mockery of the total dominance that chattel bondage implied. Slaves set the pace of work, defined standards of workmanship, and divided labor among themselves, doubtless leaving a good measure of time for their own use. The insistence of many hard-pressed frontier slaveowners that their slaves raise their own provisions legitimated this autonomy. By law, slaves had Sunday to themselves. Time allowed for gardening, hunting, and fishing both affirmed slave independence and supplemented the slave diet. It also enabled some industrious blacks to produce a small surplus and to participate in the colony's internal economy, establishing an important precedent for black life in the lowcountry.

Such independence burdened whites. They complained bitterly and frequently about blacks traveling unsupervised through the countryside, congregating in the woods, and visiting Charles Town to carouse, conspire, or worse. Yet knowledge of the countryside and a willingness to take the initiative in hunting down cattle or standing up to Spaniards were precisely the characteristics that whites valued in their slaves. They complained but they accepted. Indeed, to resolve internal disputes within their own community, whites sometimes promoted black participation in the affairs of the colony far beyond the bounds later permitted slaves or even black freeman. "For this last election," grumbled several petitioners in 1706, "Jews, Strangers, Sailors, Servants, Negroes, & almost every French Man in Craven & Berkly County came down to elect, & their votes were taken."[15] Such breaches of what became an iron law of Southern racial policy suggest how the circumstances of the pioneer lowcountry life shrank the social as well as the cultural distance between transplanted Africans and the mélange of European settlers. During the first generations of settlement, Afro-American and Anglo-American culture and society developed along parallel lines with a large degree of overlap.

If the distinction between white and black culture remained small in the lowcountry, so too did differences within black society. The absence of direct importation of African slaves prevented the emergence of African–creole differences; and, since few blacks gained their liberty during those years, differences in status within the black community were almost nonexistent. The small radius of settlement and the ease of water transportation, moreover, placed most blacks within easy reach of Charles Town. A "city" of several dozen rude buildings where the colonial legislature met in a tavern could hardly have impressed slaves as radically different from their own primitive quarters. Town slaves, for their part, doubtless had first-hand familiarity with farm work as few masters could afford the luxury of placing their slaves in livery.

Thus, during the first years of settlement, black life in the lowcountry, like black life in the North, evolved toward a unified Afro-American culture. Although their numbers combined with other circumstances to allow Carolina blacks a larger role in shaping their culture than that enjoyed by blacks in the North, there remained striking similarities in the early development of Afro-American life in both regions. During the last few years of the seventeenth century, however, changes in economy and society undermined these commonalities and set the development of lowcountry Afro-American life on a distinctive course.

The discovery of exportable staples, first naval stores and then rice and indigo, transformed the lowcountry as surely as the sugar revolution transformed the West Indies. Under the pressure of the riches that staple production provided, planters banished the white yeomanry to the hinterland, consolidated small farms into large plantations, and carved new plantations out of the malaria-ridden swamps. Before long, black slaves began pouring into the region and, sometime during the first decade of the eighteenth century, white numerical superiority gave way to the lowcountry's distinguishing demographic characteristic: the black majority.

Black numerical dominance grew rapidly during the eighteenth century. By the 1720s, blacks outnumbered whites by more than two to one in South Carolina. In the heavily settled plantation parishes surrounding Charles Town, blacks enjoyed a three to one majority. That margin grew steadily until the disruptions of the Revolutionary era, but it again increased thereafter. Georgia, where metropolitan policies reined planter ambition, remained slaveless until mid-century. Once restrictions on slavery were removed, planters imported blacks in large numbers, giving lowland Georgia counties considerable black majorities.

Direct importation of slaves from Africa provided the impetus to the growth of the black majority. Some West Indian Afro-Americans continued to enter the lowcountry, but they shrank to a small fraction of the whole. As African importation increased, Charles Town took its place as the largest mainland slave mart and the center of the lowland slave trade. Almost all of the slaves in Carolina and later in Georgia – indeed, fully 40 percent of all pre-Revolutionary black arrivals in mainland North America – entered at Charles Town. The enormous number of slaves allowed slave masters a wide range of choices. Lowcountry planters developed preferences far beyond the usual demands for healthy adult and adolescent males and concerned themselves with the regional and tribal origins of their purchases. Some planters may have based their choices on long experience and a considered understanding of the physical and social character of various African nations. But, for the most part, these preferences were shallow ethnic stereotypes. Coromantees revolted; Angolans ran away; Iboes destroyed themselves. At other times, lowland planters apparently preferred just those slaves they did not get, perhaps because all Africans made unsatisfactory slaves and the unobtainable ones looked better at a distance. Although lowcountry slave masters desired Gambian people above all others, Angolans composed a far larger proportion of the African arrivals. But, however confused or mistaken in their beliefs, planters held them firmly and, in some measure, put them into practice. "Gold Coast and Gambia's are the best, next to them the Windward Coast are prefer'd to Angola's," observed a Charles Town merchant in describing the most salable mixture. "There must not be a Callabar amongst them."[16] Planter preferences informed lowcountry slave traders and, to a considerable degree, determined the tribal origins of lowland blacks.

Whatever their origins, rice cultivation shaped the destiny of African people arriving at Charles Town. Although the production of pitch and tar played a pivotal role in the early development of the staple-based economy in South Carolina, rice quickly became the dominant plantation crop. Rice cultivation evolved slowly during the late seventeenth and early eighteenth centuries as planters, aided by knowledgeable blacks, mastered the complex techniques necessary for commercial production. During the first half of the eighteenth century, rice culture was limited to the inland swamps, where slave-built dikes controlled the irrigation of low-lying rice fields. But by mid-century planters had discovered how to regulate the tidal floods to irrigate and drain their fields. Rice production moved to the tidal swamps that lined the region's many rivers and expanded greatly. By the beginning of the nineteenth century, the rice coast stretched from Cape Fear in North Carolina to the Satilla River in Georgia. Throughout the lowcountry, rice was king.

The relatively mild slave regime of the pioneer years disappeared as rice cultivation expanded. Slaves increasingly lived in large units, and

RICE CULTURE ON THE OGEECHEE, NEAR SAVANNAH, GEORGIA.—Sketched by A. R. Waud.—[See Page 4.]

Figure 4.1 Mid-nineteenth-century representations of the processes of rice production. With the exception of the steam mill in the upper left-hand corner, the processes depicted here had not changed from the colonial era. (Photograph taken from *Harper's Weekly,* January 5, 1867.)

they worked in field gangs rather than at a variety of tasks. The strict requirements of rice production set the course of their work. And rice was a hard master. For a large portion of the year, slaves labored knee deep in brackish muck under the hot tropical sun; and, even after the fields were drained, the crops laid-by, and the grain threshed, there were canals to clear and dams to repair. By mid-century planters had also begun to grow indigo on the upland sections of their estates. Indigo complemented rice in its seasonal requirements, and it made even heavier labor demands. The ready availability of African imports compounded the new harsh realities of plantation slavery by cheapening black life in the eyes of many masters. As long as the slave trade remained open, they skimped on food, clothing, and medical attention for their slaves, knowing full well that substitutes could be easily had. With the planters' reliance on male African imports, slaves found it increasingly difficult to establish and maintain a normal family life. Brutal working conditions, the disease-ridden, lowland environment, and the open slave trade made for a deadly combination. Slave birth rates fell steadily during the middle years of the eighteenth century and mortality rates rose sharply. Between 1730 and 1760, deaths outnumbered births among blacks and only African importation allowed for continued population growth. Not until the eve of the Revolution did the black population begin again to reproduce naturally.

As the lowcountry plantation system took shape, the great slave masters retreated to the cities of the region; their evacuation of the countryside was but another manifestation of the growing social and cultural distance between them and their slaves. The streets of Charles Town, and, later, of Beaufort, Georgetown, Savannah, Darien, and Wilmington sprouted great new mansions as planters fled the malarial lowlands and the black majority. By the 1740s, urban life in the lowcountry had become attractive enough that men who made their fortunes in rice and slaves no longer returned home to England in the West Indian tradition. Instead, through intermarriage and business connections, they began to weave their disparate social relations into a close-knit ruling class, whose self-consciousness and pride of place became legendary. Charles Town, as the capital of this new elite, grew rapidly. Between 1720 and 1740 its population doubled, and it nearly doubled again by the eve of the Revolution to stand at about twelve thousand. With its many fine houses, its great churches, its shops packed with luxury goods, Charles Town's prosperity bespoke the maturation of the lowland plantation system and the rise of the planter class.

Planters, ensconced in their new urban mansions, their pockets lined with the riches rice produced, ruled their lowcountry domains through a long chain of command: stewards located in the smaller rice ports, overseers stationed near or on their plantations, and plantation-based black drivers. But their removal from the plantation did not breed the callous indifference of West Indian absenteeism. For one thing, they were no more than a day's boat ride away from their estates. Generally, they resided on their plantations during the non-malarial season. Their physical removal from the direct supervision of slave labor and the leisure their urban residences afforded appear to have sharpened their concern for "their people" and bred a paternalist ideology that at once legitimated their rule and informed all social relations.[17]

The lowcountry plantation system with its urban centers, its black majority, its dependence on "salt-water" slaves transformed black culture and society just as it reshaped the white world. The unified Afro-American culture and society that had evolved during the pioneer years disappeared as rice cultivation spread. In its place a sharp division developed between an increasingly urban creole and a plantation-based African population. The growth of plantation slavery not only set blacks further apart from whites, it also sharply divided blacks.

One branch of black society took shape within the bounds of the region's cities and towns. If planters lived removed from most slaves, they maintained close, intimate relations with some. The masters' great wealth, transient life, and seasonal urban residence placed them in close contact with house servants who kept their estates, boatmen who carried messages and supplies back and forth to their plantations, and urban artisans who made city life not only possible but comfortable. In addition, coastal cities needed large numbers of workers to transport and process the plantation staples, to serve the hundreds of ships that annually visited the lowcountry, and to satisfy the planters' newly acquired taste for luxury goods. Blacks did most of this work. Throughout the eighteenth century they composed more than half the population of Charles Town and other lowcountry ports. Probably nothing arrived or left these cities without some black handling it. Black artisans also played a large role in urban life. Master craftsmen employed them in every variety of work. A visitor to Charles Town found that even barbers "are supported in idleness & ease by their negroes...; & in fact many of the mechaniks bear nothing more of their trade than the name." Although most black artisans labored along the waterfront as ship-wrights, ropemakers, and coopers, lowcountry blacks – unlike blacks in Northern cities – also entered the higher trades, working as gold beaters, silversmiths, and cabinetmakers. In addition, black women gained control over much of the marketing in the lowcountry ports, mediating between slave-grown produce in the countryside and urban consumption. White tradesmen and journeymen periodically protested against slave competition, but planters, master craftsmen, and urban consumers who benefited from black labor and services easily brushed aside these objections.[18]

Mobile, often skilled, and occasionally literate, urban slaves understood the white world. They used their knowledge to improve their position within lowcountry society even while the condition of the mass of black people deteriorated in the wake of the rice revolution. Many urban creoles not only retained the independence of the earlier years but enlarged upon it. They hired their own time, earned wages from "overwork," kept market stalls, and sometimes even opened shops. Some lived apart from their masters and rented houses of their own, paying their owners a portion of their earnings in return for *de facto* freedom. Such liberty enabled a few black people to keep their families intact and perhaps even accumulate property for themselves. The small black communities that developed below the Bluff in Savannah and in Charles Town's Neck confirm the growing independence of urban creoles.

The incongruous prosperity of urban bondsmen jarred whites. By hiring their own time, living apart from their masters, and controlling their own family life, these blacks forcibly and visibly claimed the white man's privileges. Perhaps no aspect of their behavior was as obvious and, hence, as galling as their elaborate dress. While plantation slaves – men and women – worked stripped to the waist wearing no more than loin cloths (thereby confirming the white man's image of savagery), urban slaves appropriated their masters' taste for fine cloths and often the clothes themselves. Lowcountry legislators enacted various sumptuary regulations to restrain the slaves' penchant for dressing above their station. The South Carolina Assembly once even considered prohibiting masters from giving their old clothes to their slaves. But hand-me-downs were clearly not the problem as long as slaves earned wages and had easy access to the urban marketplace. Frustrated by the realities of urban slavery, lawmakers passed and repassed the old regulations to little effect. On the eve of the Revolution, a Charles Town Grand Jury continued to bemoan the fact that the "Law for preventing the excessive and costly Apparel of Negroes and other Slaves in this province (especially in *Charles Town*) [was] not being put into Force."[19]

Most of these privileged bondsmen appear to have been creoles with long experience in the New World. Although some Africans entered urban society, the language skills and the mastery of the complex interpersonal relations needed in the cities gave creoles a clear advantage over Africans in securing elevated positions within the growing urban enclaves. To be sure, their special status was far from "equal." No matter how essential their function or intimate their interaction, their relations with whites no longer smacked of the earlier "sawbuck equality."

Instead, these relations might better be characterized as paternal, some-times literally so.

Increasingly during the eighteenth century, blacks gained privileged positions within lowcountry society as a result of intimate, usually sexual, relations with white slave masters. Like slaveholders everywhere, lowland planters assumed that sexual access to slave women was simply another of the master's prerogatives. Perhaps because their origin was West Indian or perhaps because their dual residence separated them from their white wives part of the year, white men established sexual liaisons with black women frequently and openly. Some white men and black women formed stable, long-lasting unions, legitimate in everything but law. More often than other slaveholders on continental British North America, lowcountry planters recognized and provided for their mulatto offspring, and, occasionally, extended legal freedom. South Carolina's small free Negro population, almost totally confined to Charles Town, was largely the product of such relations. Light-skinned people of color enjoyed special standing in the lowcountry ports, as they did in the West Indies, and whites occasionally looked the other way when such creoles passed into the dominant caste. But even when the planters did not grant legal freedom, they usually assured the elevated standing of their mulatto scions by training them for artisan trades or placing them in household positions. If the countryside was "blackened" by African imports, Charles Town and the other lowcountry ports exhibited a mélange of "colored" peoples.

While one branch of black society stood so close to whites that its members sometimes disappeared into the white population, most plantation slaves remained alienated from the world of their masters, physically and culturally. Living in large units often numbering in the hundreds on plantations that they had carved out of the malarial swamps and working under the direction of black drivers, the black majority gained only fleeting knowledge of Anglo-American culture. What they knew did not encourage them to learn more. Instead, they strove to widen the distance between themselves and their captors. In doing so, they too built upon the large degree of autonomy black people had earlier enjoyed.

In the pioneer period, many masters required slaves to raise their own provisions. Slaves regularly kept small gardens and tended barnyard fowl to maintain themselves, and they often marketed their surplus. Blacks kept these prerogatives with the development of the plantation system. In fact, the growth of lowcountry towns, the increasing specialization in staple production, and the comparative absence of nonslaveholding whites enlarged the market for slave-grown produce. Planters, of course, disliked the independence truck gardening afforded plantation blacks and the tendency of slaves to confuse their owners' produce with their own, but the ease of water transportation and the absence of white supervision made it difficult to prevent.

To keep their slaves on the plantation, some planters traded directly with their bondsmen, bartering manufactured goods for slave produce. Henry Laurens, a planter who described himself as a "factor" for his slaves, exchanged some "very gay Wastcoats which some of the Negro Men may want" for grain at "10 Bushels per Wastcoat." Later, learning that a plantation under his supervision was short of provisions, he authorized the overseer "to purchase of your own Negroes all that you know Lawfully belongs to themselves at the lowest price they will sell it for." As Laurens's notation suggests, planters found benefits in slave participation in the lowcountry's internal economy, but the small profits gained by bartering with their bondsmen only strengthened the slaves' customary right to their garden and barnyard fowl. Early in the nineteenth century, when Charles C. Pinckney decided to produce his own provisions, he purchased breeding stock from his slaves. By the Civil War, lowland slaves controlled considerable personal property – flocks of ducks, pigs, milch cows, and occasionally horses – often the product of stock that had been in their families for generations.[20] For the most part, slave propertyholding remained small during the eighteenth century. But it helped insulate plantation blacks from the harsh conditions of primitive rice production and provided social distance from their masters' domination.

The task system, a mode of work organization peculiar to the lowcountry, further strengthened black autonomy. Under the task system, a slave's daily routine was sharply defined: so many rows of rice to be sowed, so much grain to be threshed, or so many lines of canal to be cleared. Such a precise definition of work suggests that city-bound planters found it almost impossible to keep their slaves in the fields from sunup to sundown. With little direct white supervision, slaves and their black foremen conspired to preserve a large portion of the day for their own use, while meeting their masters' minimum work requirements. Struggle over the definition of a task doubtless continued throughout the formative years of the lowcountry plantation system and after, but by the end of the century certain lines had been drawn. Slaves generally left the field sometime in the early afternoon, a practice that protected them from the harsh afternoon sun and allowed them time to tend their own gardens and stock. Like participation in the lowcountry's internal economy, the task system provided slaves with a large measure of control over their own lives.

The autonomy generated by both the task system and truck gardening provided the material basis for lowland black culture. Within the confines of the overwhelmingly black countryside, African culture survived well. The continual arrival of Africans into the lowcountry renewed and refreshed slave knowledge of West African life. In such a setting blacks could hardly lose their past. The distinctive pattern of the lowland slave trade, moreover, heightened the impact of the newly arrived Africans on the evolution of black culture. While slaves dribbled into the North through a multiplicity of ports, they poured into the lowcountry through a single city. The large, unicentered slave trade and the large slaveholding units assured the survival not only of the common denominators of West African culture but also many of its particular tribal and national forms. Planter preferences or perhaps the chance ascendancy of one group sometimes allowed specific African cultures to reconstitute themselves within the plantation setting. To be sure, Africans changed in the lowcountry. Even where blacks enjoyed numerical superiority and a considerable degree of autonomy, they could no more transport their culture unchanged than could their masters. But lowcountry blacks incorporated more of West African culture – as reflected in their language, religion, work patterns, and much else – into their new lives than did other black Americans. Throughout the eighteenth century and into the nineteenth, lowcountry blacks continued to work the land, name their children, and communicate through word and song in a manner that openly combined African traditions with the circumstances of plantation life.

The new pattern of creolization that developed following the rice revolution smashed the emerging homogeneity of black life in the first years of settlement and left lowcountry blacks deeply divided. One branch of black culture evolved in close proximity to whites. Urban, often skilled, well-traveled, and increasingly American-born, creoles knew white society well, and they used their knowledge to better themselves. Some, clearly a well-connected minority, pressed for incorporation into the white world. They urged missionary groups to admit their children to school and later petitioned lawmakers to allow their testimony in court, carefully adding that they did not expect full equality with whites. Plantation slaves shared few of the assimilationist aspirations of urban creoles. By their dress, language, and work routine, they lived in a world apart. Rather than demand incorporation into white society, they yearned only to be left alone. Within the quarter, aided by their numerical dominance, their plantation-based social hierarchy, and their continued contact with Africa, they developed their own distinctive culture, different not only from that of whites but also from the cosmopolitan world of their Afro-American brethren. To be sure, there were connections between the black majority and the urban creoles. Many – market women, jobbing artisans, and boatmen – moved easily between these two worlds, and most blacks undoubtedly learned something of the other world through chance encounters, occasional visits, and word of mouth. Common white oppression continually shrank the social distance that the distinctive experience created, but by the eve of the Revolution, deep cultural differences separated those blacks who sought to improve their lives through incorporation into the white world and those who determined to disregard the white man's ways. If the movement from African to creole obliterated cultural differences among Northern blacks, creolization fractured black society in the lowcountry.

Cultural distinctions between Africans and Afro-Americans developed in the Chesapeake as well, although the dimension of differences between African and creole tended to be time rather than space. Unlike in the lowcountry, white planters did not promote the creation of a distinctive group whose origins, function, and physical appearance distinguished them from the mass of plantation slaves and offered them hope, however faint, of eventual incorporation into white society. And, compared to the North, African immigration into the Chesapeake came relatively early in the process of cultural transformation. As a result, African–creole differences disappeared with time and a single, unified Afro-American culture slowly emerged in the Chesapeake.

As in the lowcountry, little distinguished black and white laborers during the early years of settlement. Most of the first blacks brought into the Chesapeake region were West Indian creoles who bore English or Spanish surnames and carried records of baptism. Along the James, as along the Cooper, the demands of pioneer life at times operated to strengthen the slaves' bargaining position. Some blacks set the condition of their labor, secured their family life, participated in the region's internal economy, and occasionally bartered for their liberty. This, of course, did not save most black people from the brutal exploitation that almost all propertyless men and women faced as planters squeezed the last pound of profit from the tobacco economy. The blacks' treatment at the hands of planters differed little from that of white bound labor in large measure because it was difficult to treat people more brutally. While the advantages of this peculiar brand of equality may have been lost on its beneficiaries, those blacks who were able to complete their terms of servitude quickly joined whites in the mad scramble for land, servants, and status.

Many did well. During the seventeenth century, black freemen could be found throughout the region owning land, holding servants, and occasionally attaining minor offices. Like whites, they accumulated property, sued their neighbors, and passed their estates to their children. In 1651, Anthony Johnson, the best known of these early Negro freemen, received a two-hundred-and-fifty-acre headright for importing five persons into Virginia. John Johnson, a neighbor and probably a relative, did even better, earning five hundred and fifty acres for bringing eleven persons into the colony. Both men owned substantial farms on the Eastern Shore, held servants, and left their heirs sizable estates. As established members of their communities, they enjoyed the rights of citizens. When a servant claiming his freedom fled Anthony Johnson's plantation and took refuge with a nearby white farmer, Johnson took his neighbor to court and won the return of his servant along with damages against the white man.

The class rather than racial basis of early Chesapeake society enabled many black men to compete successfully for that scarcest of all New World commodities: the affection of white women. Bastardy lists indicate that white female servants ignored the strictures against what white lawmakers labeled "shameful" and "unnatural" acts and joined together with men of their own condition regardless of color. Fragmentary evidence from various parts of seventeenth-century Virginia reveals that approximately one-quarter to one-third of the bastard children born to white women were mulattoes. The commonplace nature of these interracial unions might have been the reason why one justice legally sanctified the marriage of Hester, an English servant woman, to James Tate, a black slave. Some successful, property-owning whites and blacks also intermarried. In Virginia's Northampton county, Francis Payne, a Negro freeman, married a white woman, who later remarried a white man after Payne's death. William Greensted, a white attorney who represented Elizabeth Key, a mulatto woman, in her successful suit for her freedom, later married her. In 1691, when the Virginia General Assembly finally ruled against the practice, some propertied whites found the legislation novel and obnoxious enough to muster a protest.

By the middle of the seventeenth century, Negro freemen sharing and fulfilling the same ideals and aspirations that whites held were no anomaly in the Chesapeake region. An Eastern Shore tax list of 1668 counted nearly a third of black tithables free. If most blacks did not escape the tightening noose of enslavement, they continued to live and work under conditions not much different from white servants. Throughout the seventeenth and into the first decades of the eighteenth century, black and white servants ran away together, slept together, and, upon occasion, stood shoulder to shoulder against the weighty champions of established authority. Thus viewed from the first years of settlement – the relatively small number of blacks, their creole origins, and the initial success of some in establishing a place in society – black acculturation in the Chesapeake appeared to be following the nonplantation pattern of the Northern colonies and the pioneer lowcountry.

The emergence of a planter class and its consolidation of power during a series of political crises in the middle years of the seventeenth century transformed black life in the Chesapeake and threatened this pattern of cultural change. Following the legalization of slavery in the 1660s, black slaves slowly but steadily replaced white indentured servants as the main source of plantation labor. By 1700, blacks made up more than half the agricultural work force in Virginia and, since the great planters could best afford to purchase slaves, blacks composed an even larger share of the workers on the largest estates. Increased reliance on slave labor quickly outstripped West Indian supplies. Beginning in the 1680s, Africans entered the region in increasingly large numbers. The proportion of blacks born in Africa grew steadily throughout the waning years of the seventeenth century, so that by the first decade of the eighteenth century, Africans composed some three-quarters of the region's blacks. Unlike the lowcountry, African imports never threatened the Chesapeake's overall white numerical superiority, but by the beginning of the eighteenth century they dominated black society. Some eighty years after the first blacks arrived at Jamestown and some forty years after the legalization of slavery, African importation profoundly transformed black life.

Slave conditions deteriorated as their numbers increased. With an eye for a quick profit, planters in the Chesapeake imported males disproportionately. Generally men outnumbered women more than two to one on Chesapeake slavers. Wildly imbalanced sex ratios undermined black family life. Physically spent and emotionally drained by the rigors of the Middle Passage, African women had few children. Thus, as in the North and the Carolina lowlands, the black birth rate fell and mortality rate surged upward with the commencement of direct African importation.

The hard facts of life and death in the Chesapeake region distinguished creoles and Africans at the beginning of the eighteenth century. The demands of the tobacco economy enlarged these differences in several ways. Generally, planters placed little trust in newly arrived Africans with their strange tongues and alien customs. While they assigned creoles to artisanal duties on their plantations and to service within their households, they sent Africans to the distant, upland quarters where the slaves did the dull, backbreaking work of clearing the land and tending tobacco. The small size of these specialized upcountry units, their isolation from the mainstream of Chesapeake life, and their rude frontier conditions made these largely male compounds lonely, unhealthy places that narrowed men's vision. The dynamics of creole life, however, broadened black understanding of life in the New World. Traveling freely through the countryside as artisans, watermen, and domestic servants, creoles gained in confidence as they mastered the terrain, perfected their English, and learned about Christianity and other

Figure 4.2 Late nineteenth-century representation of the stages of pre-revolutionary tobacco production. (1) Sowing. (2) Hilling. (3) Transplanting. (4) Laying by and topping. (5) Worming and suckering. (6) Cutting and sticking. (7) Housing. (8) Stripping and tying. (9) Packing. (From Benjamin Butterworth, *The Growth of Industrial Art*, Washington, DC, 1892.)

cultural modes that whites equated with civilization. Knowledge of the white world enabled black creoles to manipulate their masters to their own advantage. If Afro-Americans became increasingly knowledgeable about their circumstances and confident of their ability to deal with them, Africans remained provincials, limited by the narrow alternatives of plantation life.

As in the lowcountry and the Northern colonies, Africans in the Chesapeake strove to escape whites, while creoles used their knowledge of white society for their own benefit. These cultural differences, which were reflected in all aspects of black life, can be seen most clearly in the diverse patterns of resistance. Africans ran away toward the back country and isolated swamps. They generally moved in groups that included women and children, despite the hazards such groups entailed for a successful escape. Their purpose was to recreate the only society they knew free from white domination. In 1727, Governor William Gooch of Virginia reported that about a dozen slaves had left a new plantation near the falls of the James River. They headed west and settled near Lexington, built houses, and planted a crop before being retaken. But Afro-Americans ran away alone, usually with the hope of escaping into American society. Moving toward the areas of heaviest settlement, they found refuge in the thick network of black kinship that covered the countryside and sold their labor to white yeomen with few questions asked. While the possibility of passing as free remained small in the years before the Revolution, the creoles' obvious confidence in their ability to integrate themselves into American society stands in stark contrast to that of Africans, who sought first to flee it.

As reflected in the mode of resistance, place of residence, occupation, and much else, Africans and creoles developed distinctive patterns of behavior and belief. To a degree, whites recognized these differences. They stigmatized Africans as "outlandish" and noted how creoles "affect our language, habits, and customs." They played on African–creole differences to divide blacks from each other, and they utilized creole skills to maximize the benefits of slave labor. But this recognition did not elevate creoles over Africans in any lasting way. Over the course of the century following legal enslavement, it had precisely the opposite effect. Chesapeake planters consolidated their class position by asserting white racial unity. In this context, the entry of large numbers of African – as opposed to creole – blacks into the region enlarged racial differences and helped secure planter domination. Thus, as reliance on black labor increased, the opportunities for any black – no matter how fluent in English or conversant with the countryside – to escape bondage and join the scramble for land, servants, and status diminished steadily.

By the middle of the eighteenth century, the size and character of the free Negro population had been significantly altered. Instead of a large minority of the black population, Negro freemen now composed just a small proportion of all blacks, probably not more than 5 percent. Many were cripples and old folks whom planters discarded when they could no longer wring a profit from their labor. While most were of mixed racial origins, few of these free mulattoes of the Chesapeake, in contrast to those of the lowcountry, traced their ancestry to the planter class. Instead, they descended from white servants, frequently women. These impoverished people had little status to offer their children. Indeed, planter-inspired legislation further compromised their liberty by requiring that the offspring of white women and black men serve their mother's master for thirty-one years. Those who survived the term could scarcely hope for the opportunities an earlier generation of Negro freemen had enjoyed. The transformation of the free Negro caste in the century between 1660 and 1760 measured the change in Chesapeake society as its organizing principle changed from class to race.

The free Negro's decline reveals how the racial imperatives of Chesapeake society operated to lump all black people together, free and slave, creole and African. In the Chesapeake, planters dared not grant creoles special status at the expense of Africans. Since the Africans would shortly be creoles and since creoles shared so much with whites, distinctions among blacks threatened the racial division that underlay planter domination. In the lowcountry, where geography, economy, and language separated white and black, those few blacks who spoke, dressed, acted, and looked like whites might be allowed some white prerogatives. But, if lowcountry planters could argue that no white man could do the work required to grow rice commercially, no one in the Chesapeake could reasonably deny that whites could grow tobacco. The fundamental unity of Chesapeake life and the long-term instability of African–creole differences pushed blacks together in the white mind and in fact.

During the middle years of the eighteenth century, changes in the Chesapeake economy and society further diminished differences within black society and created a unified Afro-American culture. The success of the tobacco economy enlarged the area of settlement and allowed planters to increase their holdings. The most successful planters, anxious to protect themselves from the rigors of the world marketplace, strove for plantation self-sufficiency. The great estates of the Chesapeake became self-contained enterprises with slaves taking positions as artisans, tradesmen, wagoners, and, sometimes, managers; the plantation was "like a Town," as a tutor on Robert Carter's estate observed, "but most of the Inhabitants are black." The increased sophistication of the Chesapeake economy propelled many more blacks into artisanal positions and the larger units of production, tighter pattern of settlement, and the greater mobility allowed by the growing network of roads ended the deadening isolation of the upcountry quarter. Bondsmen increasingly lived in large groups, and those who did not could generally find black companionship within a few miles' walk. Finally, better food, clothing, and shelter and, perhaps, the development of immunities to New World diseases enabled blacks to live longer, healthier lives.[21]

As part of their drive for self-sufficiency, Chesapeake slaveholders encouraged the development of an indigenous slave population. Spurred by the proven ability of Africans to survive and reproduce and pressed in the international slave market by the superior resources of West Indian sugar magnates and lowland rice growers, Chesapeake planters strove to correct the sexual imbalance within the black population, perhaps by importing a large proportion of women or lessening the burden of female slaves. Blacks quickly took advantage of this new circumstance and placed their family life on a firmer footing. Husbands and wives petitioned their owners to allow them to reside together on the same quarter and saw to it that their families were fed, beyond their masters' rations. Planters, for their part, were usually receptive to slaves' demands for a secure family life, both because it reflected their own values and because they profited mightily from the addition of slave children. Thomas Jefferson frankly considered "a woman who brings a child every two years as more profitable than the best man on the farm [for] what she produces is an addition to capital, while his labor disappears in mere consumption." Under these circumstances, the black population increased rapidly. Planters relied less and less on African importation and, by the 1740s, most of the growth of the black population came from natural increase. Within a generation, African importation was, for all practical purposes, no longer a significant source of slave labor. In the early 1770s, the period of the greatest importation into the lowcountry, only five hundred of the five thousand slaves added annually to the black population of Virginia derived directly from Africa.[22]

The establishment of the black family marked the re-emergence of Afro-American culture in the Chesapeake. Although Africans continued to enter the region, albeit at a slower pace, the nature of the slave trade minimized their impact on the development of black society in the region. Unlike those in the lowcountry, newly arrived Africans could rarely hope to remain together. Rather than funnel their cargo through a single port, Chesapeake slavers peddled it in small lots at the many tobacco landings that lined the bay's extensive perimeter. Planters rarely bought more than a few slaves at a time, and larger purchasers, usually the great planter-merchants, often acted as jobbers, quickly reselling these slaves to backcountry freeholders. The resulting fragmentation sent newly arrived Africans in all directions and prevented the maintenance of tribal or shipboard ties. Chesapeake slaveholders cared little about the origins of their slaves. In their eyes, newly arrived Africans were not Iboes, Coromantees, or Angolans, but "new Negroes." While the unicentered slave trade sustained and strengthened African culture in the lowcountry, the Chesapeake slave trade facilitated the absorption of Africans into the evolving creole society.

Differences between creoles and Africans did not disappear with the creation of a self-sustaining Afro-American population. The creoles' advantages – language skills, familiarity with the countryside, artisanal standing, and knowledge of the plantation routine – continued to propel them into positions of authority within the slave hierarchy. In some ways, the growing complexity of the Chesapeake economy widened the distance between Africans and creoles, at least at first. Most of the skilled and managerial positions within the region's expanding iron industry went to creole blacks as did the artisanal work in flour mills and weaving houses. On some plantations, moreover, artisan and house status became lodged in particular families with parents passing privileged positions on to their children. Increasingly, skilled slaves entered the market economy by selling their own time and earning money from "overwork," thereby gaining a large measure of freedom. For the most part, Africans remained on rude, backwoods plantations tending the broad-leaf weed. Since creole slaves sold at a premium price and most great planters had already established self-sustaining slave forces, small planters purchased nearly all of the newly arrived Africans after mid-century. These upward-striving men generally owned the least developed, most distant farms. Their labor requirements remained primitive compared to the sophisticated division of labor on the self-contained plantation-towns.

Over the long term, however, economic changes sped the integration of Africans into Afro-American society. Under the pressure of a worldwide food shortage, Chesapeake planters turned from the production of tobacco to that of foodstuff, especially wheat. The demands of wheat cultivation transformed the nature of labor in the region. Whereas tobacco farming required season-long labor, wheat farming employed workers steadily only during planting and harvesting. The remainder of the year, laborers had little to do with the crop. At the same time, however, wheat required a larger and more skilled labor force to transport the grain to market and to store it, mill it, and reship it as flour, bread, or bulk grain. Economic changes encouraged masters to teach their slaves skills and to hire them out during the slack season. At first, these opportunities went mostly to creoles, but as the wheat economy grew, spurring urbanization and manufacturing, the demands for artisans and hirelings outstripped the creole population. An increasing number of Africans were placed in positions previously reserved for creoles. The process of cultural transformation that earlier in the eighteenth century had taken a generation or more was considerably shorter at mid-century. Africans became Afro-Americans with increasing rapidity as the century wore on, eliminating the differences within black society that African importation had created.

Chesapeake blacks enjoyed considerably less autonomy than their lowcountry counterparts. Resident planters, small units of production, and the presence of large numbers of whites meant that most blacks lived and worked in close proximity to whites. While lowcountry planters fled to coastal cities for a large part of the year, the resident planter was a fixture of Chesapeake life. Small freeholders labored alongside slaves, and great planters prided themselves on regulating all aspects of their far-flung estates through a combination of direct personal supervision and plantation-based overseers. The latter were usually white, drawn from the region's white majority. Those few blacks who achieved managerial positions, moreover, enjoyed considerably less authority than lowland drivers. The presence of numerous nonslaveholding whites circumscribed black opportunities in other ways as well. While Chesapeake slaves commonly kept gardens and flocks of barnyard animals, white competitors limited their market and created a variety of social tensions. If lowcountry masters sometimes encouraged their slaves to produce nonstaple garden crops, whites in the Chesapeake – slaveholders and nonslaveholders alike – complained that blacks stole more than they raised and worked to curb the practice. Thus, at every turn, economy and society conspired to constrain black autonomy.

The requirements of tobacco cultivation reinforced the planters' concern about daily work routine. Whereas the task system insulated lowcountry blacks against white intervention and maximized black control over their work, the constant attention demanded by tobacco impelled Chesapeake planters to oversee the tedious process of cultivating, topping, worming, suckering, and curing tobacco. The desire of Chesapeake masters to control their slaves went beyond the supervision of labor. Believing that slaves depended on them "for every necessity of life," they intervened in the most intimate aspects of black life. "I hope you will take care that the Negroes both men and women I sent you up last always go by the names we gave them," Robert "King" Carter reminded his steward. "I am sure we repeated them so often...that everyone knew their names & would readily answer to them." Chesapeake planters sought to shape domestic relations, cure physical maladies, and form personalities. However miserably they failed to ensure black domestic tranquility and reform slave drunkards, paternalism at close quarters in the Chesapeake had a far more potent influence on black life than the distant paternalism that developed in the lowcountry. Chesapeake blacks developed no distinct language and rarely utilized African day names for their children.[23] Afro-American culture in Chesapeake evolved parallel with Anglo-American culture and with a considerable measure of congruence.

The diverse development of Afro-American culture during the seventeenth and eighteenth centuries reveals the importance of time and place in the study of American slavery. Black people in colonial America shared many things: a common African lineage, a common racial oppressor, a common desire to create the richest life possible for themselves and their posterity in the most difficult of circumstances. But these commonalities took different shape and meaning within the diverse circumstances of the North American mainland. The nature of the slave trade, the various demographic configurations of whites and blacks, and the demands of particular staples – to name some of the factors influencing the development of slave society – created at least three distinctive patterns of Afro-American life. Perhaps a finer analysis will reveal still others.

This diversity did not end with the American Revolution. While African–creole differences slowly disappeared as the centerpole of black society with the closing of the slave trade and the steady growth of an Afro-American population, other sources of cohesion and division came to the fore. Differences between freemen and bondsmen, urban and rural folk, skilled and unskilled workers, and browns and blacks united and divided black people, and made black society every bit as variable and diverse during the nineteenth century as in the eighteenth. Indeed the diversity of black life increased substantially during the antebellum years as political changes abolished slavery in some places and strengthened it in others, as demographic changes set in motion by the Great Migration across the Lower South took effect, as the introduction of new crops enlarged the South's repertoire of staples, and as the kaleidoscopic movement of the world market sent the American economy in all directions.

If slave society during the colonial era can be comprehended only through a careful delineation of temporal and spatial differences among Northern, Chesapeake, and lowcountry colonies, a similar division will be necessary for a full understanding of black life in nineteenth-century America. The actions of black people during the American Revolution, the Civil War, and the long years of bondage between these two cataclysmic events cannot be understood merely as a function of the dynamics of slavery or the possibilities of liberty, but must be viewed within the specific social circumstances and cultural traditions of black people. These varied from time to time and from place to place. Thus no matter how complete recent studies of black life appear, they are limited to the extent that they provide a static and singular vision of a dynamic and complex society.

Notes

1   Stanley Elkins, *Slavery: A Problem in American Institutional and Intellectual Life* (Chicago, 1959); John W. Blassingame, *The Slave Community: Plantation Life in the Antebellum South* (New York, 1972); Eugene D. Genovese, *Roll, Jordon, Roll: The World the Slaves Made* (New York, 1974); and Ulrich B. Phillips, *American Negro Slavery* (New York, 1918).

2 I have used these terms synonymously to refer to black people of native American birth.

3 In the discussion of the Chesapeake region and the lowcountry, scholars have employed the term "Anglo-American" to refer to the culture of white people. Because of the greater diversity of origins of white peoples in the Middle Colonies, the term "Euro-American" seems more applicable to white culture in the North.

4 Kalm, *Peter Kalm's Travels in North America*, ed. and tr. A. B. Benson, 1 (New York, 1937): 205, as quoted in Alan Tully, "Patterns of Slavehold-ing in Colonial Pennsylvania: Chester and Lancaster Counties, 1729–1758," *Journal of Social History*, 6 (1973): 286.

5 N. B. Shurtleff et al., eds., *Records of the Governor and Company of Massachu-setts Bay in New England (1628–1698)*, 1 (Boston, 1853): 79, as quoted in Carl Bridenbaugh, *Cities in the Wilderness, 1625–1742* (New York, 1938), 49.

6 New York *Weekly Post-Boy*, May 17, 1756, as quoted in Edgar J. McManus, *Black Bondage in the North* (Syracuse, NY, 1973), 38.

7 W. N. Sainsbury et al., eds., *Calendar of State Papers, Colonial Series, 1708–1709*, 110, as quoted in Lorenzo J. Greene, *The Negro in Colonial New England* (New York, 1942), 35.

8 Governor Samuel Cranston to the Board of Trade, December 5, 1708, in J. R. Bartlett, ed., *Records of the Colony of Rhode Island and Providence Plantations*, 4 (1860), 55, as quoted in William D. Miller, "The Narragan-sett Planters," *American Antiquarian Society Proceedings*, 43 (1933), 68 n. 2; and Cadwallader Colden to Mr. Jordan, March 26, 1717, in *Letters and Papers of Cadwallader Colden*, 1 (New York, 1917), 39, as quoted in Arthur Zilversmit, *The First Emancipation: The Abolition of Negro Slavery in the North* (Chicago, 1967), 22.

9 Sara Kemble Knight, as quoted in Ralph F. Weld, *Slavery in Connecticut* (New Haven, 1935), 8–9; John Watts, *Letterbook of John Watts*, New York Historical Society Collections, no. 61 (New York, 1938), 151.

10 Watts, *Letterbook of John Watts*, 31.

11 Henry Bull, "Memoir of Rhode Island," Newport *Rhode-Island Republican*, April 19, 1837, as quoted in William D. Pierson, "Afro-American Culture in Eighteenth-Century New England" (PhD dissertation, Indiana Univer-sity, 1975), 181.

12 Peter Williams, *A Discourse, Deliverd in the Death of Capt. Paul Cuffee* (New York, 1817).

13 Peter H. Wood, *Black Majority: Negroes in Colonial South Carolina from 1670 through the Stono Rebellion* (New York, 1974), 13–24, 94–7.

14 Thomas Nairne, *A Letter from South Carolina* (London, 1710), 31; Memorial of Joseph Boone and Richard Beresford to the Lord Commis-sioners of Trade and Plantations, December 6, 1716, Public Record Office, London, as quoted in Clarence L. Ver Steeg, *Origins of a Southern Mosaic: Studies of Early Carolina and Georgia* (Athens, GA, 1975), 106.

15 "The Representation and Address of Several Members of This Present Assembly," in William James Rivers, *A Sketch of the History of South Carolina* (Charleston, SC, 1856), 459, as quoted in Ver Steeg, *Origins of a Southern*

Mosaic, 38 (italics removed); and Wood, *Black Majority: Negroes in Colonial South Carolina*, 102–3.

16 Henry Laurens, *The Papers of Henry Laurens*, ed. Philip M. Hamer, George C. Rogers, Jr, and David R. Chesnutt, 7 vols. (Columbia, SC, 1970–), 1: 294–5.

17 Eugene D. Genovese has not made either regional or temporal distinctions in the development of Southern ideology but has leaned heavily on South Carolina for his understanding of Southern paternalism; see his *Roll, Jordan, Roll: The World the Slaves Made* (New York, 1976), 1–113.

18 Joseph W. Barnwell, ed., "The Diary of Timothy Ford," *South Carolina Historical Magazine*, 13 (1914): 142.

19 *South Carolina Gazette*, May 24, 1773, as quoted in John D. Duncan, "Servitude and Slavery in Colonial South Carolina, 1670–1776" (PhD dissertation, Emory University, 1971), 234; Klaus G. Leowald, Beverly Starika, and Paul S. Taylor, tr. and eds., "Johann Martin Bolzius Answers a Questionnaire on Carolina and Georgia," *William and Mary Quarterly*, 3rd ser., 14 (1957): 236; Thomas Cooper and David J. McCord, comps, *Statutes at Large of South Carolina*, 10 vols. (Columbia, SC, 1836–41), 7: 396–412; and Duncan, "Servitude and Slavery in Colonial South Carolina," 233–7.

20 Laurens, *Papers of Henry Laurens*, 4: 616, 5: 20, 41; C. C. Pinckney, Plantation Journal, 1812, and George Lucas to Charles Pinckney, January 30, 1745/6, Manuscript Division, Library of Congress, Washington, DC.

21 Philip V. Fithian, *The Journal and Letters of Philip Vickers Fithian, 1773–1774*, ed. Hunter D. Farish (Williamsburg, VA, 1943), 73.

22 Edwin M. Betts, ed., *Thomas Jefferson's Farm Book* (New York, 1953), pt 2: 46.

23 Robert Carter to Robert Jones, Robert "King" Carter Letterbooks, Alderman Library, University of Virginia, Charlottesville (I am grateful to Emory Evans for alerting me to this letter); and Robert Carter to William Carr, March 15, 1785, Carter Papers, typescript, Duke University, Durham, NC.

A New and Accurate Description of the Coast of Guinea... (1705)

William Bosman

... Not a few in our country fondly imagine that parents here sell their children, men their wives, and one brother the other: but those who think so deceive themselves; for this never happens on any other account but that of necessity, or some great crime. But most of the slaves that are offered to us are prisoners of war, which are sold by the victors as their booty.

When these slaves come to Fida, they are put in prison all together, and when we treat concerning buying them, they are all brought out together in a large plain; where, by our chirurgeons, whose province it is, they are throughly examined, even to the smallest member, and that naked too both men and women, without the least distinction or modesty. Those which are approved as good are set on one side; and the lame and faulty are set by as invalides, which are here called mackrons. These are such as are above five and thirty years old, or are maimed in the arms, legs, hands, or feet, have lost a tooth, are grey-haired, or have films over their eyes; as well as all those which are affected with any veneral distemper, or with several other diseases.

The invalides and the maimed being thrown out, as I have told you, the remainder are numbred, and it is entred who delivered them. In the mean while a burning iron, with the arms or name of the companies, lyes in the fire; with which ours are marked on the breast.

This is done that we may distinguish them from the slaves of the English, French or others; (which are also marked with their mark) and to prevent the negroes exchanging them for worse; at which they have a good hand.

I doubt not but this trade seems very barbarous to you, but since it is followed by meer necessity it must go on; but we yet take all possible care that they are not burned too hard, especially the women, who are more tender than the men.

We are seldom long detained in the buying of these slaves, because their price is established, the women being one fourth or fifth part cheaper than the men. . . .

When we have agreed with the owners of the slaves, they are returned to their prison; where from that time forwards they are kept at our charge, cost us two pence a day a slave; which serves to subsist them, like our criminals, on bread and water: So that to save charges we send them on board our ships with the very first opportunity; before which their masters strip them of all they have on their backs; so that they come aboard stark-naked as well women as men: in which condition they are obliged to continue, if the master of the Ship is not so charitable (which he commonly is) as to bestow something on them to cover their nakedness.

You would really wonder to see how these slaves live on board; for though their number sometimes amounts to six or seven hundred, yet by the careful management of our masters of ships, they are so regulated that it seems incredible: And in this particular our nation exceeds all other Europeans; for as the French, Portuguese and English slave-ships, are always foul and stinking; on the contrary ours are for the most part clean and neat.

The slaves are fed three times a day with indifferent good victuals, and much better than they eat in their own country. Their lodging-place is divided into two parts; one of which is appointed for the men the other for the women; each sex being kept a-part: Here they lye as close together as is possible for them to be crowded.

We are sometimes sufficiently plagued with a parcel of slaves, which come from a far in-land country, who very innocently persuade one another, that we buy them only to fatten and afterwards eat them as a delicacy.

When we are so unhappy as to be pestered with many of this sort, they resolve and agree together (and bring over the rest of their party) to run away from the ship, kill the Europeans, and set the vessel a-shore; by which means they design to free themselves from being our food.

I have twice met with this misfortune; and the first time proved very unlucky to me, I not in the least suspecting it; but the up roar was timely quashed by the master of the ship and my self, by causing the abettor to be shot through the head, after which all was quiet.

But the second time it fell heavier on another ship, and that chiefly by the carelessness of the master, who having fished up the anchor of a departed English ship, had laid it in the hold where the male slaves were lodged; who, unknown to any of the ships crew, possessed themselves of a hammer; with which, in a short time, they broke all their fetters in pieces upon the anchor: after this they came above deck and fell upon our men; some of whom they grievously wounded, and would certainly have mastered the ship, if a French and English ship had not very fortunately happened to lye by us; who perceiving by our firing a distress'd-gun, that something was in disorder on board, immediately came to our assistance with chalops and men, and drove the slaves under deck: Notwithstanding which before all was appeased about twenty of them were killed. . . .

The Carolina Chronicle of Dr. Francis Le Jau (1706–17)

Francis Le Jau

From letters of the Reverend Francis Le Jau to the Secretary of the Society for the Propagation of the Gospel

October 20, 1709...As for the Spiritual State of my Parish this is the Account I can give of it for the present.

The extent of it is 20 Miles in length, and from 7 to 14 in breadth. Number of families 80. of the Church of England. Dissenting families 7, if so many, I find but 4 very strict. Baptised this half year past a Marryed Woman and 17 Children. Actual Communicants in all about 50: Constant Communicants every two Months near 30, among whom are two Negroes.

Since I came I baptised in all 2 Adults & 47 Children. Our Congregation is generally of about 100 Persons, sometimes more, several that were inclinable to some of the dissenting partys shew themselves pritty constant among us, and I do what possible to edify them and give them satisfaction in their doubts. On Sunday next I design God willing to baptise two very sensible and honest Negro Men whom I have kept upon tryal these two Years. Several others have spoken to me also; I do nothing too hastily in that respect. I instruct them and must have the consent of their Masters with a good Testimony and proof of their honest life and sober Conversation. Some Masters in my parish are very well satisfyed with my Proceedings in that respect: others do not seem to be so; yet they have given over opposing my design openly; it is to be hoped the good Example of the one will have an influence over the others. I must do the Justice to my Parishioners that tho' many Young Gentlemen are Masters of Great Estates, they and almost all the heads of all our Neighbouring families are an Example of Sobriety, honest[y] & Zeal for the Service of the Church to all the province.

To remove all pretence from the Adult Slaves I shall baptise of their being free upon that Account, I have thought fit to require first their consent to this following declaration *You declare in the Presence of God and before this Congregation that you do not ask for the holy baptism out of any design to ffree yourself from the Duty and Obedience you owe to your Master while you live, but meerly for the good of Your Soul and to partake of the Graces and Blessings promised to the Members of the Church of Jesus Christ.* One of the most Scandalous and common Crimes of our Slaves is their perpetual Changing of Wives and husbands, which occasions great disorders: I also tell them whom I baptise, *The Christian Religion dos not allow plurality of Wives, nor any changing of them: You promise truly to keep to the Wife you now have till Death dos part you.* I[t] has been Customary among them to have their ffeasts, dances, and merry Meetings upon the Lord's day, that practice is pretty well over in this Parish, but not absolutely: I tell them that present themselves to be admitted to Baptism, they must promise they'l spend no more the Lord's day in idleness, and if they do I'l cut them off from the Comunion.

These I most humbly Submit to the judgment of my Superiors whose Commands and instructions I will follow while I live: I see with an incredible joy the fervor of several of those poor Slaves. . . .

[February 19, 1710] . . . We have but one single public house in this vast parish, and hear of no Scandalous doings or at least of any habitual excesses. I have proposed to the Society in some of my former Letters, some difficulties about our joyning unbaptised persons in marriage; about the declaration I caused the baptised Negroes to make that they don't pretend to any freedome from their Masters Service, and will keep to their Wives and about promoting reading among all Slaves; in my last I troubled you with a trifling Narration of the Confusion our best Negroe Scholar was like to Create here among his fellow Slaves for having put his own Construction upon some Words of the Holy Prophet's which he had read; the thing indeed is inconsiderable in itself, but I fear the Consequences. I humbly submit to the Judgment of my Superiors in all Cases. . . .

[June 13, 1710] . . . Permit me to assure My Lord President his Grace, My Lord of London and the Members of the Religious Society of my Obedience, respect & perfect gratitude. The Number of Our families the same 87. Since the 20th Octr. 1709. I baptised 19. among whom 3 Negroe Men; the Constant Number of Communicants 30. or 36, among whom 4 Negroe Men; all the Communicants together are still about 50. because some went to live in other places; Marriages 3; Buryals 2 Children; the Number of Our Negroe Slaves may be near 500. but above 1/3 part of 'em are Children.

Since it has pleased Almighty God to bless me with health I have upon Sundays, after our Divine Service invited the Negroes & Indian Slaves to stay for half an hour, the Invitation to my great Comfort has been joyfully reced by about 50 of 'em; We begin and end Our particular Assembly with the Collect *prevent us O Lord* &c. I teach 'em the Creed, the Lords Prayer, and the Commandments; I explain some portion of the Catechism, I give them an entire Liberty to ask questions, I endeavour to proportion my answers and all my Instructions to their want and Capacity: I must acknowledge that the hand of God dos visibly appear on this particular occasion. I had often attempted and proposed a time, a Method and means easy, as I thought, for the Instruction of those poor Souls, but all in vain, till this last was put in my mind by special mercy, the Most Pious among their Masters stay also and hear; others not so zealous wou'd find fault, if possible, their Murmerings sometimes reach my Ears, but I am not discouraged: The Caution I have taken & which the Society is pleased to approve of, vizt. to do nothing without the

Masters good testimony and consent, is a sufficient answer to them that oppose most the happyness of their Slaves; but the good example of some truely Religious Masters is a Check upon the others, the Alteration is so considerable of late that in general very few Masters excepted, the Slaves shall be fed and provided for by the Masters, and the whole time of the Slaves shall be their Masters; this is what I have continually urged; knowing how idly and criminally the Slaves spent the time given to them to Work for themselves. I bless God for having at last rendered the Masters sensible of their own Advantage in that respect. Four or 6 shall be soon baptised by the Consent of their Masters, and the others with the Children in time, except in danger of death, those Slaves behave themselves very well, and do better for their Masters profit than formerly, for they are taught to serve out of Christian Love & Duty; they tell me openly that they will ever bless God for their knowing good things which they knew not before. The Lord's day is no more profaned by their dancings at least about me: I asked once a pretty ancient and very fine Slave whether he cou'd read, his answer was he wou'd rather choose hereafter to practice the good he could remember. As I had the honour to represent in one of my last Letters the inconveniences which I perceive ... I forbear urging too far the exercise of reading among them leaving to the discretion of their Masters to choose the fitest persons to learn till I receive further Instructions about that point. There are 3. or 4. Portuguese Slaves in this parish very desirous to receive the Communion amongst us; I framed a short Modell of Submission grounded upon some Popish Tenets which they told me of their own Accord, without troubling them with things they know not; I require of them their renouncing of those particular points, the Chief of which is praying to the Saints and that they must not return to the Popish Worship in case they shou'd be sent to Medera again. I gave them that fform of Submission in Writing and left it to their Consideration, they come constantly to Church and are very sensible. I have proposed to some Masters a thing that seems to me very easy to be done and will prevent horrid Crimes and Confusions amongst Negroes and Indian Slaves for the future, that none of those that are not yet marryed presume to do it without his Masters consent, and likewise those that are not Marryed do not part without the like Consent (I know some will transgress) but I hope 'twill do good to many, especially in time to come; This thought of mine I most humbly Submit to the Judgment of the Society to which I will ever yield with the utmost respect. ...

[February 20, 1711/12] ... 2 Marriages. *12* Children Baptised. 2 Adults. 4 Buryals *36* Communicants at Xtmas last among whome 5 new Communicants, and near 60 in the Parish, Children Catechised at a time *10* or *12* in all above 20 Negroes Catechised 40. or *50*. The Mortality that begun to rage in Augt. is not yet over, especialy in Towne where the Commissary has attended with much zeal, and I thank God he has been preserved from dangerous sickness, the number of the White People dead of late in the Province is near *200*, and the slaves as many again, which is a Considble loss for a place, so thin Inhabited we have allso wanted Salt, and Provisions are very scarce chiefly in the Towne where no Body durst go from the Country. The Surgeons are of opinion that the Aire has been infected these 14 Yeares. I look upon a more immediat Cause that is the Irreligion and Lewdness of too many Persons, but chiefly the Barberous usage of the poor Slaves. I endeavour to urge the dutyes of mercy towards them as much as I am able, and I bless God things are upon a better ffoot in that respect about me – but still I am Contradicted by several Masters, but I trust in God these visitations will serve to make them mind better things than worldly advantages –

I have had of late an opportunity to oppose with all my might the putting of a very unhumane Law and in my Judgmt. very unjust it is in Execution, in Relation to run away Negroes, by a Law Enacted in this Province some years before I came; such an Negroe must be mutilated by amputation of Testicles if it be a man, and of Ears if a Woman. I have openly declared against such punishment grounded upon the Law of God, which setts a slave at liberty if he should loose an Eye or a tooth when he is Corrected. Exod. 21. and some good Planters are of my opinion. I must Informe you of a most Cruel Contrivance a man has Invented to punish small faults in slaves. he puts them in a Coffin where they are crushed almost to death, and he keeps them in that hellish Machine for 24 hours commonly with their ffeet Chained out, and a Lid pressing upon their stomack, this is a matter of fact universally knowen, when I look upon the ordinary cause that makes those poor Souls run away, and almost dispaire I find it is imoderate labour and want of Victualls and rest. God Alm: inspire the Honourable Society my most Illustrious Patrons to Consider those things so that they may be remedyed for the Encouragemt. of those poor Creatures. . . .

[December 11, 1712] . . . I thought to have baptized some more Negro Slaves this Advent they are well Instructed and I hear no complaint concerning them. Their Masters Seem very much Averse to my Design, Some of them will not give them Leave to come to Church to learn how to Pray to God & to Serve him, I cannot find any reason for this New Opposition but the Old pretext that Baptism makes the Slaves proud and Undutifull: I endeavour to convince them of the Contrary From the Example of those I have baptized, and Chiefly those who are Admitted to our holy Comunion who behave themselves very well, I humbly ask that if the Society Orders any Thing to be Publisht to Induce the Masters to shew more Charity towards their Slaves I may have some Copies to distribute. . . .

[February 23, 1713] . . . I will not fail to Acquaint the Society with Some Particular Things wch I think it is my Duty to lay before them And I Submit to their wise Consideration & Judgemt. what Afflicts and Discourages me beyond Expression is to see the pious Designes of the Honrble Society very much Obstructed by the rash Conduct of Some of our Inhabitants. I humbly Apprehend That it is Expected the Missionaries should Endeavour to Promote the knowledge of Christ among the Ignorant Heathens begining with the Poor Negroe & Indian Slaves that live in our ffamilies, and Seeking all Opportunites to do good to the free Indians Scattered in the Province till God Gives us meanes to Instruct those Indian Nations that are our Neighbours, Which I firmly hope shall be Accomplished in his own time, But indeed few Masters appear Zealous or even pleased with what the Missionaries try to do for the Good of their Slaves, they are more Cruel Some of them of late Dayes than before, They hamstring maim & unlimb those poor Creatures for Small faults, A man within this Month had a very fine Negroe batized, Sensible Carefull & good in all Respects who being wearyed with Labour & fallen asleep had the Mischance to loose a parcell of Rice wch by the Oversetting of a Periogua fell into a River. The man tho Intreated by the Minister of the Parish, who is Brother Maule and some Persons of the best Consideration among us to forgive the Negroe, who had Offended only through Neglect without Malice, thought fit to keep him for several Dayes in Chains, & I am told muffled up that he might not Eat, & Scourge him twice a Day, and at Night to put him into a hellish Machine contrived by him into the Shape of a Coffin where could not Stirr, The punishmt having continued Several Dayes & Nights and there being no Appearance when it should End, the poor Negroe through Despair Ask't one of his Children for a knife & manacled as he was Stabb'd himself with it; I am told this is the 5th Slave that Same man has destroyed by his Cruelty within 2 or 3 Yeares, but he is onely an hired Overseer the Owner of the Slaves lives out of this Province, I own I See everybody almost angry at So much Barbarity, Yet he pretends to go to Church, and they look upon the Man as Guilty of Murder, and So do great many of my Acquaintance who tho not So Barbarous take no Care at all of the Souls of their Slaves, and as little as the[y] can of their bodies I am at a loss when I see them in a praying posture knowing that at the same time they do not love their Neighbour, and what is most Amazeing I cannot make them Comprehend that their Neglect is an habitual state of Sin, I have Seen very Severe Judgemts. Since I came, Nothing Else almost but Judgemts. . . .

*A Narrative of the Life and Adventures of Venture,
a Native of Africa, but Resident above Sixty Years
in the United States of America (1700s)*

Venture Smith

Chapter I. Containing an Account of His Life, From His Birth to the Time of His Leaving His Native Country

I was born at Dukandarra, in Guinea, about the year 1729. My father's name was Saungm Furro, Prince of the tribe of Dukandarra. My father had three wives. Polygamy was not uncommon in that country, especially among the rich, as every man was allowed to keep as many wives as he could maintain. By his first wife he had three children. The eldest of them was myself, named by my father, Broteer. The other two were named Cundazo and Soozaduka. My father had two children by his second wife, and one by his third. I descended from a very large, tall and stout race of beings, much larger than the generality of people in other parts of the globe, being commonly considerable above six feet in height, and every way well proportioned. . . .

Before I dismiss [my] country, I must first inform my reader what I remember concerning this place. A large river runs through this country in a westerly course. The land for a great way on each side is flat and level, hedged in by a considerable rise in the country at a great distance from it. It scarce ever rains there, yet the land is fertile; great dews fall in the night which refresh the soil. About the latter end of June or first of July, the river begins to rise, and gradually increases until it has inundated the country for a great distance, to the height of seven or eight feet. This brings on a slime which enriches the land surprisingly. When the river has subsided, the natives begin to sow and plant, and the vegetation is exceeding rapid. Near this rich river my guardian's land lay. He possessed, I cannot exactly tell how much, yet this I am certain of respecting it, that he owned an immense tract. He possessed likewise a great many cattle and goats. During my stay with him I was kindly used, and with as much tenderness, for what I saw, as his only son, although I was an entire stranger to him, remote from friends and relatives. The principal occupations of the inhabitants there were the cultivation of the soil and the care of their flocks. They were a people pretty similar in every respect to that of mine, except in their persons, which were not so tall and stout. They appeared to be very kind and friendly. I will now return to my departure from that place.

My father sent a man and horse after me. After settling with my guardian for keeping me, he took me away and went for home. It was then about one year since my mother brought me here. Nothing remarkable occurred to us on our journey until we arrived safe home. I found then that the difference between my parents had been made up previous to their sending for me. On my return, I was received both by my father and mother with great joy and affection, and was once more restored to my paternal dwelling in peace and happiness. I was then about six years old.

Not more than six weeks had passed after my return, before a message was brought by an inhabitant of the place where I lived the preceding year to my father, that that place had been invaded by a numerous army, from a nation not far distant, furnished with musical instruments, and all kinds of arms then in use; that they were instigated by some white nation who equipped and sent them to subdue and possess the country; that his nation had made no preparation for war, having been for a long time in profound peace; that they could not defend themselves against such a formidable train of invaders, and must, therefore, necessarily evacuate their lands to the fierce enemy, and fly to the protection of some chief; and that if he would permit them they would come under his rule and protection when they had to retreat from their own possessions. He was a kind and merciful prince, and therefore consented to these proposals.

He had scarcely returned to his nation with the message before the whole of his people were obliged to retreat from their country and come to my father's dominions. He gave them every privilege and all the protection his government could afford. But they had not been there longer than four days before news came to them that the invaders had laid waste their country, and were coming speedily to destroy them in my father's territories. This affrighted them, and therefore they immediately pushed off to the southward, into the unknown countries there, and were never more heard of.

Two days after their retreat, the report turned out to be but too true. A detachment from the enemy came to my father and informed him that the whole army was encamped not far from his dominions, and would invade the territory and deprive his people of their liberties and rights, if he did not comply with the following terms. These were, to pay them a large sum of money, three hundred fat cattle, and a great number of goats, sheep, asses, etc.

My father told the messenger he would comply rather than that his subjects should be deprived of their rights and privileges, which he was not then in circumstances to defend from so sudden an invasion. Upon turning out those articles, the enemy pledged their faith and honor that they would not attack him. On these he relied, and therefore thought it unnecessary to be on his guard against the enemy. But their pledges of faith and honor proved no better than those of other unprincipled hostile nations, for a few days after, a certain relation of the king came and informed him that the enemy who sent terms of accommodation to him, and received tribute to their satisfaction, yet meditated an attack upon his subjects by surprise, and that probably they would commence their attack in less than one day, and concluded with advising him, as he was not prepared for war, to order a speedy retreat of his family and subjects. He complied with this advice.

The same night which was fixed upon to retreat, my father and his family set off about the break of day. The king and his two younger wives went in one company, and my mother and her children in another. We left our dwellings in succession, and my father's company went on first. We directed our course for a large shrub plain, some distance off, where we intended to conceal ourselves from the approaching enemy, until we could refresh ourselves a little. But we presently found that our retreat was not secure. For having struck up a little fire for the purpose of cooking victuals, the enemy, who happened to be encamped a little distance off, had sent out a scouting party who discovered us by the smoke of the fire, just as we were extinguishing it and about to eat. As soon as we had finished eating, my father discovered the party and immediately began to discharge arrows at them. This was what I first saw, and it alarmed both me and the women, who, being unable to make any resistance, immediately betook ourselves to the tall, thick reeds not far off, and left the old king to fight alone. For some time I beheld him from the reeds defending himself with great courage and firmness, till at last he was obliged to surrender himself into their hands.

They then came to us in the reeds, and the very first salute I had from them was a violent blow on the head with the fore part of a gun, and at the same time a grasp round the neck. I then had a rope put about my neck, as had all the women in the thicket with me, and were immediately led to my father, who was likewise pinioned and haltered for leading. In this condition we were all led to the camp. The women and myself, being submissive, had tolerable treatment from the enemy, while my father was closely interrogated respecting his money, which they knew he must have. But as he gave them no account of it, he was instantly cut and pounded on his body with great inhumanity, that he might be induced by the torture he suffered to make the discovery. All this availed not in the least to make him give up his money, but he despised all the tortures which they inflicted, until the continued exercise and increase of torment obliged him to sink and expire. He thus died without informing his enemies where his money lay. I saw him while he was thus tortured to death. The shocking scene is to this day fresh in my memory, and I have often been overcome while thinking on it. He was a man of remarkable stature. I should judge as much as six feet and six or seven inches high, two feet across the shoulders, and every way well proportioned. He was a man of remarkable strength and resolution, affable, kind and gentle, ruling with equity and moderation.

The army of the enemy was large, I should suppose consisting of about six thousand men. Their leader was called Baukurre. After destroying the old prince, they decamped and immediately marched towards the sea, lying to the west, taking with them myself and the women prisoners. In the march, a scouting party was detached from the main army. To the leader of this party I was made waiter, having to carry his gun, etc. As we were a-scouting, we came across a herd of fat cattle consisting of about thirty in number. These we set upon and immediately wrested from their keepers, and afterwards converted them into food for the army. The enemy had remarkable success in destroying the country wherever they went. For as far as they had penetrated they laid the habitations waste and captured the people. The distance they had now brought me was about four hundred miles. All the march I had very hard tasks imposed on me, which I must perform on pain of punishment. I was obliged to carry on my head a large flat stone used for grinding our corn, weighing, as I should suppose, as much as twenty-five pounds; besides victuals, mat and cooking utensils. Though I was pretty large and stout of my age, yet these burdens were very grievous to me, being only six years and a half old.

We were then come to a place called Malagasco. When we entered the place, we could not see the least appearance of either houses or inhabitants, but on stricter search found that instead of houses above ground they had dens in the sides of hillocks, contiguous to ponds and streams of water. In these we perceived they had all hid themselves, as I suppose they usually did on such occasions. In order to compel them to surrender, the enemy contrived to smoke them out with faggots. These they put to the entrance of the caves and set them on fire. While they were engaged in this business, to their great surprise some of them were desperately wounded with arrows which fell from above on them. This mystery they soon found out. They perceived that the enemy discharged these arrows through holes on the top of the dens directly into the air. Their weight brought them back, point downwards, on their enemies' heads, whilst they were smoking the inhabitants out. The points of their arrows were poisoned, but their enemy had an antidote for it which they instantly applied to the wounded part. The smoke at last obliged the people to give themselves up. They came out of their caves, first spatting the palms of their hands together, and immediately after extended their arms, crossed at their wrists, ready to be bound and pinioned. I should judge that the dens above mentioned were extended about eight feet horizontally into the earth, six feet in height, and as many wide. They were arched overhead and lined with earth, which was of the clay kind and made the surface of their walls firm and smooth.

The invaders then pinioned the prisoners of all ages and sexes indiscriminately, took their flocks and all their effects, and moved on their way towards the sea. On the march, the prisoners were treated with clemency, on account of their being submissive and humble. Having come to the next tribe, the enemy laid siege and immediately took men, women, children, flocks, and all their valuable effects. They then went on to the next district, which was contiguous to the sea, called in Africa, Anamaboo. The enemies' provisions were then almost spent, as well as their strength. The inhabitants, knowing what conduct they had pursued, and what were their present intentions, improved the favorable opportunity, attacked them, and took enemy, prisoners, flocks and all their effects. I was then taken a second time. All of us were then put into the castle and kept for market. On a certain time, I and other prisoners were put on board a canoe, under our master, and rowed away to a vessel belonging to Rhode Island, commanded by Captain Collingwood, and the mate, Thomas Mumford. While we were going to the vessel, our master told us to appear to the best possible advantage for sale. I was bought on board by one Robertson Mumford, steward of said vessel, for four gallons of rum and a piece of calico, and called VENTURE, on account of his having purchased me with his own private venture. Thus I came by my name. All the slaves that were bought for that vessel's cargo were two hundred and sixty.

Chapter II. Containing an Account of His Life from the Time of His Leaving Africa to That of His Becoming Free

The first of the time of living at my master's own place,[1] I was pretty much employed in the house, carding wool and other household business. In this situation I continued for some years, after which my master put me to work out of doors. After many proofs of my faithfulness and honesty, my master began to put great confidence in me. My behavior had as yet been submissive and obedient. I then began to have hard tasks imposed on me. Some of these were to pound four bushels of ears of corn every night in a barrel for the poultry, or be rigorously punished. At other seasons of the year, I had to card wool until a very late hour. These tasks I had to perform when only about nine years old. Some time after, I had another difficulty and oppression which was greater than any I had ever experienced since I came into this country. This was to serve two masters. James Mumford, my master's son, when his father had gone from home in the morning and given me a stint to perform that day, would order me to do *this* and *that* business different from what my master had directed me. One day in particular, the authority which my master's son had set up had like to have produced melancholy effects. For my master having set me off my business to perform that day and then left me to perform it, his son came up to me in the course of the day, big with authority, and commanded me very arrogantly to quit my present business and go directly about what he should order me. I replied to him that my master had given me so much to perform that day, and that I must faithfully complete it in that time. He then broke out into a great rage, snatched a pitchfork and went to lay me over the head therewith, but I as soon got another and defended myself with it, or otherwise he might have murdered me in his outrage. He immediately called some people who were within hearing at work for him, and ordered them to take his hair rope and come and bind me with it. They all tried to bind me, but in vain, though there were three assistants in number. My upstart master then desisted, put his pocket handkerchief before his eyes and went home with a design to tell his mother of the struggle with young VENTURE. He told that their young VENTURE had become so stubborn that he could not control him, and asked her what he should do with him. In the meantime I recovered my temper, voluntarily caused myself to be bound by the same men who tried in vain before, and carried before my young master, that he might do what he pleased with me. He took me to a gallows made for the purpose of hanging cattle on, and suspended me on it. Afterwards he ordered one of his hands to go to the peach orchard and cut him three dozen of whips to punish me with. These were brought to him, and that was all that was done with them, as I was released and went to work after hanging on the gallows about an hour.

After I had lived with my master thirteen years, being then about twenty-two years old, I married Meg, a slave of his who was about my own age. . . . At the close of that year I was sold to a Thomas Stanton, and had to be separated from my wife and one daughter, who was about one month old. He resided at Stonington Point. To this place I brought with me from my late master's, two johannes, three old Spanish dollars, and two thousand of coppers, beside five pounds of my wife's money. This money I got by cleaning gentlemen's shoes and drawing-boots, by catching muskrats and minks, raising potatoes and carrots, etc., and by fishing in the night, and at odd spells. . . .[2]

Towards the close of the time that I resided with this master, I had a falling out with my mistress. This happened one time when my master was gone to Long Island a-gunning. At first the quarrel began between my wife and her mistress. I was then at work in the barn, and hearing a racket in the house, induced me to run there and see what had broken out. When I entered the house, I found my mistress in a violent passion with my wife, for what she informed me was a mere trifle – such a small affair that I forbear to put my mistress to the shame of having it known. I earnestly requested my wife to beg pardon of her mistress for the sake of peace, even if she had given no just occasion for offence. But whilst I was thus saying, my mistress turned the blows which she was repeating on my wife to me. She took down her horse whip, and while she was glutting her fury with it, I reached out my great black hand, raised it up and received the blows of the whip on it which were designed for my head. Then I immediately committed the whip to the devouring fire.

When my master returned from the island, his wife told him of the affair, but for the present he seemed to take no notice of it, and mentioned not a word of it to me. Some days after his return, in the morning as I was putting on a log in the fireplace, not suspecting harm from any one, I received a most violent stroke on the crown of my head with a club two feet long and as large around as a chair post. This blow very badly wounded my head, and the scar of it remains to this day. The first blow made me have my wits about me you may suppose, for as soon as he went to renew it I snatched the club out of his hands and dragged him out of the door. He then sent for his brother to come and assist him, but I presently left my master, took the club he wounded me with, carried it to a neighboring justice of the peace, and complained of my master. He finally advised me to return to my master and live contented with him till he abused me again, and then complain. I consented to do accordingly. But before I set out for my master's, up he came and his brother Robert after me. The Justice improved this convenient opportunity to caution my master. He asked him for what he treated his slave thus hastily and unjustly, and told him what would be the consequence if he continued the same treatment towards me. After the justice had ended his discourse with my master, he and his brother set out with me for home, one before and the other behind me. When they had come to a by-place, they both dismounted their respective horses and fell to beating me with great violence. I became enraged at this and immediately turned them both under me, laid one of them across the other, and stamped them both with my feet what I would.

This occasioned my master's brother to advise him to put me off. A short time after this, I was taken by a constable and two men. They carried me to a blacksmith's shop and had me handcuffed. When I returned home my mistress enquired much of her waiters whether VENTURE was handcuffed. When she was informed that I was, she appeared to be very contented and was much transported with the news. In the midst of this content and joy, I presented myself before my mistress, showed her my handcuffs, and gave her thanks for my gold rings. For this my master commanded a negro of his to fetch him a large ox chain. This my master locked on my legs with two padlocks. I continued to wear the chain peaceably for two or three days, when my master asked me with contemptuous hard names whether I had not better be freed from my chains and go to work. I answered him, "No." "Well, then," said he, "I will send you to the West Indies, or banish you, for I am resolved not to keep you." I answered him, "I crossed the waters to come here and I am willing to cross them to return."

For a day or two after this not anyone said much to me, until one Hempstead Miner of Stonington asked me if I would live with him. I answered that I would. He then requested me to make myself discontented and to appear as unreconciled to my master as I could before that he bargained with him for me, and that in return he would give me a good chance to gain my freedom when I came to live with him. I did as he requested me. Not long after, Hempstead Miner purchased me of my master for fifty-six pounds lawful. He took the chain and padlocks from off me immediately after. . . .

[At Age 31, Venture Is Sold to Colonel Smith.]

As I never had an opportunity of redeeming myself whilst I was owned by Miner, though he promised to give me a chance, I was then very ambitious of obtaining it. I asked my master one time if he would consent to have me purchase my freedom. He replied that he would. . . .

The next summer I again desired he would give me a chance of going to work. But he refused and answered that he must have my labor this summer, as he did not have it the past winter. I replied that I considered it as hard that I could not have a chance to work out when the season became advantageous, and that I must only be permitted to hire myself out in the poorest season of the year. He asked me after this what I would give him for the privilege per month. I replied that I would leave it wholly to his own generosity to determine what I should return him a month. Well then, said he, if so, two pounds a month. I answered him that if that was the least he would take I would be contented.

Accordingly I hired myself out at Fisher's Island, earning twenty pounds; thirteen pounds six shillings of which my master drew for the privilege and the remainder I paid for my freedom. This made fifty-one pounds two shillings which I paid him. In October following I went and wrought six months at Long Island. In that six month's time I cut and corded four hundred cords of wood, besides threshing out seventy-five bushels of grain, and received of my wages down only twenty pounds, which left remaining a larger sum. Whilst I was out that time, I took up on my wages only one pair of shoes. At night I lay on the hearth, with one coverlet over and another under me. I returned to my master and gave him what I received of my six months' labor. This left only thirteen pounds eighteen shillings to make up the full sum of my redemption. My master liberated me, saying that I might pay what was behind if I could ever make it convenient, otherwise it would be well. The amount of the money which I had paid my master towards redeeming my time, was seventy-one pounds two shillings. The reason of my master for asking such an unreasonable price, was, he said, to secure himself in case I should ever come to want. Being thirty-six years old, I left Colonel Smith once more for all. I had already been sold three different times, made considerable money with seemingly nothing to derive it from, had been cheated out of a large sum of money, lost much by misfortunes, and paid an enormous sum for my freedom.

Notes

1 Captain George Mumford and his family lived on Fisher's Island, off the coast of Connecticut.
2 After a year and a half, Thomas Stanton purchased Venture's wife and daughter.

Further Reading

Berlin, Ira, *Many Thousands Gone: The First Two Centuries of Slavery in North America*. Cambridge, MA: Harvard University Press, 1998.
Gomez, Michael A., *Exchanging Our Country Marks: The Transformation of African Identities in the Colonial and Antebellum South*. Chapel Hill: University of North Carolina Press, 1998.
Landers, Jane, *Black Society in Spanish Florida*. Urbana: University of Illinois Press, 1999.
Morgan, Philip D., *Slave Counterpoint: Black Culture in the Eighteenth-century Chesapeake and Lowcountry*. Chapel Hill: University of North Carolina Press, 1998.
Mullin, Michael, *Africa in America: Slave Acculturation and Resistance in the American South and the British Caribbean, 1736–1831*. Urbana: University of Illinois Press, 1992.

Olwell, Robert, *Masters, Slaves, and Subjects: The Culture of Power in the South Carolina Low Country, 1740–1790*. Ithaca: Cornell University Press, 1998.

Piersen, William, *Black Yankees: The Development of an Afro-American Subculture in Eighteenth-century New England*. Amherst: University of Massachusetts Press, 1988.

Thornton, John, *Africa and Africans in the Making of the Atlantic World, 1400–1680*, 2nd edn. New York: Cambridge University Press, 1998.

European Immigration

Introduction

The movement of people across the Atlantic to the Americas is, as Bernard Bailyn points out, one of the most significant phenomena in the history of the modern world. His essay focuses on European immigration to Britain's North American colonies. This flow of people proceeded throughout the colonial period, its sources, destinations, and magnitude shifting as local conditions changed in both Europe and America. Prior to 1700, approximately 80 percent of the population of the mainland colonies originated in England and Wales; another 11 percent was African in origin. Just fifty-five years later, England and Wales accounted for barely half the colonial population, the proportion of Africans had increased to about 20 percent, and migrants from other parts of Europe and the British Isles had grown substantially in numbers. Colonists of Scottish and Irish origin together accounted for about 16 percent of the colonies' people, while Germans – most of them concentrated in Pennsylvania, Maryland, and Virginia – made up about 7 percent of the population. Overall numbers also increased dramatically in this period, from about 100,000 in 1700 to 2 million in 1770.

The dramatic growth and diversification of the colonial population after 1700 depended upon three preconditions: there had to be "push factors" encouraging prospective emigrants to leave their homes; there had to be a strong demand for laborers and settlers in the colonies; and there had to be a network of transatlantic shippers and merchants capable of organizing the transportation of large numbers of immigrants, coming not just from London and Bristol but also from the north of England, Scotland, and Ireland, from European ports like Rotterdam, and from the growing slave-trading outposts of West Africa. Bailyn's essay distinguishes between two broad emigration streams out of the British Isles. The first, centered in London (the *metropolitan* pattern), carried primarily single young men to the colonies to serve as indentured servants. Most went to Pennsylvania, Maryland, and Virginia. The second stream, which originated in the north of England and in Scotland (the *provincial* pattern), brought mostly free families to areas where newly opened farmlands were available on reasonable terms. Bailyn notes that the vast process of transatlantic immigration is made up of countless *local* stories, that broad patterns can be broken down into an almost endless number of tales about individuals, communities, and localities that can only be understood through careful study.

The experiences of individuals who immigrated to North America varied widely. It has been estimated that over half of all European migrants to the British colonies came as indentured servants. William Moraley (document 1), like many of his fellow migrants, signed an indenture contract before he left England that committed him to four years of service to a master. Technically, therefore, he arrived in Philadelphia an unfree man. Yet his experiences in the colony belie his status as a bound servant. What aspects of his story seem especially surprising or unlikely given his status? Certainly Moraley's experience was not typical, yet it reminds us that the scarcity of labor in the colonies sometimes allowed even indentured servants to enjoy remarkably good working and living conditions.

Others suffered great hardships. Gottlieb Mittelberger was a free German migrant to Pennsylvania – he had enough money to pay for his own passage –

but he traveled on a boat with many indentured servants. The conditions of their voyage were so appalling that he wrote a book pleading with his fellow Germans *not* to come to America (document 2). What experiences in this account seem most surprising to you? Compare the motives of Moraley and Mittelberger as authors. What goals did each have in mind, and how might those goals have influenced the stories they tell?

A substantial number of immigrants came as free families, especially from northern England and Scotland. The final document (document 3) is taken from a tract promoting settlement in North Carolina to prospective settlers. What "push" factors does the author identify that might lead a family to leave Scotland? What "pull" factors might attract such migrants to North Carolina?

Worlds in Motion

Bernard Bailyn

I would like to introduce my subject with a flight of fancy. I would like to imagine a satellite circling the globe from the early medieval period to the advent of industrialism, equipped with a camera of perfect accuracy, a camera capable of scanning vast areas in a single sweep and yet of focusing on the smallest region or community at any point of time. I want to imagine that this circling eye could bring together into a single view groups, individuals, and places scattered over hundreds, even thousands, of miles and over decades, even centuries of time, and that it could catch not only the outward appearance of people, their physical movements, and their palpable way of life, but also their interior experiences, the quality of their culture, the capacity of their minds, the patterns of their emotions.

With such a camera, one could grasp the essence of historical change, the evanescence that is the heart and soul of history, and the elusive ambiguity of historical movement. But what, from that vantage point, would impress one as the most sweeping and striking development in this millennium of Western history? The most visible physically, I think, would be deforestation and the extension of arable land. Less visible but equally striking would be the breakup of Christian unity and, even more striking, the forming of nation states, with all the political, administrative, military, and ideological consequences that flowed from that development. Yet I do not think these would be the only transformations that would impress a cosmic eye surveying pre-industrial Western history.

Running through these famous, world-historical developments, and accelerating, with occasional setbacks, for a thousand years, was a more elemental development, a movement of another dimension altogether and one that is more difficult to isolate and describe.

I do not know when it began – sometime in the early Middle Ages. It moved forward with varying speeds for several hundred years; was thrown back for a century or more after the first third of the fourteenth century; took a sudden lurch forward in the sixteenth century; slowed in the mid-seventeenth century; then sped precipitately ahead in the later seventeenth century to form in the eighteenth and nineteenth centuries a mighty flow that transformed at first half the globe, ultimately the whole of it, more fundamentally than any development except the Industrial Revolution. This transforming phenomenon was the movement of people outward from their original centers of habitation – the centrifugal *Völkerwanderungen* that involved an untraceable multitude of local, small-scale exoduses and colonizations, the continuous creation of new frontiers and ever-widening circumferences, the complex intermingling of peoples in the expanding border areas, and in the end the massive transfer to the Western Hemisphere of people from Africa, from the European mainland, and above all from the Anglo-Celtic offshore islands of Europe, culminating in what Bismarck called "the decisive fact in the modern world," the peopling of the North American continent.[1]

The westward transatlantic movement of people is one of the greatest events in recorded history. Its magnitudes and consequences are beyond measure. From 1500 to the present, it has involved the displacement and resettlement of over fifty million people, and it has affected indirectly the lives of uncountable millions more. It forms the foundation of American history and is basic, too, in ways we are only now beginning to understand, to the history of Europe, Africa, and even, to a lesser extent, of Asia.

This massive, global movement of people to North America and their settlement in new communities on that continent have of course attracted the attention of historians since American social history has been written. But the first, formative stage of this story – from the beginnings until the Industrial Revolution – only now, I believe, comes into sharp focus as a central historical theme: which is no criticism of the historians who have described aspects of the story as it has heretofore been seen. For scholarship proceeds dialectically; new lines of force develop to overcome deficiencies that only become visible in the wake of successful solutions to earlier deficiencies. And the outlines of such a very large subject as this come into a new configuration only at a peculiar conjunction of emerging lines of research.

Such a configuration is now taking shape, I believe, within the present creative ferment of scholarship in early American history – a wealth of research and writing concentrated on a relatively short period of time that is perhaps unique in western historiography. Books and articles on the first two centuries of European life in North America appear in a constant flow, some framed by narrowly conceived disputes with previous writers, some concluding in portentous generalities that take no account of other, similarly derived conclusions, but almost all containing new details, new information. There is an extraordinary richness in the current scholarship of this traditional field of study, and also a great confusion in understanding.

The profusion and the disarray in early American history are partly the result of the sheer number of historians at work in the field. They are partly, too, the result of the fact that the subject is inevitably a battleground for general notions of the "meaning" of American life. And they are also the result of the influence of European scholarship of the same period, which has stimulated a wide array of comparative or parallel studies in American history, unintegrated into the structure of the subject as a whole. But the main reason for the disarray, I think, is simply that the sheer amount of accumulated information has overwhelmed the effective organizing principles, the major themes or interpretative structures, that have heretofore contained it. And consequently what is most urgently needed is not, at the moment, more technical studies but a fresh look at the whole story, and a general interpretation or set of related interpretations that draws together the great mass of available material – literary and statistical, new and old, local and cosmopolitan; that links latent with manifest events; and that provides a framework for a comprehensive, developmental narrative of early American history.

"The Peopling of British North America" – itself but a small segment of the saga of Western man's restless expansion across the globe – seems to contain within it the materials for one such unifying theme. The title itself is familiar, but in the context of the entire range of presently available information it takes on new meaning. It brings together the major aspects of life in the American colonies – social structure and settlement patterns, demography and politics, agriculture and religion, mobility, family organization, and ethnic relations – and places the whole evolving story of American life within the broadest possible context of Western history. "Peopling" means recruitment, emigration, and immigration, hence the whole world of overseas migration associated with the scholarship of Marcus Lee Hansen and Oscar Handlin. It implies settlement, the opening up and uses of land, mobility, and the frontier, hence the world of Frederick Jackson Turner updated by two generations of historians, most recently by the younger historical geographers, Carville

Earle, R. Cole Harris, James Lemon, D. W. Meinig, H. Roy Merrens, and Robert Mitchell. But it implies, too, the mingling and clashing of diverse groups and races, the evolution of social patterns, of community and family organization, population characteristics – the whole world of cultural-anthropological, social-structural, and demographic history which lies scattered in hundreds of books and articles written over the past quarter century by scholars in several disciplines pursuing separate paths of inquiry.

"Peopling" means motion, process, evolution in time, but it is not abstract: it concentrates on individuals and their fortunes. And it enlarges the perspective of early American history to the broadest possible range. For the transatlantic crossings and settlements of the colonial years were but the middle links in immense chains of related displacements and adjustments. From the jagged, wind-swept Butt of Lewis on the far northern tip of the Outer Hebrides to the Lunda kingdom deep in equatorial Africa, from Prussia south to the Danube, and from the Elbe to the Mississippi, tens of thousands of people were moving over great distances, to resettle in the alien environment of the North American seaboard communities and then to help open to initial cultivation millions of acres in the wilderness to the west. It was the greatest population movement in early modern history, and yet, despite all the recent writing on early American history, our understanding of this great westward transfer of people is a blur, lacking in structure, scale, and detail. We know only in the vaguest way who the hundreds of thousands of individuals who settled in British North America were, where precisely they came from, why they came, and how they lived out their lives. The few patches of concrete information we have bring out by contrast the vastness of our general ignorance.

The most extensive run of detailed information about any large group of immigrants in the colonial period was produced just before the Revolution by the British government, responding to fears that the mass exodus to America then under way would depopulate the realm. Such fears were exaggerated, but they were by no means ridiculous. The migration to America in the fifteen years between the end of the Seven Years War and the Revolution was remarkable by the standards of the time. Between the end of warfare in the mainland colonies and the disruption of the empire in 1775, over 55,000 Protestant Irish emigrated to America, over 40,000 Scots, and over 30,000 Englishmen – a total of approximately 125,000 from the British Isles – in addition to at least 12,000 immigrants from the German states and Switzerland who entered the port of Philadelphia, and 84,500 enslaved Africans imported to the southern mainland colonies. This grand total of about 221,500 arrivals in the fifteen-year period (a conservative figure, yet almost 10 percent of the entire estimated population of mainland America in 1775) meant an average *annual* influx of approximately 15,000 people, which was close to the total estimated population of Boston during these years; and, except for the slaves, the great majority of these tens of thousands of newcomers crowded initially into a few small port towns, almost all of them south of New England.[2]

It is therefore not at all surprising that landlords in Britain were becoming apprehensive and that pressure was exerted on the government to do something decisive to resolve the problem. By the fall of 1773, as I have elsewhere explained, it was generally believed that Parliament was considering a bill to ban all emigration to North America. The mere rumor touched off widespread debate on the legality and wisdom of such a move. Questions of national identity, of the relation of subjectship to geographical location, and of the legitimate limits of governmental power, all were discussed in newspaper columns, pamphlets, and local provincial meetings. Benjamin Franklin, then in London, wrote a carefully argued piece denouncing the contemplated legislation. And internal memoranda on the subject within the government moved the heavy inertia of the state closer to the point of action. In the end, faced with opposition and legal uncertainties, the government decided to postpone action until it knew more of the facts involved. And so, on December 9, 1773, the Treasury ordered the customs officers in England and Scotland to record the "name, age, quality, occupation, employment, and former residence" of every person leaving Great Britain for the colonies, and to register each individual's destination and reasons for leaving. The resulting data were forwarded to the Treasury, where an officer was assigned the task of scrutinizing and refining the information, and entering it in a single large workbook.

This was a pre-statistical age, and the data are faulty in many ways. In all, 9,364 permanent emigrants from Britain to the Western Hemisphere were entered on the books between December 1773 and March 1776, but comparison with newspaper notices of ship arrivals and studies of passenger lists reveal an underregistration of between 15 and 30 percent. And the Scottish records, though they contain some of the most interesting information the officials recorded, were particularly deficient in coverage. Yet, though faulty, and though they relate only to England and Scotland, these are the most detailed transatlantic migration records we have for the eighteenth century, and they are extremely revealing.

Results of computer analysis of these records form a sketch of essential characteristics. A few are predictable: the youth of these British emigrants to mainland North America (over half were under twenty-five; over a quarter between the ages of twenty and twenty-four); the unbalanced sex distribution (three out of four were male); their legal status (almost half were indentured servants or redemptioners). While almost a third traveled in family groups, very few of the families included servants of any kind. As to their geographical origins, just under a third came from London and the six Home Counties of south-eastern England; almost a quarter of the total came from metropolitan London itself. On the other hand, two-fifths of the entire group came from Scotland, and the majority of the Scots came from the Highlands and the northern and western islands.

These are gross figures for the recorded migration as a whole – informative but in themselves not very surprising, and difficult to fit together into a meaningful pattern. The more significant figures are masked by these overall totals, and emerge only from successive stages of computer analysis. In the end, the picture as a whole proves to be highly differentiated. This was no singular migration from the British Isles to North America but two separate, quite distinctive processes in motion at the same time, distinctive not only sociologically and econom-ically but geographically as well. One consisted of emigrants who trav-eled outward to America from the main population center of Britain in the Thames Valley; the other group was drawn from the northern British provinces. The differences form a spectrum stretching in continuous gradations from the urban concentration of London, north across the Midlands, and into the northern counties and Scotland. At the extrem-ities – London on the one hand, Yorkshire and the Scottish Highlands on the other – there are two distinctive patterns; the former may be desig-nated *metropolitan*, the latter *provincial*. And these differences profoundly shaped the way these emigrants would enter into American life and the impact they would have in the new land.

The *metropolitan* pattern, which characterizes the central migration from the Thames Valley, is typified by a young man, in his early twenties, acting individually. He is not, usually, drawn from among London's most desperate, destitute slum dwellers; nor is he from the more stable or substantial segments of the population. He is, rather, an impecunious young artisan or craftsman who has served all or some part of his apprenticeship, or in a less formal way learned something of a trade, has found employment irregular or nonexistent, and, without prospects, still unmarried and without family encumbrances, has decided to head out to the colonies alone. In doing so, whether to preserve a small modicum of savings for settlement in the new land or out of sheer necessity, he has assumed a burden of debt for his transportation, to be paid off by four years of bonded labor. There are few children of either sex in this metropolitan migration, few women, and few families. The families that can be found are of the simplest possible structure – almost all of them only husband and wife or siblings traveling together.

In economic terms the typical metropolitan emigrant, though un-
bound by family ties or responsibilities, was not autonomous. Committed, typically, to four years of bonded servitude in the colonies, he was
highly responsive to the needs of the labor market – indeed, he had no
choice but to be absolutely responsive to the market in the particular
corner of the colonial economy in which he found himself. Vigorous and
at least in some minor way skilled in the productive work of the pre-
industrial economy, these emigrants were bound to contribute to its
productivity yet were prevented for four years from drawing personal
gain from it, hence limited in their consumption for that period. And
their natural contribution to population growth was also delayed for the
period of their servitude, hence significantly diminished.

Such is the "ideal type" of the metropolitan emigrant. At the other
extreme there is a different pattern altogether. In this provincial pattern
the characteristic unit is not, as in the metropolitan migration, an isolated male worker in his early twenties, a bondsman for several years of
unlimited servitude. It is, rather, a family, and a family that contains not
only mature women but also small children, including a remarkable
number of young girls. There are 7 males for every female in the metropolitan migration, but only 1.6 males for every female in the provincial.
The size of these families emigrating from northern England and Scotland is surprising. The average was almost as large as the average English
family in the non-emigrating population, and hence it would appear that
these family units of the English population were moving essentially
intact. Consistent with this fact is the economic condition of these
migrating families. There are relatively few indentured servants among
these provincial emigrants, even among those who were traveling alone
and were in their early twenties. There would appear to have been a
sufficient mobilization of resources among these families and individuals
to permit freedom of movement without the severe encumbrance of
bonded servitude. In one way or another – often by liquidating all their
possessions, real and personal – they had raised enough, often just
enough, funds to retain their freedom.

The provincial emigration was predominantly the transfer of farming
families that were still in process of growth, hence likely to contribute
quickly to the increase of the American population. And they would
contribute quickly, too, to the growth of the American economy, not
only by their constructive enterprise but by the demand they created, the
markets they enlarged, as consumers. Above all, they were eager to take
advantage from the start of opportunities created by the opening up of
new land in America. They were likely to seek out new settlements and
to move into the most attractive areas available in the backcountry.
They, and not the many isolated emigrants bound in indentures to

serve any master who could buy their services, were destined to be the frontiersmen in this new segment of the American population.

So much emerges clearly from the computer analysis of the customs register of emigrants of 1773–1776. But questions abound. Why did *families* leave from the northern countries and Scotland but not from the Thames Valley and the southeast generally, which in the seventeenth century had been the center of family emigrations? And why, within the northern provinces, did some families leave but not others? Is there a pattern to the immediate precipitation of decision to uproot oneself or one's family? And the questions multiply when one looks even casually at the pattern of destinations. The metropolitan migrants went mainly to a contiguous group of mid-Atlantic colonies: Pennsylvania, Maryland, and Virginia. The provincial migrants went heavily, overwhelmingly, to others: Nova Scotia, New York, and North Carolina. Why? Half of all the indentured servants and two-fifths of all the English emigrants went to the single colony of Maryland, in whose histories there is no indication that amid the political tumult of the years 1774 and 1775 approximately 2,300 immigrants (minus deaths in passage) from Britain alone (we do not know how many from elsewhere), crowded into the colony's ports and were somehow distributed along the wagon and river routes into the countryside. Why Maryland? And why was Yorkshire in particular exporting people in such numbers over such great distances? The questions arise from the computer printouts like a cloud of gnats, and one wishes one were alone, as of old, with a few literary documents that might be analyzed exhaustively, if impressionistically, down to the last syllable.

Similar questions can be asked of all of the nonslave westward-bound emigrants to North America. An estimated 10 percent of the pre-Revolutionary population was German-speaking. Why did some Germans feel impelled to leave their native villages, but not others, their immediate neighbors in apparently identical situations? About 500,000 people emigrated from southwestern Germany and Switzerland in the eighteenth century. The majority – three-fifths – went a few hundred miles north or east, to Prussia, to the Habsburg lands along the lower Danube, and, at the end of the period, at the invitation of Catherine the Great, to Russia. But two-fifths – that is, 200,000 people – from almost the identical regions, moved 4,000 miles north and then west to such exotic places as "the island," as it was commonly called in the villages of the Palatinate, of Pennsylvania. Why? Were these migrations, and the similar movements of other groups – the Protestant Irish, the Dutch, and indeed the enslaved Africans – simply products of economic entrepreneurship responding rationally to developing opportunities and the need for labor? Or were there social, cultural, and economic forces behind all these movements, making them possible and determining their specific form?

And what shaped the patterns of dispersal within America – the lines of exploration and settlement? Geography, to some extent, of course; but geography did not create the impulse to move, the dynamics of expansion; nor did sheer economic necessity or sheer demographic pressure. Nowhere in this thinly settled land did stable communities approach Malthusian limits to population growth; yet people moved continuously as if there were such pressure.

The shifts of population within the colonies seem strange, irrational. In the decade preceding the Revolution, North Carolina supplied most of the first European settlers of Kentucky, but at the same time North Carolina was itself being deluged by emigrants from Pennsylvania, Virginia, Scotland, and Germany, and its population shot up from around 88,000 to somewhere between 175,000 and 185,000. Connecticut families suddenly appeared not only in northeastern Pennsylvania and the far north of the Vermont–New York border area, but also on the shores of the Gulf of Mexico. New Jerseyites settled Natchez, and were joined there by Pennsylvanians and North Carolinians. And newcomers from overseas were everywhere: Germans and Scotch-Irish could be found in almost every colony. Inland North Carolina, near present-day Fayetteville and Hillsboro, was in effect a colony of Scottish Highlanders; West Indians settled in Georgia, a colony whose population was so polyglot that a successful magistrate needed to speak fluently in at least three languages and preferably four; and Yorkshiremen and Scots arrived in increasing numbers in Nova Scotia. The road networks, once a compact tangle along the eastern seaboard, threw out new tentacles hundreds of miles across half the continent, quickly enclosing within a single communication system much of the half-billion acres east of the Mississippi.

The same almost frantic expansion can be seen in every direction. For a century and a half the peopling of New England had been a gradual process, reflecting a high natural population growth without significant immigration. By the end of the seventeenth century the population had reached 90,000 to 100,000. For half a century thereafter new towns had been settled at an average rate of six a year; by 1760 the vacant central area had been filled and the population had reached an estimated 500,000. In the next decade and a half, while the population rose another 20 percent, no fewer than 264 new towns were settled, an average of 18 a year. Who settled these remote towns? Where did the settlers come from, and why? We know something about Benning Wentworth's entrepreneurship in creating these townships and we know something of the efforts that were made to recruit settlers for them from overseas. But we know nothing of how Wentworth and his associates in New Hampshire assembled the several thousand proprietors' names, or what the relationships between the settlers and the proprietors were, or what conditions had set in motion this remarkable domestic migration into these isolated northern villages.

There are occasional patches of light – a few faces, a few statistics here and there in the current literature to illuminate the peopling of America over the first century and a half of European settlement. There are some excellent regional studies that bear on migration, written mainly by historical geographers; a comprehensive and illuminating study of over seven hundred participants in the great Puritan migration; an economic analysis of the recruitment characteristics of indentured servants, which complements an older, less statistical study; two highly suggestive probes by Mildred Campbell – bold, innovative, seminal studies which, twenty years after their appearance, have become the focuses of interpretative controversies; a few imaginative studies of slavery and the recruitment of slaves; and a number of reliable community studies, some of the most interesting of which relate not to New England, the subject of the first of such efforts, but to Virginia and especially to Maryland, the work of the excellent group of historians associated with the St. Mary's City Commission.

Still, despite all of these writings, and, in addition, my own effort to describe comprehensively the emigration from Britain on the eve of the Revolution, the population movements of the pre-industrial era, multitudinous and complex almost beyond description, remain mysterious and chaotic. There are no structural lines, no general propositions, to frame the history as a whole – nor will there be until the dimensions of the subject are recognized for what they are and the possibility of a unified organization for the story as a whole clearly seen.

It is in order to suggest something, at least, of these dimensions in concrete terms, and to sketch a few of the general elements in the overall story, that I would like to put forward [the following proposition as] . . . a limited starting point in approaching a very large subject. [It is] meant simply to [suggest] the dimensions of the subject and the possibility of controlling it within certain discrete lines of interpretation.

The peopling of British North America was an extension outward and an expansion in scale of domestic mobility in the lands of the immigrants' origins, and the transatlantic flow must be understood within the context of these domestic mobility patterns. Ultimately, however, its development introduced a new and dynamic force in European population history, which permanently altered the traditional configuration.

If there is one uncontroversial fact that has emerged from the past four decades of research in European social history, it is that the traditional society of early modern Europe was a mobile society – a world in motion. Professor E. E. Rich, in a perceptive article on the population of Elizabethan England written [half a century] ago, stressed the relationship between domestic migration and overseas migration. Rich found a persistence rate in selected Elizabethan villages over a ten-year period of no more than 50 percent. He estimated that only 16 percent of all Elizabethan families had remained in the same village as long as a century. Since Rich wrote, the picture has been greatly elaborated – by local historians like Alan Everitt, by historical geographers like John H. C. Patten, and by members of the Cambridge Group for the History of Population and Social Structure.

We now know not simply that the English population was mobile in the pre-industrial era but that its mobility was a composite of three closely interwoven patterns. First, there was a pattern of short-distance movements found everywhere in the English countryside, resulting from population growth; decline in real wages; the extension of commercial farming, which demanded, and helped create, an army of rural wage laborers; and the uprooting effect of domestic industry. Everywhere unattached farmworkers roamed the countryside seeking employment. Among more established groups, too, short-distance mobility in the countryside was common, in part the result of the circulation of the young among households of higher or equal status, compounded by the ubiquity of servitude. Roger Schofield has estimated that, in the typical English village of the eighteenth century, three out of every four males between the ages of fifteen and nineteen had left home and were in service of some kind; typically, two out of every three children of both sexes left their home parishes, to be replaced by children of other parishes. Overall, at any given time in the seventeenth century, 14 percent of the total population was in service, and around one-half of all the people in England were, or had been, servants. This generality of servitude meant widespread movement – yet movements that did not totally disconnect individuals from their original environments. Most of those who left home young to labor in other households or enterprises remained within half a day's walking distance of their homes.

The second pattern was regional: mobility over longer distances, funneling a significant portion of the mobile population of the countryside into provincial towns and cities. Thus the historical geographer John H. C. Patten, in his study of mobility in seventeenth-century East Anglia – the original source of much of the New England population – demonstrates that the constant flow of country people into the three urban centers of Norwich, Great Yarmouth, and Ipswich had its sources in communities within a range of eight to twenty miles of those towns. He suggests that the larger the urban magnet the wider the geographical range of recruitment and the deeper the poverty of the migrants, especially among those beyond the usual early years of high mobility. A further specification is offered by Peter Clark, examining the flow of people into and out of three Kentish towns at the time of the first British American settlements. He too finds a direct correlation between size of towns and the distances traveled by immigrants into them, the main recruitment range for these Kentish towns being a radius of sixteen miles; but he goes beyond that to establish a further correlation between socio-economic level and distance of recruitment.

He distinguishes between, on the one hand, the "betterment migration" of the quite young sons of stable rural families moving short distances into towns, usually for apprenticeship training; and, on the other hand, the "subsistence migration" of groups of much poorer people forced to move over greater distances simply to survive – to move more frequently, and to move more commonly from town to town rather than from country to town. These are true wanderers, isolated individuals far from their original residences, dislodged originally by poverty or the fear of poverty, roaming the land alone or in small groups, seeking employment and security, picking up casual labor whenever possible and repelled back, after temporary employment, into the migrating stream of poor people wandering through the countryside.

But the high correlation between distance and poverty was significantly reduced in the passage of time. By the early eighteenth century these long-distance subsistence migrants – common in the sixteenth and early seventeenth centuries – had largely disappeared as population had grown, agriculture had expanded, the mortality crises in the towns had diminished, the demand for manufactured goods had increased, and vagrancy legislation had become more stringent. By the mid-eighteenth century, "long distance migration [was] . . . no longer closely identified with the lower orders. Instead, upper social groups – gentlemen and merchants, as well as professional men – registered the greatest average distances travelled." But all of these regional migrations, whatever their socio-economic character and their spatial dimensions, tended to remove people from their immediate home environments, despite the efforts that were made to preserve connections of some sort, especially within extended kin networks.

The third and by far the most dynamic pattern was superimposed over all the local and regional movements. This "dominant node in the national migration system" was the great flow of people into the vast and constantly growing catch basin of London. London grew enormously in this era: reasonable population estimates are 60,000 in the early sixteenth century, 200,000 in 1600, 350,000 in 1650, and 575,000 in 1700, at which time greater London contained 11 percent of the entire population of England and Wales. And this growth was no product of natural population surpluses in the city itself. London devoured people. Disease devastated the slums; yet ever more people flocked in from all over the realm to restore the losses. Plague deaths of some 15 percent of the total were made up, in the seventeenth century, within two years.[3]

One can only guess at the overall numbers of those who left the countryside or small towns for London. Patten estimates that one million migrants came to London between 1550 and 1750. E. A. Wrigley calculates that in the period 1650–1750 deaths so far exceeded births in London that only a *net* immigration into the city of eight thousand persons a year can account for London's growth, and therefore that London was absorbing approximately one-half of the entire natural increase in England's population. One in every six English adults in this period had a direct experience of life in London, and one-third of London's population at any point in the century were recent arrivals. The movement to London flowed predominantly from northwest to southeast across Scotland and England, and as it flowed it drew off elements of the lesser mobility patterns by means of subnetworks connecting it to the migrations to provincial cities like Norwich, Sheffield, and York.

All of this may seem remote from the settling of the farms and villages of colonial America, but in fact it is essential to understanding it. For, in its earliest phase, the peopling of North America was a spillover – an outgrowth, an extension – of these established patterns of mobility in England. It tapped into these existing flows without basically altering them or modifying their magnitudes.

Thus, while it is of course true that religion shaped the leadership, organization, and ethos of the Puritan migration of the early seventeenth century, the human constituents were available in the East Anglian population accustomed for generations to move geographically in search of employment, opportunity, and stability. In the context of the mobility of the time, the famous Puritan exodus – which, to judge by the weight of subsequent scholarship, must have been a world-historical event – as an organized migration was nothing remarkable. The traditional figure (which is probably high) is 21,200 emigrants to Puritan New England in the twelve years before 1642; but during those same years three times that number left England for other colonies in America and the West Indies, and almost six times that number of Englishmen and Scots (120,000) migrated to Ireland. In one 24-*month* period in the 1630s, at least 10,000 Scots migrated to Ireland, roughly half the total of the entire Puritan migration.

Amid this continuous circulation of people throughout the greater British world, the relocation of religious groups like the Puritans, seeking relief and self-determination, was by no means "unique in the annals of migration."[4] Such events were in fact commonplace in this highly mobile society. Most Puritan emigrants, one English historian has written, were normal Englishmen acting normally. Unemployed west-country laborers flocked into Bristol just as East Anglians did into Norwich, and since Bristol had long been the departure point for western voyages it was natural for them to extend their search for employment to the shores of Virginia and Maryland. The Atlantic became a highway like the Great North Road, and it was a highway rather easier to cross, despite all the dangers of ocean voyages, than the land passages across the British Isles. People learned to move west naturally, just as they moved north, south, and east, seeking employment, security, and a hopeful future.

We do not yet have a detailed explanation of precisely how, in these early years, the transition from domestic to overseas migration – the bulging out in an unaccustomed direction – took place in England. We do know how it happened elsewhere. Just such a transition from domestic mobility to overseas migration has been described in the case of Spain. We know how it was that impoverished Andalusian farmworkers and the idle *hidalgos* and tradesmen of the overcrowded southern cities moved off to Spain's American colonies. And students of French population movements have explained the nature of such transitions in mobility patterns, and particularly the shift from temporary movements to permanent migrations. Yet, though the connections between domestic mobility and overseas migration have not been explained in detail in the English case, there are some revealing clues in the available material.

When poverty in the countryside led to severe population pressure in the towns, indigent migrants were dealt with harshly – expelled from town to town, thrown into houses of correction, isolated in disreputable slums, banished to riotous suburbs. The farther away the better: some town authorities managed by one means or another to ship some of these "subsistence migrants," already used to long-distance migration, to America.[5] More important, the normal workings of the labor market, by a natural extension, somehow reached overseas. For it appears that the incidence of emigration in the seventeenth century relates positively to harvest failures in England and negatively to rises in wage levels. And there seems to be some degree of correlation between the movements of seventeenth-century Chesapeake tobacco prices and the flows of indentured servants – a correlation that can be explained only by the presence of a ready pool of available recruits and well-established mechanisms for translating the demands of the labor market into the movements of large numbers of people. Such mechanisms operated in the domestic labor markets: the ebb and flow of seasonal labor migrations depended upon them; somehow they were extended to the developing labor markets overseas, with the result that the Chesapeake tobacco fields in the seventeenth century became an annex to the labor markets of south-western England.

Though the precise workings of the links between the domestic and overseas labor markets remain somewhat vague, the fact seems undeniable that migration to British North America in its first phases was a bulging out, an extension, of domestic mobility patterns into overseas territories, with results of the greatest importance. We now know, for example, that it was the failure of the southern English labor supply to provide the manpower needed in the expanding Chesapeake tobacco fields that led to the first large-scale importation of black slaves. All the correlations are consistent: the rising numbers of indentured servants through the 1650s, then the falling away in the sixties, as English population growth slackened, as fire and plague both reduced the available labor supply in London and created a greater demand there, and hence as real wages rose. All of this tended to consume what labor there was in domestic markets, while the imports of slaves in Virginia and Maryland rose significantly. Blacks did not outnumber whites in the labor force of the tobacco colonies until the 1680s, and thereafter, as the scale of production continued to rise, the dependence on an almost endless supply of black laborers became permanent.

Again and again major issues, apparently unresolvable paradoxes in the peopling process, can be resolved by reference to the *domestic* scene in the land of origin. The situation in the Scottish Highlands in the mid- to late eighteenth century appears at first bewildering. Emigration was said to be a universal phenomenon, an epidemic, a madness that gripped the minds of ordinary people, celebrated in song and poetry, denounced in endless newspaper columns and official statements, and the object of desperate concern by landlords and officials. But were the thousands who were leaving rich or poor, transient or permanent, burdens or benefits to the community, hence losses or gains in their exodus for the country at large? On the one hand, the explanations offered at the time stressed the dreadful poverty of those who left, the desperation of their living conditions, and the devastation they had faced from the new rent rises and other economic changes. On the other hand, there were constant complaints that the emigrants were draining off thousands of pounds a year in loose capital. And indeed a single shipload, about which we happen to know a great deal, leaving from the barren, austere north-Scottish county of Caithness, almost devoid of surplus capital, drained off approximately £1,000 in cash or its equivalent. Paradox – but it is resolved if one views the whole of the Highlands emigration, domestic and overseas, comprehensively.

The Highlanders, their lives badly dislocated by the destruction of the clan system after the suppression of the Jacobite rebellion of 1745 and dislocated too by the increasing rationalization of agricultural production, were moving away in droves – but not all to the same areas. The overseas migration was managed largely by tacksmen (primary lessees) or shipping entrepreneurs, who organized expeditions of freight-paying passengers, and a shipload of such emigrants was obliged to pay up to £800 collectively for their passage. Many, in addition, took an "overplus" of funds with them for accidents and extras along the way. To manage this, often they sold all their possessions: but they were not the abject poor. Yet the truly impoverished left too – not commonly, however, for America. Instead, they moved off to the Lowlands, where they helped to provide the labor force needed in the growing industries and the service markets of the cities. The distinction was explained, in 1805, by Francis Horner, who knew the facts. With the breakup of the clan system and the commercialization of agriculture, he wrote in an essay on Lord Selkirk's *Observations . . . on Emigration* (Edinburgh, 1805), a large part of the working population, especially in the Highlands, was displaced and rendered economically redundant.

> Two prospects present themselves. In the Low Country of Scotland, the wages of manufacturing labour; in America, the easy acquisition of land in absolute property . . . but the execution of the latter plan must be attended with more expense than the other. It will be practicable, therefore, to those only who can afford this expense. . . . The cotters have seldom property enough for the necessary expenses of emigration; and few of them have ever been able to emigrate: they have, in general, removed into the manufacturing districts of the Low Country of Scotland. But the population of the Highlands was composed, in a very large proportion, of the small tenants; and all of these are possessed of something that might be denominated capital. Most of them live much more wretchedly, as to habitation and diet, than the labourers who earn daily wages in other parts of the island; but they have property of greater value. . . . By disposing of all this stock, especially if the price of cattle happens to be high, [the small tenant] is enabled to embark in undertakings which cannot be thought of by the cotter, and which are not within the reach of the peasantry, even in the more improved and richer parts of the island.
>
> To those who can thus afford the expenses of the passage and first settlement, the low price of land in America presents the prospect of speedily attaining a situation and mode of life similar to that in which all their habits have been formed. . . . By their ability or inability to afford the expenses of their passage to America, the choice of the Highlanders, with a very few exceptions, has been entirely regulated. Even among those whose poverty forced them to go at first into the manufacturing towns, some of the most remarkable exertions of industry have been prompted, only by

the desire of accumulating as much money as might enable them to join their friends beyond the Atlantic.[6]

So when the tacksmen on the MacLeod estates on the island of Harris in the Outer Hebrides, prosperous before the MacLeods elevated the rents, contemplated drastic action, they refused to consider buying property in the Lowlands. Like so many Highlanders, they had been affected by that "spirit of emigration," a contemporary reported, "which in a few years will carry the inhabitants of the Highlands and Islands of Scotland into North America. Disdaining to become possessors of farms in the low countries [of Scotland] and follow the customs of its inhabitants which they held in contempt, they launched out into a new world breathing a spirit of liberty and a desire of every individual becoming a proprietor, where they imagine they can still obtain land for themselves and their flocks of cattle at a triffling rent or of conquering it from the Indians with the sword."[7] The migration to North America, in this case as in others, was not an isolated phenomenon but one element in a larger configuration, the whole of which explains the differences among the parts.

Similar dispersals took place in other areas that contributed significantly to the peopling of British North America – Ireland and the German states particularly; in these cases too emigration was at first a spillover of domestic population movements.

Mobility was endemic in southwestern Germany, throughout the Rhine Valley, in parts of Switzerland, and in the Low Countries. Many of the most "traditional" German villages had long been the scenes of high mobility. Through the whole broad band of central Europe there was a constant short-distance flow of village workers seeking seasonal employment and permanent improvement; here too, as in Britain, regional urban centers drained off the mobile population of the local hinterlands; and here too religion gave shape to small portions of the general mobility – all of this quite without reference to the special problems created by persecution, wars, and famine in the Palatinate at the end of the seventeenth century. Sects in central Europe, stimulated in their mobility by the political and religious fragmentation of the German-speaking world, drew aside in self-protection just as the Pilgrims and Puritans had done; many sought resolutions of their problems in more extensive movements than they had originally intended.

A thousand local rivulets fed streams of emigrants moving through northern and central Europe in all directions – *east* more commonly than west. A sampling of the sources of the first sizable German migration to British territory, which scattered ultimately to Ireland and New York – that of 1709–1710 – shows a remarkable range of communities from which the migrants came. Approximately 42 percent of the immigrants came from the Palatinate proper, west of the Rhine and south of the Mosel. But as many came from east of the Rhine, and there were groups from the farthest borderlands of the German-speaking world – from as far north as Flensburg, the Baltic port a few miles from Denmark; from as far east as the Czech border towns of Dresden and Görlitz; and from as far west and south as Montbéliard, an Alsatian Huguenot community in the suzerainty of Württemberg, close to Basel and Besançon. This was no concentrated exodus with a singular impetus, but a kind of seepage from an otherwise almost invisible but continuous and normal flow of people from village to village, from village to town, and from town to city. The Palatinate, it has been suggested – long before America was thought of in such terms – was a melting pot of European peoples.

At times, in the general swirl, the very identity of the migrants got lost, compounding the difficulty of identifying particular motives and distinctions. The so-called "Palatines" were by no means all from the two Palatinates: anyone voyaging down the Rhine was likely to acquire that name – Swiss as well as Westphalians, Alsatians and Bavarians as well as Hessians. Similarly, some of the so-called "Germans" who settled in Pennsylvania were not "Pennsylvania Dutch" (that is, *Deutsch* = German) at all, but, paradoxically, *really* Dutch – that is, Netherlanders, Dutch-speaking migrants from the border region of the Netherlands, who had moved first to German territory before going overseas as "Germans." The same kind of jumble took place in the eastward migrations; emigrants to Hungary and then to Russia from Württemberg, Baden, Hesse, the Palatinate, and even Alsace were lumped together as "Swabians" or "Saxons." And when a group of French Protestants, having left France for the Rhineland, ended up, after a second migration, on the banks of the Kennebec River in Maine, their sponsors chose to refer to them as "Germans," though they could not have been more French, and apparently succeeded in passing them off as Germans – happily, since it helped remove New Englanders' suspicions that they might be clandestine Catholics or secretly sympathetic to New France.

All of this is particularly well documented. For, in the mosaic of small princedoms and dukedoms that made up Germany, the continuing allegiance of taxpaying subjects and agricultural workers was considered to be essential, and consequently movement was scrutinized and recorded. Departures were legalized by the issuance of formal documents, most often letters of manumission, many hundreds of which have survived. Through them one can trace the departures and destinations of large numbers of people who were in motion in these German principalities, establish their economic and social status by noting the taxes they were obliged to pay upon their departures, and perhaps find clues to their motivations and expectations. And the manumission records contain only the most obvious of the many traces that remain of this widely dispersed emigration. Church records and court files on both sides of the Atlantic extend the documentation, as do shipping lists, arrival records, and correspondence sent back from America to relatives, friends, and officials in a hundred German villages and towns.

At times the seepage that made up the early German migrations can be studied almost microscopically. One finds, for example, in the records of the obscure hamlet of Heuchelheim in the northeastern corner of the Palatinate, official notice of the legal emigration of seventy-four adults and at least fourteen children in the twenty-two years after 1749. Most of the adults declared their intention of marrying and settling in villages of the Palatinate or in the neighboring Archbishopric of Worms; but there were a few exceptions. One man left to join the Prussian army; one family with numerous children went four miles off to the town of Frankenthal to work in a porcelain factory; and three unattached men and two complete families departed – we do not know why – for Pennsylvania, four thousand miles away. Of these future American families – about to confront over forty toll barriers on the Rhine, profiteering shippers and Dutch authorities in Rotterdam, British officials in Cowes or Portsmouth, and then an ocean voyage of many weeks – one was declared to be so poor it could not be charged the usual tax. All four members, therefore, would be sold into servitude if the cost of their passage was not "redeemed" upon their arrival in Philadelphia.

The same natural spillover of domestic population movements, whatever the determination of direction, is found everywhere. The first movements to America from Scotland and Ireland, whenever they occurred, were not different from those from England, from the German states, from Switzerland, or from the Low Countries. In the early phases of the migrations the existing *patterns* of mobility in these homelands were unaffected by the American magnet, the demographic *structure* remained constant. The North American colonies were simply another destination available to people in motion.

But in time the dynamics of the situation changed. Everywhere, though in different phasings, the pull of the American colonies grew to the point where it shaped the patterns of European domestic mobility. It became an independent force acting on the demographic configurations of the Old World, a powerful and ungovernable prod outside all indigenous propulsions, created by entrepreneurship, promotion, and the sheer magnetism of economic betterment and religious toleration.

The slave trade was only the extreme expression of the deliberate engineering of overseas migration. William Penn's famous efforts at promoting emigration and settlement, like the earlier efforts of the Virginia Company and of the other early proprietors, were relatively passive: in effect Penn ran an advertising campaign sufficient to mobilize elements of a readily available population. But in time truly dynamic entrepreneurs of migration appeared, and the flows of emigration to North America were propelled forward by them. Agents for shippers and land companies combed the Rhineland and the British Isles for emigrants, and lent support to emigration organizations formed by would-be migrants themselves. At this stage there was no spontaneous, mechanical relationship between poverty and emigration. The only correlation that can be firmly established is between the activities of recruiting agents and the flow of emigrants from areas with a high degree of actual or latent mobility, especially areas from which people had already emigrated to America. And the recruiters could succeed because the maturing American economy, while superficially providing less of an open opportunity than it had earlier, was basically more expansive, more elaborate, more attractive than it had been before, and its magnetism persisted, at times grew.

Parcels of prime coastal land obtainable in freehold tenure were obviously less easily available in the eighteenth century than they had been in the early and mid-seventeenth century; in many areas such land was completely unobtainable. But there were millions of open acres east of the Mississippi, and the growing scale of enterprise, both in commerce and agriculture, and the multiplying and maturing towns created opportunities that had not existed when coastal property had been almost free for the taking. In the mid-eighteenth century the opportunities available in the American world were opening up, not closing down, though they were taking different form. This fact radiated out into susceptible populations in great sweeps of enticing information propagated by paid recruiters, and the impact on the established mobility patterns in Europe was profound.

So in Paisley, Scotland, in 1773, when weavers struck for higher wages and blocked employers' efforts to use scab labor, the authorities undertook a resolute, all-out prosecution of the ringleaders for creating "an unlawful combination" – until they discovered that several thousand of the workers "threatened to go off in a body to America." At that point the trial became, in the words of one of the judges, "very delicate." The court drew back and imposed lenient sentences, and not on all but only on some of the leaders, freeing the rest; the judges contented themselves with lecturing all concerned on "the criminality of their conduct." Privately, the chief judge breathed a sigh of relief that "all thoughts of going over to America are for the present laid aside."[8]

The presence of the powerful American magnet had become a wild card, an autonomous force in the demographic situation. The question is not why the British government undertook a comprehensive study of the causes and consequences of emigration to America in 1773 but why it had not done so before. For, while the fact that the mainland North American colonies were British led to the natural assumption that movement from Britain to America should be as free as from England to Scotland or Ireland, it took no great insight to see that the effect of continuing mass emigration might prove to be extremely complicated for Britain. And indeed, by 1767 there was concern enough about the consequences of "so great a number of useful inhabitants ... daily emigrating to the American colonies" for the British government to disallow an act of the Georgia legislature subsidizing the immigration and resettlement of British subjects in newly opened territories, a common practice that had been engaged in by South Carolina since 1731. But there were no general guidelines for regulating mobility within British territory, and landlords like the powerful Anglo-Irish secretary of state for the colonies, Lord Hillsborough, contemplating the possible depopulation of their estates, were beginning to demand them. It was an awkward and difficult problem which few in authority in Britain fully understood.[9]

For other nations, which could not imagine profiting even indirectly from the exodus to America except by the elimination of criminals and indigents, there were no such complications. Officials in the German states had long been aware of the danger posed by what one of them called "the frivolous itch of emigration" to such outlandish places as "*Bintzel Vannier*," as Pennsyl-vania was called in the Main River Valley. They tried to control the flow. They levied stiff *Steuer* (taxes) on the emigrants, followed by stiffer *Nachsteuer*; tied up manumissions and exits in all sorts of red tape; and frequently prohibited emigration altogether.[10] But given the weakness of state power in the eighteenth century, the exodus could not be stopped. It continued forcefully until the outbreak of the Revolutionary War.

Thus Wrigley's assertion that London in the years 1650–1750 was absorbing one-half of the entire natural increase of population in the English countryside reflects one of the basic facts of eighteenth-century social life in Britain. But in the period 1640–1699, Wrigley has more recently shown, 69 percent of all of England's natural increase was drawn off not by London but by emigration to North America, and over the whole period from 1695 to 1801 emigration consumed 20 percent of the natural increase of England. Hence there was in effect not *one* "dominant node in the national migration system"; there were *two*. The whole configuration of British mobility was fundamentally affected by the exodus to America. London was the most common source of American immigrants – it had been that at the beginning and it remained that throughout the colonial period. Much of the movement to London, it now appears, was only a stage in the migration to America. And indeed I wonder, if we had all the information we needed – if we could establish the magnitude and phasing of transatlantic migration from all parts of Britain, and if we could establish the precise relation of overseas migration to other aspects of population movements – I wonder if we would not conclude that the peopling of North America became a dominant force in the history of British mobility in the later years of colonial rule, a powerful determinant of its shape.

The key element in this complex picture is the linkage between local migrations and overseas emigration, and that association, as I say, is extraordinarily difficult to isolate and describe. But a certain eighteenth-century Shetlander, John Harrower, whose career is particularly well documented, would, I think, have understood it precisely. His experiences exemplify at least one aspect of this process vividly, and he was a reflective man.

One of the ten thousand emigrants registered by the customs officials, he recorded his experiences and feelings in a detailed and expressive diary. He was an impoverished forty-year-old shopkeeper and tradesman who in December 1773 left his home in Lerwick in the far Shetland Islands, north of the Scottish mainland, "in search of business," carrying with him his total capital of $8\frac{1}{2}$ pence cash and £3 worth of woolen stockings for sale along the way. He never intended to go to America: his aim was to find employment in Britain or the Low Countries, restore his finances, and then return home. After repeated failures to find work in Scotland or to obtain a passage across the North Sea, he took a free berth to Portsmouth and then, hopeful of employment in the capital, walked the eighty miles to London. There he found a mass of similarly unemployed and desperate artisans and tradesmen, some of them reduced to beggary. He held out as long as he could, but having spent his last shilling without finding work, alone "in a garret room . . . frendless and forsaken," he sold himself for four years of bonded servitude to a shipmaster going to Virginia in return for the cost of his voyage.

On board the *Planter* he found seventy-four other indentured servants drawn from all over the British Isles but recruited also from among the lesser artisans of London. A wide range of trades was represented – a glass-blower from Surrey, a wigmaker from Southwark, a watchmaker from London, a breeches-maker from Wiltshire, a butcher from Ireland, a footman, a groom, a boatmaker, a painter – but no one without a stated occupation, no simple laborer or farmworker below the status of a husbandman. After a voyage lasting two months, the ship docked at the town of Fredericksburg, Virginia, on the Rappahannock River, where the shipmaster disposed of his human cargo. Most of the servants on board were bought by a merchant jobber, who resold them individually and with careful calculation of the interests of potential buyers. Harrower's years of service were bought by Colonel William Daingerfield, who needed a tutor for his children, and the Scotsman ended up on the Daingerfield plantation, Belvidera, where he found security and even a measure of gentility, though not the independence he sought. He was still in service there, a schoolteacher and respected domestic servant, when he died in 1777, possessed of £70 with which he was planning to bring over his wife and three children.[11]

So in complex ways the American magnet exerted its force. For some, it was a distant but positive goal somehow to be reached; for others, it was a last resort, a refuge when all else failed; for still others, it was a mystery full of vague possibilities, to be explored, considered, realized, or rejected. But for everyone in this mobile world it was an irreducible fact of life, ever present and ever potent.

Notes

1 Quoted in A. L. Rowse, "Tudor Expansion: The Transition from Medieval to Modern History," *William and Mary Quarterly*, 3rd ser., 14 (1957), 312. (This periodical will be cited hereafter as *WMQ*.)
2 The information in this and the following paragraphs summarizes sections of my *Voyagers to the West* (New York, 1986), which presents the full documentation.
3 John H. Patten, *Rural-Urban Migration in Pre-industrial England* (Oxford University School of Geography *Research Papers* no. 6, 1973), p. 23; Lawrence Stone, "Social Mobility in England, 1500–1700," *Past & Present*, 33 (1966), 30–1; E. A. Wrigley, "A Simple Model of London's Importance in Changing English Society and Economy, 1650–1760," ibid., 37 (1967), 44; Andrew B. Appleby, "Nutrition and Disease: The Case of London, 1550–1750," *Journal of Interdisciplinary History*, 6 (1975), 1–22 (for mortality tables see appendix, pp. 20–22).
4 Carl Bridenbaugh, *Vexed and Troubled Englishmen, 1590–1642* (New York, 1968), p. 434.
5 Peter Clark, "The Migrant in Kentish Towns, 1580–1640," in *Crisis and Order in English Towns, 1500–1700*, ed. Peter Clark and Paul Slack (London, 1972), pp. 149, 151–152.
6 *The Economic Writings of Francis Horner*, ed. Frank W. Fetter (London, 1957), pp. 120–2. Selkirk himself had touched on the point in his *Observations* (pp. 57–8); Horner developed and explained it.
7 Anon., "Observes or Remarks upon the Lands and Islands which Compose the Barrony Called Harries, the Property of Norman McLeod of McLeod, Esqr," Lee Papers, MS. 3431, f. 180, National Library of Scotland, Edinburgh.
8 Thomas Miller to the Earl of Suffolk, October 25, 1773, Public Record Office (London), SP 54/46, f. 248.

9   E. R. R. Green, "Queensborough Township: Scotch-Irish Emigration and the Expansion of Georgia, 1763–1776," *WMQ*, 17 (1960), 188.

10 Otto Langguth, "Auswanderer aus der Grafschaft Wertheim" (1932), tr. and supp. Donald H. Yoder, "Pennsylvania German Pioneers from the County of Wertheim," [*Yearbook of*] *the Pennsylvania German Folklore Society*, XII (1947), pp. 169–70, 180.

11 Edward M. Riley, ed., *The Journal of John Harrower...1773–1776* (Williamsburg, VA, and New York, 1963).

The Infortunate: The Voyage and Adventures of William Moraley, an Indentured Servant (1743)

William Moraley

I left *Philadelphia*, to go to *Burlington* to my Master; I went in a Boat, where I got my self Drunk for the first time after my Arrival, and then first experienced the Strength of Rum. About Twelve we landed there, and I was conveyed to my Master, where I dined upon Dumplings, boil'd Beef, and Udder; when I became enamour'd with Mrs *Sarah*, the Daughter. I was stripp'd of my Rags, and received in lieu of them a torn Shirt, and an old Coat. They tell me, it was only for the present, for I might expect better.

I went to bed that Night, being the first Time I had seen one since I left *London*, which was fifteen Weeks. The next day I had leave, upon my Desire, to walk about the Town: It is close to the River, and contains about 300 Houses; the Number of inhabitants was 800. It has a key and Wharf, where Ships of 500 Tun may anchor: At the Upper-End, is the Prison, built of Brick. Every House has a Garden and Orchard, stored with Apples, Peaches, and Cherries. Cyder is the common Drink here; some Houses making one hundred and fifty Barrels in the Year....

My Master employed me in his Business: I continued satisfied with him for sometime; but being desirous to settle at *Philadelphia*, during the rest of my Servitude, I declared to him, I would stay no longer, and desired him to dispose of me to some other Master, and insisted upon it, agreeably to the Tenour of my Indenture. This Demand made him cross to me, and I attempted an Escape, but was taken, and put into Prison; but was soon released, with a promise to satisfy my Demand. About a Fortnight after, we went to the Mayor of *Philadelphia*, his Name was *Griffith*, a Man of exact Justice, tho' an Irishman, who reconciled us; so I returned back to *Burlington*, and continued with him three Years, he forgiving me the other Two: I was ever after perfectly pleased with my Master's Behaviour to me, which was generous.

There lived in the Family a Relation of his, named *Hannah Lambert*, a Gentlewoman of Beauty, good Parts, and a good Fortune, Daughter to Mr Thomas Lambert, a Native of Yorkshire. One Day as this Lady and myself was crossing [the] *Delaware*, in a Canoe, it overset; so being in Danger, I forgot my own for her Safety, and taking her round the Small of the Waist, with one Arm, swam by the help of the other to the other Side of the River. She so sensibly remembered this Service, that all the Time of my stay in this Family, I never wanted Money. Her Father gave me five Pounds, and when ever I went into the Country, I generally made his House my resting Place, where I was very civilly treated.

Our Family consisted of a Wife and two Daughters, with a Nephew, a Negro Slave, a bought Servant, and myself, with the aforesaid Gentlewoman. We had a next Door Neighbour, called William Cullum, a *Lincolnshire* Man, and a Baker: He came to us one Day, as my master and myself were making Nails for a Bellows for a Forge; and laying down upon the Bellows Board Three-Pence and Sugar writ the following Words in Chalk, and left the Place, we not knowing from whence the money came.

> *Here's Money, Sugar, fetch some Rum,*
> *And when the Liquors made, I come.*

My Master perceiving it, said, Well, this is *William Cullum's*, in order to shew his Wit, and order'd me to answer it Extempore. I first fetched the Rum, then made the Liquor, which was *Bombo*, and writ under the foregoing Lines.

> *The Liquor's made, besure to come,*
> *Or send more Sugar, and more Rum.*

Which my Friend perceived, laughed, and gave me a Shilling, with which I merrily quaffed.

One Night as I was in Bed with my Fellow Servant, being awake, the Chamber Door opened without any Noise, and I perceiv'd something coming across the Floor, like a Ghost, in White, with a black Face. The Sight was so terrifying, that I shrunk under the Bed Cloaths, and sweated heartily, and endeavoured to wake my Friend, but to no Purpose. It came to the Bedside, and stooping, grin[n]ed, and stared me in the Face, and beckened with its Hand: At which I shiver'd so much, and my Chops chatter'd, as if beating a March; but recollecting myself, I demanded of it what it wanted. Then it beckoned again, and left the Room; but soon after came again, looked earnestly at me. When I said, *Lord! why do you come here?* It answer'd, *Nothing with you,* as I well remember, and then went away, the Door shooting after it, without any Noise. I was very positive it was a Spirit, and told the Family the next Morning; who said, it was a Negro killed some Years since by her Master, and that they had often seen it. . . .

At the first Peopling [of] these Colonies, there was a Necessity of employing a great Number of Hands, for the clearing the Land, being overgrown with Wood for some Hundred of Miles; to which Intent, the first Settlers not being sufficient of themselves to improve those Lands, were not only obliged to purchase a great Number of *English* Servants to assist them, to whom they granted great Immunities, and at the Expiration of their Servitude, Land was given to encourage them to continue there; but were likewise obliged to purchase Multitudes of Negro Slaves from *Africa*, by which Means they are become the richest Farmers in the World, paying no Rent, nor giving Wages either to purchased Servants or Negro Slaves; so that instead of finding the Planter Rack-rented, as the *English* Farmer, you will taste of their Liberality, they living in Affluence and Plenty.

The Condition of the Negroes is very bad, by reason of the Severity of the Laws, there being no Laws made in Favour of these unhap[p]y Wretches: For the least Trespass, they undergo the severest Punishment; but their Masters make them some amends, by suffering them to marry, which makes them easier, and often prevents their running away. The Consequence of their marrying is this, all their Posterity are Slaves without Redemption; and it is in vain to attempt an Escape, tho' they often endeavour it; for the Laws against them are so severe, that being caught after running way, they are unmercifully whipped; and if they die under the Discipline, their Masters suffer no Punishment, there being no Law against murdering them. So if one Man kills another's Slave, he is only obliged to pay his Value to the Master, besides Damages that may accrue for the Loss of him in his Business.

The Masters generally allow them a Piece of Ground, with Materials for improving it. The Time of working for themselves, is *Sundays*, when they raise on their own Account divers Sorts of Corn and Grain, and sell it in the Markets. They buy with the Money Cloaths for themselves and Wives; as for the Children, they belong to the Wives Master, who bring them up; so the Negro need fear no Expense, his Business being to get them for his Master's use, who is as tender of them as his own Children. On *Sundays* in the evening they converse with their Wives, and drink Rum, or Bumbo, and smoak Tobacco, and the next Morning return to their Master's Labour.

They are seldom made free, for fear of being burthensome to the Provinces, there being a Law, that no Master shall manumise them, unless he gives Security they shall not be thrown upon the Province, by settling Land on them for their Support.

Their Marriages are diverting; for when the Day is appointed for the Solemnization, Notice is given to all the Negroes and their Wives to be ready. The Masters of the new Couple provide handsomely for the Entertainment of the Company. The Inhabitants generally grace the Nuptials with their Presence, when all Sorts of the best Provisions are to be met with. They chuse some *Englishman* to read the Marriage Ceremony out of the Common Prayer Book; after which they sing and dance and drink till they get drunk. Then a Negro goes about the Company and collects Money for the Use of the Person who marry'd them, which is laid out in a Handkerchief, and presented to him.

This is the only free Day they have, except Sundays, throughout the whole Course of their Lives, for then they banish from them all Thoughts of the Wretchedness of their Condition. The Day being over, they return to their Slavery. I have often heard them say, they did not think God made them Slaves, any more than other Men, and wondered that Christians, especially *Englishmen*, should use them so barbarously. But there is a Necessity of using them hardly, being of an obdurate, stubborn Disposition; and when they have it in their Power to rebel, are extremely cruel.

The Condition of bought Servants is very hard, notwithstanding their indentures are made in *England* wherein it is expressly stipulated, that they shall have, at their Arrival, all the Necessaries specified in those Indentures, to be given 'em by their future Masters, such as Clothes, Meat, and Drink; yet upon Complaint made to a Magistrate against the Master for Nonperformance, the Master is generally heard before the Servant, and it is ten to one if he does not get his Licks for his Pains, as I have experienced upon the like Occassion, to my Cost.

If they endeavor to escape, which is next to impossible, there being a Reward for taking up any Person who travels without a Pass, which is extended all over the *British* Colonies, their Masters immediately issue out a Reward for the apprehending them, from Thirty Shillings to Five Pound, as they think proper, and this generally brings them back again. Printed and Written Advertisements are also set up against the Trees and publick Places in the Town, besides those in the News-papers. Notwithstanding these Difficulties, they are perpetually running away, but seldom escape; for a hot Pursuit being made, brings them back, when a Justice settles the Expences, and the Servant is oblig'd to serve a longer time.

Journey to Pennsylvania (1754)

Gottlieb Mittelberger

[W]hat really drove me to write this little book was the sad and miserable condition of those traveling from Germany to the New World. . . .

Once people have read all this I have no doubt that those who might still have some desire to go over there will stay at home and will carefully avoid this long and difficult voyage and the misfortunes connected with it; since such a journey will mean for most who undertake it the loss of all they possess, of freedom and peace, and for some the loss of their very lives and, I can even go so far as to say, of the salvation of their souls. . . .

In Rotterdam, and to some extent also in Amsterdam, the people are packed into the big boats as closely as herring, so to speak. The bedstead of one person is hardly two feet across and six feet long, since many of the boats carry from four to six hundred passengers, not counting the immense amount of equipment, tools, provisions, barrels of fresh water, and other things that also occupy a great deal of space.

Because of contrary winds it sometimes takes the boats from two to four weeks to make the trip from Holland to Cowes [England]. But, given favorable winds, that voyage can be completed in eight days or less. On arrival everything is examined once more and customs duties paid. It can happen that ships have to ride at anchor there from eight to fourteen days, or until they have taken on full cargoes. During this time everyone has to spend his last remaining money and to consume the provisions that he meant to save for the ocean voyage, so that most people must suffer tremendous hunger and want at sea where they really feel the greatest need. Many thus already begin their sufferings on the voyage between Holland and England.

When the ships have weighed anchor for the last time, usually off Cowes in Old England, then both the long sea voyage and misery begin in earnest. For from there the ships often take eight, nine, ten, or twelve weeks sailing to Philadelphia, if the wind is unfavorable. But even given the most favorable winds, the voyage takes seven weeks.

During the journey the ship is full of pitiful signs of distress – smells, fumes, horrors, vomiting, various kinds of sea sickness, fever, dysentry, headaches, heat, constipation, boils, scurvy, cancer, mouth-rot, and similar afflictions, all of them caused by the age and the highly-salted state of the food, especially of the meat, as well as by the very bad and filthy water, which brings about the miserable destruction and death of many. Add to all that shortage of food, hunger, thirst, frost, heat, dampness, fear, misery, vexation, and lamentation as well as other troubles. Thus, for example, there are so many lice, especially on the sick people, that they have to be scraped off the bodies. All this misery reaches its climax when in addition to everything else one must also suffer through two to three days and nights of storm, with everyone convinced that the ship with all aboard is bound to sink. In such misery all the people on board pray and cry pitifully together.

In the course of such a storm the sea begins to surge and rage so that the waves often seem to rise up like high mountains, sometimes sweeping over the ship; and one thinks that he is going to sink along with the ship. All the while the ship, tossed by storm and waves, moves constantly from one side to the other, so that nobody aboard can either walk, sit, or lie down and the tightly packed people on their cots, the sick as well as the healthy, are thrown every which way. One can easily imagine that these hardships necessarily affect many people so severely that they cannot survive them.

I myself was afflicted by severe illness at sea, and know very well how I felt. These people in their misery are many times very much in want of solace, and I often entertained and comforted them with singing, praying, and encouragement. Also, when possible, and when wind and waves permitted it, I held daily prayer meetings with them on deck, and, since we had no ordained clergyman on board, was forced to administer baptism to five children. I also held services, including a sermon, every Sunday, and when the dead were buried at sea, commended them and our souls to the mercy of God.

Among those who are in good health impatience sometimes grows so great and bitter that one person begins to curse the other, or himself and the day of his birth, and people sometimes come close to murdering one another. Misery and malice are readily associated, so that people begin to cheat and steal from one another. And then one always blames the other for having undertaken the voyage. Often the children cry out against their parents, husbands against wives and wives against husbands, brothers against their sisters, friends and acquaintances against one another.

But most of all they cry out against the thieves of human beings! Many groan and exclaim: "Oh! If only I were back at home, even lying in my pig-sty!" Or they call out: "Ah, dear God, if I only once again had a piece of good bread or a good fresh drop of water." Many people whimper, sigh, and cry out pitifully for home. Most of them become homesick at the thought that many hundreds of people must necessarily perish, die, and be thrown into the ocean in such misery. And this in turn makes their families, or those who were responsible for their undertaking the journey, oftentimes fall almost into despair – so that it soon becomes practically impossible to rouse them from their depression. . . .

One can scarcely conceive what happens at sea to women in childbirth and to their innocent offspring. Very few escape with their lives; and mother and child, as soon as they have died, are thrown into the water. On board our ship, on a day on which we had a great storm, a woman about to give birth and unable to deliver under the circumstances, was pushed through one of the portholes into the sea because her corpse was far back in the stern and could not be brought forward to the deck.

Children between the ages of one and seven seldom survive the sea voyage; and parents must often watch their offspring suffer miserably, die, and be thrown into the ocean, from want, hunger, thirst, and the like. I myself, alas, saw such a pitiful fate overtake thirty-two children on board our vessel, all of whom were finally thrown into the sea. Their parents grieve all the more, since their children do not find repose in the earth, but are devoured by the predatory fish of the ocean. It is also worth noting that children who have not had either measles or smallpox usually get them on board the ship and for the most part perish as a result. . . .

It is not surprising that many passengers fall ill, because in addition to all the other troubles and miseries, warm food is served only three times a week, and at that is very bad, very small in quantity, and so dirty as to be hardly palatable at all. And the water distributed in these ships is often very black, thick with dirt, and full of worms. Even when very thirsty, one is almost unable to drink it without loathing. It is certainly true that at sea one would often spend a great deal of money just for one good piece of bread, or one good drink of water – not even to speak of a good glass of wine if one could only obtain them. I have, alas, had to experience that myself. For toward the end of the voyage we had to eat the ship's biscuit, which had already been spoiled for a long time, even though in no single piece was there more than the size of a thaler that was not full of red worms and spiders' nests. . . .

When at last after the long and difficult voyage the ships finally approach land, when one gets to see the headlands for the sight of which the people on board had longed so passionately, then everyone crawls from below to the deck, in order to look at the land from afar. And people cry for joy, pray, and sing praises and thanks to God. The glimpse of land revives the passengers, especially those who are half-dead of illness. Their spirits, however weak they had become, leap up, triumph, and rejoice within them. Such people are now willing to bear all ills patiently, if only they can disembark soon and step on land. But, alas, alas!

When the ships finally arrive in Philadelphia after the long voyage only those are let off who can pay their sea freight or can give good security.

The others, who lack the money to pay, have to remain on board until they are purchased and until their purchasers can thus pry them loose from the ship. In this whole process the sick are the worst off, for the healthy are preferred and are more readily paid for. The miserable people who are ill must often still remain at sea and in sight of the city for another two or three weeks – which in many cases means death. Yet many of them, were they able to pay their debts and to leave the ships at once, might escape with their lives. . . .

This is how the commerce in human beings on board ship takes place. Every day Englishmen, Dutchmen, and High Germans come from Philadelphia and other places, some of them very far away, sometime twenty or thirty or forty hours' journey, and go on board the newly arrived vessel that has brought people from Europe and offers them for sale. From among the healthy they pick out those suitable for the purposes for which they require them. Then they negotiate with them as to the length of the period for which they will go into service in order to pay off their passage, the whole amount of which they generally still owe. When an agreement has been reached, adult persons by written contract bind themselves to serve for three, four, five, or six years, according to their health and age. The very young, between the ages of ten and fifteen, have to serve until they are twenty-one, however.

Many parents in order to pay their fares in this way and get off the ship must barter and sell their children as if they were cattle. Since the fathers and mothers often do not know where or to what masters their children are to be sent, it frequently happens that after leaving the vessel, parents and children do not see each other for years on end, or even for the rest of their lives. . . .

It often happens that whole families – husband, wife, and children – being sold to different purchasers, become separated, especially when they cannot pay any part of the passage money. When either the husband or the wife has died at sea, having come more than halfway, then the surviving spouse must pay not only his or her fare, but must also pay for or serve out the fare of the deceased.

When both parents have died at sea, having come more than halfway, then their children, especially when they are still young and have nothing to pawn or cannot pay, must be responsible for their own fares as well as those of their parents, and must serve until they are twenty-one years old. Once free of service, they receive a suit of clothing as a parting gift, and if it has been so stipulated the men get a horse and the women a cow. . . .

No one in this country can run away from a master who has treated him harshly and get far. For there are regulations and laws that ensure that runaways are certainly and quickly recaptured. Those who arrest or return a fugitive get a good reward. For every day that someone who runs away is absent from his master he must as a punishment do service an extra week, for every week an extra month, and for every month a half year. But if the master does not want to take back the recaptured runaway, he is entitled to sell him to someone else for the period of as many years as he would still have had to serve.

Occupations vary, but work is strenuous in this new land; and many who have just come into the country at an advanced age must labor hard for their bread until they die. I will not even speak of the young people. Most jobs involve cutting timber, felling oak trees, and levelling, or as one says here, clearing, great tracts of forest, roots and all. . . .

Thus let him who wants to earn his piece of bread honestly and in a Christian manner and who can only do this by manual labor in his native country stay *there* rather than come to America.

For, in the first place, things are no better in Pennsylvania. However hard one may have had to work in his native land, conditions are bound to be equally tough or even tougher in the new country. . . .

I want to say that those people who may let themselves be talked into something and seduced into the voyage by the thieves of human beings are the biggest fools if they really believe that in America or Pennsylvania roasted pigeons are going to fly into their mouths without their having to work for them.

How sad and miserable is the fate of so many thousand German families who lost all the money they ever owned in the course of the long and difficult voyage, many of whom perished wretchedly and had to be buried at sea and who, once they have arrived in the new country, saw their old and young separated and sold away into places far removed one from the other!

Informations Concerning the Province of North Carolina (1773)

Scotus Americanus

Migrations to America from many parts of Britain, particularly to the province of North Carolina, from the Highlands and isles of Scotland, have, of late, become very frequent and numerous, and are likely to continue so. Whatever this may be owing to, the matter is serious, and, to some, the consequences are very alarming. The natives of the

Highlands and isles have always been remarkable for the strongest attachment to the place of their nativity, and for the highest respect towards their masters and superiors. In these, they were wont to find kind patrons and protectors, and cherishing, indulgent fathers to themselves and families. This endeared to them a soil and climate to which nature has not been very liberal of its favours, in somuch, that they have ever shewn the utmost aversion at leaving their country, or removing to happier regions, and more indulgent climates. That this is true of the Highlanders in general, will be acknowledged by those who are in the least acquainted with them. The cause, then, that could induce a people of this cast, to forsake their native lands, in such numbers, and make them seek for habitations in countries far distant and unknown, must, doubtless, be very cogent and powerful. And, here, let the present landholders and proprietors consider, whether, of late, they are not greatly to blame? whether they have not begun to shake the iron rod of oppression too much over them? Let proprietors of the largest estates among them, such whose fortunes enables them to figure it away in life, ask themselves, if they have not used every means to estrange the affections of the Highlanders from them? whether they have not contributed all in their power, and, in a manner, exerted themselves to make their home intolerable and disagreeable to them, and lessen their once strong attachment towards their beloved, though poor country, so as to make them forget their native prejudices, surmount every apparent difficulty, and become emigrants and adventurers to other climes and regions far remote.

The luxury, dissipation, and extravagance of the times, may chiefly account for this change of conduct in the land-holders towards their tenants. Formerly the proprietors resided mostly among them upon their estates, conversed freely, and were familiar with them, were tender of them, cherished, and patronized them; to them the tenants were devoted; to them they had recourse upon every emergency: they were happy, they grew up and prospered under them. The modern lairds, unlike their fore-fathers, live at a great distance from their estates. Whatever misfortunes may befal the tenants, whatever grievances they have to complain of, whatever oppression they may groan under, they have no access to their masters; they scarce know where he lives, or where to find him; or, if they should, it is a long and expensive journey to go where he is; and complaints at a distance are seldom listened to, or properly redressed. Careless and unconcerned the master lives in the circle, as it is called, of the gay and the great. There, is a round of merriment and whim, in a vortex of airy amusements, of giddy and unsubstantial pleasures, and at the height of an expensive, though false and unnatural taste, he squanders away his fortune, and wastes his time and his health at once. . . .

These gentlemen too, accustomed to live in large and wealthy cities, or in the most fertile and best cultivated provinces of Britain, are greatly shocked, in their visits, at the rude aspect, and steril face of the Highlands, and at the small progress that agriculture makes in these remote parts. The natives are exclaimed against, as an intractable, idle, and useless set of beings. Without means, without encouragement, at a distance from market, against climate, and soil too, in many places, it is expected of them, that they should cultivate and enclose wide extended heaths, rugged mountain, and large barren morasses. But, may it not be asked, if the proprietors themselves have shewn any extraordinary specimen or examples of this sort among them? have they done any thing effectual towards bringing on, or establishing fisheries, trade, or manufactories on their estates? Such of them as do improve and enclose their ground, is it not at an immense expence, far beyond the reach of most tenants in the Highlands? Are not these things carried on from father to son, through a long tract of time? And, in general, may it not be asked, whether much advantage has, as yet, been made of them? . . .

It is a well known and received maxim, in farming, that the gross produce of the land should be, at least, equal to three of the current rents, or by what means shall the farmer support himself? But, in these modern schemes, this maxim is quite laid aside, and another of a very different and strange complexion is attempted to be substituted in its place, viz. "That the more rent is laid upon any farm, the better shall the tenant be able to improve the land, to pay his rent, and to live well, than when he paid a small rent." In conformity to this refined maxim, some of these gentlemen set part of their lands, and soon found their expectations disappointed. With true tyrannic perseverance, they have tried one set of tenants after another, by the same rule, and have seen them all beggared in their circumstances. . . .

And now, is there any wonder, if, under their present discouraging circumstances, and considering the dark and gloomy prospects they have before them at home, that the Highlanders should seek for refuge in some happier land, on some more hospitable shore, where freedom reigns, and where, unmolested by Egyptian taskmasters, they may reap the produce of their own labour and industry. For this purpose, where can they better betake themselves than to the large continent of America, to that part of it especially, to which some of their countrymen went sometime ago, where their posterity still live well and independently, and to which, of late, numbers have gone, who shew no inclination to return; but, on the contrary, send the most favourable accounts to their friends and acquaintance in the Highlands, and the most pressing invitations for them to follow after them across the Atlantic. Here they still belong to the British empire, and are happy under the benign influence of its administration. Here, at ease, they may enjoy all those civil blessings which the noblest constitution under heaven was intended to communicate to all ranks belonging to it, and to make these blessings permanent and sure.

In the following pages, I mean to give my countrymen a short sketch of the province of North Carolina, with regard to its climate, soil, produce, and manner of settling there, founded upon unquestionable evidence, as well as personal observation, by which it will appear how little credit is due to the ridiculous and discouraging accounts given in the public papers, at the desire of some of the land-holders, by which also will be shewn, that of all our colonies it is the most proper for Highlanders of any degree to remove to, if they want to live in a state of health, ease, and independence. . . .

. . . The climate is agreeable and wholesome in general; and, compared with the rest of the northern hemisphere, may be looked upon as the most temperate part of the earth on the north side of the equator. It agrees, in general, with that of Virginia; but where they differ, it is much to the advantage of Carolina. The summers are warmer than in Virginia; but the winters are milder and shorter; nor are there such sudden transitions from heat to cold, nor such violent extremes as in Virginia. The winters are seldom severe enough to freeze any considerable body of water, and affect only the mornings and evenings, when the air is felt as sharp as in the Highlands; but the frosts have seldom strength to resist the noon-day sun; so that many tender plants, that do not stand the winter of Virginia, flourish here. The sky in winter is commonly clear and serene, and no deep snow is to be seen. The climate in summer is said, by people of observation, to resemble that of Italy and Lisbon, and indeed they lye in pretty near the same latitude. . . .

. . . Its commodities and general produce are very valuable, consisting of rice, indico, hemp, tobacco, fir, deer skins, turpentine, pitch, tar, raw hides, tanned leather, flower, flax-seed, cotton, corn, pease, pottatoes, honey, bees-wax, Indian corn, barrelled beef and pork, tallow, butter, rosin, square timber of different sorts, deals, staves, and all kind of lumber. This short description will not admit of entering into the manner in which the above commodities are cultivated; but the late settlers there from the Highlands are assiduous in their employments; and this, joined with the hospitality, friendship and harmony, that subsists among them in general, from whatever country, cannot fail, in a short time, of making the province flourish, and of rewarding their labour with independence and wealth, the offspring of ingenuity and industry. . . .

. . . The land, in general, along the sea coast, is light and sandy, and promises little in appearance to a stranger; it is, however, of a generous nature, and helped by a kindly sun, yields corn and tobacco extremely well, and, when flooded, yield rice plentifully. But, along the sides of rivers and creeks, there is a fine black mold, and rich soil, for about a mile and a half back from either bank of the river, which, without manure, returns plentifully whatever is committed to it. This good soil spreads still wider, and improves continually, as you advance into the country, and then it is uniformly good and fertile for immense tracts of land. The whole country is in a manner one forest, where our planters have not cleared it. And at a 100 miles from the sea, where it begins to grow hilly, and mixed with rising grounds, the soil is of an amazing fertility, fitted for every purpose of human life. Nor can any thing be imagined more pleasant to the eye; than the variegated appearance of this back country. The air is here pure and wholesome, and the heat in summer much more temperate than on the flat sandy coast. It is diversified in the most agreeable manner, with arable lands, meadows, and woods; here and there appear rising hills; and its forests abound with excellent timber, such as oak of several sorts, cyprus, hickory, the pine, the walnut, the ash, the poplar, the beech, the elm, the sycamore, the laurel, the bay, the gum, and the mulberry, with many others not mentioned. This furnishes the inhabitants with plenty of fire-wood, and the best of timber for ship-building and other uses. The woods in general wear a refreshing verdure through the year: and the earth is rendered rich and delightful by the fine rivers and streams which glide through them. Where I travelled, the banks of the rivers from Wilmington to far above Cross Creek, were agreeably adorned with fine seats, villas, and pleasant farm-houses, at moderate distances, on either side, which afforded a most enchanting scene of the ease and happiness which the present settlers enjoy: and, in general, most of the present planters may be said to have a river at their door, and easy conveyance for their commodities to market. ...

The method of settling in Carolina, is to find out a space of King's land, or unpatented land, and to get an order from the governor, which order is given to a surveyor; when the survey is finished, he draws a plan of that space of land, which plan is returned into the office for recording patents, &c. then he gets his patent or right signed by the governor, which is good for ever after; the expence of all this is commonly about ten guineas, and sometimes not so much: supposing the run of land taken up be 640 acres, only there is 2s. and 6d. quit rents paid yearly for the hundred acres.

... I have been informed, that if a settler can keep three servants or negroes clearing his grounds for two years, he may sell 700 bushels of wheat, and 5000 weight of tobacco for every year afterwards, besides many other articles. Two men and four horses will work a large plantation in their best land, after cleared. They often plow with one horse.

Wheat is sown in October and November, and some in March. They plant Indian corn and tobacco between April and May. Some lands give three crops in the year. They sow flax-seed the first of March, which they pull the first of May; then they plant the ground with corn, which is ripe the latter end of September, and then sow it with turnip for the winter, which grow very large.... I may here observe, that there were neither horses, cows, sheep, or hogs, in America, till carried thither by the Europeans; and now they are multiplied so extremely, that many of them are allowed to run wild in some provinces. Here the settlers have plenty of all European animals. To have 2 or 300 cows is very common; some have 1000 and upwards. I knew a few planters who had 500 calves in a season, and some have more. . . .

Young healthy negroes are bought there for between 25 and 40 l. Five of these will clear and labour a plantation the first year, so as you shall have every thing in abundance for your family, with little trouble to yourself, and be able to spare many articles for market; to which every year again, as the ground advances in being cleared, you may send great quantities of flower, flax-seed, indico, rice, butter, tallow, pease, pota-toes, live stock, pork, beef, and tobacco. And I cannot help mentioning here, the happiness in which blacks live in this and most of the provinces of America, compared to the wretchedness of their condition in the sugar islands. Good usage is what alone can make the negroes well attached to their masters interest. The inhabitants of Carolina, sensible of this, treat these valuable servants in an indulgent manner, and something like rational beings. . . .

. . . As in every rising colony, so in this, tradesmen are much wanted; and the demand for them must increase in proportion to the number of settlers that resort to it. Accordingly, at present, tradesmen of all kinds have the greatest encouragement here; those most in request, are mill-wrights, coopers, wheel-wrights, house and ship-carpenters, black-smiths. Here farmers would get good employment; fullers, dyers, and stocking-weavers, are much wanted. The ship-carpenters get 13s. per day; the cooper half-a-crown for every barrel he makes; the taylor from 30 to 40s. for the bare making of a suit of clothes; the shoe-maker from 5 to 6s. for making a pair of shoes; wrights and masons 5s. a-day; weavers get every 4th yard for working either woolen or linen cloth, and so on. To enter into more particulars would require a volume.

. . . Here we see, that a man of small substance, if upon a precarious footing at home, can, at once, secure to himself a handsome, independ-ent living, and do well for himself and posterity. The poorest man, if he can but work, procures, at once, plenty of subsistence, which grows yearly upon his hands, until, by gentle and agreeable labour, he arrives, at last, at a state of affluence and ease. None of either sex or profession need fear the want of employment, or an ample reward and encouragement in their different occupations and callings. All modes of Christian worship, not detrimental to society, are here tolerated, as in the other royal governments in North America. The church of England is the established religion; but the Presbyterians are most numerous; and divines of that order might here find decent livings; lawyers and physicians are here respected; professors of the sciences are as yet few; teachers of youth are much caressed, and wanted. A rising colony is always reckoned a proper field for the honest, industrious merchant to prosper. Tradesmen, mechanics, and labourers of all sorts, have here an ample range before them: hither then they may repair, and no longer remain in a starving and grovelling condition at home: they may hasten across the Atlantic, and carry over with them some remains of the true old British spirit before it be totally vitiated and extinguished: thither let them import their yet generous and liberal sentiments: let them transport thither the polite arts and sciences, that they may grow up and flourish in a happier clime, and under more benign skies. Here each may sit safe, and at ease, under his own fig-tree, indulging himself in the natural bent of his genius, in patronizing the useful arts of life, and in practicing the virtues of humanity. In a word, let the Highlanders only compare the situation of the country they now live in, to the country of which I have given them but a rude and imperfect draught, and then, if they can, let them long hesitate about the choice they are to make.

Portaskaig in Islay   Scotus Americanus
May 24th, 1773

Further Reading

Altman, Ida and James Horn (eds.), *"To Make America": European Emigration in the Early Modern Period*. Berkeley: University of California Press, 1991.

Bailyn, Bernard, *Voyagers to the West: A Passage in the Peopling of America on the Eve of Revolution*. New York: Alfred A. Knopf, 1986.

Bailyn, Bernard and Philip D. Morgan (eds.), *Strangers within the Realm: Cultural Margins of the First British Empire*. Chapel Hill: University of North Carolina Press, 1991.

Ekirch, A. Roger, *Bound for America: The Transportation of British Convicts to the Colonies, 1718–1775*. New York: Oxford University Press, 1990.

Fogleman, Aaron, *Hopeful Journeys: German Immigration, Settlement, and Political Culture in Colonial America, 1717–1775*. Philadelphia: University of Pennsylvania Press, 1996.

Games, Alison, *Migration and the Origins of the English Atlantic World*. Cambridge, MA: Harvard University Press, 1999.

Pestana, Carla Gardina and Sharon V. Salinger (eds.), *Inequality in Early America*. Hanover, NH: University Press of New England, 1999.

Salinger, Sharon, *"To Serve Well and Faithfully": Labor and Indentured Servitude in Pennsylvania, 1682–1800*. New York: Cambridge University Press, 1987.

Wokeck, Marianne S., *Trade in Strangers: The Beginnings of Mass Migration to North America*. University Park: Pennsylvania State University Press, 1999.

6

Awakening

Introduction

Article
Frank Lambert, " 'Pedlar in Divinity': George Whitefield and the Great Awakening, 1737–1745," *Journal of American History* 77 (1990): 812–37.

Documents
1 Nathan Cole, "The Spiritual Travels of Nathan Cole," ed. Michael J. Crawford, *William and Mary Quarterly*, 3rd ser., 33 (1976): 89–126 (excerpts).

2 Charles Chauncy, *A Letter...to Mr. George Wishart* (1742), in Richard Bushman (ed.), *The Great Awakening: Documents on the Revival of Religion, 1740–1745* (New York: Atheneum, 1970), pp. 116–21 (excerpts). [Source given: (Charles Chauncy), *A Letter from a Gentleman in Boston, to Mr. George Wishart, One of the Ministers of Edinburgh, Concerning the State of Religion in New-England* (Edinburgh, 1742), pp. 5–15, 17–24.]

3 Jonathan Edwards, *The Distinguishing Marks* (1741), in Richard Bushman (ed.), *The Great Awakening: Documents on the Revival of Religion, 1740–1745* (New York: Atheneum, 1970), pp. 121–7 (excerpts). [Source given: Jonathan Edwards, *The Distinguishing Marks of a Work of the Spirit of God...* (Boston, 1741), pp. 62–4, 66–79.]

Further Reading

Introduction

Beginning in the 1730s, Britain's colonies experienced a series of religious revivals that came to be collectively known as the "Great Awakening." The revivals were stimulated by a growing number of itinerant preachers, the most influential and widely known of whom was an English evangelist named George Whitefield. While the Awakening has often been cast by historians as a reaction against the growing commercialization of colonial life, which many preachers believed was undermining religious values, Frank Lambert argues that Whitefield's genius lay in his ability to apply commercial methods and ideas to the process of spreading God's word. Whitefield was a central figure in the emergence of a transatlantic evangelical movement that generated enormous popular appeal through the use of advance publicity, printed materials, and a commercial vocabulary. Lambert's essay shows how Whitefield drew on Christian sentiments with deep roots in colonial communities, but relied upon new systems of communication, travel, and trade for their dissemination.

Whitefield's effectiveness depended upon an audience's immediate, emotional response to the power of his words. Most of his sermons were structured to make his hearers painfully conscious of their moral failings, to emphasize the grace of God, and to communicate the joy of deliverance through faith. This structure, which carried his audiences through a cycle of emotional responses, differed sharply from that of most preaching in the colonies, which generally offered logical explications of biblical texts. The impact of Whitefield's preaching was also heightened by the excitement that surrounded his brief visit to a community, in contrast with the experience of regular clergymen who preached to the same congregation Sunday after Sunday. Whitefield delivered his favorite sermons hundreds of times, until they were perfectly crafted dramatic performances. The cumulative effect could be overwhelming and life-changing, as it was for Nathan Cole (document 1). What aspects of Whitefield's visit most impressed him? What message did he take from the sermon he heard? How did his encounter with Whitefield change Cole's life?

Controversy followed Whitefield on his travels. His own journals often broadcast local conflicts to a wider reading public and helped to stimulate a public debate on his methods. For many regular clergy, including Charles Chauncy, Whitefield's evangelizing produced little except enthusiasm, confusion, and distraction from the steady virtues of a mature Christian faith (document 2). Others, including Jonathan Edwards, were convinced that the spiritual impact of the "awakening" was real and its fruits lasting (document 3). How did Chauncy and Edwards disagree about the proper methods for bringing about Christian conversion? How did each regard Christian enthusiasm? Which view do you find more persuasive?

"Pedlar in Divinity": George Whitefield and the Great Awakening, 1737–1745

Frank Lambert

When the Anglican evangelist George Whitefield arrived at Lewis Town, Pennsylvania, on October 30, 1739, he brought with him more than his zeal to declare the necessity of a spiritual new birth. His cargo in the hold of the *Elizabeth* contained boxes of evangelical books and pamphlets, including Benjamin Jenks's *Prayers and Offices of Devotion for Families*, John Flavel's *Husbandry Spiritualised*, Isaac Watts's *Divine Songs*, William Law's *A Practical Treatise Upon Christian Perfection*, John Norris's *A Treatise Concerning Christian Prudence*, 200 copies of the *Country-parson's advice to his parishioners*, and 150 volumes of the *Book of Common Prayer*. He also transported cartons of his own printed sermons, journals, letters, and prayers. These items represented just part of the apparatus he employed to generate religious enthusiasm in the intercolonial revivals known as the Great Awakening.

Whitefield's shipload of consumer merchandise symbolizes his immersion in a thoroughly commercialized society, one that provided him with the means of constructing a new religious discourse – modern revivalism. Recent works have illuminated how Whitefield and other evangelicals shaped the Great Awakening. One imaginative volume has focused on Whitefield's innovations in rhetoric and social communication that challenged local distinctions and authority relations. Case studies have explored the revivalist's audiences, in particular those factors influencing the colonists' attitudes toward the awakening – a complex interaction of age, gender, church membership, and social standing. And one landmark in early American historiography has indicated that commerce long viewed as destructive of traditional values, including piety – served as a means of promoting community and religion. However, Whitefield's appropriation of new commercial techniques to publicize the revivals has only been alluded to (often in passing) without systematic development. What was new about Whitefield was the skill as an entrepreneur, an impresario, that made him a full-fledged forerunner to evangelists like Charles Grandison Finney and Billy Graham.

One recent writer asserted that "crowds materialized out of nowhere to hear [Whitefield] speak in the most stirring terms about the 'New Birth,'" adding an offhanded acknowledgment that "word" of Whitefield's successes "prepared" new regions to receive him. However, by applying means from the world of commerce to publicize his meetings, Whitefield generated large, enthusiastic crowds. Like the rest of us, the evangelist constructed his social reality with the elements at hand, and in the mid-eighteenth century, commercial language and techniques abounded, affording him a new way of organizing, promoting, and explaining his evangelical mission. Thus, the spreading market enabled him to conceive of organizing a revival spanning the Atlantic, making "the whole world his parish."[1] Improvements in marketing organization and practices provided the means of relieving the suffering of "strangers at a distance," transforming mere awareness of distant needs into a moral imperative to deliver spiritual and material aid. In Whitefield's case, that meant preaching the gospel to the "uttermost parts of the earth," including the wilderness of Georgia. Drawing upon the experience of enterprising merchants selling their wares at great distances, Whitefield prepared remote auditors to receive the spoken word through advance publicity, especially that of newspaper advertising. And he employed a commercial vocabulary to convey the necessity of the New Birth to his listeners who themselves thought in categories of market exchange.

An argument that advance publicity and self-promotion alone explain the Grand Itinerant's attraction of unprecedented crowds is unfounded and reductionist. However, an examination of his promotional strategies does provide a new understanding not only of Whitefield's success but also of the diffusion of commercialism throughout mid-eighteenth-century society. It indicates a need to view the Great Awakening in a larger context, as part of an evangelical stirring that occurred throughout the Atlantic world. And such a study points toward a reexamination of the relation between commerce and religion, challenging the interpretation that the two were antithetical, suggesting instead a creative tension whereby evangelists such as Whitefield, while preaching against a selfish preoccupation with the pursuit of wealth, employed the tools of trade to promote the gospel.

Contemporaries observed and commented on the extent and importance of Whitefield's advance publicity. Opponents and supporters alike remarked on the evangelist's use of print to promote his work. In early 1740, the antirevivalist, Timothy Cutler, an Anglican minister in Boston, complained in a letter to the bishop of London that Whitefield's "Journals, Sermons, and Pamphlets are reprinted and eagerly bought here," adding that "the enthusiastic Notions [were] very much kindled . . . and propagated by his Writings, dispersed everywhere." Six months after the evangelist's departure from New England in October 1740, Cutler lamented that the "ill effects of Mr. Whitefield's visit might to some measure have worn off could we have been preserved from his Writings, and those of his Converts and Followers now spread all over our Country." As a tribute to Whitefield's success in employing print to disseminate his message, Cutler requested a shipment of "orthodox" books to neutralize enthusiastic influence.[2]

Thomas Prince, Jr., the prorevivalist editor of the Boston magazine Whitefield inspired, the *Christian History*, recounted the advance publicity that prepared New Englanders for the evangelist's trip in 1740. Prince recalled the succession of written works that arrived in Boston in the months preceding Whitefield's arrival. First Whitefield mailed copies of his journals and printed sermons to prominent ministers such as Benjamin Colman and Jonathan Edwards. Then Boston newspapers furnished New Englanders accounts of the preacher's successes in the middle and southern colonies – self-promoting reports written by Whitefield himself or his traveling companion William Seward, a London stockjobber, and transmitted through Benjamin Franklin's intercolonial newspaper network. Then supporters such as the Reverend Josiah Smith, heeding Whitefield's plea to "take up [their] pen[s]" on behalf of the revival, published glowing testimonials extolling Whitefield's evangelism and humanitarianism – works that recommended the itinerant to New Englanders. Thus when Whitefield began his services, Bostonians, indeed, "were prepared to embrace him."[3]

By 1739 Whitefield had discovered that "the meanest instruments," especially the press, promoted the gospel by "excit[ing] people's curiosity, and serv[ing] to raise their attention." He explained to Colman his motives for publishing accounts of the revivals, expressing his confidence that "our Lord's cause might be promoted thereby." Whitefield believed that his mission was so great that his publicity should exceed that of "the world." Admonishing his business agent for mishandling the release of a promotional pamphlet, Whitefield wondered, "when will the children of light be as wise in their generation as the children of the world?" His opponents, however, chafed under Whitefield's control of the press. One antirevivalist complained that Whitefield so dominated the newspapers in Philadelphia in 1740 that "printers would not publish anything for [opponents of the revival] and that the press [was] shut against them," a charge Whitefield denied even as he supplied a steady stream of self-serving articles to the publishers.[4]

In the first year of Whitefield's public ministry, press coverage helped elevate him and his revival to an unprecedented level of popular acceptance. While Whitefield was not yet ordained as an Anglican minister and little known outside his hometown of Gloucester, England, he became the best-known evangelist in the Atlantic world in large part because of newspaper advertising, which interpreted his preaching as a second

Reformation. The evangelical bookseller, James Hutton, recorded Whitefield's emergence as the dominant figure in the early stirrings of the revival. In 1737 Whitefield came from Oxford to London "amongst other young awakened preachers," not yet distinguished from the zealous band of aspirants to the ministry. Meanwhile John Wesley, Whitefield's mentor, who had traveled as a missionary to the new colony of Georgia, had written requesting his assistance in Savannah. Whitefield had accepted, forgoing "some advantageous proposals, which were designed to hold him back in England." Hutton reported that "notice of this was given in the papers, with some prominence . . . which brought together great numbers." A wealthy businessman who promoted charity schools – Seward – had placed that advertisement in the London newspapers. Seward introduced Whitefield to the readers as "a young gentleman of distinguished piety, very eminent in his profession, and a considerable fortune [going] voluntarily to preach the gospel in Georgia." Hutton noted that because Seward presented Whitefield as undertaking "a cause . . . without selfish interest, everybody ran after him." Hutton further observed that Seward "also had the result [of Whitefield's performance] put in, viz. that much money was collected at the preaching" for charity schools. For Hutton, it was the "novelty of the thing" – the bold advertising of Whitefield and his success – that attracted "many hundred people . . . curious to hear this Whitefield." The bookseller noted that the other young revivalists also "preached in a more than ordinarily earnest way," but Whitefield, benefiting from the prominent publicity, "was everywhere made known" and emerged as the leading evangelical preacher.[5]

Although the London clergy had long employed newspapers to publicize charity sermons, under Seward's guidance Whitefield transformed mere notices into advertisements rivaling those promoting the latest consumer goods. Typical ecclesiastical entries in the *London Daily Advertiser* announced sermons by presenting the bare essentials: who was to preach, for what charity, in which church, and at what time. And rarely did the ministers provide the press with a report of the services, such as the number attending and the amount collected. By contrast, Seward "sold" Whitefield to the readers, complete with advertising "puffs," appealing details designed to pique interest. Seward's paid advertisements appeared on the front page in the form of news articles written by a third party. The format recounted recent successes and announced upcoming events. In describing Whitefield's performance at St. Swithin's church in September 1737, Seward reported that the evangelist preached an *"excellent"* charity sermon before a *"crowded"* congregation whose contributions were *"remarkable."* He noted that Whitefield's sermon on the *"greatness* of the charity of the poor widow's mites" inspired the auditors to contribute over five pounds including "no less than 800 halfpence." He concluded by announcing Whitefield's next sermon as a continuation of the evangelist's *"truly pious"* undertaking to promote the *"good effects* [charity schools] have on the lower ranks of the people." Seward employed similar language in promoting his own stockjobbing business. His advertisement of November 11, 1739, for instance, announced that he offered for sale shares "in a *new method*, much *more advantageous* to the purchaser than they can *possibly* be bought *any other way*." Whether publicizing sermons or securities, London's daily newspapers provided a powerful means of self-presentation, a lesson Whitefield learned and applied even after Seward's death in October 1740.[6]

Noting that following the press coverage "there was no end of the people flocking to hear the Word of God," Whitefield developed a sustained advertising campaign to promote his charity sermons in London prior to departing on his second American trip. Early in 1739, while collecting for an orphan house he had founded in Georgia, Seward placed two or three notices per week in the *London Daily Advertiser*, relying also on verbal communication at the services to publicize upcoming meetings. However, because of an embarrassing episode, Whitefield's "press agent" announced in the May 3 edition that "daily notice [would] be given in [the] paper." Although Whitefield had announced at a Sunday sermon when and where he would preach over the next few days, many people, including several "persons of distinction," awaited the evangelist at the wrong site. Thenceforward, daily newspaper advertising became a standard feature of Whitefield's publicity until his sailing for America almost three months later.[7]

Whitefield also benefited from the extensive advertising of his printed works, which both contributed to his growing popularity and resulted from his spreading fame. Booksellers recognized Whitefield as an author who had "made sermons, once a drug, a vendible commodity." Consequently, enterprising publishers vied with each other to exploit the lucrative demand for the evangelist's writings. In one issue of the *Daily Advertiser*, for instance, a printseller advertised a portrait of Whitefield, "neatly engrav'd from a drawing taken by an excellent painter," and on the same page, a bookseller advertised two of the evangelist's sermons plus a collection of prayers "recommended by George Whitefield." In the summer of 1738, competition between publishers over which had the right to publish Whitefield's first journal resulted in a windfall of publicity. The rivals, Thomas Cooper and James Hutton, advertised their editions on the same pages of the *Daily Advertiser* for a full week. They also engaged in a front-page debate over whose edition offered the more faithful rendering of Whitefield's manuscript. While no evidence points to Seward's involvement, someone as zealous and shrewd as he must have placed a copy of Whitefield's diary in the hands of the non-Methodist Cooper. The itinerant had mailed the document to Hutton, at the time an ardent supporter. Whatever the case, the competing advertisements heightened interest in the journals, increasing their sales and thus promoting the revival.[8]

By the beginning of 1738, colonial newspapers reprinted Whitefield's advertisements, almost two years before his preaching tour that triggered the Great Awakening. Philadelphia's *American Weekly Mercury* included Seward's initial report of Whitefield's success at St. Swithin's, complete with the superlatives describing the evangelist's preaching and fund raising. The *Williamsburg Virginia Gazette* highlighted the revivalist's commitment to go to Georgia and his attraction of "so great a concourse of people." William Parks, the Williamsburg editor, may have selected the report about Whitefield because it stood out from the blander announcements of other Anglican clergymen. Or, he may have received the advertisement through Whitefield's expanding letter-writing network, a transatlantic chain of correspondence by which evangelicals circulated revival news, recommended devotional literature, and exchanged successful strategies. A year later, Whitefield provided Parks with material – sermons, pamphlets, newspaper reports, and journals – to reprint in his newspaper or to publish and sell through his bookstore. Whatever the case, press coverage on both sides of the Atlantic prepared men and women to receive the spoken word from this extraordinary evangelist.[9]

Upon arriving in America in October 1739, Whitefield continued to promote his revivals through vigorous newspaper coverage. Though Whitefield's associates, John Syms and James Habersham, handled "press relations" while traveling with the itinerant, Seward proved the most aggressive and effective agent. In his own journal, published in 1740 in England and America, the zealous businessman recorded his role in newspaper reporting and press relations. Successive entries during 1740 reveal the nature and extent of his activities. "April 27. Wrote paragraph for the News, of our Brother's Preaching, etc., particularly the following to be published in New York. April 29. Wrote and examined sundry things for the Press; Particularly Mr. Whitefield's Letter. . . . May 2. Call'd at Mr. Franklin's the Printer."[10]

While advance men and merchants performed the role of press agents, Whitefield himself exercised direct control over press coverage. After he dispatched Seward to England in April 1740 to raise money, the itinerant reported his own performances and successes, producing third-person accounts of his latest preaching tour in the middle colonies, complete with puffs. He opened a typical report with a statistical account of his activities, indicating he was on shore thirty-three days, traveled "hundreds" of miles, preached fifty-eight sermons, attracted crowds of up to twenty thousand, and collected "near 500 pounds sterling." Then, assessing the power of the revival, he wrote, "Great and visible effects followed his preaching. There was never such a general awakening, and concern for the things of God known in America before." He closed by announcing his intention to visit New England in the fall and return to Philadelphia afterwards. Thus, Whitefield advertised his revivals under the guise of a newspaper article – just the kind of "objective" third-party report Josiah Wedgwood instructed his associates to secure to promote pottery sales because he considered it the most powerful of advertisements.[11]

Although print runs remained small for mid-eighteenth-century newspapers, seldom numbering more than a few hundred, improvements in marketing and distribution meant that Whitefield could reach a wide audience. Parliament's failure to renew the Licensing Act of 1694 prompted a proliferation of newspapers in London. The first daily was published in 1702, and by 1740 London boasted of "three dailies, five weeklies, seven thrice a week, and three thrice a week halfpenny posts, or fifty-three issues of various papers per week." And the number of provincial and colonial newspapers mushroomed as well. But the number of subscribers does not indicate the readership of newspapers and books. Coffeehouses, which sprang up throughout England in the half century before Whitefield's revivals, operated as circulating libraries where gentlemen gathered to read the latest newspapers and books. And entrepreneurial booksellers offered books for loan as well as for sale, enabling those who could not afford the purchase price to read the latest works. In Whitefield's evangelical circles, religious societies and itinerant preachers served a similar function, widening the readership of evangelical papers and books. By the mid-1740s, after their well-publicized theological split, both Whitefield and John Wesley maintained "book rooms" that distributed their works through their separate "connexions."[12]

Most of the fourteen colonial newspaper publishers played important roles in promoting Whitefield's revivals, advertising his writings, and soliciting contributions. As the major intercolonial event in 1740–1, Whitefield's revival enjoyed extensive coverage. For example, 60 percent of the *Pennsylvania Gazette*'s issues of that period devoted space to Whitefield, often including reports of his successes and itineraries, reprints of his publications, and advertisements for his writings. And though Whitefield conducted most of his preaching tours in northern cities, the *Virginia Gazette* carried stories of the evangelist in a third of its issues. But, more than frequency, the space allotted Whitefield within single editions attested to the widespread interest he generated. For instance, during 1740, Andrew Bradford often devoted the entire front page of the *American Weekly Mercury* to the evangelist's letters, journals, endorsements, and testimonials. In seventeen of fifty-two issues of the *South Carolina Gazette* published between the summers of 1740 and 1741, the lead story was a heated controversy pitting Whitefield and his supporters against his opponents. The disputes centered on whether Whitefield's "enthusiasm" was acceptable behavior for an Anglican minister. Its persistence as a news item suggests revival controversy was good business for the newspaper.

No one was a more aggressive Whitefield promoter than Franklin. Though differing in religious views, Franklin and Whitefield enjoyed a lasting and profitable relationship that satisfied both men – the publisher sold more newspapers and books, and the evangelist reached a wider audience. Franklin sent sermons, pamphlets, and journals through his intercolonial booksellers' network, insuring fast and widespread dissemination. And Franklin's newspaper coverage of the revival was so favorable and extensive he was forced to print a defense against charges of editorial bias in the *Pennsylvania Gazette*. But the printer's support went beyond publishing. He helped Whitefield raise money through an effective subscription by which evangelicals covenanted to make installment payments to underwrite the revival. He also defended the preacher's integrity when opponents accused Whitefield of misappropriating funds donated for the orphan house. However, Whitefield also helped Franklin. From 1739 to 1741, Franklin published 110 titles – as many as he printed during the previous seven years. Almost all the increase came from Whitefield. The itinerant's works sold well. Franklin projected sales of two hundred for an expensive four-volume collection of two volumes each of sermons and journals, but actual sales exceeded the forecast by more than 25 percent. And according to Franklin's ledgers, Whitefield's works generated more revenue in some cities, for example, Charleston, South Carolina, and Newport, Rhode Island, than did his popular *Poor Richard's Almanac*.

Desiring a vehicle dedicated to the propagation of his revivals, in 1741 Whitefield assumed management of the London-based evangelical magazine, the *Weekly History*. His action inspired similar periodicals in Scotland and New England. In taking this initiative Whitefield responded to an expressed desire among evangelicals for a periodical dedicated to their cause. One subscriber noted that the "polite world have their Spectators, Tatler's, Guardian's, and Comedies," adding that "the Children of God also [should have] their proper entertainment, their weekly amusement, their divine miscellany, and the historical account of the progress of their Lord's kingdom." Whitefield responded to such demands by supplying the editor, John Lewis, "fresh matter every week," including sermons, journals, and letters. But by 1742 the evangelist had assumed editorial control and determined the magazine's contents and format. And the paper became the official organ of the Whitefield Methodists, as the Calvinist branch of the movement became known. In the autumn of 1743, the paper assumed a new title, describing its purpose and scope: *Christian History or General account of the Progress of the Gospel in England, Scotland, and America as far as the Reverend Mr. Whitefield, his fellow-labourers and Assistants are Concerned.*[13]

Whether Whitefield published his magazine or other printed matter such as sermons, he considered the reader as a consumer. He wrote for a mass audience that included the poor. In a letter to his fellow evangelist, William Hervey, Whitefield disclosed his plans to sell four sermons for just sixpence, noting that he wrote "for the poor, you for the polite and noble." Thus while Hervey selected for one of his works "a very neat paper, with an elegant type," Whitefield instructed his printer to reduce the paper costs for a sermon "designed for the poor... [because] the poor must have them cheap." The evangelist also expressed his consciousness of the reader as he contemplated the length of his printed works. In explaining the brevity of one pamphlet, he noted, "I wrote short, because I know long compositions generally weary the reader." His sensitivity to readers as consumers resulted in the wide diffusion of his works throughout the Atlantic world, attested to by booksellers, followers, and opponents alike.[14]

Whitefield promoted his revivals through the widespread distribution of sermons and journals. The significance of the evangelist's printed sermons is of particular interest because of Franklin's well-known criticism of them. Focusing on the heated controversy the published discourses sparked, Franklin believed the itinerant's sermons gave advantage to his enemies. The printer pointed out that they could not attack "unguarded expressions and erroneous opinions" delivered in oration. But his critics dissected his writings, leading Franklin to conclude, "I am of the opinion if he had never written anything, he would have left behind him a much more numerous and important sect." However, Whitefield did not desire to create another denomination or church nor to swell the ranks of an existing denomination. Indeed, he incurred the wrath of the Scottish evangelist, Ebenezer Erskine, by refusing to join the Presbyterian church. Whitefield's intention was to replace the "bad books" written by such rationalists as John Tillotson, archbishop of Canterbury, for example, with "good books" adhering to Calvinist tenets, thus strengthening Calvinist tendencies within the Anglican communion. Whitefield encouraged his followers to display the badges of their New Birth through material goods – the books they carried and the dress they wore. He exhorted them to "put on [their] cockades" that men and women would know them "to be Christ's." His own books could be displayed as just such cockades. And his written sermons advertised the kind of discourse auditors could expect at his services.[15]

To thousands, the printed sermons also had important symbolic significance. They represented the principles of the revival – the primacy of the individual in salvation, renunciation of unconverted ministers, and emotional experience as the basis of religion. Opponents like Charles Chauncy and Timothy Cutler of Boston noted the symbolic nature of the sermons, crediting their ubiquitous presence with perpetuating religious "enthusiasm." Printed sermons in Whitefield's revivals were analogous to consumer goods displayed by the followers of the radical English politician, John Wilkes. Pro-Wilkes potters sold mugs, punch bowls, and other ceramic articles adorned with the candidate's political slogans. Mercers marketed such Wilkite clothing as coats with special buttons, cuffs, and handkerchiefs. Other merchandise symbolizing the radical cause included tobacco pipes, candlesticks, and tankards. All of these goods served as visible means by which supporters identified with and participated in a movement.

Whitefield disseminated his sermons in large numbers, with publishers eager to satisfy the demand during the revival's peak years. From the first year of his ministry in 1737, the evangelist's discourses sold well. Of his sermon on the necessity of a new birth, the evangelist noted, "This sermon sold well to persons of all denominations, and was dispersed very much both at home and abroad." As he provided his bookseller, Hutton, a steady supply of homilies for publication he observed that they "were everywhere called for." On his first landing in Philadelphia, Whitefield authorized Franklin's rival, the publisher Bradford, to print two of his sermons when Bradford forecast sales of one thousand, a significant press run for any publication in the mid-eighteenth century. In the spring of 1740, the itinerant reported to a London supporter that "God is pleased to give a great blessing to my printed sermons. They are now in the hands of thousands in these parts." And Cutler lamented to the bishop of London, "His Journals, Sermons, and Pamphlets are reprinted and eagerly bought here."[16]

Through his publications, Whitefield did more than publicize his revivals. For some people, his writings represented the primary means of receiving his message. While traveling through the southern colonies in 1739, the evangelist noted the difficulty of holding revivals among a sparse and scattered population. Though he conducted services, the absence of sizable towns and difficulty of travel limited the crowds. While in Virginia, the evangelist preached in Williamsburg, unaware of a small group of evangelicals just sixty miles away in Hanover County who were unable to come to hear him preach. The lay leader of the group, Samuel Morris, observed that Whitefield's "fame was much spread abroad, as a very warm and alarming Preacher, which made such of us in Hanover as had been awakened, very eager to see and hear him." Despite Morris's eloquent statement of the efficacy of Whitefield's promotional campaign, the group did not hear him. They procured, however, from a Scottish traveler a "book of his sermons preached in Glasgow and taken from his mouth in short Hand."[17] Thus Whitefield's publications circulated through unexpected routes and with surprising consequences.

Through reading Whitefield's sermons, the Virginians spread the revival. Acting as a surrogate preacher, Morris began to read the sermons aloud at meetings attended by ten to twelve faithful souls. While the writings of reformers like Martin Luther had introduced the members to "the Way of Justification," the "Concern was not very extensive." But when Morris read Whitefield's works, "many were convinced to seek deliverance with the greatest solicitude." As the readings continued, the group grew too large to meet in homes and built its first meetinghouse. Unable to find a suitable pastor – that is, one who was evangelical and Calvinist – these dissenting evangelicals continued to rely on Whitefield's printed sermons. "When the report of these Sermons and the Effects occasioned by reading them was spread Abroad," Morris reported, he was invited to several places to read them, and "by this Means the concern was propagated." Through the aid of Whitefield's printed sermons, the group survived and evolved into the first Presbyterian church in Virginia.[18]

By preceding the oral message with the printed word, Whitefield's journals were effective in raising expectations for the revivals. Upon reading Whitefield's journals, Benjamin Colman wrote, "I lov'd and honour'd [you] from the first sight I had of your Journal to Gibraltar." He continued, "when I read your Journals, my Heart tells me, if God were not with you of a Truth, neither could your bodily Strength hold out and less the Powers of your Mind." Thomas Prince, editor of Boston's evangelical magazine, the *Christian History*, recalled that in 1738 New Englanders began reading about the remarkable success of the evangelist in "his first two Journals." In the weeks before the first Boston preaching tour, lengthy journal extracts in the newspapers traced the revival's northward progress.[19]

Whitefield disseminated his journals in various forms and through several media. The evangelist and his assistants circulated his latest journals through the letter-writing network. Often he mailed extracts from the version in process to give his supporters a current account of the revival. And on occasion the evangelist even read from his journals to religious societies. He also sent copies to newspapers where they sometimes appeared in successive issues on the front page. Eager to print anything with Whitefield's name on it, book publishers facilitated the dispersion of the journals. Though all sixteen printed versions emanated from Boston and Philadelphia presses, they radiated through an intercolonial bookseller network. Franklin published the seven journals in a two-volume set and distributed it to other printers and booksellers in Massachusetts, Connecticut, Rhode Island, Pennsylvania, Delaware, Maryland, Virginia, and South Carolina. He also issued an eighth volume for a regional audience, covering only Whitefield's travels in the environs of Philadelphia. Franklin's colonywide network was a new scheme in America, just as Whitefield's open-air preaching was novel. These two innovators naturally joined their intercolonial interests to serve each other.

Not only did Whitefield exploit a wide variety of printed forms, he also employed several merchandising techniques to promote his evangelical activities. One marketing strategy Whitefield favored was serial publication of his sermons and journals. Introduced by imaginative publishers earlier in the eighteenth century, "this method of weekly publication allure[ed] multitudes to peruse books, into which they would otherwise never have looked." Through serialization, Whitefield increased demand two ways. First, the low price for each segment made it affordable for a larger group of people than could purchase the two-volume collection. Second, the serialized journals created a heightened sense of anticipation as readers followed the evangelist's progress toward their own communities. From 1737 through 1741, the formative years of his transatlantic revivals when promotion was most needed, he wrote and published seven different volumes. At the end of the first, describing events from his departure to his arrival at Savannah, he wrote, "I . . . close this part of my Journal," setting the stage for an ongoing account. He also serialized his spiritual autobiography. In 1740, during his second passage to America, he wrote for publication the first part of his life, *A Short Account of God's dealings with the Reverend Mr. George Whitefield*, designed to inform the reader of important events and influences up to those described in his first journal. At the close of the first of two volumes, he wrote, "I shall hereafter relate God's further dealings with my soul, and how He led me into my present way of acting." Advertisements for subsequent volumes of both the journals and the autobiography emphasized the "latest edition" or "most recent account."[20] About every six months, the itinerant sent new editions to his publishers on both sides of the Atlantic.

Whitefield increased publication sales through a variety of creative pricing schemes. Seeking widespread distribution in a mass market,

Whitefield instructed his publisher to "print so as to sell cheap." In the preface to his hymnal, he made explicit the connection between price and purchaser, "As the generality of those who receive the Gospel are commonly the poor of the flock, I have studied cheapness, as well as conciseness." However, raising money for the orphanage through a private subscription for a collection of sermons, the itinerant set a high price of four shillings. Recognizing that merchants such as Thomas Noble of New York bought hundreds of books and sermons for free distribution to those who could not afford them, Whitefield and his booksellers offered quantity discounts. The sermon on the new birth sold for "six pence; or two guineas per hundred for those who give them away," the latter terms representing a 16 percent discount. Through his London printer, Lewis, Whitefield offered a cash discount to encourage early payment on subscription sales. Through flexible pricing Whitefield expanded the market for his publications, facilitating widespread publicity.[21]

Whitefield best displayed his merchandising acumen in efforts to increase the *Weekly History's* sagging circulation and bolster its anemic revenue. After Whitefield returned to London in 1741, the magazine's management began to reflect his consumer-driven mentality. Late in 1742, editor Lewis announced, "we purpose to begin next in a more commodious manner as we are likely to be furnished with more materials," no doubt from the evangelist himself. The editor pledged "to let our readers have more reading for their money" by removing the large title, resulting in "much [more] room for useful reading." And for consumer convenience, the magazine would be made available in pocket size, perhaps an innovation Whitefield borrowed from Franklin, who produced a pocket-sized version of his almanac. And Lewis promised home delivery, dispensing the magazine at "people's houses, at the price of one penny."[22] Through such imaginative merchandising, Whitefield and his associates reversed the fortunes of the publication, which survived well past the revival's decline.

Whitefield was an innovator in advertising. Merchants who viewed markets as restricted to a fixed number of customers did not advertise to create consumer demand. Instead, they merely provided information about the availability of their goods and the terms of sale. However, English capitalists in the eighteenth century expanded both domestic and foreign markets and advertised in order to exploit what they considered to be an elastic consumer demand. With a similar view, Whitefield sought to generate interest in his revivals through aggressive advertising. Opponents protested "the various methods taken up by Mr. Whitefield and his adherents, for trumpeting abroad his fame, and magnifying his person and performance."[23]

Whitefield recognized that negative as well as positive publicity could generate interest in his revivals. Especially during his first three American trips, the evangelist engaged in polemics to differentiate his message of the new birth from what he considered to be the "stirrings of dry bones," rattling from unconverted ministers. In a published letter to the students at Harvard and Yale, he charged both colleges with allowing their "light [to] become darkness." That incendiary tract attacking cherished institutions sparked a heated exchange of supporting and opposing publications. Whitefield wrote of the debate, "A few mistaken, misinformed good old men are publishing halfpenny testimonials against me." However, Whitefield agreed with Colman that such opponents had done him "a real service" by giving the evangelist's friends an opportunity "to publish testimonials in [his] favour." Whitefield recorded in his journal that opponents' charges served in the end to benefit him and the revival because they kept readers' attention focused on him.[24]

On occasion, Whitefield and his associates manipulated the news to publicize the revival. William Seward wrote an account of a dancing school's closing in Philadelphia and attributed its demise to Whitefield's charge that its activities were "inconsistent" with the gospel. Franklin inserted the unedited article in the May 1, 1740, *Pennsylvania Gazette*, sparking a dispute that dominated the paper's front page for the entire month. The school's proprietor accused Franklin of biased coverage and Seward of planting the story to "spread his master's fame."[25] That astute observation proved accurate as the story was reprinted from Boston to Charleston.

Testimonials and endorsements were key elements in Whitefield's advertisement program. They introduced and recommended him to a local community. For instance, when he first arrived in Boston in 1740, he brought with him a strong testimonial from Josiah Smith, a Harvard-educated minister in Charleston, South Carolina. Smith, a friend of Colman, testified to the positive changes Whitefield's preaching had wrought in Charleston. He extolled the itinerant's oratorical prowess and pronounced his theology orthodox. Whitefield delivered the document to Colman and another leading clergyman, Thomas Cooper. Both Colman and Cooper wrote their own endorsements of the evangelist as a preface to Smith's testimony and published the whole as a pamphlet promoting the revival. Whitefield continued to benefit from the testimony by reprinting it in the *Christian Weekly* and circulating it throughout the letter-writing network.

Whitefield's writings initiated a chain of events leading to unsolicited endorsements. A New Yorker in 1739 "read two or three of Mr. Whitefield's Sermons and Part of his Journal, and from thence . . . obtain'd a settled opinion he was a good man." Inspired by what he read, the man attended one of the revival services. After he heard Whitefield, he wrote a strong endorsement of the itinerant's theology and oratory. Philadelphia and Boston newspapers published the endorsement, further extending the influence of a single testimonial.[26]

How Whitefield managed the revival's funds illustrates a final important commercial influence on his ministry. After announcing his intention to evangelize in America, the itinerant preached a series of charity sermons in England, collecting donations of more than a thousand pounds for the orphanage John and Charles Wesley had suggested for Georgia. At the prompting of a merchant, Whitefield bought consumer goods, which he transported on the *Elizabeth*, intending to sell them in America where demand for English merchandise ran high. Upon arriving in Philadelphia, he advertised his wares, conducted an auction, and made a profit sufficient to finance his preaching tour. On a subsequent fund-raising journey, Whitefield purchased a five-hundred-acre plantation in South Carolina with donations he collected in Charleston. Using slave labor, he hoped to generate a surplus to provide working capital for the orphanage. Thus Whitefield the entrepreneur significantly shaped the contours of the ministry of Whitefield the evangelist.

Whitefield exploited the growing consumer demand to help finance the revivals. He found opportunities for profits at almost every level of the distribution chain. As a producer of raw materials for English textile manufactories and provisions for the West Indies market, the master of the Georgia orphanage generated 20 percent of the institution's revenues from such exports. His superintendent, James Habersham, who by the 1750s had become one of Savannah's wealthiest merchants, placed the orphanage schooner in the service of the expanding coastal trade to realize additional earnings from shipping fees. And at the Tabernacle, Whitefield's London headquarters, a bookkeeper managed the evangelist's book-selling business, preparing a weekly report of revenues from the sales of printed material throughout the Atlantic evangelical community.

As a tireless fund raiser, Whitefield not only funded his evangelical and humanitarian interests, he amassed an estate in excess of £3,300 – exclusive of his lands and buildings in England and America. Such a sum was significant in 1770 when an artisan's house and lot in Savannah cost £250 and a teacher at the Georgia orphan house received an annual stipend of £50.

Whitefield's extensive application of the new merchandising techniques set him apart from his evangelical predecessors and contemporaries. Although the revivalist exploited the power of newspaper publicity to "spread his fame" abroad, even his early colleagues in English pietism,

John and Charles Wesley, rejected advertising as a means of promoting their religious enterprises, viewing it as a tasteless "sounding [of] a trumpet."[27] What influenced Whitefield to employ innovations from the marketplace? How and from whom did the evangelist learn the commercial strategies he employed so successfully?

Whitefield's initial inspiration for appropriating commercial means to promote his revivals stemmed from his family's involvement in the market. His father was a wine merchant in Bristol before moving to Gloucester, where he purchased the Bell Inn, whose income placed the elder Whitefield's name near the top of the town's tax rolls. After his father died during George's childhood, the youngster's mother married a man who traded in hardware, who immediately assumed ownership of the tavern. There, George worked as a "common drawer," under both his stepfather and, after the latter's death, his brother Richard, who gained title to the business. Before his departure to begin his studies at Oxford University, Whitefield ran the tavern in his brother's absence for almost a year. In addition to his direct experience in running a local business, Whitefield had at least a glimpse into overseas trade. He spent several months in Bristol with his older brother, James, who was a ship's captain trading in the American and West Indies markets. James sold English manufactured goods, Barbados rum, and muscovado, or raw sugar, at his store on the Charleston, South Carolina, wharf. Indeed, his advertisements appeared in the *South Carolina Gazette* before those of his evangelist brother. James gave financial support to the young minister, but his more important contribution may have been the knowledge he imparted regarding the world of commerce.

Whitefield's childhood friends introduced him to the spreading world of book selling and newspaper publishing. Gabriel Harris, whose father owned Gloucester's most prominent book store, remained a faithful supporter throughout Whitefield's ministry. As a youngster, Whitefield spent considerable time in the Harris home and gained the approbation of the elder Harris, who provided both books and money toward George's studies at Pembroke College at Oxford. He helped promote the young minister by sending one of Whitefield's early sermon manuscripts to an older clergyman, who not only liked the discourse but also paid Whitefield a guinea for the document. Whitefield also associated with Robert Raikes, whose father founded the town's first newspaper, the *Gloucester Journal*. After assuming control of the paper following his father's death, Raikes attended Whitefield's first public sermon and wrote a favorable report in the next edition. At Whitefield's urging, Raikes published extracts from William Law's treatises on practical piety in six successive issues during 1737. Whitefield noted that "God was pleased to give [the reprints] His Blessing."[28] Thus, Whitefield's early friendships introduced him to the print trade, which would later become the most important agent of his advertising and publicity.

Beyond the influence of family and friends in Gloucester, Whitefield was shaped by the spreading commercialized society itself – the world of Daniel Defoe and Bernard Mandeville – where "more [people] than ever was known in former years . . . [engaged] in buying and selling." Because of rising incomes and easy credit, consumers on both sides of the Atlantic had the means to purchase the new consumer goods coming on the market. As the cost of food declined throughout the 1730s and 1740s, the English enjoyed greater purchasing power. And, by the American Revolution, the colonists' per capita income matched that of the British. Further, American merchants made available "a large amount of credit extended for the purchase of all kinds of commodities and services for consumption purposes."[29]

By the second quarter of the eighteenth century, household producers throughout the English countryside turned out "small consumer goods on an unprecedented scale" to meet the demand of a very large and growing market. Defoe noted in 1722 that 120,000 people were employed in the woolen and silk manufactures of Norwich alone. Most worked out of their country homes, spinning yarn or operating looms. They sold their goods through merchants not only in London and the provinces but throughout the Atlantic world as well. One visitor to Maryland observed that "the quick importation of fashions from the mother country is really astonishing. I am almost inclined to believe that a new fashion is adopted earlier by the polished and affluent American than by many opulent persons in the great metropolis." Lorena Walsh's examination of probate inventories in the Chesapeake Bay area revealed that by the 1730s, "middling families got into the act [of consuming] and by the 1750's, even the poorer sorts were finding a wide variety of non-essentials increasingly desirable." Carole Shammas estimated that by 1774, "the average American spent over one quarter of his or her budget on imports from outside his or her colony of residence."[30]

Consumer demand spurred enterprising merchants to restructure the marketplace, creating institutions Whitefield found useful in promoting his religious enterprises. The scope and nature of advertising changed. Print capitalists published newspapers throughout provincial England and colonial America and made their readers aware of the latest London fashions. Generic descriptions of products, such as cloth, paper, and ceramics, characterized advertisements in the 1720s, but by the 1750s, New York advertisers publicized the availability of "purple gloves, rough gloves, chamois gloves, buff gloves, 'Maid's Black Silk' gloves, 'Maid's Lamb Gloves,' and even 'Men's Dog Skin Gloves.'" Retailers introduced "bright, glass-fronted and bow-windowed" shops, "enabling English householders to obtain goods from the length and breadth of the country." And Scottish merchants extended the retail network to the sparsely populated Virginia countryside. In 1743 Francis Jerdone, a merchant in Hanover County, observed, "There are 25 stores within 18 miles round me . . . and 4 or 5 more expected next year from some of the [British] outports." Middlemen became more important links in the lengthening distribution chain, as their warehouses and credit smoothed the flow of goods from manufacturers to final consumer. A new breed of wholesalers, traveling merchants, carried with them goods worth upwards of a thousand pounds sterling, supplied country shops with goods in bulk (called "whole pieces"), and gave "large credit" to shopkeepers. And as they had for centuries, itinerant hawkers and peddlers continued to sell their wares directly to consumers in London and beyond. Communications improvements enabled merchants to expand the flow of goods to the widening market. English businessmen raised funds through subscriptions to build the canals and turnpikes necessary to make exchanges easier and to mobilize effective demand.[31]

Consumer demand also prompted businessmen to develop new merchandising techniques that Whitefield applied to the propagation of religion. Prior to the mid-eighteenth century, many manufacturers were content to remain at home and "let the orders come to them." But by 1780 William Hutton, observing business practices in Birmingham, could write, "The merchant stands at the head of the manufacturer . . . [and] travels the whole island to promote the sale; a practice which would have astounded our forefathers." The brass manufacturer Matthew Boulton and the potter Josiah Wedgwood pioneered many of the aggressive sales strategies that characterized what Neil McKendrick has called the "birth of a consumer society." Boulton seized such special occasions as royal birthdays to conduct spectacular London sales "to boost demand and to win the attention of the fashion spreaders." Advertisements included familiar references to royal patronage to "milk the effects of social emulation." But advertising alone was insufficient in warding off competitors who sought their share of the growing consumer demand. Wedgwood concluded that "various means must be unremittingly made use of to awake, and keep up the attention of the world to the fine things we are making." He and other entrepreneurs employed a range of selling ploys that sound anachronistically modern, including market research, product differentiation, giveaways to promote sales, advanced credit, three-tier discount schemes, solicited puffs, and even "false attacks organized to provide the opportunity to publicize the counter-attack."[32]

The new commercialism produced a language of goods that extended to human endeavors beyond the business world. John Brewer has claimed that Wilkes "cribbed from the tradesman's copybook" to fund his campaign and capture votes.[33] And George Whitefield linked religion and commerce to organize and promote the transatlantic revivals. The young Anglican's message of the necessity of a spiritual new birth was not new. Jonathan Edwards of Northampton, Massachusetts, had sounded a similar theme in the regional awakening he led in 1735. Whitefield's innovation lay in the commercialization of his revivals. Although the eighteenth-century English world underwent significant demographic and economic change, churches clung to tradition. The norm was a settled ministry serving local parishioners who gathered at fixed times for worship. With a commercialized perspective strengthened by his familiar association with merchants, Whitefield developed a different vision – one informed by patterns of thought gleaned from the expanding market. Like the merchants who generated their own consumer demand by planting colonies and advertising their wares at home and abroad, Whitefield applied the latest marketing strategies to create and exploit a transatlantic audience for evangelicalism.

Whitefield heightened his familiarity with the world of commerce as he immersed himself in the Atlantic market to promote and fund his favorite charity, the Georgia orphan house (which he called Bethesda). Whitefield sharpened his entrepreneurial skills as he sought a commercial enterprise to make the orphanage self-sustaining. Throughout the 1740s, Whitefield's correspondence reflected his preoccupation with such mundane matters as profits from book sales, bills of exchange to settle transatlantic accounts, and the high cost of labor. Whitefield tried to keep track of funds being raised and disbursed on both sides of the Atlantic. While in Charleston in 1745, for instance, he requested his London agent, John Syms, to send "a short sketch of my accompts that I may know how my affairs stand." To balance his books, the evangelist sought to increase his revenue and decrease his expenses. Whitefield wrote Boston supporters concerning his latest publications, expressing his expectation that "some profit will accrue to me from my sermons, etc." But to improve their profitability, Whitefield urged a trusted Bostonian to "make what bargain with [the printers] you think proper" to reduce printing costs. Whitefield also fretted over reducing expenditures, at one point proposing smuggling and illegally introducing slavery into Georgia as a way to lower Bethesda's labor costs. To a South Carolina planter, Whitefield expressed his opinion that although Georgia prohibited slavery, "no notice [was] taken of Negroes at all." Therefore, he suggested if the planter would "give [him] a Negroe, [he would] venture to keep him, and if he should be seized" the itinerant would buy him again. Like merchants of the day, Whitefield relied on credit to operate in overseas trade. He, for example, drew bills on William

Seward's brother, Benjamin, a London merchant, to remit funds to Syms to satisfy British suppliers. Thus, Whitefield's own experience in the market influenced his favorable attitude toward merchants and their role in propagating the gospel.[34]

Whitefield deepened his immersion in the commercial culture through consumption – purchases for himself as well as those for Bethesda. Unlike some of the radical revivalists, such as James Davenport of Long Island, who preached against spreading consumerism, Whitefield not only did not condemn consumption, he enjoyed material possessions. After securing the orphan house's financial position in the mid-1750s, the evangelist spent more freely on himself. Concluding that his "one-horse chaise [would] not do for [him]," Whitefield ordered a closed four-wheeled carriage with improved springs to make his trips over England's rough roads more comfortable. It cost "thirty or forty pounds," equivalent to the annual income of some of the lesser clergy. After taking delivery, the itinerant indicated he "like[d] the purchase exceedingly well." And he cherished a handsome watch adorned with a beautiful gold case, though he covered it with leather so the "delicacy [would] not offend." Whitefield also delighted in personal gifts his supporters gave him, including books, horses, and even a slave. One of his most treasured gifts was a slave whom his co-laborer William Hervey purchased for him at a cost of thirty pounds sterling. To remember the donor, Whitefield named the servant Weston, after Hervey's parish, Weston-Flavel. At times, Whitefield even demonstrated great anxiety over his personal goods. While in America in 1746, he wrote successive letters to his mother, brother-in-law, and finally his agent, Syms, requesting that his "padlocked chest . . . [and] portable furniture" be sent to Charleston. The letters expressed a growing sense of urgency by one attached to his possessions.[35]

Contrary to the interpretations of many contemporaries and historians alike, Whitefield viewed commerce and revivalism as compatible. Edwin S. Gaustad, agreeing with Perry Miller's thesis that there was a steady decline in the vitality of colonial Puritanism as third- and fourth-generation laymen and clergymen alike turned from the faith of their spiritual forefathers to the pursuit of profits and pleasure, argued that the "thriving West Indian trade . . . brought a measure of prosperity to the New England colonies" that led to such evils as pride and economic oppression. As a result of the expansion of the market, "God became less respected as man became more respectable." Writing on the Great Awakening in the major seaports, Gary Nash concluded that the awakening became "class specific," embraced by the laboring poor and shunned by the merchant elites of colonial cities. However, many merchants did support Whitefield and the early Methodists. Whitefield and John Wesley counted among their most ardent supporters in Bristol, for example, businessmen attracted not only by their proclamation of the Puritan ethic but also by their energy, dedication, and organization – qualities essential to mercantile success. And, Whitefield enjoyed no greater acceptance and support than that accorded him by the Brattle Street Church in Boston, a congregation dominated by merchants. Discovering a creative tension between profits and piety, Whitefield's entrepreneurial evangelism accommodated Christians who pursued their callings in the marketplace.[36]

Not only did Whitefield view commerce and religion as compatible, he maintained that trade was an essential feature of the divine economy. He argued that God would have deemed creation incomplete if his human creatures lacked company. Therefore, the Almighty made it impossible that "communities be kept up, or commerce carried on, without society." Indeed, "Providence seem[ed] wisely to have assigned a particular product to almost each particular Country, on Purpose, as it were to oblige us to be social." Whitefield concluded that the mutual dependence of commerce and society demonstrated that "the one great end of [human] existence," consisted in individuals' being useful to each other in social life.[37] Toward that end, he determined to share his "particular product" – his evangelical message – with the widest possible audience through the means at hand.

Whitefield's acquaintance with the spreading market influenced his conception of evangelism. It provided him the language to define his "business" as that of propagating the gospel to a parish that encompassed the whole world. It also shaped his view that merchants were necessary to the spread of evangelical religion. Whitefield held that Christian merchants were called to their vocation, arguing that their success in profitable trade promoted soul winning by generating the funds necessary to conduct the transatlantic revivals. Whitefield expressed his regard for honorable exchange through the liberal sprinkling of commercial metaphors in his sermons and correspondence. In one self-conscious application of mercantile imagery, Whitefield thanked God for converting one supporter into a "Christian merchant, and teaching him the art of trafficking for the Lord."[38]

As his ministry progressed in partnership with supporters from the world of commerce, Whitefield inserted commercial language more frequently into his discourses. Employing the vocabulary of trade and finance, the revivalist assured one merchant that the trader's "all [was] insured, and [he would] receive [his] own with good usury at the great day." He encouraged the businessman to "spend and be spent for Christ's people," declaring evangelism to be a "glorious employ."

Departing for his fifth visit to America in 1754, Whitefield exhorted his followers to be "laudably ambitious, and get as rich as [they could] towards God." He declared the "bank of heaven . . . a sure bank" on which he had "drawn thousands of bills . . . and never had one sent back protested." Before embarking on his last American journey, Whitefield lamented losing "the sale of some gospel goods at Gravesend market-place" and urged his fellow laborers to "meet with thousands of money-less customers" to "sell" the gospel. Then, referring to his own mission to the colonies, the evangelist voiced his desire for a fruitful "trading voyage [wherein he would] sail into harbour with a well full and choice cargo of heavenly wares."[39]

Whitefield's use of commercial language sounded exactly like what ministers such as Cotton Mather and Benjamin Colman had preached a generation before the awakening. What was new about Whitefield was not his appropriation of the language of the market, but his adaptation of marketing techniques. Yet, Whitefield's commercialization of religion need not suggest a secular orientation. Rather it indicates a zeal for propagating the gospel through the most powerful means available. Therefore, he intuitively and self-consciously appropriated merchandising strategies for igniting the transatlantic revivals.

Whitefield profited from a close association with businessmen. They followed the revivalist for a variety of reasons and provided him with valuable merchandising assistance. His major benefactor, Seward, an ardent supporter of charity schools as a means of elevating the "poorer sorts," recognized Whitefield's ability to solicit funds. James Hutton suggested that while Whitefield's "chief object was at the time to convert souls," Seward and others sought merely "to get money for their schools." However, Seward demonstrated his commitment to the cause of broadcasting the need for the New Birth. Not only did he leave his lucrative business as a stockjobber to travel to America with Whitefield, he played a major role in financing and publicizing White-field's revivals. In Philadelphia in 1739, he purchased a sloop and gave it to the evangelist, enabling the preacher and fellow travelers to itinerate between Savannah and Boston at their convenience. At Whitefield's request, Seward bought five thousand acres on the forks of the Delaware River to establish a school for Negroes and a community for English evangelicals. He also gave monetary and spiritual encouragement to the religious societies that formed the nucleus of the itinerant's informal organization in towns throughout Britain and America. As a respected member of the evangelical community, Seward extended the evangelist's letter-writing network, corresponding with sympathetic business associates about Whitefield's successes and needs. From Philadelphia, for example, he sent letters to "Savannah, Charleston, Frederica, Virginia,

Cape Fear, New Brunswick, and New York," enclosing both newspaper accounts and Whitefield's latest publications.[40]

Whitefield, shaped by the world of trade, also influenced lay followers in their business enterprises. James Lackington, a successful London bookseller, traced his initial encouragement in business to the early Methodist revivals of Whitefield and Wesley. While attending a revival meeting in the 1740s, Lackington underwent a conversion experience, which "caused [him] to embrace every opportunity to learn to read." His determination to read evangelical works led him to collect religious books, the foundation for the modest initial inventory of his first bookstore. Whitefield and Wesley encouraged evangelical entrepreneurs by inviting them to advertise their wares in evangelical magazines and by advancing them interest-free loans. Lackington "borrowed five pounds" from one of the Methodist society's funds, adding that the advance "was of great service" in increasing his stock.[41]

In a more direct way, Whitefield helped Habersham launch a successful commercial career, resulting in his becoming one of Savannah's leading merchants. Habersham accompanied Whitefield to Georgia on his first American trip and remained to lay the foundation for the orphan house. Just as Bethesda was "the means of first bringing [Whitefield] out" as an evangelist, it provided the enterprising Habersham the means of beginning his trading business. As he engaged in the coastal and West Indies trade on behalf of the orphanage, he also traded on his own account. By 1744 Habersham had left the orphan house and formed a partnership that participated in the transatlantic trade, exporting tobacco and rice and importing English manufactures. The link between commerce and evangelical religion stands in bold relief in the relationship between Whitefield and Habersham. On the initial voyage to Georgia, Whitefield taught Habersham the Bible and Latin so he would be effective in teaching the orphans. Then in the 1750s, Habersham, by that time a savvy businessman, taught Whitefield how to solve Bethesda's financial difficulties. Beset by funding problems exacerbated by the war with the Spanish, Whitefield turned to Habersham to devise a plan to reduce the orphan house's expenses and increase its revenues.[42] As a result of his plan, the orphanage became self-sustaining.

Printers supported Whitefield in part because he was good business. As the revival spread in the colonies, Whitefield and American booksellers profited from the commercial appeal of the evangelist's publications, fostered by his well-publicized successes – huge crowds, numerous conversions, and liberal contributions. Each year from 1739 through 1745, American publishers released more works by Whitefield than by any other writer. The total number of publications printed in the colonies increased by 85 percent from 1738 to 1741, with most of the increase attributable to the Grand Itinerant. In the peak revival year, 1740, Whitefield wrote or inspired thirty-nine titles, or 30 percent of all works published in America. For many printers, Whitefield's writings constituted a significant proportion of their business. For instance, from 1739 to 1742, one of the largest publishers in the colonies, Daniel Henchman of Boston, spent more than 30 percent of his printing budget producing the evangelist's books. Whitefield not only profited from the sale of his works, he also benefited from Henchman's and Franklin's generous contributions to Bethesda. However, the relationship between business and theology was a complicated one with both commerce and religion influencing decisions. Hutton, who had printed most of Whitefield's early works, refused to produce further writings after 1741, when he sided with Wesley's rejection of Whitefield's Calvinism. Although he had, according to Whitefield, "made hundreds" from the revivalist's publications, Hutton forswore future profits, refusing to print religious matters "except what [he] believed and approved."[43]

Whitefield shared with the new merchants of the consumer revolution both similar strategies and a common view of the market as elastic. Improvements in communications and marketing enabled traders to escape the "cosseted constraints" of local markets and sell their goods to strangers at great distances. And the increased disposable income of urban consumers resulting from falling agricultural prices in the first half of the eighteenth century prompted merchants to consider means of selling consumer goods to the middling and even poorer people, not just the better sort. In a similar way, Whitefield discovered in the new merchandising techniques vehicles for conveying the necessity of a new birth to people far beyond the confines of a single local parish, or the entire Anglican church, or even the very boundaries of Britian itself. Although he subscribed to the Calvinist doctrine of election, Whitefield believed that God used the "meanest instruments" to awaken sinners to his grace. Thus, the evangelist felt compelled to employ every means – even those "the world" used to merchandise its baubles – to deliver the gospel to all people.[44]

As Whitefield succeeded in generating unprecedented crowds, he raised the ire of those who opposed his violation of traditional ecclesiastical boundaries and clerical conduct. The eminent Boston rationalist, Charles Chauncy, protested the way Whitefield hawked religion like a traveling salesman peddling his wares, objecting especially to the itinerant's giving "Public Notice" of his preaching activities. An anonymous writer to the *Boston Weekly News-Letter* proposed a remedy for the evangelist's blatant commercial activities in the name of religion. The correspondent wrote that as there was "a very wholesome law in the province to discourage Pedlars in Trade," the time had arrived "to enact something for the discouragement of Pedlars in Divinity also."[45] These outcries point to one of the greatest ironies of the Great Awakening: the Calvinist Whitefield embraced mass marketing. While Chauncy and other proto-Unitarians rejected Whitefield's Calvinism as narrow and decidedly unenlightened, they also denounced his innovative, rational adaptations of the latest commercial means to propagate his message to vast audiences.

Notes

1 Harry S. Stout, *The New England Soul: Preaching and Religious Culture in Colonial New England* (New York, 1986), 189; George Whitefield, *Journals* (London, 1960), 439; John Gillies, ed., *The Works of the Reverend George Whitefield* (6 vols., London, 1771–2), 1, 312; John Gillies, ed., *Memoirs of the Reverend George Whitefield* (Middletown, 1838), 88.

2 William S. Perry, ed., *Historical Collections Relating to the American Colonial Church* (4 vols., Hartford, 1870), II, 350–60.

3 "Accounts of the Rev. Mr. Whitefield," *Christian History*, January 5, 1744/5; "Accounts of the Rev. Mr. Whitefield Continued," ibid., January 12, 1744/5.

4 *Pennsylvania Gazette*, May 1, May 8, 1740; Gillies, ed., *Works of Whitefield*, I, 291, II, 180; Whitefield, *Journals*, 407.

5 "James Hutton's Account of 'The Beginning of the Lord's Work in England to 1746,'" *Proceedings of the Wesley Historical Society*, 15 (1926), 183–4; *London Daily Advertiser*, September 19, 1737.

6 For a typical sermon notice, see, for example, *London Daily Advertiser*, September 24, 1737. Ibid., September 28, 1737, November 11, 1737 [italics added]; "A List of Deaths in the Year 1740," *Gentleman's Magazine*, 10 (November 1740), 571.

7 William Seward, *Journal of a Voyage from Savannah to Philadelphia, and from Philadelphia to England in 1740* (Boston, 1740), 16–22; *London Daily Advertiser*, May 3, 1739.

8 Josiah Smith, *The Character, Preaching, etc., of the Reverend Mr. George Whitefield, Impartially Represented and Supported, in a Sermon, Preach'd in Charlestown, South-Carolina, March 26th 1740* (Boston, 1740); *London Daily Advertiser*, December 25, 1737.

9 *Williamsburg Virginia Gazette*, December 30, 1737–January 6, 1738.

10 Seward, *Journal*, 16–22.

11 Gillies, ed., *Works of Whitefield*, I, 179.

12 Louis Wilfrid Moffit, *England on the Eve of the Industrial Revolution: A Study of Economic and Social Conditions from 1740 to 1760 with Special Reference to Lancashire* (London, 1925), 246–7.

13 Letter to editor, *Weekly History*, July 6, 1741, p. 3; "Postscript," ibid., April 25, 1741, p. 3; Gillies, ed., *Works of Whitefield*, II, 90.

14 Gillies, ed., *Works of Whitefield*, II, 141, 479; Luke Tyerman, *The Oxford Methodists: Memoirs of the Rev. Messrs. Clayton, Ingham, Gambold, Hervey, and Broughton, with Biographical Notices of Others* (New York, 1873), 250; Gillies, ed., *Works of Whitefield*, II, 265.

15 Benjamin Franklin, *Autobiography*, ed. Larzer Ziff (New York, 1959), 111; Gillies, ed., *Works of Whitefield*, I, 277, VI, 406–7.

16 Whitefield, *Journals*, 86–9, 360; Gillies, ed., *Works of Whitefield*, I, 167; Perry, ed., *Historical Collections*, II, 348.

17 Samuel Davies, "The State of Religion Among the Protestant Dissenters in Virgina" [1751] in *The Great Awakening: Event and Exegesis*, ed. Darrett Rutman (New York, 1970), 46–51.

18 Ibid.

19 Benjamin Colman, *Three Letters to the Rev. Mr. George Whitefield* (Philadelphia, 1739), 5; *Christian History*, January 5, 12, 19, 1744/5.

20 Whitefield, *Journals*, 70, 152; George Whitefield, *A Short Account of God's dealings with the Reverend Mr. George Whitefield, late of Pembroke College, Oxford. From his infancy, to the time of his entering into Holy Orders* (Glasgow, 1741).

21 Gillies, ed., *Works of Whitefield*, II, 77; George Whitefield, *A Collection of Hymns for Social Worship More Particularly design's for the Use of the Tabernacle Congregation in London* (London, 1756), n.p.; Gillies, ed., *Works of Whitefield*, I, 508; George Whitefield, *Nature and Necessity of Our new Birth in Christ Jesus, in order to Salvation* (London, 1738), 1; *Weekly History*, September 18, 1742.

22 *Weekly History*, November 13, 1742.

23 *South Carolina Gazette*, June 18, 1741.

24 Gillies, ed., *Works of Whitefield*, I, 296, II, 76; Whitefield, *Journals*, 373.

25 *Pennsylvania Gazette*, May 1, May 8, 1740.

26 *Christian History*, January 5, 12, 19, 1744/5; *American Weekly Mercury*, December 20, 1739.

27 Whitefield, *Journals*, 86–9; Thomas Jackson, ed., *The Journal of Charles Wesley* (2 vols, London, 1849), I, 159.

28 Whitefield, *Journals*, 63.

29 Neil McKendrick, "Introduction," in *The Birth of a Consumer Society: The Commercialization of Eighteenth-Century England*, ed. Neil McKendrick, John Brewer, and J. H. Plumb (Bloomington, 1982), 2; Wilbur C. Plummer, "Consumer Credit in Colonial Philadelphia," *Pennsylvania Magazine of History and Biography*, 46 (October, 1942), 390.

30 Daniel Defoe, *A Tour through England and Wales*, ed. Ernest Rhys (London, 1927), 62; William Eddis, *Letters from America*, ed. Aubrey C. Land (Cambridge, MA., 1969), 57–8; Lorena Walsh, "Urban Amenities and Rural Sufficiency: Living Standards and Consumer Behavior in the Colonial Chesapeake, 1643–1777," *Journal of Economic History*, 43 (March 1983), 111; Carole Shammas, "How Self-Sufficient Was Early America?" *Journal of Interdisciplinary History*, 13 (Autumn 1982), 266.

31 T. H. Breen, "'Baubles of Britain': The American and Consumer Revolutions of the Eighteenth Century," *Past and Present*, 119 (May 1988), 80;

Roy Porter, *English Society in the Eighteenth Century* (New York, 1982), 206; T. H. Breen, "An Empire of Goods: The Anglicization of Colonial America, 1690–1776," *Journal of British Studies*, 25 (October 1986), 492; Defoe, *Tour through England*, ed. Rhys, 207–8.

32 Neil McKendrick, "The Commercialization of Fashion," in *Birth of a Consumer Society*, ed. McKendrick, Brewer, and Plumb, 66–7, 72–3; Neil McKendrick, "Josiah Wedgwood and the Commercialization of the Potteries," in *Birth of a Consumer Society*, ed. McKendrick, Brewer, and Plumb, 141.

33 Brewer, "Clubs, Commercialization, and Politics," in *Birth of a Consumer Society*, ed. McKendrick, Brewer, and Plumb, 231–62, esp. 232.

34 John W. Christie, ed., "Newly Discovered Letters of George Whitefield, 1745–1746," *Journal of the Department of History of the Presbyterian Historical Society*, 32 (June 1954), 73, 171, 183, 248, 76–7, 251–2.

35 Gillies, ed., *Works of Whitefield*, III, 232–4; "Letters of the Hon. James Habersham," 138–9; Tyerman, *Oxford Methodists*, 277–8; Christie, ed., "Newly Discovered Letters," 252–5; Whitefield, *Journals*, 48, 296.

36 Edwin S. Gaustad, *The Great Awakening in New England* (New York, 1957), 15; Gary Nash, *The Urban Crucible: Social Change, Political Consciousness, and the Origins of the American Revolution, 1760–1800* (Princeton, 1979), 198–232; Geoffrey E. Milburn, "Piety, Profit, and Paternalism: Methodists in Business in the North-East of England, c.1760–1920," *Proceedings of the Wesley Historical Society*, 44 (December 1983), 45–6.

37 J. E. Crowley, *This Sheba, Self: The Conceptualization of Economic Life in Eighteenth-Century America* (Baltimore, 1974), 112.

38 Gillies, ed., *Works of Whitefield*, I, 316; II, 134.

39 Ibid., II, 134; III, 397, 404.

40 "James Hutton's Account of 'The Beginning of the Lord's Work,'" 207; Seward, *Journal*, 10; Whitefield, *Journals*, 89, 361; Seward, *Journal*, 10.

41 *Memoirs of the Forty-Five First Years of the Life of James Lackington* (London, 1794), 59, 129.

42 Gillies, ed., *Works of Whitefield*, III, 309, 452.

43 "James Hutton's Account of 'The Beginning of the Lord's Work,'" 212.

44 Brewer, "Clubs, Commercialization, and Politics," 198; Whitefield, *Journals*, 372.

45 Charles Chauncy, *A Letter From a Gentleman in Boston to Mr. George Wishart, concerning the state of religion in New England* (Edinburgh, 1742); *Boston Weekly News-Letter*, April 22, 1742.

The Spiritual Travels of Nathan Cole (1741)

Nathan Cole

I was born Feb 15th 1711 and born again Octo 1741 –

When I was young I had very early Convictions; but after I grew up I was an Arminian until I was *near* 30 years of age; I intended to be saved by my own works such as prayers and good deeds.

Now it pleased God to send Mr Whitefield into this land; and my hearing of his preaching at Philadelphia, like one of the Old apostles, and many thousands flocking to hear him preach the Gospel; and great numbers were converted to Christ; I felt the Spirit of God drawing me by conviction; I longed to see and hear him, and wished he would come this way. I heard he was come to New York and the Jerseys and great multitudes flocking after him under great concern for their Souls which brought on my Concern more and more hoping soon to see him but next I heard he was at long Island; then at Boston and next at Northampton.

Then on a Sudden, in the morning about 8 or 9 of the Clock there came a messenger and said Mr Whitfield preached at Hartford and Weathersfield yesterday and is to preach at Middletown this morning[1] at ten of the Clock, I was in my field at Work, I dropt my tool that I had in my hand and ran home to my wife telling her to make ready quickly to go and hear Mr Whitfield preach at Middletown, then run to my pasture for my horse with all my might; fearing that I should be too late; having my horse I with my wife soon mounted the horse and went forward as fast as I thought the horse could bear, and when my horse got *much* out of breath I would get down and put my wife on the Saddle and bid her ride as fast as she could and not Stop or Slack for me except I bad her and so I would run until I was *much* out of breath; and then mount my horse again, and so I did several times to favour my horse; we improved every moment to get along as if we were fleeing for our lives; all the while fearing we should be too late to hear the Sermon, for we had twelve miles to ride double in little more than an hour and we went round by the upper housen parish.[2]

And when we came within about half a mile or a mile of the Road that comes down from Hartford weathersfield and Stepney to Middletown; on high land I saw before me a Cloud or fogg rising; I first thought it came from the great River,[3] but as I came nearer the Road, I heard a noise something like a low rumbling thunder and presently found it was the noise of Horses feet coming down the Road and this Cloud was a Cloud of dust made by the Horses feet; it arose some Rods into the air over the tops of Hills and trees and when I came within about 20 *rods* of the Road, I could see men and horses Sliping along in the Cloud like shadows and as I drew nearer it seemed like a steady Stream of horses and their riders, scarcely a horse more than his length behind another, all of a Lather and foam with sweat, their breath rolling out of their nostrils every Jump; every horse seemed to go with all his might to carry his rider to hear news from heaven for the saving of Souls, it made me tremble to see the Sight, how the world was in a Struggle; I found a Vacance between two horses to Slip in mine and my Wife said law our Cloaths will be all spoiled see how they look, for they were so Covered with dust, that they looked almost all of a Colour Coats, hats, Shirts, and horses.

We went down in the Stream but heard no man speak a word all the way for 3 miles but every one pressing forward in great haste and when we got to Middletown old meeting house there was a great Multitude *it was said to be 3 or 4000* of people Assembled together; we dismounted and shook of[f] our Dust; and the ministers were then Coming to the meeting house; I turned and looked towards the Great River and saw the ferry boats Running swift backward and forward bringing over loads of people and the Oars Rowed nimble and quick; every thing men horses and boats seemed to be Struggling for life; *The land and banks over the river looked black with people and horses* all along the 12 miles I saw no man at work in his field, but all seemed to be gone.

When I saw Mr Whitfield come upon the Scaffold he Lookt almost angelical; a young, Slim, slender, youth before some thousands of people with a bold undaunted Countenance, and my hearing how God was with him every where as he came along it Solemnized my mind; and put me into a trembling fear before he began to preach; for he looked as if he was Cloathed with authority from the Great God; *and a sweet sollome solemnity sat upon his brow.* And my hearing him preach, gave me a heart wound; By Gods blessing: my old Foundation was broken up, and I saw that my righteousness would not save me; then I was convinced of the doctrine of Election: and went right to quarrelling with God about it; because that all I could do would not save me; and he had decreed from Eternity who should be saved and who not.

I began to think I was not Elected, and that God made some for heaven and me for hell. And I thought God was not Just in so doing, I thought I did not stand on even Ground with others, if as I thought; I was made to be damned; My heart then rose against God exceedingly, for his making me for hell; Now this distress lasted Almost two years: – Poor – Me –

Miserable me. – It pleased God to bring on my Convictions more and more, and I was loaded with the guilt of Sin, I saw I was undone for ever; I carried Such a weight of Sin in my breast or mind, that it seemed to me as if I should sink into the ground every step; and I kept all to my self as much as I could; I went month after month mourning and begging for mercy, I tryed every way I could think to help my self but all ways failed: – Poor me it took away *most* all my Comfort of eating, drinking, Sleeping, or working. Hell fire was most always in my mind; and I have hundreds of times put my fingers into my pipe when I have been smoaking to feel how fire felt: And to see how my Body could bear to lye in Hell fire for ever and ever. Now my countenance was sad so that others took notice of it.

Sometimes I had some secret hope in the mercy of God; that some time or other he would have mercy on me; And so I took some hopes, and thought I would do all that I could do, and remove all things out of the way that might possibly be an hindrance; and I thought I must go to my Honoured Father and Mother and ask their forgiveness for every thing I had done amiss toward them in all my life: if they had any thing against me; I went and when I came near the house one of my Brothers was there, and asked me what was the matter with me: I told him I did not feel well, and passed by; But he followed and asked again what was the matter. I gave him the same answer, but said he something is the matter more than Ordinary for I see it in your Countenance: I refused to tell at present – Poor me – I went to my Father and Mother and told them what I came for: and asked them to forgive me every think [*sic*] they had against me concerning my disobedience or whatsoever else it might be; they said they had not any thing against me, and both fell aweeping like Children for Joy to see me so concerned for my Soul.

Now when I went away I made great Resolutions that I would forsake every thing that was Sinfull; And do to my uttermost every thing that was good; And at once I felt a calm in my mind, and I had no desire to any thing that was sin as I thought; But here the Devil thought to Catch me on a false hope, for I began to think that I was converted, for I thought I felt a real Change in me. But God in his mercy did not leave me here to perish; but in the space of ten days I was made to see that I was yet in the Gall of bitterness; my Convictions came on again more smart than ever – poor me – Oh then I long'd to be in the Condition of some good Man.

Notes

1   Thursday, October 23, 1740.
2   Middletown Upper Houses Parish, the present town of Cromwell.
3   The Connecticut River.

A Letter... to Mr. George Wishart (1742)

Charles Chauncy

Reverend Sir,

I Perceive by a printed Letter from a Friend in *Edinburgh*, containing *Excerpts of Letters concerning the Success of the Gospel in these Parts*, that marvellous Accounts have been sent Abroad of a most glorious Work of Grace going on in *America*, as begun by Mr. *Whitefield*, and helpt forward by those in his way of preaching and acting. I should be glad there had been more Truth in those Accounts. . . .

The Minds of People in this Part of the World, had been greatly prepossest in Favour of Mr. *Whitefield*, from the Accounts transmitted of him, from time to time, as a *Wonder of Piety, a Man of God*, so as *no one was like him:* Accordingly, when he came to *Town*, about two Years since, he was received as though he had been an *Angel of God*; yea, *a God come down in the Likeness of Man.* He was strangely flocked after by all Sorts of Persons, and much admired by the *Vulgar*, both *great* and *small.* . . .

. . . Wherever he went he generally moved the *Passions*, especially of the *younger* People, and the *Females* among them; the Effect whereof was, a great Talk about Religion, together with a Disposition to be perpetually hearing Sermons, to neglect of all other Business; especially, as preach'd by those who were Sticklers for the *new Way*, as it was called. And in these things *chiefly* consisted the Goodness so much spoken of. . . . I could not discern myself, nor many others whom I have talked with, and challenged on this Head, but that there was the same Pride and Vanity, the same Luxury and Intemperance, the same lying and tricking and cheating, as before this Gentleman came among us. . . .

A Number of Ministers, in one Place and another, were by this Time formed into Mr. *Whitefield*'s Temper, and began to appear and go about preaching, with a Zeal more flaming, if possible, than his. One of the most famous among these was Mr. *Gilbert Tennent*, a Man of no great Parts or Learning; his preaching was in the *extemporaneous* Way, with much Noise and little Connection. If he had taken suitable Care to prepare his Sermons, and followed Nature in the Delivery of them, he might have acquited himself as a *middling* Preacher; but as he preached, he was an *awkward Imitator* of Mr. *Whitefield*, and too often turned off his Hearers with *mere Stuff*, which he uttered with a Spirit more bitter and uncharitable than you can easily imagine; all were *Pharisees, Hypocrites, carnal unregenerate Wretches*, both Ministers and People, who did not think just as he did, particularly as to the Doctrines of *Calvinism*; and those who opposed him, and the Work of God he was sure he was carrying on, would have opposed *Christ Jesus himself* and *his Apostles*, had they lived in their Day. . . .

And now it was, that Mr. *Whitefield*'s Doctrine of *inward Feelings* began to discover itself in Multitudes, whose *sensible Perceptions* arose to such a Height, as that they *cried out, fell down, swooned away*, and, to all Appearance, were like Persons in *Fits*; and this, when the Preaching (if it may be so called) had in it as little well digested and connected good Sense, as you can well suppose. Scores in a Congregation would be in such Circumstances at a Time; nay some hundreds in some Places, to the filling the Houses of Worship with Confusion not to be expressed in Words, nor indeed conceived of by the most lively Imagination, unless where Persons have been Eye and Ear-witnesses to these Things. Though I may add here, that to a Person in possession of himself, and capable of Observation, this surprising Scene of Things may be accounted for: The *Speaker* delivers himself, with the *greatest Vehemence* both of *Voice* and *Gesture*, and in the most *frightful Language* his Genius will allow of. If this has its intended Effect upon *one* or *two weak Women*, the Shrieks catch from one to another, till a great Part of the Congregation is affected; and some are in the Thought, that it may be too common for those *zealous in the new Way* to *cry out themselves*, on purpose to move others, and bring forward a *general Scream*. *Visions* now became common, and *Trances* also, the Subjects of which were in their own Conceit transported from Earth to Heaven, where they saw and heard most glorious Things; conversed with *Christ* and *holy Angels*; had opened to them the *Book of Life*, and were permitted to read the Names of Persons there, and the like. And what is a singular Instance (so far as I remember) of the working of Enthusiasm, *laughing, loud hearty laughing*, was one of the Ways in which our *new Converts*, almost every where, were wont to join together in expressing their Joy at the Conversion of others.

'Tis scarce imaginable what Excesses and Extravagancies People were running into, and even encouraged in; being told such Things were Arguments of the *extraordinary Presence of the Holy Ghost* with them. . . .

At these Times there were among the People what we call here EXHORTERS; these are such as are esteemed to be *Converts* in the *new Way*. Sometimes they are *Children, Boys* and *Girls*, sometimes *Women*; but most commonly *raw, illiterate, weak* and *conceited young Men*, or *Lads*. They pray with the People, call upon them to come to Christ, tell them they are dropping into Hell, and take upon them what they imagine is the Business of preaching. They are generally much better thought of than any Ministers, except those in the *new Way*, I mean by the Friends to the *Extraordinaries* prevalent in the Land; and they are the greatest Promoters of them. . . .

Various are the Sentiments of Persons about this *unusual Appearance* among us. Some think it to be a *most wonderful Work of God's Grace*; others a *most wonderful Spirit of Enthusiasm*; some think there is a *great deal* of *Religion*, with some *small Mixture* of Extravagance; others, a *great deal of Extravagance* with some *small Mixture* of that which may be called *good*; some think the *Country* was never in such a *happy* State on a *religious* account, others that it was never in a *worse*.

For my self, I am among those who are clearly in the Opinion, that there never was such a *Spirit* of *Superstition* and *Enthusiasm* reigning in the Land before; never such *gross Disorders* and *barefaced Affronts* to *common Decency*; never such *scandalous Reproaches* on the *Blessed Spirit*, making him the Author of the greatest *Irregularities* and *Confusions*: Yet, I am of Opinion also, that the Appearances among us (so much out of the ordinary Way, and so unaccountable to Persons not acquainted with the History of the World) have been the Means of awakening the Attention of many; and a good Number, I hope, have settled into a truly *Christian* Temper: Tho' I must add, at the same time, that I am far from thinking, that the Appearance, in *general*, is any other than the Effect of *enthusiastick Heat*. The Goodness that has been so much talked of, 'tis plain to me, is nothing more, in general, than a *Commotion in the Passions*. I can't see that Men have been made *better* if hereby be meant, their being formed to a nearer Resemblance to the *Divine Being* in *moral Holiness*. 'Tis not evident to me, that Persons, generally, have a better Understanding of Religion, a better Government of their Passions, a more Christian Love to their Neighbour, or that they are more decent and regular in their Devotions towards God. I am clearly of the Mind, they are worse in all these Regards. They place their Religion so much in the *Heat* and *Fervour* of their *Passions*, that they too much neglect their *Reason* and *Judgment*: And instead of being more kind and gentle, more full of Mercy and good Fruits, they are more bitter, fierce and implacable. And what is a *grand discriminating Mark of this Work*, wherever it takes Place, is, that it makes Men *spiritually proud* and *conceited* beyond Measure, infinitely *censorious* and *uncharitable*, to *Neighbours*, to *Relations*, even the nearest and dearest; to *Ministers* in an especial Manner; yea, to all Mankind, who are not as they are, and don't think and act as they do: And there are few Places where *this Work* has been in any *remarkable* manner, but they have been filled with Faction and Contention; yea, in some, they have divided into Parties, and openly and scandalously separated from one another. . . .

The Distinguishing Marks (1741)

Jonathan Edwards

As to this Work that has lately been carried on in the Land, there are many Things concerning it that are notorious, and known by every Body, (unless it be some that have been very much out of the Way of observing and hearing indeed) that unless the Apostle *John* was out in his Rules, are sufficient to determine it to be in general, the Work of God. 'Tis notorious that the Spirit that is at work, takes off Persons Minds from the Vanities of the World, and engages them in a deep Concern about a future and eternal Happiness in another World, and puts them upon earnestly seeking their Salvation, and convinces them of the Dreadfulness of Sin, and of their own guilty and miserable State as they are by Nature. It is notorious that it awakens Mens Consciences, and makes 'em sensible of the Dreadfulness of God's Anger, and causes in them a great Desire, and earnest Care and Endeavour to obtain his Favour. It is notorious, that it puts them upon a more diligent Improvement of the Means of Grace which God has appointed. It is also notorious, that in general, it works in Persons a greater Regard to the Word of God, and desire of hearing and reading of it, and to be more conversant with the holy Scriptures than they used to be. And it is notoriously manifest that the Spirit that is at work, in general, operates as a Spirit of Truth, making Persons more sensible of what is really true, in those Things that concern their eternal Salvation: As that they must die, and that Life is very short and uncertain; that there is a Great, Sin-hating God, that they are accountable to, and will fix them in an eternal State in another World, and that they stand in great Need of a Saviour. It is furthermore notorious, that the Spirit that is at work makes Persons more sensible of the Value of that Jesus that was crucified, and their Need of him; and that it puts them upon earnestly seeking an Interest in him. . . .

Those in whom have been these uncommon Appearances, have been of two Sorts; either those that have been in great Distress, in an Apprehension of their Sin and Misery; or those that have been overcome with a sweet Sense of the Greatness, Wonderfulness and Excellency of divine Things. Of the Multitude of those of the former Sort, that I have had Opportunity to observe, and have been acquainted with, there have been very few, but that by all that could be observed in them, in the Time of it, or afterwards, their Distress has arisen from real, proper Conviction, and a being in a Degree sensible of that which was the Truth. And tho' I don't suppose, when such Things were observed to be common, that Persons have laid themselves under those violent Restraints, to avoid outward Manifestations of their Distress, that perhaps they otherwise would have done; yet there have been very few in whom there has been any Appearance of feigning or affecting such Manifestations, and very many for whom it would have been undoubtedly utterly impossible for 'em to avoid them. Generally those that have been in these Agonies have appeared to be in the perfect Exercise of their Reason; and those of them that have been able to speak, have been able to give an Account of the Circumstances of their Minds, and the Cause of their Distress, in the Time of it, and well able to remember, and give an Account afterwards. I have known a very few Instances of those, that in their great Extremity, have for a short Space been deprived, in some Measure of the Use of Reason; but among the many Hundreds, and it may be Thousands, that have lately been brought to such Agonies, I never yet knew one, lastingly deprived of their Reason. ...

Those that are in such Extremity, commonly express a great Sense of their exceeding Wickedness, the Multitude and Aggravations of their actual Sins, and the dreadful Pollution, Enmity and Perverseness of their Hearts, and a dreadful Obstinacy and hardness of Heart; a Sense of their great Guilt in the Sight of God; and the Dreadfulness of the Punishment that Sin exposes to: Very often they have a lively Idea of the horrible Pit of eternal Misery; and at the same Time it appears to them, that a Great God that has them in his Hands, is exceeding Angry with them; his Wrath appears amazingly terrible to them; God appearing to them so much provoked, and his great Wrath so incensed, they are apprehensive of great Danger, that we will not bear with them any longer; but will now, forthwith, cut 'em off, and send them down to the dreadful Pit they have in View; at the same Time seeing no Refuge: They see more of the Vanity of every Thing they used to trust to, and flatter themselves in; 'till they are brought wholly to despair in all, and to see that they are at the Disposal of the meer Will of the God that is so angry with them. Very many, in the midst of their Extremity, have been brought to an extraordinary Sense of their fully deserving that Wrath and Destruction, which is then before their Eyes; and at the same Time, that they have feared every Moment, that it would be executed upon them, they have been greatly convinced that it would be altogether just that it should, and that God is indeed absolutely Sovereign: and very often, some Text of Scripture expressing God's Sovereignty, has been set home upon their Minds, whereby their Minds have been calm'd, and they have been brought as it were to lie at God's Foot; and after great Agonies, a little before Light has arisen, they have been composed and quiet, in a

Kind of Submission to a Just and Sovereign God; but their bodily Strength much spent; and sometimes their Lives, to Appearance almost gone; and then Light has appeared, and a glorious Redeemer, with his wonderful, all-sufficient Grace, has been represented to them, often, in some sweet Invitation of Scripture. Sometimes the Light comes in suddenly, sometimes more gradually, filling their Souls with Love, Admiration, Joy and Self-Abasement; drawing forth their Hearts in Longing after the excellent lovely Redeemer, and Longings to lie in the Dust before him; and Longings that others might behold him, and embrace him, and be delivered by him; and Longings to live to his Glory: but sensible that they can do nothing of themselves; appearing Vile in their own Eyes, and having much of a Jealousy over their own Hearts. And all the Appearances of a real Change of Heart have followed; and Grace has acted, from Time to Time, after the same Manner that it used to act in those that were converted formerly, with the like Difficulties, Temptations, Buffetings, and like Comforts; excepting that in many, Light and Comfort has been in higher Degree than ordinary. Many very young Children have been thus wro't upon. There have been some Instances very much like those Demoniacks that we read of, *Mar.* 1. 26. and *Chap.* 9. 26. of whom we read, that *when the Devil had cried with a loud Voice, and rent them fore, he came out of them.* And probably those Instances were designed for a Type of such Things as these. Some have several Turns of great Agonies, before they are delivered: and some have been in such Distresses, and it has passed off, and no Deliverance at all has followed. . . .

And as to the Imprudences and Irregularities and Mixture of Delusion that have been; it is not at all to be wondered at that a Reformation, after a long continued, and almost universal Deadness, should at first when the Revival is new, be attended with such Things. In the first Creation God did not make a compleat World at once; but there was a great deal of Imperfection, Darkness, and Mixture of *Chaos* and Confusion, after God first said, *Let there be Light,* before the whole stood forth in perfect Form. When God at first began his great Work for the Deliverance of his People, after their long continued Bondage in *Egypt,* there were false Wonders mix'd with true, for a while; which harden'd the unbelieving *Egyptians,* and made 'em doubt of the Divinity of the whole Work. When the Children of *Israel* first went about bringing up the Ark of God, after it had long been neglected, and had been long absent, they *sought not the Lord after the due Order,* I Chron. 15. 13. At the Time when the Sons of God came to present themselves before the Lord, *Satan came also among them.* And *Solomon*'s Ships when they *brought Gold and Silver and Pearls,* also brought *apes and Peacocks.* When Day Light first appears, after a Night of Darkness, we must expect to have Darkness mixt with Light, for a while, and not to have perfect Day, and the Sun risen at once. The

Fruits of the Earth are first green, before they are ripe, and come to their proper Perfection gradually; and so Christ tells us, *is the Kingdom of God.* Mark 4. 26, 27, 28. *So is the Kingdom of God; as if a Man should cast Seed into the Ground, and should Sleep, and rise Night and Day; and the Seed should spring and grow up, he knoweth not how: for the Earth bringeth forth Fruit of her self; first the Blade; then the Ear; then the full Corn in the Ear.*

The Imprudences and Errors that have attended this Work, are the less to be wonder'd at, if it be considered, that it is chiefly young Persons that have been the Subjects of it, who have less steadiness and Experiences, and are in the Heat of Youth, and much more ready to run to Extreams. Satan will keep Men secure as long as he can; but when he can do that no longer, he often endeavours to drive them to Extreams, and so to dishonour God, and wound Religion that Way. And doubtless it has been one Occasion of much of the Misconduct there has been, that in many Places, People that are the Subjects of this Work of God's Spirit, see plainly that their Ministers have an ill Opinion of the Work; and therefore with just Reason, durst not apply themselves to 'em as their Guides in this Work; and so are without Guides: and no Wonder that when a People are as Sheep without a Shepherd, they wander out of the Way. A People, in such Circumstances especially, stand in great and continual Need of Guides, and their Guides stand in continual Need of much more Wisdom than they have of their own. And if a People have Ministers that favour the Work, and rejoyce in it, yet 'tis not to be expected that, either People or Ministers should know so well how to conduct themselves in such an extraordinary State of Things, while it is new, and what they never had any Experience of before, as they may, after they have had Experience, and Time to see the Tendency, Consequences, and Issue of Things. The happy Influence of Experience is very manifest at this Day, in the People among whom God has settled my Abode. The Work of God that has been carried on there this Year, has been much purer than that which was wrought there six Years before; It has seem'd to be more purely spiritual; freer from natural and corrupt Mixtures, and any Thing favouring of enthusiastick Wildness and Extravagance: It has wrought more by deep Humiliation and Abasement before God and Men; and they have been much freer from Imprudences and Irregularities. And particularly there has been a remarkable Difference in this Respect, That whereas many before, in their Comforts and Rejoycings, did too much forget their Distance from God, and were ready in their Conversation together of the Things of God, and of their own Experiences, to talk with too much of an Air of Lightness, and something of Laughter; now they seem to have no Disposition to it, but rejoyce with a more solemn, reverential, humble Joy; as God directs the Princes of the Earth, *Psal.* 2. 11. 'Tis not because the Joy is not as great, and in many of them much greater: There are many among us, that were wro't upon in that former Season, that have now had much greater Communications from Heaven than they had then; but their Rejoycing operates in another Manner: it only abases and solemnizes them; breaks their Hearts, and brings them into the Dust: Now when they speak of their Joys, it is not with Laughter, but a Flood of Tears. Thus those that laughed before, weep now; and yet, by their united Testimony, their Joy is vastly purer and sweeter than that which before did more raise their animal Spirits.

Further Reading

Bonomi, Patricia, *Under the Cope of Heaven: Religion, Society, and Politics in Colonial America*. New York: Oxford University Press, 1986.

Butler, Jon, *Awash in a Sea of Faith: Christianizing the American People*. Cambridge, MA: Harvard University Press, 1990.

Lambert, Frank, *Inventing the "Great Awakening."* Princeton: Princeton University Press, 1999.

Lambert, Frank, *"Pedlar in Divinity": George Whitefield and the Transatlantic Revivals*. Princeton: Princeton University Press, 1994.

Larson, Rebecca, *Daughters of Light: Quaker Women Preaching and Prophesying in the Colonies and Abroad, 1700–1775*. New York: Alfred A. Knopf, 1999.

Lovejoy, David S., *Religious Enthusiasm in the New World: Heresy to Revolution*. Cambridge, MA: Harvard University Press, 1985.

Sensbach, Jon F., *A Separate Canaan: The Making of an Afro-Moravian World in North Carolina, 1763–1840*. Chapel Hill: University of North Carolina Press, 1998.

Stout, Harry S., *The Divine Dramatist: George Whitefield and the Rise of Modern Evangelicalism*. Grand Rapids, MI: Wm. B. Eerdmans, 1991.

7

Creating Gentility

Introduction

Gentility, as Richard Bushman notes, is a familiar yet elusive concept. To understand the term, he examines a set of practices that defined genteel persons in the eighteenth century. Many of these practices are familiar; as you read the essay, you will be reminded of individuals like Ben Franklin, Abigail Adams, and Thomas Jefferson. The idea of gentility allows us to see how these people were able to set themselves apart so clearly from the great majority of their contemporaries. It also reveals how consciously they *strove* to set themselves apart. Bushman shows us that genteel behavior was carefully cultivated in social performances that were intended to lend distinction to its practitioners, to distinguish them from the mass of humanity, and to create settings in which elites could communicate with one another and criticize one another's actions.

The rise of gentility after about 1700 helped to define a new social order in which a small minority of colonists began to build elaborate homes, surround themselves with expensive furnishings, dress in elegant costumes, and carry themselves in more mannered ways. These same people began to identify common interests and communicate with one another in new ways. Gentility developed alongside a metropolitan print culture in the colonies, which carried news and ideas from London to the maturing port towns of Portsmouth, Boston, New York, Philadelphia, Charlestown, Bridgetown, and Port Royal. It depended upon the expansive network of manufacturers and merchants who supplied colonial ports with a growing array of fine material trappings: silver tea sets and Turkey carpets, ribbons and silks, wigs and hats, tropical woods and Madeira wines. All these things made up the cultural universe of genteel colonists, who defined themselves apart from their neighbors but in connection with like-minded individuals.

Reading and self-improvement were essential to the production of gentility. Benjamin Franklin's *Autobiography* (document 1) offers an account of the process by which he educated himself as a youth and acquired the underpinnings of a genteel bearing. Franklin passed through a series of stages that must have been common to literate young men of his generation. He sampled his father's library of religious tracts, but preferred stories of voyages; he read books by Daniel Defoe and Cotton Mather on the value of "projects" and good works; he was enchanted by the *Spectator*, the famous periodical by Joseph Addison and Richard Steele, which for the two years of its publication served as an introduction to gentility and wit for thousands of readers; he went on to read Locke, Shaftesbury, and Pope, three of the leading lights of eighteenth-century genteel rationalism. What were the steps by which Franklin developed the ability to write and debate effectively? What qualities did he consider most valuable in those undertakings? What, in Franklin's mind, were the purposes of conversation?

Travelers' accounts from this period often reveal the clash between genteel men and women, on the one hand, and ordinary folk (whom they often regarded as boorish or clownish) on the other. One of the most engaging of these accounts was written by Alexander Hamilton (document 2), a Scot who graduated from the University of Edinburgh before moving to Annapolis, Maryland, to practice medicine. In ill health himself, Hamilton traveled north in the summer of 1744 to escape the Maryland heat and see more of the colonies. Hamilton's journal reveals both a keen wit and a critical eye, which he cast on every scene he reports. In what ways does Hamilton reveal himself to the reader to be a genteel observer of his surroundings? Only in the towns he visited did Hamilton encounter like-minded gentlemen and gentlewomen; in the countryside, we see him snickering into his handkerchief at the foibles of ordinary men and women. What qualities in other people was he most likely to ridicule? What traits did he most admire?

Gender roles and expectations shaped the practice of gentility. Superficially, it might appear that gentility encouraged men and women to cultivate surface appearances to the neglect of their characters. But, as Bushman notes, appearances were regarded by the genteel to be reflections of inner qualities. Men and women of taste and refinement cultivated a deeply critical stance toward one another, based as much on judgments of character as on appearance and performance. Elizabeth Magawley, a middle-aged Pennsylvania widow, challenged the prevailing tendency among men to regard women as frivolous creatures, unworthy of sensible discourse (document 3). How does she make her case for the intelligence of women? What, according to Magawley, is the ideal form of discourse between men and women of sense?

Bodies and Minds

Richard Bushman

The word "gentility" derives from the French *gentil*, which entered English usage twice, first in the thirteenth century, when it turned into the English "gentle," and again in the late sixteenth century, when *gentil* kept more of its French pronunciation and became "genteel." This second migration occurred when Renaissance courtesy books were being translated into English and the word was useful to sum up the new style. Frequency of favorable usage seems to have peaked in the eighteenth century, at the time of the broad effort of the English middle class to assimilate courtly ideals and civility. By then it was enmeshed in a complex web of meaning involving kindred terms like "polite," "polished," "refined," "tasteful," "well-bred," "urbane," "civil," "fashionable," "gay," "beau monde," words that highlighted one or another facet of gentility.

By the eighteenth century, "genteel" was used to describe a host of objects, situations, persons, and habits. There were genteel wigs, genteel saddles, genteel speech and letters. Martha Washington ordered a genteel nightgown from a genteel shop in London. Genteel persons with genteel educations practiced genteel professions. Strangers in taverns or boardinghouses were able to evaluate the gentility of the other guests, or of the host, the food, the furnishings. There were genteel schools and genteel towns. The word had vast scope and energy.

In addition to its reach, "genteel" was powerful in the sense of commanding value. Not until the nineteenth century did the word take on a negative cast. In 1766, when a new innkeeper advertised her intention to keep "a very genteel plentiful house," she was promoting its virtues and appealing to the best people to patronize her establishment. She could charge more for genteel rooms and fare, and the same was true for all genteel objects. A genteel salver was a greater worth than a plain, neat tray; a genteel house on a genteel street commanded a higher price than a plain house. By the same token, genteel people were more highly valued than plain people and elicited better treatment from innkeepers and shopkeepers. At an inn in New Castle, Delaware, in 1744, Dr Alexander Hamilton noted with amusement that a fellow traveler who came to breakfast "in a greasy jacket and breeches and a dirty worsted cap" got "scraps of cold veal for breakfast," rather than the better food served to other guests.[1] Gentility bestowed social power.

What did all this mean? The extensive use and social power of the word "genteel" leads us to surmise that it occupied a central position in a far-reaching cultural system, but the precise definition of gentility is elusive. The gathering of a wide variety of objects, actions, and people under the single head of gentility implies that all of the nouns modified by the adjective "genteel" had something in common. But the exact nature of that quality, like the essences of many culturally influential words, is difficult to define.

All that can be said for certain is that genteel things and actions were associated with genteel people. Close association with polite society was likely to invest objects or practices with an aura of gentility. But that answer begs the question, for what made polite people genteel in the first place, giving them the power to make other things genteel? If a wig acquired genteel qualities when genteel people wore it, what other than the wig made people genteel? Their clothes, their posture, their speech perhaps, but what in each of these was genteel? The extensive use of the word and its verifiable social power is evidence of its cultural importance, but how are we to understand gentility's basic nature?

If gentility is difficult to grasp abstractly, perhaps it can be understood concretely, beginning with the actions and qualities of specific individuals who were reputedly genteel. One such person was Alexander Graydon, a young Philadelphian who gained a reputation as a dashing man-about-town while training as a lawyer. Sent to York, Pennsylvania, in 1773 for practical experience, he encountered at his boardinghouse a fellow attorney. "He was an Irishman," Graydon wrote in his memoirs, "a man of middle age – the extent of whose attainments was certainly nothing more, than in a coarse, vulgar hand, to draw a declaration; and in equally vulgar arithmetic, to sum up the interest due upon a bond. His figure was as awkward as can well be imagined, and his elocution exactly corresponded with it." Though the description began disparagingly, Graydon actually admired the man. "Justice, however, requires it should be added, that his want of brilliant qualities, was compensated by an adequate portion of common sense, by unblemished integrity, and liberality in his dealings with the poor."

With such honorable qualities, why did Graydon not immediately recognize the Irishman's virtues? Why did he begin the description disparagingly? Graydon had to defend the Irishman because the man lacked genteel qualities: he wrote in a coarse, vulgar hand; his arithmetic was vulgar; his figure was awkward and his speech the same. Graydon's sharp eye noted one specific deficiency after another which together comprised vulgarity, a failing for which only a number of sterling virtues could compensate. Gentility required that handwriting, speech, and posture all be properly composed, and the Irishman's lacks in each of these details disqualified him as a genteel person.[2]

Graydon's comments imply that the genteel person was a set of aspects, almost a checklist of desirable traits and abilities. There seems to be no other way to recapture gentility than to assemble these diverse and at times confusing aspects and attempt to see how they came together in a unified whole. The courtesy books resorted to the same mode of analysis when they reduced their lessons to a set of maxims, as in Washington's "Rules of Civility" or Chesterfield's letters to his son. The acquisition of gentility required attention to a hundred details of conduct which the well-trained eye instantly observed and which courtesy-book writers summed up in their rules. A French courtesy book for young women, republished in America, informed readers that "there are Rules for all our Actions, even down to *Sleeping with a good Grace*. Life is a continual Series of Operations, both of Body and Mind, which ought to be regulated and performed with utmost Care."[3] In instructing neophytes, the courtesy books set out the rules for body and mind, and we can seek to delineate gentility by the same method, examining the specifics of the genteelly regulated body and the gentle mind.

Regulated Bodies

Among the aims of the courtesy books, as we have seen, was the creation of an immaculate body through cleansing and isolation. Alexander Hamilton's inn mate at New Castle in 1744 bore the certain mark of vulgarity in the grease on his jacket. The man failed to keep himself clean and paid the price in loss of respect. Recipe books, which began to circulate in the colonies in the eighteenth century, provided formulas for removing grease spots from clothes. Washstands, a new furniture form, appeared in Thomas Chippendale's *Gentleman and Cabinet-Maker's Director* (1754), implying that washing the body merited a unique and elaborate furniture form. While washstands of this quality do not appear in American inventories, beautiful dressing tables do. These last emerged in late-seventeenth-century England as the upper middle class embraced gentility. Along with special shaving furniture, which was the male equipment for accomplishing one's toilet, the dressing table speaks for a heightened attention to the cleanliness, the adornment, and the fashionable manipulation of the immaculate body.

All of the cleanliness exercises were part of a larger campaign to regulate the body. Clean hands and greaseless clothes were aspects of bringing the body to perfection through careful discipline. Regulation of the mouth received particular attention. In the matter of yawning, for example, the books advised learners to "Speak not in your Yawning, but put Your handkercheif or Hand before your face and turn aside." The rules forbade people from talking with their mouths full, stuffing so much into the mouth that the jowls bulged out, rinsing their mouths in the presence of others, spitting into the fire, walking with the mouth open, or breathing loudly. In every way the mouth had to be kept under firm control. "Do not Puff up the Cheeks, Loll not out the tongue rub the Hands, or beard, thrust out the lips, or bite them or keep the Lips too open or too Close."[4]

The mouth seemed to be associated with the base parts of the body and would have been concealed if speaking and eating had not made accessibility necessary. Short of hiding the mouth altogether, strict regulation had to bring it under perfect control. Rule after rule in Washington's book told the young man to keep his mouth closed, not to let his tongue hang out or jaw go slack. The look of a sagging mouth gave one the visage of an ignorant peasant. The firm, composed mouth, so indelibly associated with Washington, was the facial posture of a gentleman, a model for the treatment of the genteel person's entire body.

Chesterfield said that the limits on bodily actions were innumerable. "It would be endless to particularise all the instances in which a well-bred man shews his politeness in good company, such as not yawning, singing, whistling, warming his breech at the fire, lounging, putting his legs upon the chairs and the like, familiarities every man's good sense must condemn, and good-breeding abhor." Chesterfield objected to laughter, partly again because of the open mouth. He thought frequent, loud laughter the mark of a "weak mind" and a "low education." Wit "may create a smile, but as loud laughter shews, that a man has not the command of himself, every one, who would wish to appear sensible, must abhor it."[5] Failure to regulate the body left one looking clownish and ridiculous.

To achieve artistic control of one's physical being, a primary rule was to remain erect, to keep the line from the base of the spine through the neck to the back of the head as straight as possible. To add to the upright posture, the chin was held up. While sitting for portraits, people turned their heads and even inclined them but without allowing their chins to fall. Shoulders were kept down and back with the chest and abdomen protruding. Hips were held back behind the line of the chest; when observed from the side, the body formed a slight S curve, from shoulders down the spine to the hips. As students of posture have observed, the genteel stance resembled the positions of formal ballet. Ballet received its first impetus from Louis XIV, himself a devoted dancer who received his sobriquet the "Sun King" from a role he danced in a court ballet. At the time, the dancers were aristocratic members of the court, and dancers assumed the ideal body positions of all who aspired to grace of movement.

Colonial portraits, especially before 1760, almost invariably display this upright posture. If the colonial gentry did not always hold the ideal pose, we can still believe that they assumed it for formal occasions. At their entertainments, on occasions of state, and in the presence of superiors who required respect, genteel people stood and sat with their backs and heads straight, their chins up, and their shoulders down and back, much as they appear in their portraits. "The proper Posture of one that sits," one courtesy book said, "is to have that Part of his Body from the Waste upwards, upright, tho' free and moveable, and the lower Part firm, close to his Seat, and motionless, without crossing his Legs; for this is the respectful Behaviour which Civility exacts from an inferiour, in the presence of his Superiour."[6] Portraitists obligingly placed their clients in genteel poses, just as they clothed sitters in fashionable dress. Nancy Shippen's mother wrote to ask whether she was learning to hold her head and shoulders properly along with how to enter and leave a room. The charge for teaching all of this fell upon the dancing masters, whose influence grew year by year, judging from the ubiquity of itinerant instructors. By the time of the Revolution even rural gentry families like the Ridgelys took dancing instruction.

Fashionable clothing helped genteel people to hold their bodies in place. Men's coats pulled the shoulders down and back into the prescribed postures, and under their suit coats, men wore snug waistcoats. Before mid-century, the waistcoat, which reached from the shoulders nearly to the knees, ordinarily hung unbuttoned at the top with some lacy shirtfront showing. After mid-century, the waistcoat was invariably buttoned at the waist, and the name waistcoat, rather than vest, suggests that this place on the coat had special significance. An unbuttoned front would have been exceedingly informal, an affront to a visitor. Beyond that, the buttoned coat held the lower back in its proper position, serving for men something of the same function as stays did for women. The frame of bone stays, fastened tightly around women's midriffs, held them in the proper erect position, and their dresses usually fit as tightly at the waist as the waistcoats did.

Erect posture was essential, but sometimes it was overdone. Urban gentlemen smiled at overly correct country people for holding themselves too stiffly. Ease of bearing was as important to the gentleman as ease of the company was to a brilliant entertainment. The bent elbow, the hand on the hip, the feet at an angle, and the open relaxed hand with palm up signified the sitter's ease. In the last half of the eighteenth century, the desire for ease grew stronger. Striking portraits exist of elegant women leaning against pillows or on the upholstered arms of sofas; John Singleton Copley painted Mrs. Thomas Gage resting her head upon her hand. Copley portrayed John Hancock at his desk with his legs crossed, a posture which would have been highly informal and unsuitable a century earlier. In this later period, Matthew Pratt depicted himself leaning forward with his elbows on a table and arms crossed. The genteel thought it the height of elegance to relax their formal standards and move into these easy poses.

But body regulation was not to be entirely relaxed. The recognized modes of vulgar dress and deportment had to be avoided. A coatless man with a free-flowing shirt and an unbuttoned vest would be instantly identified as a tradesman or laborer, never a gentleman. The flowing shirt or smock freed the arms to reach, lift, and swing, as was necessary for the work of commoners but unnecessary and unsuitable for gentry. A gentleman would no more appear with his vest unbuttoned than he would laugh aloud with mouth wide open. Copley pictured Paul Revere with his shirt loose on his body, his vest open, with no coat to confine his shoulders, and so stripped him of all pretensions to gentility, at least for the purpose of the picture. A British musician was shocked when a group of German farmers attended a performance in Lancaster, Pennsylvania. "At our first concert, three clownish-looking fellows came into the room, and, after sitting a few minutes, (the weather being warm, not to say hot) very composedly took off their coats: they were in the usual summer dress of farmer's servants in this part of the country; that is to say, without either stockins or breeches, a loose pair of trowsers being the only succedaneum. As we fixed our admission at a dollar each, (here seven shillings and six pence,) we expect this circumstance would be sufficient to exclude such characters."[7]

Figure 7.1 Charles W. Peale, portrait of Richard Bennett Lloyd, 1771. (Courtesy Winterthur Museum.)

A member of one of Maryland's wealthiest families, Richard Bennett Lloyd combined perfect ease with disciplined erectness. Two years later he purchased a commission in the Coldstream Guards, married a woman from the Isle of Wight, and subsequently moved to France before returning to America in 1780.

Posture was important because slumped shoulders and a hung head denoted a servility that was out of keeping with a gentleman's dignity and honor. The genteel person, who might appear sometimes in shirt

Figure 7.2   William Williams, Jr, portrait of William Hall, Philadelphia, 1766. (Courtesy Winterthur Museum.)

William Hall, the son of David Hall, Benjamin Franklin's partner in the printing business. Shown here in 1766, the young man has the right posture and correct clothing but lacks the polish of Richard Lloyd. The rising provincial gentry always stood in danger of falling short of genteel standards, risking the scorn of more practiced ladies and gentlemen.

sleeves, could never allow himself to be seen in degrading postures. Nor was he to "loll," which implied relaxing the upright stance by leaning far back, putting up one's legs, lying down in public, curling up, or leaning far out of a window and resting on the sill. Chesterfield distinguished between vulgar slovenliness and self-indulgent lolling on the one hand and genteel ease on the other. He observed to his son that "you may also know a well-bred person by his manner of sitting. Ashamed and confused, the awkward man sits in his chair stiff and bolt upright, whereas the man of fashion, is easy in every position; instead of lolling or lounging as he sits, he leans with elegance, and by varying his attitudes, shews that he has been used to good company." The easy poses of the later eighteenth century, while a departure from the erect formality of earlier times, still required the straight back line, permitting one to lean to one side or the other, but not to loll.[8]

The posture of the body comprised only a portion of the protocol of body regulation; proper motion was the other part. We can confidently speak of the erect stance because of the portraits; we can only read about the motions. For these, we must turn to written instructions on how to remove a hat, to bow, to walk, and above all to dance, the most severe test of body mastery. Social dances were far more elaborate then than now, approaching the complexity of theatrical dancing, and yet they had to be carried off with grace and ease, making the services of a dancing master a necessity for young ladies and gentlemen. To get the full picture of the genteel body, we must picture the people in the portraits walking, dancing, and gesturing with the same practiced ease as they stand or sit in the paintings.

The lengthy descriptions of the movement of great men and women suggest the hypnotic power of simple physical presence. Richard Rush remembered watching for Washington to open a session of Congress in Philadelphia in 1794 or 1795. An immense crowd gathered at Chestnut and Sixth to await his white carriage attended by liveried servants and drawn by four bay horses.

> Washington got out of his carriage, and slowly crossing the pavement, ascended the steps of the edifice, upon the upper platform of which he paused, and turning half round, looked in the direction of a carriage which had followed the lead of his own. Thus he stood for a minute, distinctly seen by every body. He stood in all his civic dignity and moral grandeur, erect, serene, majestic. His costume was a full suit of black velvet; his hair, in itself blanched by time, powdered to a snowy whiteness, a dress sword at his side, and his hat held in his hand. Thus he stood in silence; and what moments those were! Throughout the dense crowd a profound stillness reigned. Not a word was heard, not a breath. Palpitations took the place of sounds. It was a feeling infinitely beyond that which vents itself in shouts.

> Every heart was full. In vain would any tongue have spoken. All were
> gazing, in mute unutterable admiration. Every eye was riveted on that
> form – the greatest, purest, most exalted of mortals. It might have
> seemed as if he stood in that position to gratify the assembled thousands
> with a full view of the father of their country. Not so. He had paused for his
> secretary, then, I believe, Mr. Dandridge or Colonel Lear, who got out of
> the other carriage, a chariot, decorated like his own. The secretary,
> ascending the steps, handed him a paper – probably a copy of the speech
> he was to deliver – when both entered the building. Then it was, and not
> until then, that the crowd sent up huzzas, loud, long, earnest, enthusi-
> astic.[9]

Much contributed to the power of that hushed moment on the steps:
Washington's history, his authority, the beauty of the carriage, his dress.
But the slow walk across the pavement, the dignified ascent of the stairs,
the pause and half turn, and his serene, majestic bearing were part of the
moment's magic. His presence stopped every sound until the spell broke
and cheers burst forth.

On the other hand, the expectation of perfect grace was so high that
any momentary lapse was noted. Senator William Maclay, ever the close
observer, recorded an instance at Washington's house when he read a
statement to a delegation from Congress.

> The President took his reply out of his coat-pocket. He had his spectacles
> in his jacket-pocket, having his hat in his left hand and the paper in the
> right. He had too many objects for his hands. He shifted his hat between
> his forearm and the left side of his breast. But taking the spectacles from
> the case embarrassed him. He got rid of this small distress by laying the
> spectacle-case on the chimney-piece. Colonel Humphreys stood on his
> right, Mr. Lear on his left. Having adjusted his spectacles, which was not
> very easy, considering the engagements of his hands, he read his reply with
> tolerable exactness and without emotion. I thought he should have re-
> ceived us with his spectacles on, which would have saved the making of
> some uncouth motions. Yet, on the whole, he did nearly as well as anybody
> could have done the same motions. Could the laws of etiquette have
> permitted him to have been disencumbered of his hat, it would have
> relieved him much.[10]

Reflecting on the occasion, Maclay considered how the awkward inter-
play of body and objects might have been eased. Above all, he did not
want Washington to make "uncouth motions." Judging from the length
and detail of the diary entry, the artistic management of a regulated body
in the drama of everyday gentility meant as much to Maclay as the affairs
of state.

Dress

The genteel presence created by bearing and graceful motion was further enhanced by clothing; dress signaled rank and character as surely as posture did. The meaning of the feel, the color, the cut, and the expense of clothing was clear enough to have been earlier codified in law. Sumptuary legislation, which detailed acceptable apparel as related to rank, was first enacted in England in the thirteenth century. The laws went through many revisions and varied efforts at enforcement before extraneous concerns about prerogative power led to repeal in 1604. Under the 1510 statute, the basic sixteenth-century legislation, only lords were permitted to wear gold or silver cloth or bone lace, and only knights blue or red velvet. Later statutes restricted silk, even in small patches, to men of adequate wealth. People lower in the social scale had to limit the cost of the materials in their clothing and the amount of fabric in a given garment. The legislation partly aimed to inhibit foreign imports and to protect English textile producers, but the main purpose was to stabilize the outward signs of rank and to stop extravagance among people who would suffer from dressing beyond their means. The legislation suggests how materials and colors bore well-defined social meaning from an early date.

The genteel culture of the eighteenth century inherited and partially incorporated this code of meaning. Scarlet had traditionally signified royalty and grandeur in Western Europe, and bright rich colors, especially when worked into elaborate designs, continued to mark people of high birth and wealth. Indian cottons and especially chintz, which became immensely popular at the end of the seventeenth century, appealed to the English upper classes because of the vivid designs that could be painted or printed on them. Wool could also be impressed with color, but it held the hues less well under repeated washings. The chintzes brought the luxury of vivid color and elaborate design to the public in a more practical form and at less expense. Bright colors instantly marked a person of rank and fashion. Poorer people wore the dull, natural browns, greens, and off-whites of homespun clothing colored with vegetable dyes which blended with the hues of the natural world.

Color, however, was not essential for gentility in the eighteenth century. Many portraits of American gentry present the sitters in browns, grays, and, later in the century, black. The gentry did not invariably dress in brilliant colors, although the plums and cocoa tans of their clothes were richer, stronger hues than the poor could manage with their vegetable dyes. Color was more firmly associated with rank than with gentility, and rank and gentility were not synonymous. Very wealthy Americans or those few with titles do appear in bright colors or elaborately patterned fabrics in their portraits, but the middling great planter or merchant and wife, who would certainly claim gentility, contented themselves with conservative hues. A person of gentility had to understand his or her exact position in the social order and never overstep it. A bright silk suit on an ordinary Boston merchant would have been a breach of good taste and decidedly ungenteel. The wearer of the plain brown suit was no less genteel for his lack of color. The principle of gentility almost required that the use of bright colors should be more restrained in the clothing of the American gentry, who, by English standards, were only upper-middle-class.

American gentry also were few ornaments. Brocade trim, lace, and gold and silver buttons and buckles were a part of aristocratic dress and unsuitable for lower ranks. But the American gentry did add small brilliant touches of adornment. Good buckles were necessary, and buttons were apparently an obsession. Eighteenth-century storekeepers stocked buttons by the thousands; large bags of them turn up in their inventories. But brocade trim rarely appeared in portraits, and buttons did not usually glitter. The principle of restraint operated in these details too.

The genteel, however, were required to wear clean, fine linen at throat and wrists. Every male and female portrait shows fine white fabric at these points, and usually lace at the sleeve ends. Although Nicholas Ridgely had only two suits when he died, he had nine fine holland shirts. When George Washington visited Belvoir as a young man, he packed nine white shirts and white stockings. The genteel image required fine white fabric where skin met suit or dress, revealing that the immaculate body was covered by a film of white cloth.

Aristocratic dress was traditionally characterized by smoothness. The fabrics regulated by sumptuary legislation were the smoothest available, silk satins and velvets. Restrictions on other fabrics were described by cost and amount, but silk fabrics were forbidden outright to the lower classes, as if finish, aside from price, set the fabric apart. People at the lower end of the scale wore enough homespun and coarse osnaburgs and fustians, establishing in effect a textural polarity between rough and smooth. This distinction in early sumptuary legislation entered wholly into the genteel aesthetic of dress in the eighteenth century. Fabric was ranged along a spectrum of increasing value and prestige according to the degree of smoothness. Stockings were priced according to their smoothness, as were women's straw hats. In the eighteenth century the English gentry took up the plaited straw hats of country women for informal wear, but chose imported leghorn plaiting, noted for its fineness, thus giving a genteel straw a distinguishing finish. Similarly, silk fabrics were preeminent for a woman's finest dresses, and velvet or superfine wool for a man's suit.

Claudia Kidwell and Margaret Christman observe that virtually all the fabrics "used by the poorer sort shared a common quality of coarseness": osnaburg (a coarse linen), fustian (a mixture of cotton and linen), and linsey-woolsey, made of linen and wool, were all coarse. Plain cottons and wools of the poorer sort were also heavier and coarser than the chintzes and superfine wools of the polite. There were other important differences too, Kidwell and Christman say: "The floral patterns and chintzes on the one hand were arrayed against a mass of striped and checked and 'speckl'd' fabrics; the pure white linens versus the uncertain colors of country cloth; the rich red from expensive cochineal standing out against the neutral colors produced by most vegetable dyes." But most notable was "the very obvious difference in texture, the smooth as opposed to the rough."[11]

The expense and effort of spinning fine yarns and weaving smooth fabric raised the price of silks and velvets. But the price does not account for the inherent value of smoothness that made it worth the trouble and expense. The etymology of the word "coarse" suggests that the physical quality was linked to broader cultural values. It is thought that "coarse" derived from "course," meaning plain and ordinary, and came in time to mean rude or vulgar. The feel of coarse cloth was associated with the lower ranks of society and with rude personal traits. Meanings and feelings radiating from a debased social position and vulgar personal characteristics infused the sensory experience of the fabric through the word "coarse." By the same token, "polished" and "polite" linked smooth fabric with well-finished personal qualities. The application of the same words to materials and to persons suggests that fabrics became metaphors for personality. In paying higher prices for smooth fabrics, the gentry wished to reflect in their clothing the personal qualities they sought in their conduct.

As articulated by Edmund Burke, smooth and flowing surfaces went beyond clothing and personality to a much more general aesthetic. As a young man trying to distinguish the qualities of beauty, he identified smoothness as an essential trait of all beautiful things.

The next property constantly observable in such objects is *Smoothness*. A quality so essential to beauty, that I do not now recollect any thing beautiful that is not smooth. In trees and flowers, smooth leaves are beautiful; smooth slopes of earth in gardens; smooth streams in the land-scape; smooth coats of birds and beasts in animal beauties; in fine women, smooth skins; and in several sorts of ornamental furniture, smooth and polished surfaces. A very considerable part of the effect of beauty is owing to this quality; indeed the most considerable. For take any beautiful object, and give it a broken and rugged surface, and however well formed it may be in other respects, it pleases no longer. Whereas let it want ever so many of the other constituents, if it wants not this, it becomes more pleasing than almost all others without it. This seems to me so evident, that I am a good deal surprised, that none who have handled the subject have made any mention of the quality of smoothness in the enumeration of those that go to the forming of beauty. For indeed any ruggedness, any sudden projection, any sharp angle, is in the highest degree contrary to that idea.[12]

Burke may be unique among eighteenth-century observers in articulating the place of smoothness in beauty. But his assertion was based on observation; many desirable objects within genteel culture were smooth. Besides fabrics, ceramics ranged along a smooth–rough continuum from the finest porcelains to crude earthenwares. Burke enunciated an aesthetic principle that craftsmen of all kinds, without conscious collusion, had already incorporated into their products. Combined with shapes characterized by gradual variation, something smooth, like the shape and feel of a bird or a woman's neck, became irresistibly beautiful, as if an innate quality automatically called forth the pleasing sensation of beauty.

Despite these ingrained distinctions, a visitor walking up High Street in Philadelphia in the middle of the eighteenth century might not always have been able to distinguish commoners from genteel people of fashion. Plain people doubtless fell heir to clothing once worn by ladies and gentlemen, and the irresistible urge to emulate people in power moved lesser men and women to wear cheaper or shabbier versions of fashionable dress. Pictures of High Street show street traders in knee breeches and waistcoats.

Yet it remained true in general that people carried the marks of their social position on their backs. If in individual cases people passed for something they were not, the polarities of polished and coarse were well understood by all. Trained by dancing masters to hold torsos and heads erect, the genteel did not amble or loll on a public street. Genteel clothing, with its color, rich adornment, smooth texture, and aristocratic cut and pattern, was easily distinguished from craftsmen's leather aprons over shirts with open vests, the smocks of farmers and drovers, the trousers of seamen and laborers, and the coarse jackets and petticoats of the serving girls.

Eating

Inside Philadelphia houses, the physical activity of the inhabitants would also have informed a visitor of their degree of gentility, but such a visitor

Figure 7.3 Southeast corner of Third and Market Streets, Philadelphia. (From William Russell Birch and Thomas Birch, *The City of Philadelphia in the State of Pennsylvania North America; as it appeared in the Year 1800 consisting of Twenty Eight Plates*, Philadelphia, 1800.)

A mixed company mingled in the streets of Philadelphia in 1800. The dress of ladies and gentlemen set them apart, but people of middling standing who acquired genteel attire in one way or another took on some of the airs of the gentry.

would not have found one class distinction common in Europe: the meals of rich and poor would not have differed as greatly as in England or on the Continent. In everyday fare, the menus of upper-class and lower-class people traditionally had been defined by one important difference – meat. Upper-class people ate meat regularly while peasants mostly ate grain, prepared in various ways as bread, gruel, or porridge. Vegetables in season garnished the cereals, as did occasional touches of meat and cheese.

Plain farmers and the poor in America also subsisted primarily on cereals prepared as breads or as porridges, as the European peasantry long had done, but poor Americans ate much better than poor Englishmen. Sarah McMahon found meat in 65 to 80 percent of the estate inventories after the fall slaughtering period. She also discovered that wills called for meat in 70 to 90 percent of widow's dower provisions, an indication of the common view of a standard diet. In both instances, the percentages increased through the century. In 1728 the Boston *News Letter* summarized the diet of a respectable middle-class family as consisting typically of bread and milk for breakfast and supper, with pudding, bread, meat, roots, pickles, vinegar, salt, and cheese for dinner. Many farm families replicated that menu.

More than menu, the visitor would have seen differences in presentation going from plain to genteel houses. If the food on a gentleman's table might not be entirely different from common food, the tables themselves in gentry and plebeian houses – the dishes, platters, drinking vessels, and flatware – would never be confused. The poor in the eighteenth century continued the primitive eating modes that were standard in seventeenth-century households, and these were a far cry from the manner of genteel dining. In the seventeenth century, many households lacked tables on which to place food as it came from the fireplace, and that condition was not unknown in some regions halfway through the eighteenth century. In Wethersfield, Connecticut, from 40 to 50 percent of the estate inventories showed no table before 1670, and as many as a quarter lacked a table as late as 1730. A third of the inventories in New Castle County, Delaware, in the 1750s listed no tables. Chairs were nearly as uncommon. Over 80 percent of the inventoried Wethersfield households had chairs by the 1680s, but the average (mean) number was 2.6, meaning that many households had one or two.

Planks laid on trestles for each meal, then dismantled to open up more space, can be hypothesized to account for this gap in furnishings. A visitor to the Western Reserve in 1811 saw a woman stick poles through the crevices in two of the cabin walls and rest a couple of oak planks on the poles to serve her guests breakfast. Or food might have been placed on a chest or left on the floor in front of the fireplace, especially in view of the fact that cooks at the fireplace ordinarily used the floor in place of a table. A Springfield, Massachusetts, man in 1650 said that he "took up my dinner and laid it on a little table made on the cradle head." There was little reason for tables of any kind when most of the diners lacked chairs. Stools and the long benches called forms appear no more frequently in the inventories. Probably people made do, sitting on chests, kegs, and other furniture not designed specifically for sitting. The visitors to the tableless Western Reserve cabin "sat down on the bed, for chairs or stools there were none." In tiny one-room houses, which were the norm for most people, family members may have carried their food outside in good weather and sat on the ground to eat. The orderly gathering of the family around a table, each with a place and a chair, would have been an exception for the poorest quarter of the population even in the early years of the eighteenth century.[13]

For the ordinary family, we should not think of the food being dished out onto plates for each eater. The inventories do not provide detailed information on individual eating utensils because the appraisers grouped plates and platters under woodenware and pewter. Individual wooden trenchers and pewter plates may be hidden under those words, but it would be wrong to assume that they were present. The individualization of eating arrangements for people at ordinary meals was still in process. In Europe spoons had not come into common use until the sixteenth century; before then people ate with their fingers from common pots. The recommended eating utensils for immigrants to New England in the early seventeenth century included spoons and bowls, but not plates.

The simpler mode of eating was long in disappearing. The studies of Plymouth, Massachusetts, inventories from 1660 to 1760 list very few plates. Since more than half of the inventories in most places show no knives or forks even in the eighteenth century, plates, which served primarily as surfaces for cutting, were unneeded. Food that required no cutting – porridge, mush, or the various pottages – could be eaten as easily from bowls or dishes with spoons. Most commonly, then, people in poor households well into the eighteenth century probably ate their partially liquid meals from bowls with spoons, or perhaps in still more primitive ways.

Alexander Hamilton, the Annapolis physician, was invited to a meal with the ferryman's family while crossing the Susquehanna River in Maryland in 1744. The ferry, Hamilton said, was

> kept by a little old man whom I found att vittles with his wife and family upon a homely dish of fish without any kind of sauce. They desired me to eat, but I told them I had no stomach. They had no cloth upon the table, and their mess was in a dirty, deep, wooden dish which they evacuated

with their hands, cramming down skins, scales, and all. They used neither knife, fork, spoon, plate, or napkin because, I suppose, they had none to use.

Hamilton went on to comment that "I looked upon this as a picture of that primitive simplicity practiced by our forefathers long before the mechanic arts had supplyed them with instruments for the luxury and elegance of life," suggesting that in his experience, the ferryman's eating habits had an air of quaint antiquity. Scooping out a homely dish of fish by hand seemed rare in 1744, but it still occurred. Hamilton would have seen more of it if he had ventured farther from the main roads. In more settled areas, the poor likely ate their porridges and pottages from bowls with spoons.[14]

These conditions changed through the eighteenth century as tables and chairs increased in frequency. By the end of the century both items were nearly as common as beds in more settled areas. By the middle of the century irregular seating and eating from bowls with spoons and fingers remained mainly as an image at the lower end of the refinement spectrum to which genteel dining could be compared. Gentility regulated dining as it did the body, including the wish to keep the food clean, separated from dirt and fingers. The growing spirit of refinement placed people on chairs at tables, gave each individual utensils, and put the food on platters and in serving bowls. Bodies were placed before the food with knives and forks in hand separating the person from tactile contact with the food, and on chairs that encouraged people to sit upright in the proper erect posture. Genteel aesthetic principles thus took over the process of dining in its entirety, and refined and exalted it.

The advance of regulated and refined dining can be measured through the proliferation of the tools that made it possible: tables and chairs, knives and forks, and porcelain plates and serving dishes. Dining accoutrements were added one by one, usually beginning with chairs that lifted people from the floor and brought them to order around a table. Then rough plates of some kind, normally of pewter, were added and about the same time knives and forks, to separate bodies from the food. Smooth porcelain serving dishes and plates, with their fine polished surfaces, usually came last.

Differences in the rate of adoption varied sharply according to the sophistication of the region and proximity to international trade routes. Nearly 90 percent of the inhabitants of Wetherfield, Connecticut, one of the first towns settled in the Connecticut Valley and a prosperous minor trading center right on the river, had tables (88 percent) and chairs (90 percent) in their houses by the 1750s, only a few percentage points less than inventories with beds (91 percent). The average (mean) number of chairs was over ten and of tables two and a half. In the two northern Delaware counties, Kent and New Castle, and in Chester County, Pennsylvania, immediately north of New Castle, the figures were lower. In the middle decades of the eighteenth century, between 65 and 68 percent of inventories listed chairs, a figure probably more typical of settled rural areas of the coastal plain. By the 1790s the percentage of inventories with chairs and tables for this region had risen to 90 percent. Lewis Miller's sketches of rural Pennsylvania households gathered for meals at tables with each person on a chair represented the condition of middling and upper families between 1795 and 1810, a style of eating available to virtually everyone in the region by the end of the century. In more remote areas the figure would be lower.

The assemblage of knives, forks, and plates, to go with individual chairs, became more common about the same time. Forks were used in Boston before the end of the seventeenth century, but were rare: only a gentleman's inventory listed a fork in 1721. Forks appeared much more commonly in the 1750s and 1760s. By that decade, between 32 and 57 percent of the decedents in the three-county region in Delaware and Pennsylvania had knife-and-fork sets in their estates. In Massachusetts, about half the inventories in 1774 showed knives and forks. In the Chesapeake the incidence of knives and forks was higher at mid-century and later, but probably a third of the population still lacked them. Bowls and spoons and fingers must have prevailed for many common people through most of the century.

Because of the obscuring names earthenware, woodenware, and pewter, the frequency of plates is more difficult to measure, but evidence from archaeological excavations conducted by James Deetz suggests more common usage after 1760 in the Plymouth region. By the middle of the eighteenth century, about 43 percent of the inventories in Kent County listed fine ceramics of some sort (delftware, stoneware, or "china"), which most often would have included plates. In Massachusetts in 1774, a third of the inventories included ceramics and over half had tea equipment. A substantial population ate with knife and fork from finer ceramic plates, at least for formal dining. Another, larger group continued with pewter plates and trenchers.

Altogether the evidence from Plymouth, Pennsylvania, Delaware, and the Chesapeake permits us to picture roughly half of the colonial population at mid-century eating from plates with knives and forks while sitting at tables. A smaller group of this knife-and-fork population ate from some kind of refined earthenware like creamware which imitated the prized surfaces of imported porcelains. The rest of the knife-and-fork group ate from coarse earthenware, pewter, or wood. A tiny population dined on imported porcelains.

Among the half of the people who used knives and forks, some refined even their simple meals. The pewter and silver porringers that survive in such great numbers, 95 percent of them from after 1750, were made for porridges and mushes, the simplest of foods, as well as for the more genteel beverages of chocolate and coffee. Benjamin Franklin's wife believed that he deserved to eat his breakfast bread and milk with a silver spoon from a china bowl rather than from an earthen porringer. As the process of refinement spread through their lives, some people brought to every meal the silver and fine ceramic tablewares used to exalt the most formal dining.

At the other end of the spectrum, a third to a half of the population ate with spoons or fingers, though likely sitting up at tables. They had no fine finishes on their tables or tablewares. They dressed in rough linens, linsey-woolseys, and leather. Their skin had likely been roughened by weather, fireplace heat, and work. They bent over their bowls unconcerned about posture or manners. Only on Sundays did they dignify their appearance with better suits of clothes or gowns, and then in simple blues or blacks. Under the beneficent influence of American plenitude, a common diet of simply prepared cereals and meat brought people together, but the modes of presenting food and the manner of eating it divided the polite classes of society from the vulgar and coarse.

Gentle Minds

In 1744 Alexander Hamilton, the Edinburgh-trained physician living in Annapolis whom we have met before, prescribed a horseback journey for himself to improve his frail health. While riding north he met the ferry-

Figure 7.4 Lewis Miller, Dr John Ranse and Family, 1807. (Courtesy York County Historical Society.)

By the end of the century, a large proportion of families had enough chairs, knives, and forks to sit at a table with individual place settings.

man at the Susquehanna who offered a meal of fish from a common pot, and later at New Castle in Delaware he encountered Morison, the would-be gentleman who was served veal scraps for breakfast because of his greasy jacket and dirty worsted cap. The episode with Morison, because it sheds additional light on the essentials of gentility and moves us beyond the body to the mind, is worth recounting in some detail.

At the inn, Morison tried without success to present himself as a gentleman. Hamilton saw at once that Morison was "a very rough spun, forward, clownish blade, much addicted to swearing, at the same time desirous to pass for a gentleman." When the landlady, seeing his shabby clothes and observing his "heavy, forward, clownish air and behaviour," presented him with veal scraps for breakfast, Morison flew into a rage. "'Damn him,'" he swore, "'if it wa'n't out of respect to the gentleman in company,' (meaning me) he would throw her cold scraps out at the window and break her table all to pieces should it cost him 100 pounds for damages." "Taking off his worsted night cap, he pulled a linnen one out of his pocket and clapping it upon his head, 'Now,' says he, 'I'm upon the borders of Pennsylvania and must look like a gentleman.'"

Morison believed that clothes were responsible for his treatment. He also sensed that his conversation was lacking and to redeem himself "made a transition to politicks and damnd the late Sr. R[obert] W[alpole] for a rascall. We asked him his reasons for cursing Sr. R[obert], but he would give us no other but this, that he was certainly informed by some very good gentlemen, who understood the thing right well, that the said Sr. R[obert] was a damnd rogue." Having made a pass at political conversation, Morison returned to his possessions.

> He told us that tho he seemed to be but a plain, homely fellow, yet he would have us know that he was able to afford better than many that went finer: he had good linnen in his bags, a pair of silver buckles, silver clasps, and gold sleeve buttons, two Holland shirts, and some neat night caps; and that his little woman att home drank tea twice a day; and he himself lived very well and expected to live better.

Others like Morison must have thought that a linen nightcap, silver buckles, holland shirts, and the drinking of tea, the physical accoutrements of gentility, would enable a person to pass for a gentleman. But of course none of these persuaded Hamilton. There was the "heavy, forward, clownish air and behaviour," the "naturall boorishness," and Morison's violent speech as well. Morison seemed to sense that his conversation lacked something and so turned to politics, where his ignorance only compounded his difficulties. But he was on the right track, for besides the regulation of the body and its adornment with fine linens and silver buckles, the mind needed polish. Gentility required a person to rise above boorishness and dullness, to display an abundant mind, especially in conversation, and to reveal a vivacious, sweet, and generous spirit. A parvenu could hire a tailor to dress his body and a dancing master to teach physical deportment. But to acquire the spiritual and mental traits of a well-bred gentleman required years of tutoring the intellect as well.

In its true and most refined form, gentility was meant to be a spiritual condition. A proper education, Locke said in *Some Thoughts Concerning Education*, formed the mind in its innermost core, and everything else about the person – manners, speech, dress – expressed the temper of the spirit. The pleasures the well-bred person gave to a company were the pleasures of knowing a refined being. "The Actions, which naturally flow from such a well-formed Mind, please us ... as the genuine Marks of it; and being as it were natural Emanations from the Spirit and Disposition within." "This seems to me to be that Beauty, which shines through some Men's Actions," Locke went on, not tricks or flourishes or luxurious dress, but "little Expressions of Civility and Respect," which "seem not Artificial or Studied, but naturally to flow from a Sweetness of Mind, and a well turn'd Disposition." That quality, rare even among the well-bred, Morison lacked entirely. He could purchase linen and buckles without end and never come close to the essence of gentility. Probably few of the American gentry met Locke's high standards for good breeding, but many understood that houses, plates, knives and forks, posture, and polite speech were insufficient unless they became the outward signs of an inward grace.[15]

Delicacy, Sensibility, and Taste

Gentility borrowed heavily from traditional Christianity for its inventory of personal virtues. In admonishing his student to "Let Chearfulness, Sweetness, and Modesty, be always blended in your Countenance and Air," the author of *The Lady's Preceptor* called on a common stock of Christian qualities. The popularity of *The Whole Duty of Man* among the American gentry shows how easily Christianity and gentility blended in the depiction of genteel character. The literature on the subject assumed that the true gentleman was a Christian – though his piety was regulated as closely as his body, to restrain, for example, the emotional excesses of evangelical religion. Instead, the gentleman embodied the Christian moral virtues of compassion, kindness, and humility. Good manners expressed a Christian regard for the happiness of others.[16]

At the same time, some genteel virtues went beyond the usual store of Christian qualities, and these were the ones most lacking in Morison. Three interrelated words sum up these peculiarly genteel qualities: "delicacy," "sensibility," and "taste." With them we come to the heart of genteel culture.

Delicacy was the eighteenth-century word for the rising "threshold of embarrassment" that Norbert Elias finds central to the civilizing process. The delicate person flushed with shame at the mere mention of the grosser bodily processes that civilization had driven from the conversation of polite people. Delicacy, in this vein, was aversion to every form of coarse behavior or thought, and even the suggestion of erotic passion. The strongest constraints were laid on young women. "One of the chiefest beauties in a female character," one conduct book insisted, "is that modest reserve, that retiring delicacy, which avoids the public eye, and is disconcerted even at the gaze of admiration."

Delicacy in the larger sense meant the capacity for fine discriminations and an appreciation for all that was refined and gentle. While suppressing the base, delicacy delighted in everything sweet and lovely. Delicacy caused the princess to suffer from the pea under the stack of mattresses. Delicacy required a sensitivity to human feelings, an exact discernment of the emotional effects of a word or an action, and a desire to protect people from every hurt. Delicacy forbade an individual to assert superiority or to degrade another. Delicacy detected the slightest shadow of blame or derogation and acted to lift that shadow from any across whom it fell. *A Father's Legacy* warned that wit, because it ridiculed its targets, "must be guarded with great discretion and good-nature, otherwise it will create you many enemies. It is perfectly consistent with softness and delicacy; yet they are seldom found united." Humor was "often a great enemy to delicacy" because it broke the first rule of gentility, complaisance, the wish to please. Delicate discriminations enabled the polite to put all company at ease.[17]

Sensibility, the second quality of the three, was interwoven with delicacy; a person with sensibility reacted strongly to experience and might be overcome with feeling. Sensible people wept easily at suffering or were carried away with compassion or gratitude. Delicacy, in the sense of fine discriminations, caused the sensitive spirit of the refined person to react powerfully. "There is a certain Delicacy of Passion," Hume wrote, "to which some People are subject, that makes them extremely sensible to all the Accidents of Life...And When a Person that has this Sensibility of Temper, meets with any Misfortune, his Sorrow or Resentment takes intire Possession of him."[18]

Being overcome with feeling in consequence of delicate sensibilities was a pleasurable indulgence of the genteel life, all the more pleasurable because the surge of strong emotion attested to the possession of genteel virtues. Nancy Shippen, whose diary entries were a record of her considerable sorrows as well as the happiness of her life, candidly noted the pleasure she took in her sensibilities. "Sweet Sensibility! source of a thousand heaven born sensations, for the wealth of the Indies I wou'd not be without thee! – " Her mother-in-law cautioned Nancy to discipline her own daughter gently, "as she has so much sensibility that it would make her unhappy without complaining of it." Bad behavior must be curbed, but not sensibility, which was prized in a young spirit.

Feelings that arose from compassion for suffering or love for one's children were especially honored. In Susanna Rowson's *Charlotte Temple*, an old gentleman is outraged by the attempt of a worthless rake to court his daughter. After hearing of the old man's strong feelings, Charlotte's father comments that "the truly brave soul is tremblingly alive to the feelings of humanity," a perfect description of the combination of delicacy and sensibility that gentility prized. The old man goes on to say that "painful as these feelings are, I would not exchange them for that torpor which the stoic mistakes for philosophy. How many exquisite delights I should have passed by unnoticed but for these keen sensations, this quick sense of happiness or misery." We call this pursuit of emotion for the sheer pleasure of feeling sentimentalism. By the middle of the eighteenth century, sentimentalism had deeply ingrained itself into genteel culture, adding a rich emotionality to the cooler temperament of courtly civility.[19]

Taste and delicacy were interwoven just as delicacy and sensibility were, for delicacy aided in the detection of beauty. If delicacy of perception aroused strong feelings, it also made one aesthetically sensitive. Philip Fithian, the Robert Carter family tutor in the 1770s, in describing briefly the houses and gardens of Nomini Hall, said that "they discover a delicate and Just Tast."[20] The implication was that the owners had that fine appreciation of all the delicate touches required to create beautiful houses and gardens. In everyday discourse where the word had frequent usage, no effort was made to define taste, as perplexing a problem in that day as now, and yet good taste was always admired and it was a requisite of a refined personality. Such a person recognized beauty through the exercise of the powers of discrimination, and could unerringly evaluate the aesthetic qualities of a vase, an opera, a face, or a suit of clothes. More important still, such a person created beauty in all he or she possessed. The rooms, the furnishings, the exterior architecture, the gardens, and even the barns and fields of a genteel family exhibited a just taste, as those of the Carters did at Nomini Hall.

Figure 7.5 Charles W. Peale, portrait of Mrs Benjamin Rush (Julia Stockton), Philadelphia, 1776. (Courtesy Winterthur Museum.)

Charles Willson Peale's portrait of Julia Rush turns the qualities of taste and delicacy into a visual reality. The posture of body and face, her dress, the lute, the book, and the flower at her bosom testify to her refined qualities. Both her husband and her father, Richard Stockton, were signers of the Declaration of Independence.

Conversation

Delicacy and sensibility, although more closely tied to individual minds than taste, similarly interacted with society and the world beyond the person. All three virtues enhanced the most self-conscious and practiced art of eighteenth-century polite life, conversation. In conversation the

most finely honed discriminatory powers and the delicately attuned
sensibilities of the genteel spirit exhibited and confirmed themselves.
The rules for conducting conversation were discussed at length in the
courtesy books and exemplified in the dialogue of genteel novels like
those of Samuel Richardson. Actual people, while they did not record
complete conversations, did frequently comment on the conversational
abilities of their associates, just as they judged the beauty of refined
women. The Charleston newspaper, in extolling the virtues of Eliza
Pinckney, said of her that "her understanding, aided by an uncommon
strength of memory, had been so highly cultivated and improved by
travel and extensive reading, and was so richly furnished, as well with
scientific, as practical knowledge, that her talent for conversation was
unrivalled."[21] Conversation was, in a sense, the culminating genteel art.

The ideal gentle mind was notable for vivacity, implying constant
intellectual and emotional vitality. A vivacious mind, while composed
and peaceful, also operated at a high pitch, displaying wit, repartee,
knowledge, and lively emotional responses. A perfectly genteel person
might hold back from conversation out of modesty, but would never
lapse into torpor or dullness. One advice book cautioned a reader that
"people of sense and discernment will never mistake . . . silence for dul-
ness. One may take a share in conversation without uttering a syllable.
The expression in the countenance shews it, and this never escapes an
observing eye." Nancy Shippen disliked those days when she "felt dull
and disagreeable, very low spirited and out of humor," for she knew that
her vivacious spirit was a large part of her attractiveness. Dullness was
painful as well as shameful.[22]

Peasants were torpid; the genteel were supposed to be gay, meaning
high-spirited or vivacious. They sought amusement to keep their spirits
high, and disliked dull times and boring people. The primary reason why
people needed the arts, one person wrote, was "to awaken their Wit, and
enliven their Taste." But among all activities, conversation offered the
vivacious soul the most suitable field of play. In his essay on taste,
Montesquieu commented that "esprit – wit and talent in their various
connotations – enjoys exercising itself, as does curiosity." In conversation, genteel people exercised their sensibility, taste, vivacity, and their
capacities for discernment and appreciation.[23]

The guides to genteel conduct spoke of conversation as "the Cement
and Soul of Society," or as "the greatest commerce of our lives." Every
courtesy book offered directions and rules, and a number made conversation the center of attention, as in *The Conversation of Gentlemen* (1738),
Henry Fielding's *Essay on Conversation* (1743), or Jonathan Swift's sa-
tiric *Complete Collection of Genteel and Ingenious Conversations* (1738).
Books catalogued figures of speech, maxims, rhymes, witticisms, and

bons mots to aid those lacking ingenuity. The ultimate source book for genteel conduct, Castiglione's *Book of the Courtier*, praised the merits of good conversation and was itself written as a model of refined conversation among well-bred courtiers. Commonly courtesy books offered examples of sample conversations for learners who could pick up the rhythm and tone or memorize actual speeches for later use.[24]

Because conversation is ephemeral, the effect of these standards on the talk of the colonial gentry can only be inferred. There is little evidence of specialized books on conversation coming to America. *The Academy of Complements* was repeatedly imported from the late seventeenth century on, and the first of six eighteenth-century printings of *The American Test Book* appeared in Philadelphia in 1789, and *The New Academy of Compliments* had two printings in the 1790s, but the more elaborate works on the subject were never reprinted here. Ideas about refined conversation, insofar as they were gleaned from books, had to be deduced from classic guidebooks such as Chesterfield's *Letters* or from novels. Samuel Richardson's *Clarissa*, *Pamela*, and *Sir Charles Grandison* together went through thirty or more American printings in addition to the copies imported from England. Richardson devoted page after page to conversation, not usually of the grave or learned kind, but raillery, compliments, flirtation, and wit.

We cannot determine how much Americans learned from such books, but we know they valued conversation. A Boston paper in 1731, doubtless echoing London, declared that "to avoid conversation is to Act against the Intention of nature . . . to live then as men we must confer with men; conversation must be one of the greatest pleasures of life." The recurrent references to the quality of conversation in the brief evaluations of people in letters and diaries suggest that some took the admonition seriously. An acquaintance was liked because "his conversation is interesting and agreable," or accepted for other good qualities despite the fact that he had "nothing to say of his own." Chastellux, a visiting French aristocrat, praised Elizabeth Willing Powel for "her taste for conversation, and the truly European use she knows how to make of her understanding and information." He thought her unusual among American women, but Philadelphia must have offered inducements for her to have learned to converse in the European mode. While not everyone acquired fluency, some had "the reputation of being witty and sharp," or made conversation which, as in the case of one young lady, was said to be "as pleasing as her figure."[25]

Polite conversation had various purposes, one being to show one's parts – that is, one's knowledge and opinions. At the beginning of the seventeenth century Henry Peacham recommended to young gentlemen the knowledge of antiquities, particularly statues, inscriptions, and coins.

Peacham recognized that only the wealthy could afford such rarities, but to converse with the owners required some knowledge. "Sure I am that he that will travel must both heed them and understand them if he desire to be thought ingenious and to be welcome to the owners." Nor did vague familiarity suffice: "It is not enough for an ingenuous gentleman to behold these [rarities] with a vulgar eye, but he must be able to distinguish them and tell who and what they be." The Peacham principle applied to scores of other topics, politics, the arts, geography, animals, and gardens. The well-finished gentleman necessarily had to have some knowledge "to be thought ingenious and to be welcome" by well-informed people.[26]

So strong was the desire to show off that young people were tempted to trot out their information prematurely. Experienced men of the world had acquired knowledge of places, governments, people, and art, had formed their judgments, and so shone in conversation. A young man, entering into the world, risked humiliation in bringing up a subject which he understood imperfectly. Chesterfield advised his son not to take the initiative at first. "If you have parts, you will have opportunities enough of shewing them on every topic of conversation, and if you have none, it is better to expose yourself upon a subject of other people's than of your own." On the other hand, one could not simply hold back. One must prepare oneself by storing away knowledge. Chesterfield urged his son to read carefully, reviewing the material until it was mastered, to enable him to converse intelligently. Chesterfield scoffed at dimwits who read lightly and went into company without having brought the matter under control. Those with a command of general topics and some wit in discussing them won favor. The governor of Pennsylvania took an interest in Benjamin Franklin when he was only a printer's apprentice because of his ability to talk about books, a trait probably still uncommon in the colonies in the 1720s. But an inept performance subjected one to the silent scorn of the company.[27]

The need to sustain conversation as the cement of society played upon many aspects of genteel life. To begin with, conversation required subject matter, grist for its conversational mills, and grave subjects would not always do. Chesterfield told his son to cultivate small talk on trivial subjects. "By small-talk, I mean a good deal to say on unimportant matters; for example, foods, the flavour and growth of wines, and the chit-chat of the day." To overcome boredom at Versailles, it was said, the court talked with animation about the bleeding of the king or a cold of Mme de Maintenon. What a relief when an enterprising sea captain put a rhinoceros on display, which everyone, including the king and queen, went to see. The beast provided conversation for a week. The magic-lantern shows, peep shows, and models of distant places like

Jerusalem or Rome that traveled through the colonies served the same purpose. An advertisement for John Bonnin's series of French scenes viewed through a "Philosophical Optical Machine" claimed that after a performance "instead of the common Chat, there is nothing scarce mentioned now, but the most entertaining Parts of Europe." After Mr. Bonnin exhibited scenes of New York City in 1748, the newspaper observed that ladies insisted on seeing the show.

> In short, there's nobody can set up the least face for politeness and conversation without having been with Mr. Bonnin; and embellishing their discourse with making judicious and elaborate observations and criticisms on this, that, and the other building, improvement, or dress.

The curiosities gave a double delight: the excitement of the first view and the pleasure of talking about them afterward.[28]

Polite people often assembled "conversation pieces" in their own houses. While the phrase is usually applied to paintings of domestic scenes, with the implication that viewers would react to the picture and talk about it among themselves, the term may be more generally applied to other objects used to start conversation. A well-planned garden, besides exhibiting the delicate and just taste of its owner, was a place and a subject for conversation. Philip Fithian recorded his pleasant walks with Mrs Carter in the family garden, where they conversed about the plants. A vista from a house or a place with a view fixed a subject which might evoke questions and around which conversation might circle, as did books, prints, maps, and scientific instruments. One courtesy book was so specific as to instruct young men how to react when a jewel was brought into company for discussion. In England the virtuosi had whole cabinets of curiosities to which they might introduce their friends. The collection practice was less common in the colonies, but any picture on the wall, a vase on a shelf, a plant in the garden served the purpose. As refinement advanced in America, thoughtful hosts assembled various conversation pieces for the amusement of their guests.

The needs of conversation thus motivated sundry gentry activities – reading, collecting, and the planting of gardens or designing of landscapes. The objects afforded the guests as well as the hosts opportunities to show their taste, sensibility, and discernment. Judging mainly from letters and diary entries as we must, the proper reaction was a succinct, discerning judgment of the object, cleverly expressed. At its best the comment would show one's familiarity with other objects of the same kind, a comparison of one vase with another seen elsewhere, for example, or of Hudson Valley vistas with those of the Rhine. In a model conversation in a French courtesy book, an educated young woman observed of

Descartes, "I like him well, because he is intelligible." No more was required than the sharp, clear point revealing her personal sensibility and judgment. She elaborated with another dictum: "I like him the better also, because he does not pretend to search too far into the Secrets of the Omnipotent." The conversation could then move on.[29]

This spirit pervades Josiah Quincy's diary entries during his coastal tour in 1774. After visiting Charleston he noted "there is a colossal statue of Mr Pitt at Charleston, much praised by many. The drapery was exquisitely well done; but to me the attitude, air, and expression of the piece was bad." He wrote in the same faintly imperious spirit in New York after the theater. "The actors make but an indifferent figure in tragedy, – a much better in comedy. Hallam has merit in every character he acts." The comments mixed perception, personal reactions, and judgment.[30] Quincy might well have delivered the same judgments in person. Morison attempted similar comments on Walpole in his conversation with Hamilton. He tried to deliver a quick judgment of Sir Robert's character, thinking it might pass for polite talk. Hamilton called his bluff, and Morison failed at the game for lack of a supporting comment. In more expert hands such comments, mixed with wit and pleasantry, would crackle around the circle for the amusement and edification of the company.

Conversation, where wit, vivacity, taste, and sensibility all might show themselves in full splendor, organized the acquisition of knowledge in polite society. Men of learning, clergymen, authors of books, statesmen, and doctors had other purposes in reading; the ordinary members of polite society read to talk. The admonition for young women in a standard courtesy book applied equally to men reading outside of their professional interests.

> For young Ladies when they have arrived to some knowledge by reading, afford great pleasure in their Conversation to others, and receive no less when they are alone by themselves; for Reading assisteth Conversation, and is absolutely necessary to make the Spirit acceptable and gratefull; for as in Reading they do gather and find, almost on all occasions, a fit subject for discourse, so by conversation they find a happy and easie method to deliver themselves with Ornament, and to joyn plenty to facility: And without this Education, Conversation is an intolerable Tyrant; for we cannot without torment intertain any Discourse with those Gentlewomen, who if they be of the Countrey, can administer no other Discourse unto you, but of their Ducks, or their Geese; or if they be of the City, can talk of nothing, unless it be of their Whisks, or their Gorgets, or those Attires that are most in Fashion.[31]

Reading raised a person's conversation above the boorish talk of rustics and the shallow obsession with fashion of city beaux and so-called fine ladies. Conversation gave a social point to books and to the study of paintings, scenery, horticulture, or anything beautiful or curious.

Conversational knowledge was acquired for social display and engagement. Familiarity with a wide range of materials enabled one to formulate a clever personal judgment for presentation in conversation so as to exhibit one's taste, sensibility, and discernment. In time cultural entrepreneurs recognized the market for the broad, shallow knowledge created by the needs of polite conversation, and organized museums, lyceums, libraries, and magazines. The participants may have noted only an object or two in a collection or heard only an hour's lecture on Egyptian culture, but that enabled them to show their capacity for illuminating judgments in the conversation that ensued, and added to the store of information on hand for polite talk.

Personal relations also supplied conversational material. Richardson's novels and later Jane Austen's contain page after page of dialogue lacking any reference to books or art or even scenery. The talk might be flirtatious, gently mocking, sometimes full of gossipy comments on current romances, but in straying from books to people, polite conversation did not shed its gentility. Conversation remained an art form, characterized at its best by wit, grace, and ingenuity. The author of *The Academy of Complements*, in a book made up of 255 pages of graceful little speeches for every occasion written for the English aristocracy during the time of Charles I, noted that "it is eloquence which adornes our discourse; gives a grace and life to our actions." "Without this," he went on, "we resemble walking rocks, all our actions being dull and heavie." The popularity of the little volume in Boston bookstores at the end of the seventeenth century suggests that some members of the colonial gentry were striving to beautify their speech.[32]

The governing principle in this more lighthearted persiflage, as in every form of polite conversation, was, as Fielding put it, "the Art of pleasing, or contributing as much as possible to the Ease and Happiness of those with whom you converse." In the model conversation on Descartes in the French courtesy book, every proffered opinion was followed immediately by an expression of deference to the superior knowledge of the other. By the same token, ridicule and derogation were strictly forbidden. Raillery presented a problem because, while amusing to the company, it discomfited its target. Fielding said "the Raillery which is consistent with Good-Breeding, is a gentle Animadversion on some Foible; which while it raises a Laugh in the rest of the Company, doth not put the Person rallied out of Countenance, or expose him to Shame and Contempt." Another courtesy book, as we have seen, advised against any raillery; Fielding admitted it on condition that the jest "be so delicate, that the Object of it should be capable of joining in the Mirth it occasions." Running through Fielding's essay on conversation, and its injunctions against gossip and indecency as well as raillery, is an evident struggle between an older form of bawdy and derisive talk and the more recent demands of good breeding with its high-strung sensitivity to the ease of everyone in the company.[33]

Swift mocked the ungainly efforts of English polite society to speak stylishly when he offered a set of "polite Speeches which beautify Conversation," but his real intent was to improve social discourse.[34] He desired, along with all who wrote about good breeding, that taste, discernment, vivacity, and complaisance be evident in every word, just as beauty and taste were to shine through the details of one's personal appearance and every aspect of one's domestic setting. Conversation became an art, for which one read, collected objects, formulated opinions, practiced graceful phrases, and above all developed those delicate responses that enabled one to show constant regard for the feelings of all in the company.

Letter Writing

The refinement of spoken words carried over into letter writing. Because "style is the dress of thoughts," Chesterfield told his son, writing told as much about a person as clothing. Ill-dressed thoughts had little chance of success. "If your style is homely, course, and vulgar, they will appear to as much disadvantage, and be as ill received as your person, though ever so well proportioned, would, if dressed in rags, dirt, and tatters." Letters became performances as did dancing and conversation, a means of judging a person's character and grace. When Benjamin Rush met his future wife Julia, she was a girl of seventeen, "engaging in her manners and correct in her conversation." But her letter made her irresistible. "I had seen a letter of her writing to Mrs. [Elizabeth Graeme] Ferguson which gave me a favorable idea of her taste and understanding.... From this moment I determined to offer her my hand."[35]

Letter writing emerged as an aristocratic art in sixteenth-century Italy, along with so much else later associated with gentility. The collections of Italian letters were, in turn, modeled on classical authors, notably Cicero, Pliny, and Seneca. By the seventeenth century the published letters of three modern authors had emerged to set the standard for later writers – the Spaniard Antonio de Guevara (1539–45), and the Frenchmen Jean Louis Guez de Balzac (1624) and Vincent Voiture (translated in 1655). These three men's letters were read and emulated in England for a century. By the middle of the eighteenth century scores of English letter collections were in print, and letters had been accepted as a minor literary form. Handbooks like *The Compleat Letter-Writer* gave examples of "Elegant Letters" for every occasion. People with no prospect of publication themselves were conscious as they wrote letters that they were undertaking small literary performances. Writing a letter resembled entering a room or engaging a polite company in conversation. The act had to be adorned with the proper gestures and carried off with aplomb and style.

Abigail Adams, normally a candid and pungent correspondent like her husband, assumed a most self-conscious literary posture when she opened a correspondence with the formidable Mercy Otis Warren, already famous in 1773 for her literary achievements. The kind of hospitality Adams had already received gave her the courage to write. "Thus imbolden'd I venture to stretch my pinions, and tho like the timorous Bird I fail in the attempt and tumble to the ground yet sure the Effort is laudable." Although she included a sixteen-line poem, perhaps of her own composition, in the letter, Adams still apologized that "I have so long neglected my pen that I am conscious I shall make but a poor figure."

Warren's diction was no less formal and self-conscious. In a passing comment on the recent hot weather she hoped that "as the gentle showers of the afternoon Extended to the River, as you kindly wished, so I hope they shed there benign influence over the mountains and Valleys of Scadden," using a local name for the South Precinct of Braintree because of its poetic ring. The two proceeded on the same high level of eloquence to conduct the kind of exchange we can imagine going on in genteel conversation. Adams sent Warren a copy of Juliana Seymour's *On the Management and Education of Children*, asking that Warren "give me your Sentiments upon this Book." All the proper rhetorical flourishes adorned the request: "May the Natural Benevolence of your Heart, prompt you to assist a young and almost inexperienced Mother in this Arduous Business." In proper style Warren entered the demurral that her opinion of a book which "is Generally admired I think is of very Little Consequence." She despaired "of Reaching those more perfect plans Exhibited by superior Hands," and then went on to deliver her judgment as people of parts did in polite conversation. She observed that Seymour put generosity above truth among the virtues, while Warren believed "a careful Attention to fix a sacred regard to Veracity in the Bosom of Youth the surest Guard to Virtue." So the two women danced the genteel dance, offering opinions on books and politics, accompanied by deferrals to the other's superior judgment and protests of their own deficiencies, all couched in a high diction and formal syntax that sustained the exchange on a lofty plane.[36]

Later in their acquaintance, familiarity led Adams to moderate her prose to a more conversational tone. Six months after the first letter she asked for another reaction. "I send with this the I volume of Molière, and should be glad of your oppinion of them. I cannot be brought to like them, there seems to me to be a general Want of Spirit." That style was more typical. With other correspondents, her letters contained family news, expressions of love, political opinions, plans, feelings, all expressed in a more natural and candid tone, as in most collections of family letters. Whichever collection of genteel correspondence we pick up, the letters contain the usual business of life and friendship.[37]

But even in the most casual exchanges between close friends, the formal note returns, reminding us that the writers never completely forgot that their writings were a performance. Sally Fisher of Duck Creek Cross Roads in Kent County, Delaware, who was to become William Corbit's second wife in 1784, corresponded with Debby Norris in Philadelphia in the late years of the Revolution when the two were twenty-two and nineteen. The girls talked of parties, male admirers, prospective visits, and the expected family news, but then from time to time ascended into the elaborate sentences of high sensibility. Sally wrote after the death of an uncle that "I thought then as well as at many other times that nothing so exalts the human soul except the genuine flame of piety as the sweet emotions of humanity which affords a kind of pleasing pain and leaves serenity almost divine." For her part, Debby Norris, commenting a few months later on Sally's admired aunt, went into raptures: "How sweetly amiable and pleasing [is] sensibility, how beautifully does it gild and add lustre to other accomplishments; like the sun beam to the trembling dew drop!" Genuine affection and youthful energy radiate on every page of these letters. So does the inclination for literary affectations and pleasure in sententious eloquence.[38]

Informal letters of friendship among the colonial gentry proliferated in the eighteenth century. The letters served to enhance friendship and family ties to be sure, but as a secondary message, the letters presented a refined spirit in the act of revealing its sensibility, its vivacity, and its delicacy. These writers knew that they were practicing a genteel art, although they had no expectation of publication. The gracefully turned phrases, the high sentiments, the touches of wit were contrived to confirm the writers' sense of themselves as ladies and gentlemen of fashion.

Handwriting

Beyond the words, the writing itself in polite correspondence shows evidence of instruction and pains; a good hand was necessary to grace a genteel correspondence. Alexander Graydon had noted in the uncouth Irish lawyer at York a coarse, vulgar handwriting and an equally vulgar arithmetic, and so judged him no gentleman. Polite people learned to form their letters as they learned to form their phrases and their sentiments. George Bickham, a famous London engraver and writing master of the seventeenth century, said a good hand will "give in Writing, what we admire in fine Gentlemen; an Easiness of Gesture, and disengag'd Air, which is imperceptibly caught from frequently conversing with the Polite and Well-bred." Chesterfield insisted that his son engage a writing master to improve the boy's handwriting, "which is indeed shamefully bad, and illiberal; it is neither the hand of a man of business, nor of a gentleman, but of a truant schoolboy." Chesterfield preferred "a genteel, legible, liberal hand." George Washington's "Rules of Civility" were as much an exercise in writing as instruction in polite conduct, and he copied them to improve his hand. Nancy Shippen's daughter learned penmanship from a steward on the Livingston estate who was "a very fine penman."[39]

The interest in refined handwriting began during the Italian Renaissance when Florentine humanists took their models from the scripts practiced in Charlemagne's empire. These stood in marked contrast to what they considered the barbaric "Gothic" scripts of their own time. The Caroline scripts received a wider currency when Pope Eugenius IV (1431–47) authorized a cursive style for documents issued by the Apostolic Chancery. The new writing, known as humanist, or chancery, or simply Italian, rapidly spread with Renaissance culture to other countries of Europe. Writing masters encoded Italian in copybooks, the first of which appeared in England in 1571 as *A Booke containing divers sortes of bands*, adapted by John Baildon from a French book by Jean de Beauchesne. In England the Italian hand met remnants of Gothic and a nearly illegible native writing called secretary. Through the seventeenth century both Gothic and Italian styles appeared in copybooks along with many variants and combinations, one appropriately called bastard Italian. In 1700 Gothic and secretary still crossed the pages of many public records; by the mid-eighteenth century anglicized versions of Italian had driven rivals from the field. This transition to a genteel script makes documents of the late eighteenth century much easier reading for modern eyes than those written a hundred years earlier.

Handwriting copybooks were addressed to the scribes and clerks who carried the great burden of official and commercial correspondence but also to the "Gentlemen and Ladies and to the Young Masters and Misses." At first, Italian was the aristocratic hand; Queen Elizabeth and Charles I both took pride in their mastery of that script. In early Stuart England the writing master Martin Billingsley (1591–1622) taught a delicate Italian hand for ladies, a stronger Italian hand for cavaliers, and versions of Gothic for secretaries, lawyers, and ordinary people. As Italian gained ascendance in all realms, the distinctions became less marked; generally, narrower rather than broadly spaced uprights and a stronger slant marked genteel and feminine hands.

In 1748 Benjamin Franklin, who practiced penmanship as a youth while trying to emulate the style of the *Spectator* papers, pirated an edition of a well-known English manual for "Persons of Business" by George Fisher that included handwriting specimens. Franklin added the word "American" to the title to make it *The Instructor, or American Young Man's Best Companion* and inserted his own variant of a commercial version of Italian known as "Round Hand." He also included an "Italian Hand" with more flourishes than practical for commercial writing and with narrower spacing than Round Hand, presumably for the benefit of aspiring gentry. Washington's elegant hand was a form of Round Hand. Polite Americans did not necessarily respect these formal distinctions, but gracefully executed Italian writing was expected in some form from a gentleman or a lady. The invariably graceful signatures on the great political documents at the end of the eighteenth century, led off by John Hancock on the Declaration of Independence, testify to the attention the American gentry of that generation had devoted to penmanship.

The gentry penman needed instruction to achieve this facility, and the craft of penmanship became an established vocation in England by the early seventeenth century. Not only the copybooks but actual writing masters arrived in America not long after settlement. Ordinary schoolmasters taught writing too, but in 1667 William Howard received permission to keep a "wrighting schoole" in Boston, and from then on specialists regularly augmented instruction from other sources. In the first two decades of the eighteenth century more than a dozen freelance writing masters advertised instruction in Boston. In the 1730s and 1740s Peter Pelham, the famous mezzotint artist, regularly advertised his "Writing and Arithmetick School, near the Town House." In 1755, 216 pupils were enrolled in Boston's "South Writing School" and another 237 in the "North Writing School."

Outside of cities like Boston, scores of copybooks supplemented the instruction of people like the Livingston's steward who taught Peggy Shippen. Most such books came from England; there were twenty-one different English copybooks in the library of a single Boston writing master, Abiah Holbrook of the South Writing School. George Fisher's *Young Man's Best Companion* came out in seventeen American editions over nearly a century. Not counting Franklin's American variant of Fisher in 1748, the first genuinely American copybook came from the press of Isaiah Thomas in Worcester in 1785. Often the books and the writing masters combined arithmetic with penmanship as Pelham did, which may account for Graydon's comment about the vulgar arithmetic of his York acquaintance. Not the addition and subtraction but the form of the numbers made the difference.

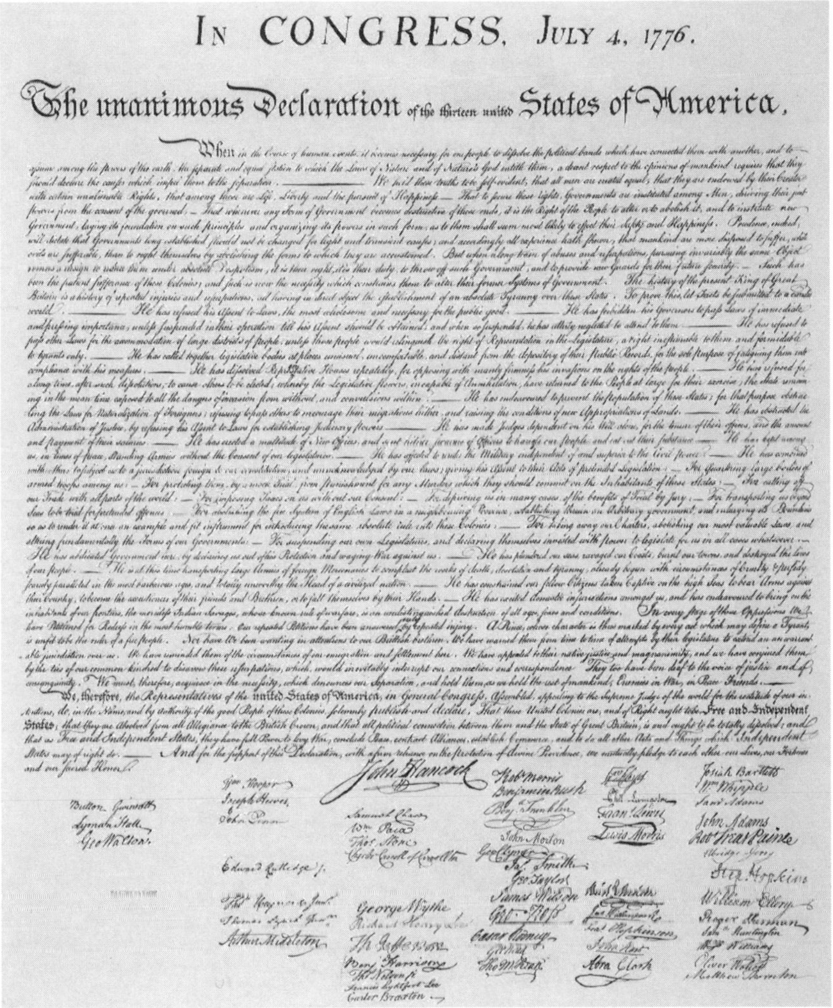
IN CONGRESS, JULY 4, 1776.

The unanimous Declaration of the thirteen united States of America,

Figure 7.6 The Declaration of Independence. (Courtesy National Archives, Washington, DC.)

By 1776 all of the signers had learned the art of fine writing, one of the marks of a gentleman.

The implications of polite letter writing lead to furniture. Nothing attests more eloquently to the significance of writing and correspondence in the eighteenth-century mentality than the appearance of a new furniture

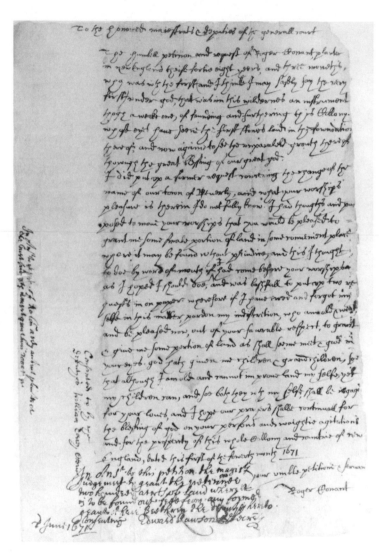

Figure 7.7 Petition of Roger Conant, 1671. (From William Bradford, *History of Plymouth Plantation, 1620–1647*, Boston, 1912, vol. 1, p. 418.)

One of the earliest settlers of New England, Roger Conant, sometimes called a gentleman in the records, wrote in the crabbed older style.

form to honor those activities – the desk. In the seventeenth century, papers had been kept in boxes, many of them well constructed and adorned. A slant lid on some boxes facilitated writing and made a kind of a desk that could be mounted on an open frame to bring it up to the right height. Near the end of the seventeenth century desks enjoyed a marvelous flowering. The simple joined boxes gave way to desks built onto chests of drawers and sometimes called bureau desks. Sometimes bookcases were mounted on top of these desks, the combined form rising six or seven feet from the floor. Inside the slant lid were drawers and openings of a size to hold folded papers. Desks were made of the best woods, mahogany, walnut, cherry, and maple, fitted with brass pulls, and adorned with pilasters, carved shells, and undulating fronts. The desks matched in workmanship any case pieces in the house and were often among the most costly.

Beyond any question, these forms were meant to honor the activities associated with them. As households adopted gentility in the eighteenth century, some aspects of life like cooking and washing disappeared into the back of the house. Writing, like dining, was not among the suppressed behaviors. The owners of desks wished to advertise their correspondence, to display their writing instruments, and to let it be known that they wrote and received letters. Desks placed in the formal front rooms of the house signified the presence of letter writers in the household. Commercial correspondence continued on desks of unpretentious pine mounted on simple open frames in shops and warehouses. Elegant residential desks spoke more for a genteel correspondence, written in a fine Italian hand, containing gracefully expressed sentiments, and written by women as well as by men.

Beautification

With all of this before us, the composure of the body, the personal traits of delicacy, sensibility, and taste, and the genteel skills of conversing and writing, we can return to the question of gentility's basic nature. Does anything hold the diverse traits of so many activities and objects together? Do they have anything in common that approaches a definition? Perhaps of all the personal qualities, taste holds the most promise for shedding light on this puzzle. For one thing, "taste" was an active word, implying responsibilities. Taste required a person to change the world. A person who chose to live with ugliness and disorder could not claim to be tasteful. The word "taste" implicitly incorporated an elaborate cultural project. It implied a mission for the refined population to beautify the world, beginning with their own persons and radiating to all they possessed and influenced.

Though rarely articulated in America in the eighteenth century, the pursuit of this mission was in evidence everywhere. Whenever Washington's military and civic responsibilities permitted, he gave concentrated attention to the adornment of Mount Vernon – the house, the gardens, the room furnishings, and the table. As deeply engaged in public affairs and business as he was, he still devoted himself generously to the beautification of his environment. And Washington was not exceptional. Men of substance everywhere occupied themselves with the details of architecture, furniture design, and landscaping. The title of Thomas Chippendale's *Gentleman's and Cabinet-Maker's Director* implied that design was the province of gentlemen, not just craftsmen, and the American gentry took up the charge.

They did not act dutifully or out of self-sacrificing idealism. A grand house, properly laid out and decorated, anchored a person's standing in the community and even sustained political power. Gentility was interwoven with the totality of gentry culture. By the Revolution, those who lacked taste generally lacked power. A magnate who erected an expensive but hideous house lost strength. Power and the tasteful ideal were interrelated. Sir Charles Grandison's equipage was "perfectly in taste" because everything about that paragon of gentility had to be. Without taste he would have commanded little respect.[40]

In addition to the political support of beautification, intellectual backing came from distinguished intellectuals in England and on the Continent. Increasing use of the word "taste" in polite speech coincided with the appearance of a spate of treatises about aesthetics, a branch of philosophy that received renewed attention in the eighteenth century. In England, Joseph Addison, Francis Hutcheson, Sir Joshua Reynolds, David Hume, William Hogarth, Edmund Burke, and many lesser lights addressed the problem in the same years when the broad-based campaign to beautify houses, gardens, and persons was reaching a peak. In fact, the gentry's preoccupation with beauty may have prompted the efforts to define its nature. In an essay on taste in *The Spectator* in 1712, Addison commented that "as this Word arises very often in conversation, I shall endeavour to give some Account of it," and then proceeded to his discourse. On the other hand, the writers on beauty also wished to offer guidance and inspiration for the beautification campaign. One anonymous work on "the polite arts" stated explicitly the simple grounding of the project. "Taste has every where the same Rules. It wills, that we erase every thing that can give an unlovely impression, and that we offer all that can produce an agreeable one."[41] That was the imperative, inherent in genteel taste, that drove the beautification program.

Edmund Burke was one who sought to define the nature of beauty. His *Philosophical Enquiry into the Origin of Our Ideas of the Sublime and the*

Beautiful influenced aesthetic philosophy both in England and on the Continent. The work is particularly helpful in understanding gentility because of the peculiar twist Burke gave to the meaning of beauty; he contrasted beauty not only to its polar opposite, ugliness, but to the sublime, which is exalted and aesthetic without being beautiful, and this distinction between the sublime and the beautiful serves to reveal more clearly the nature – and the limitations – of gentility.

Burke compiled a list of attributes that set beauty apart from ugliness. Smoothness, softness, and gently flowing curves are among the qualities that make an object beautiful rather than ugly. Sublimity, on the other hand, is distinguished from beauty by quite different traits. Sublimity is power and terror: great craggy peaks with their menacing shadows, sharp angles, and abrupt drops; ferocious storms at sea, with crashing waves and blasts of destructive wind. The exercise of power – the church at the judgment of a sinner, or civil government at an execution – arouses sublime emotions: dread, reverence, awe. Beauty is situated in a tranquil and peaceful region between ugliness and sublimity. The sublime and the beautiful, Burke observed, arise from different principles, "one being founded on pain, the other on pleasure."[42] Beauty pleases the human spirit rather than repulsing or terrifying it.

Gentility, being neither ugly nor sublime, belonged wholly to the beautiful. Gentility, whether in dress, personal manners, or architecture, was harmony, smoothness, polish, gradual rather than abrupt variation, the subduing of harsh emotions. Gentility beautified the world in Burke's sense. Eighteenth-century portraits, with their graceful and easy postures, fine clothes, and composed faces, present people who have overcome their baser impulses and learned to conceal the fearful secrets of their hearts. Painters consciously sought to make sitters neither ugly nor sublime, but smooth and beautiful.

Gentility beautified the persons of the sitters, then went on to beautify the environment, starting with the furnishing of formal rooms and extending outward into gardens and grounds. Outdoors, genteel nature was neither sublimely rugged nor ugly and coarse. While fashion might permit, say, a rough grotto on the grounds of a large estate, the predominant aim was to create a regulated landscape that repressed the sublime in favor of beauty's gentle curves and smooth surfaces. The aim of the polite arts, one theorist offered, was the imitation of *"beautiful* nature," neither the rugged, ominous nature of the sublime nor unkempt, disordered, ugly nature.[43] The harmony and beauty that genteel culture looked for in nature paralleled the ease and harmony in which genteel society took pleasure.

The aesthetic of the beautiful outlined in Burke's *Enquiry* was thus a philosophical expression of the spirit of gentility. At the same time, the

Enquiry helps us to understand gentility's limitations. Gentility's devotion to beautiful nature put it at odds with both the ugly and the sublime. Horror and awe, emotions evoked by the sublime, were repressed in genteel natures, as were all things base and disturbing – the dissonant, the plebeian, the filthy. All had to be concealed in the interest of beauty and harmony. But the attempt to control nature and society for the sake of a beautiful appearance necessarily made denial and repression essential traits of gentility. Even though in the service of a worthy purpose, the wish to conceal was, in the last analysis, shallow. Gentility hid what it could not countenance and denied whatever caused discomfort. That deficiency in candor and courage, however commendable the impulse behind it, was the flaw at the core of gentility, the reason why it proved at last to be weak and superficial.

Notes

1   Kym S. Rice, *Early American Taverns: For the Entertainment of Friends and Strangers* (Chicago, 1983), 55; Carl F. Bridenbaugh, ed., *Gentleman's Progress: The Itinerarium of Dr. Alexander Hamilton, 1744* (Chapel Hill, NC, 1948), 13.

2   Alexander Graydon, *Memoirs of His Own Time*, ed. John Stockton Littell (New York, 1969 [reprint of 1846 edn; orig. pub. as *Memoirs of a Life*, 1811]), 102.

3   Abbé d'Ancourt, *The Lady's Preceptor* (Woodbridge, NJ, 1759), 6.

4   Antoine de Courtin, *The Rules of Civility; or, The Maxims of Genteel Behaviour, As They Are Practis'd and Observ'd by Persons of Quality, upon Several Occasions*...(London, 1703, from the 12th French edn), 89–90; Charles Moore, ed., *George Washington's Rules of Civility and Decent Behaviour in Company and Conversation* (Boston and New York, 1926), 3, 5, 11, 19, 21.

5   Lord Chesterfield [Philip Dormer Stanhope], *Principles of Politeness, and of Knowing the World; by the Late Lord Chesterfield. Methodised and Digested under Distinct Heads, with Additions, by the Reverend Dr. John Trusler: Containing Every Instruction Necessary to Complete the Gentleman and Man of Fashion, to Teach Him a Knowledge of Life, and Make Him Well Received in All Companies* (Portsmouth, 1786), 18, 55–6.

6   Courtin, *Rules of Civility*, 208.

7   Quoted in Norman Arthur Benson, "The Itinerant Dancing and Music Masters of Eighteenth-century America" (Ph.D. dissertation, University of Minnesota, 1963), 237–8.

8   Chesterfield, *Principles of Politeness*, 23.

9   Rufus Wilmot Griswold, *The Republican Court; or, American Society in the Days of Washington* (New York, 1868), 311–12.

10 Quoted in Stephen Decatur, Jr, *Private Affairs of George Washington: From the Records and Accounts of Tobia Lear, Esquire, his Secretary* (Boston, 1933), 48–9.

11 Claudia B. Kidwell and Margaret C. Christman, *Suiting Everyone: The Democratization of Clothing in America* (Washington, DC, 1974) 23.

12 Edmund Burke, *A Philosophical Enquiry into the Origin of our Ideas of the Sublime and Beautiful*, ed. James T. Boulton (London, 1958 [reprinted 1968; rev. edn, Oxford, 1987]), 114.

13 David D. Hall, ed., *Witch-hunting in Seventeenth-century New England: A Documentary History, 1638–1692* (Boston, 1991), 40; Phillip R. Shriver, ed., *A Tour to New Connecticut in 1811: The Narrative of Henry Leavitt Ellsworth* (Cleveland, 1985), 66–7.

14 Bridenbaugh, ed., *Gentleman's Progress*, 8.

15 John Locke, *Some Thoughts Concerning Education*, 5th edn (London, 1705) in James L. Axtell, ed., *The Educational Writings of John Locke* (Cambridge, England, 1968), 160.

16 D'Ancourt, *Lady's Preceptor*, 11.

17 Dr Gregory, *A Father's Legacy to his Daughters* (Portsmouth, NH, 1786) [bound with Chesterfield, *Principles of Politeness*], 102, 104.

18 Quoted in "Sensibility," *The Oxford English Dictionary*, 14: 981–2.

19 Ethel Armes, ed., *Nancy Shippen, Her Journal Book: The International Romance of a Young Lady of Fashion of Colonial Philadelphia with Letters to Her and about Her* (Philadelphia, 1935), 169, 246; Susanna Rowson, *Charlotte Temple: A Tale of Truth*, ed. Clara M. and Rudolph Kirk (Schenectady, NY, n.d. [orig. pub. 1791]), 45–6.

20 Hunter Dickinson Farish, ed., *Journals and Letters of Philip Vickers Fithian, 1773–1774* (Williamsburg, VA, 1957), 77–8.

21 Elise Pinckney, ed., *The Letterbook of Eliza Lucas Pinckney, 1739–1762* (Chapel Hill, NC, 1972), xv–xvi.

22 Gregory, *A Father's Legacy*, 103; Armes, ed., *Nancy Shippen, Her Journal Book*, 175.

23 *The Polite Arts, or, a Dissertation on Poetry, Painting, Musick, Architecture, and Eloquence* (London, 1749), 8. Montesquieu quote from Peter Gay, *The Enlightenment: An Interpretation*, vol. 2: *The Science of Freedom* (New York, 1969), 300.

24 D'Ancourt, *Lady's Preceptor*, 9; *Art of Complaisance*, quoted in Rice, *Early American Taverns*, 78–9.

25 *The Weekly Rehearsal* (Boston) is quoted in David H. Flaherty, *Privacy in Colonial New England* (Charlottesville, VA, 1972), 111. Armes, ed., *Nancy Shippen, Her Journal Book*, 170, 176, and Chastellux quoted on 309; Griswold, *Republican Court*, 79–80.

26 Henry Peacham, *The Complete Gentleman*, ed. Virgil B. Heltzel (Ithaca, NY, 1962 [orig. pub. 1622; this is from the 1634 edn]), 117, 121.

27 Chesterfield, *Principles of Politeness*, 10 (quote), 71–2.

28 Ibid., 35; Jacques Levron, *Daily Life at Versailles in the Seventeenth and Eighteenth Centuries*, tr. Claire Elaine Engel (New York, 1968), 61; Bonnin quote from Rice, *Early American Taverns*, 117; Courtin, *Rules of Civility*, 32–3; New York newspaper quote from Esther Singleton, *Social New York under the Georges, 1714–1776: Houses, Streets and Country Homes, with Chapters on Fashions, Furniture, China, Plate and Manners* (New York, 1902), 323.

29 Courtin, *Rules of Civility*, 68–75.
30 Josiah Quincy, *Memoirs of the Life of Josiah Quincy, Junior, of Massachusetts, 1774–1775*, 2nd edn (Boston, 1874), 116, 138.
31 *Youth's Behavior, of Decency in Conversation Amongst Men...*, tr. Francis Hawkins, 8th printing (London, 1663), 3.
32 Philomusus, *The Academy of Complements. Wherein Ladyes, Gentlewomen, Schollers, and Strangers May Accomodate Their Courtly Practice with Most Curious Ceremonies, Complementall, Amorous, High Expressions, and Formes of Speaking, or Writing* (London, 1640), preface.
33 Henry Fielding, "An Essay on Conversation," in *Miscellanies by Henry Fielding, Esq.; Volume One*, ed. Henry Knight Miller ([Middletown, CT] 1972), 123, 150; Chesterfield, *Principles of Politeness*, 34.
34 Jonathan Swift, *A Complete Collection of Genteel and Ingenious Conversation, According to the Most Polite Mode and Method Now used at Court, and in the Best Companies of England. In Three Dialogues* (London, 1738), in *Polite Conversation*, ed. Eric Partridge (London, 1963), 23.
35 Bonamy Dobree, ed., *The Letters of Philip Dormer Stanhope, 4th Earl of Chesterfield* (n.p., 1932), November 24, 1749, 4: 1442–3. Benjamin Rush quoted in Wayne Craven, *Colonial American Portraiture: The Economic, Religious, Social, Cultural, Philosophical, Scientific and Aesthetic Foundations* (Cambridge, England, 1986), 396.
36 Abigail Adams to Mercy Otis Warren, Boston, July 16, 1773, and Mercy Otis Warren to Abigail Adams, Plymouth, July 25, 1773, in L. H. Butterfield, Wendell D. Garrett, and Marjorie E. Sprague, eds., *Adams Family Correspondence* (Cambridge, MA, 1963), 1: 84–7.
37 Abigail Adams to Mercy Otis Warren, Boston, December 11, 1773, in ibid., 1: 89.
38 Sally Fisher, Duck Creek Cross Roads, to Deborah Norris, Duck Creek Cross Roads, March 1780, and Deborah Norris to Sally Fisher, Philadelphia, May 6, 1780, in John A. H. Sweeney, ed., "The Norris–Fisher Correspondence: A Circle of Friends, 1779–82," *Delaware History*, 6 (March 1955): 200, 204.
39 Graydon, *Memoirs*, 102; Bickham quoted in Ambrose Heal, *The English Writing-Masters and Their Copy-Books, 1570–1800: A Biographical Dictionary and a Bibliography* (Hildesheim, 1962 [orig. pub. 1931]), x; Chesterfield quoted in Wilfrid Blunt, *Sweet Roman Hand: Five Hundred Years of Italic Cursive Script* (London, 1952), 33; also in Chesterfield, *Principles of Politeness*, 60; Ray Nash, *American Writing Masters and Copybooks: History and Bibliography Through Colonial Times* (Boston, 1959), 23; Moore, ed., *George Washington's Rules of Civility*, xii, xiii; Armes, ed., *Nancy Shippen, Her Journal*, 282–3.
40 Samuel Richardson, *The History of Sir Charles Grandison*, ed. Jocelyn Harris, 3 vols. (London, 1972), pt. I, 182.
41 Joseph Addison, "No. 409," June 19, 1712, *The Spectator*, ed. Donald F. Bond, 3 (Oxford, 1965): 527; *The Polite Arts, or, a Dissertation on Poetry, Painting, Musick, Architecture, and Eloquence* (London, 1749), 5.
42 Burke, *Philosophical Enquiry*, 124.
43 *The Polite Arts*, 9.

Autobiography and Other Writings (1790)

Benjamin Franklin

From my infancy I was passionately fond of reading, and all the little money that came into my hands was laid out in the purchasing of books. I was very fond of voyages. My first acquisition was Bunyan's works in separate little volumes. I afterwards sold them to enable me to buy R. Burton's historical collections; they were small chapmen's books and cheap, forty or fifty in all. My father's little library consisted chiefly of books in polemic divinity, most of which I read. I have since often regretted that at a time when I had such a thirst for knowledge, more proper books had not fallen in my way, since it was now resolved I should not be bred to divinity. There was among them Plutarch's *Lives*, in which I read abundantly, and I still think that time spent to great advantage. There was also a book of Defoe's called an *Essay on Projects* and another of Dr. Mather's called *Essays to do Good*, which perhaps gave me a turn of thinking that had an influence on some of the principal future events of my life.

This bookish inclination at length determined my father to make me a printer, though he had already one son (James) of that profession. In 1717 my brother, James, returned from England with a press and letters to set up his business in Boston. I liked it much better than that of my father, but still had a hankering for the sea. To prevent the apprehended effect of such an inclination, my father was impatient to have me bound to my brother. I stood out some time, but at last was persuaded and signed the indenture, when I was yet but twelve years old. I was to serve as apprentice till I was twenty-one years of age, only I was to be allowed journeyman's wages during the last year. In a little time I made a great progress in the business and became a useful hand to my brother. I now had access to better books. An acquaintance with the apprentices of booksellers enabled me sometimes to borrow a small one, which I was careful to return soon and clean. Often I sat up in my room reading the greatest part of the night, when the book was borrowed in the evening and to be returned early in the morning, lest it should be found missing or wanted.

After some time a merchant, an ingenious, sensible man, Mr. Matthew Adams, who had a pretty collection of books and who frequented our printing house, took notice of me, invited me to see his library, and very kindly proposed to lend me such books as I chose to read. I now took a fancy to poetry and made some little pieces. My brother, supposing it might turn to account, encouraged me and induced me to compose two occasional ballads. One was called the "Lighthouse Tragedy," and contained an account of the shipwreck of Capt. Worthilake with his two daughters; the other was a "Sailor's Song on the Taking of the Famous *Teach*, or Blackbeard, the Pirate." They were wretched stuff, in street ballad style; and when they were printed, he sent me about the town to sell them. The first sold prodigiously, the event being recent and having made a great noise. This success flattered my vanity, but my father discouraged me by ridiculing my performances and telling me verse-makers were generally beggars. Thus I escaped being a poet and probably a very bad one. But as prose writing has been of great use to me in the course of my life and was a principal means of my advancement, I shall tell you how in such a situation I acquired what little ability I may be supposed to have in that way.

There was another bookish lad in the town, John Collins by name, with whom I was intimately acquainted. We sometimes disputed, and very fond we were of argument, and very desirous of confuting one another – which disputatious turn, by the way, is apt to become a very bad habit, making people often extremely disagreeable in company, by the contradiction that is necessary to bring it into practice; and thence besides souring and spoiling the conversation, it is productive of disgusts and perhaps enmities where you may have occasion for friendship. I had caught it by reading my father's books of dispute on religion. Persons of good sense, I have since observed, seldom fall into it, except lawyers, university men, and men of all sorts who have been bred at Edinburgh. A question was once somehow or other started between Collins and me on the propriety of educating the female sex in learning and their abilities for study. He was of opinion that it was improper and that they were naturally unequal to it. I took the contrary side, perhaps a little for dispute sake. He was naturally more eloquent, having a greater plenty of words, and sometimes, as I thought, I was vanquished more by his fluency than by the strength of his reasons. As we parted without settling the point and were not to see one another again for some time, I sat down to put my arguments in writing, which I copied fair and sent to him. He answered and I replied. Three or four letters on a side had passed, when my father happened to find my papers and read them. Without entering into the subject in dispute, he took occasion to talk with me about my manner of writing, observed that though I had the advantage of my antagonist in correct spelling and pointing (which I owed to the printing house) I fell far short in elegance of expression, in method, and in perspicuity – of which he convinced me by several instances. I saw the justice of his remarks and thence grew more attentive to my manner of writing, and determined to endeavour to improve my style.

About this time I met with an odd volume of the *Spectator*. It was the third. I had never before seen any of them. I bought it, read it over and over, and was much delighted with it. I thought the writing excellent and wished if possible to imitate it. With that view, I took some of the papers, and making short hints of the sentiment in each sentence, laid them by a few days, and then without looking at the book, tried to complete the papers again by expressing each hinted sentiment at length and as fully as it had been expressed before, in any suitable words that should occur to me. Then I compared my *Spectator* with the original, discovered some of my faults, and corrected them. But I found I wanted a stock of words or a readiness in recollecting and using them, which I thought I should have acquired before that time if I had gone on making verses; since the continual search for words of the same import but of different length to suit the measure, or of different sound for the rhyme would have laid me under a constant necessity of searching for variety, and also have tended to fix that variety in my mind, and make me master of it. Therefore I took some of the tales in the *Spectator* and turned them into verse, and after a time, when I had pretty well forgotten the prose, turned them back again. I also sometimes jumbled my collections of hints into confusion, and after some weeks endeavoured to reduce them into the best order before I began to form the full sentences and complete the paper. This was to teach me method in the arrangement of the thoughts. By comparing my work afterwards with the original, I discovered many faults and corrected them; but I sometimes had the pleasure of fancying that in certain particulars of small import I had been lucky enough to improve the method or the language, and this encouraged me to think that I might possibly in time come to be a tolerable English writer, of which I was extremely ambitious.

The time I allotted for these exercises and for reading, was at night after work, or before it began in the morning, or on Sundays, when I contrived to be in the printing house alone, avoiding as much as I could the common attendance on public worship which my father used to exact of me, when I was under his care – and which, indeed, I still thought a duty, though I could not, as it seemed to me, afford the time to practise it.

When about sixteen years of age I happened to meet with a book written by one Tryon, recommending a vegetable diet.[1] I determined to go into it. My brother, being yet unmarried, did not keep house but boarded himself and his apprentices in another family. My refusing to eat flesh occasioned an inconveniency, and I was frequently chid for my singularity. I made myself acquainted with Tryon's manner of preparing some of his dishes, such as boiling potatoes or rice, making hasty pudding, and a few others; and then proposed to my brother that if he would give me weekly half the money he paid for my board, I would board myself. He instantly agreed to it, and I presently found that I could save half what he paid me. This was an additional fund for buying of books. But I had another advantage in it. My brother and the rest going from the printing house to their meals, I remained there alone, and dispatching presently my light repast (which often was no more than a biscuit or a slice of bread, a handful of raisins or a tart from the pastry cook's, and a glass of water) had the rest of the time till their return for study, in which I made the greater progress from that greater clearness of head and quicker apprehension which generally attend temperance in eating and drinking. Now it was that being on some occasion made ashamed of my ignorance in figures, which I had twice failed in learning when at school, I took Cocker's book of arithmetic, and went through the whole by myself with the greatest ease. I also read Seller's and Sturmy's book on navigation and became acquainted with the little geometry it contains, but I never proceeded far in that science. I read about this time Locke *On Human Understanding*, and *The Art of Thinking* by Messrs. du Port Royal.

While I was intent on improving my language, I met with an English grammar (I think it was Greenwood's) at the end of which there were two little sketches on the arts of rhetoric and logic, the latter finishing with a dispute in the Socratic method. And soon after I procured Xenophon's *Memorable Things of Socrates*, wherein there are many examples of the same method. I was charmed with it, adopted it, dropped my abrupt contradiction and positive argumentation, and put on the humble enquirer. And being then, from reading Shaftsbury and Collins, made a doubter, as I already was in many points of our religious doctrines, I found this method the safest for myself and very embarrassing to those against whom I used it; therefore, I took a delight in it, practised it continually, and grew very artful and expert in drawing people, even of superior knowledge, into concessions the consequences of which they did not foresee, entangling them in difficulties out of which they could not extricate themselves, and so obtaining victories that neither myself nor my cause always deserved. I continued this method some few years but gradually left it, retaining only the habit of expressing myself in terms of modest diffidence, never using when I advance anything that may possibly be disputed the words, "certainly," "undoubtedly," or any other that give the air of positiveness to an opinion; but rather say, "I conceive or apprehend a thing to be so or so," "It appears to me," or "I should think it so or so, for such and such reasons," or "I imagine it to be so," or "It is so if I am not mistaken." This habit, I believe, has been of great advantage to me when I have had occasion to inculcate my opinions and persuade men into measures that I have been from time to time engaged in promoting. And as the chief ends of conversation are to *inform*, or to *be informed*, to *please* or to *persuade*, I wish well-meaning and sensible men would not lessen their power of doing good by a positive, assuming manner that seldom fails to disgust, tends to create opposition, and to defeat every one of those purposes for which speech was given to us. In fact, if you wish to instruct others, a positive, dogmatical manner in advancing your sentiments may provoke contradiction and prevent a candid attention. If you desire instruction and improvement from the knowledge of others, you should not at the same time express yourself as firmly fixed in your present opinions; modest and sensible men, who do not love disputation, will probably leave you undisturbed in the possession of your error. In adopting such a manner you can seldom expect to please your hearers, or to persuade those whose concurrence you desire. Pope judiciously observes,

> Men must be taught as if you taught them not,
> And things unknown propos'd as things forgot.

He also recommends it to us,

> To speak, though sure, with seeming diffidence.

And he might have joined with this line that which he has coupled with another, I think less properly,

> For want of modesty is want of sense.

If you ask why *less properly*, I must repeat the lines,

> Immodest words admit of *no defence*,
> *For* want of modesty is want of sense.

Now is not the "want of sense" (where a man is so unfortunate as to want it) some apology for his "want of modesty"? and would not the lines stand more justly thus?

> Immodest words admit *but* this defense
> That want of modesty is want of sense.

This, however, I should submit to better judgements. . . .

Note

1   Thomas Tryon (1634–1703) published various pamphlets on health.

Gentleman's Progress: The Itinerarium of Dr. Alexander Hamilton (1744)

Alexander Hamilton

Annapolis, Wednesday, May 30th. I set out from Annapolis in Maryland upon Wednesday, the 30th of May, att eleven a'clock in the morning, contrary winds and bad weather preventing my intended passage over Chesapeak Bay, so taking the Patapscoe road, I proposed going by way of Bohemia to Newtown upon Chester, a very circumflex course, but as the journey was intended only for health and recreation, I was indifferent whether I took the nearest or the farthest route, having likewise a desire to see that part of the country. I was in seeming bad order att my first seting out, being suspicious that one of my horses was lame, but he performed well and beyond my expectation. I travelled but 26 miles this day. There was a cloudy sky and an appearance of rain. Some miles from town I met Mr. H[ar]t going to Annapolis. He returned with me to his own house where I was well entertained and had one night's lodging and a country dinner.

Mr. H[asel]l, a gentleman of Barbadoes, with whom I expected to have the pleasure of travelling a good part of my intended journey, had left Annapolis a week or ten days before me and had appointed to meet me att Philadelphia. He went to Bohemia by water and then took chaise over land to Newcastle and Willimington, being forbid for certain physicall reasons to travell on horseback. This was a polite and facetious gentleman, and I was sorry that his tedious stay in some places put it out of my power to tarry for him; so I was deprived of his conversation the far greatest part of the journey.

Mr. H[ar]t and I, after dinner, drank some punch and conversed like a couple of virtuosos. His wife had no share in the conversation; he is blessed indeed with a silent woman, but her muteness is owing to a defect in her hearing, that, without bawling out to her, she cannot understand what is spoke, and therefor not knowing how to make pertinent replys, she chuses to hold her tongue. It is well I have thus accounted for it; else such a character in the sex would appear quite out of nature. Att night I writ to Annapolis and retired to bed att 10 a'clock. . . .

Susquehanna Ferry

. . . The lower ferry of Susquehanna, which I crossed, is above a mile broad. It is kept by a little old man whom I found att vittles with his wife and family upon a homely dish of fish without any kind of sauce. They desired me to eat, but I told them I had no stomach. They had no cloth upon the table, and their mess was in a dirty, deep, wooden dish which they evacuated with their hands, cramming down skins, scales, and all. They used neither knife, fork, spoon, plate, or napkin because, I suppose, they had none to use. I looked upon this as a picture of that primitive simplicity practiced by our fore-fathers long before the mechanic arts had supplyed them with in-struments for the luxury and elegance of life. I drank some of their syder, which was very good, and crossed the ferry in company with a certain Scots-Irishman by name Thomas Quiet. The land about Susquehanna is pritty high and woody, and the channell of the river rockey.

Mr. Quiet rid a little scrub bay mare which he said was sick and ailing and could not carry him, and therefore he 'lighted every half mile and ran a couple of miles att a footman's pace to spell the poor beast (as he termed it). He informed me he lived att Monocosy and had been out three weeks in quest of his creatures (horses), four of which had strayed from his plantation. I condoled his loss and asked him what his mare's distemper was, resolving to prescribe for her, but all that I could gett out of him was that the poor silly beast had choaked herself in eating her oats; so I told him that if she was choaked, she was past my art to recover.

This fellow, I observed, had a particular down hanging look which made me suspect he was one of our New Light biggots. I guessed right, for he introduced a discourse concerning Whitfield and inlarged pritty much and with some warmth upon the doctrines of that apostle, speak-ing much in his praise. I took upon me, in a ludicrous manner, to impungn some of his doctrines, which, by degrees, put Mr. Quiet in a passion. He told me flatly that I was damnd without redemption. I replyed that I thought his name and behaviour were very incongruous and desired him to change it with all speed, for it was very impropper that such an angry, turbulent mortall as he should be called by the name of Thomas Quiet.

Principio Iron Works – North East

In the height of this fool's passion, I overtook one Mr. B[axte]r, a proprietor in the iron works there, and, after mutual salutation, the topic of discourse turned from religious controversy to politicks; so putting on a little faster, we left this inflammed bigot and his sick mare behind. This gentleman accompanied me to North East and gave me directions as to the road. . . .

Pensylvania – Newcastle

Tuesday, June 5th. I took horse a little after 5 in the morning, and after a solitary ride thro stonny, unequall road, where the country people stared att me like sheep when I enquired of them the way, I arrived att Newcastle upon Delaware att 9 a'clock in the morning and baited my horses att one Curtis's att the Sign of the Indian King, a good house of entertainment.

This town stands upon stonny ground just upon the water, there being from thence a large prospect eastward towards the Bay of Delaware and the province of the Jerseys. The houses are chiefly brick, built after the Dutch modell, the town having been originally founded and inhabited by the Dutch when it belonged to New York government. It consists chiefly of one great street which makes an elbow att right angles. A great many of the houses are old and crazy. There is in the town two publick buildings, viz., a court house and church.

Att Curtis's I met company going to Philadelphia and was pleased att it, being my self an utter stranger to the roads. This company consisted of three men: Thomas Howard, Timothy Smith, and William Morison. I treated them with some lemmon punch and desired the favour of their company. They readily granted my request and stayed some time for me till I had eat breakfast. Smith, in his hat and coat, had the appearance of a Quaker, but his discourse was purged of thee's and thou's tho his delivery seemed to be solemn and slow paced. Howard was a talkative man, abounding with words and profuse in compliments which were generally blunt and came out in an awkward manner. He bestowed much panegyrick upon his own behaviour and conduct.

Morison (who, I understood, had been att the Land Office in Annapolis enquiring about a title he had to some land in Maryland) was a very rough spun, forward, clownish blade, much addicted to swearing, att the same time desirous to pass for a gentleman; notwithstanding which ambition, the conscientiousness of his naturall boorishness obliged him frequently to frame ill tim'd apologys for his misbehaviour, which he termed frankness and freeness. It was often, "Damn me, gentlemen, excuse me; I am a plain, honest fellow; all is right down plain dealing, by God." He was much affronted with the landlady att Curtis's who, seeing him in a greasy jacket and breeches and a dirty worsted cap, and withall a heavy, forward, clownish air and behaviour, I suppose took him for some ploughman or carman and so presented him with some scraps of cold veal for breakfast, he having declared that he could not drink "your damnd washy tea." As soon as he saw his mess he swore, "Damn him, if it wa'n't out of respect to the gentleman in company," (meaning me) he would throw her cold scraps out at the window and break her table all to pieces should it cost him 100 pounds for dammages. Then taking off his worsted night cap, he pulled a linnen one out of his pocket and clapping it upon his head, "Now," says he, "I'm upon the borders of Pensylvania and must look like a gentleman; 'tother was good enough for Maryland, and damn my blood if ever I come into that rascally province again if I don't procure a leather jacket that I may be in a trim to box the saucy jacks there and not run the hazard of tearing my coat." This showed, by the bye, that he payed more regard to his coat than his person, a remarkable instance of modesty and self denyall.

He then made a transition to politicks and damnd the late Sr. R[obert] W[alpole] for a rascall. We asked him his reasons for cursing Sr. R[obert], but he would give us no other but this, that he was certainly informed by some very good gentlemen, who understood the thing right well, that the said Sr. R[obert] was a damnd rogue. And att the conclusion of each rodomontade, he told us that tho he seemed to be but a plain, homely fellow, yet he would have us know that he was able to afford better than many that went finer: he had good linnen in his bags, a pair of silver buckles, silver clasps, and gold sleeve buttons, two Holland shirts, and some neat night caps; and that his little woman att home drank tea twice a day; and he himself lived very well and expected to live better so soon as that old rogue B——t dyed and he could secure a title to his land. . . .

Philadelphia

The country round the city of Philadelphia is level and pleasant, having a prospect of the large river of Delaware and the province of East Jersey upon the other side. You have an agreeable view of this river for most of the way betwixt Philadelphia and Newcastle. The plan or platform of the city lyes betwixt the two rivers of Delaware and Skuylkill, the streets being laid out in rectangular squares which makes a regular, uniform plan, but upon that account, altogether destitute of variety.

Att my entering the city, I observed the regularity of the streets, but att the same time the majority of the houses mean and low and much decayed, the streets in generall not paved, very dirty, and obstructed with rubbish and lumber, but their frequent building excuses that. The State House, Assembly House, the great church in Second Street, and Whitefield's church are good buildings.

I observed severall comicall, grotesque phizzes in the inn wher[e] I put up which would have afforded variety of hints for a painter of Hogarth's turn. They talked there upon all subjects – politics, religion, and trade – some tollerably well, but most of them ignorantly. I discovered two or three chaps very inquisitive, asking my boy who I was, whence come, and whether bound.

I was shaved by a little, finicall, hump backed old barber who kept dancing round me and talking all the time of the operation and yet did his job lightly and to a hair. He abounded in compliments and was a very civil fellow in his way. He told me he had been a journyman to the business for 40 odd years, notwithstanding which, he understood how to trim gentlemen as well (thank God) as the best masters and dispaired not of preferment before he dyed.

I delivered my letters, went to dine with Collector Alexander, and visited severall people in town. In the afternoon I went to the coffee house where I was introduced by Dr. Thomas Bond to severall gentlemen of the place, where the ceremony of shaking of hands, an old custom peculiar to the English, was performed with great gravity and the usuall compliments. I took private lodgings att Mrs. Cume's in Chestnut Street.

Thursday, June 7th. I remarked one instance of industry as soon as I got up and looked out att my chamber window, and that was the shops open att 5 in the morning. I breakfasted with Mrs. Cume and dined by invitation with Dr. Thomas Bond where, after some talk upon physicall matters, he showed me some pritty good anatomical preparations of the muscles and blood vessels injected with wax.

After dinner Mr. V[ena]bles, a Barbadian gentleman, came in who, when we casually had mentioned the free masons, began to rail bitterly against that society as an impudent, assuming, and vain caball pretending to be wiser than all mankind besides, an *imperium in imperio*, and therefore justly to be discouraged and suppressed as they had lately been in some foreign countrys. Tho I am no free mason myself, I could not agree with this gentleman, for I abhorr all tyrrannicall and arbitrary notions. I believe the free masons to be an innocent and harmless society that have in their constitution nothing mysterious or beyond the verge of common human understanding, and their secret, which has made such a noise, I imagine is just no secret att all. . . .

Friday, June 8. I read Montaign's Essays in the forenoon which is a strange medley of subjects and particularly entertaining.

I dined att a tavern with a very mixed company of different nations and religions. There were Scots, English, Dutch, Germans, and Irish; there were Roman Catholicks, Church men, Presbyterians, Quakers, New-lightmen, Methodists, Seventh day men, Moravians, Anabaptists, and one Jew. The whole company consisted of 25 planted round an oblong table in a great hall well stoked with flys. The company divided into comittees in conversation; the prevailing topick was politicks and conjectures of a French war. A knott of Quakers there talked only about selling of flower and the low price it bore. The[y] touched a little upon religion, and high words arose among some of the sectaries, but their blood was not hot enough to quarrell, or, to speak in the canting phraze, their zeal wanted fervency. A gentleman that sat next me proposed a number of questions concerning Maryland, understanding I had come from thence. In my replys I was reserved, pretending to know little of the matter as being a person whose business did not lye in the way of history and politicks. . . .

Here is no publick magazine of arms nor any method of defence, either for city or province, in case of the invasion of an enimy. This is owing to the obstinacy of the Quakers in maintaining their principle of non-resistance. It were a pity but they were put to a sharp triall to see whether they would act as they profess.

I never was in a place so populous where the gout for publick gay diversions prevailed so little. There is no such thing as assemblys of the gentry among them, either for dancing or musick; these they have had an utter aversion to ever since Whitefield preached among them. Their chief employ, indeed, is traffick and mercantile business which turns their thoughts from these levitys. Some Virginia gentlemen that came here with the Commissioners of the Indian Treaty were desirous of having a ball but could find none of the feemale sex in a humour for it. Strange influence of religious enthusiasm upon human nature to excite an aversion at these innocent amusements, for the most part so agreeable and entertaining to the young and gay, and indeed, in the opinion of moderate people, so conducive to the improvement of politeness, good manners, and humanity. . . .

I dined att the tavern, and returning home after dinner I read part of a book lately writ by Fielding entituled The Adventures of Joseph Andrews, a masterly performance of its kind and entertaining; the characters of low life here are naturally delineated, and the whole performance is so good that I have not seen any thing of that kind equal or excell it. . . .

I must make a few remarks before I leave this place. The people in generall are inquisitive concerning strangers. If they find one comes there upon the account of trade or traffic, they are fond of dealing with him and cheating him if they can. If he comes for pleasure or curiosity, they take little or no notice of him unless he be a person of more than ordinary rank; then they know as well as others how to fawn and cringe. Some persons there were inquisitive about the state of religion in Maryland. My common reply to such questions was that I studied their constitutions more than their consciences so knew something of the first but nothing of the latter.

They have in generall a bad notion of their neighbouring province, Maryland, esteeming the people a sett of cunning sharpers; but my notion of the affair is that the Pensylvanians are not a whit inferior to them in the science of chicane, only their method of tricking is different. A Pensylvanian will tell a lye with a sanctified, solemn face; a Marylander, perhaps, will convey his fib in a volley of oaths; but the effect and point in view is the same tho' the manner of operating be different.

In this city one may live tollerably cheap as to the articles of eating and drinking, but European goods here are extravagantly dear. Even goods of their own manufacture such as linnen, woolen, and leather bear a high price. Their government is a kind of anarchy (or no government), there being perpetual jarrs betwixt the two parts of the legislature. But that is no strange thing, the ambition and avarice of a few men in both partys being the active springs in these dissentions and altercations, tho a specious story about the good and interest of the country is trumpt up by both; yet I would not be so severe as to say so of all in generall.

Mr. T[homa]s, the present gov[erno]r, I believe is an upright man and has the interest of the province really att heart, having done more for the good of that obstinate generation, the Quakers, than any of his predecessours have done. Neither are they so blind as not to see it, for he shares more of their respect than any of their former governours were wont to do.

There is polite conversation here among the better sort, among whom there is no scarcity of men of learning and good sense. The ladies, for the most part, keep att home and seldom appear in the streets, never in publick assemblies except att the churches or meetings; therefor I cannot with certainty enlarge upon their charms, having had little or no opportunity to see them either congregated or separate, but to be sure the Philadelphian dames are as handsome as their neighbours.
. . .

American Weekly Mercury *(Philadelphia)*, no. 575 *(January 5, 1730/1)*

Generosa [Elizabeth Magawley]

I have observ'd of late, that our unfortunate Sex have been the Subject of almost all the Satyr that has dropt from your [the magazine's writers'] Pen for some Months past; I do assure you notwithstanding, that as I am your constant Reader, so I am your hearty Well-wisher: I am not sorry to find Vice or even Fooleries put in odious Colours; nor more Angry to see ill Women expos'd, than a Valiant Soldier would be to see a Cowardly one call'd Coward. But as there is an Insinuation in one of your Papers, which I think is entirely groundless: I hope you will Pardon me the Freedom of telling you it is. The Sum of the Charge is, *That Fools and Coxcombs are most acceptable to the Ladies.* The Word Ladies is an ambiguous Term, to which no single Idea can be affix'd; as in your Sex there are several Classes of Men of Sense, Rakes, Fops, Coxcombs, and down-right Fools, so I hope, without straining your Complaisance, you will allow there are some Women of Sense comparatively, as well as Coquets, Romps, Prudes, and Idiots. If you had said Fools and Coxcombs are most acceptable to Coquets and Romps I readily grant it: Men of Sense value themselves too much to be used as Tools, they cannot stoop to the little Fooleries impos'd on them by their imaginary Goddesses, and their Resentments are too strong to bear Contempt and Insults. As to the Women of Sense (if you allow any to be so) you will also own THEY are more delighted with Conversation of Men of Sense, than with that of Coxcombs or Fools, since the contrary takes away their Character of Sense. But Men of Sense are scarce Sir, very scarce indeed, and those few that are, are too proud or think their Time ill bestow'd, in the Conversation of Ladies. They very often Think for Want of Trial, that what I argue against is true: the Vulgar Error has impos'd even upon them. This is our lamentable Case, and what must we do? Must we resolve never to Converse with the opposite Sex, or go under the Reproach of favouring Coxcombs? It may be said that we love Fops and Fools, because we play with them, and so we do with Parrots, Monkeys and Owls; and if we cannot procure objects of Admiration and Esteem, we divert our[s]elves with those of Redicule and Contempt: But, Oh, Sir, if you knew the exquisite Pleasure that we Women receive from the Conversation of a Man of Sense; what Raptures we conceive upon the least Imagination of being belov'd by him, you will confess with me, that

Coxcombs are merely indulged out of meer Necessity; and the ill success of Men of Sense, is owing to their want of Courage.

Further Reading

Brewer, John, *The Pleasures of the Imagination: English Culture in the Eighteenth Century.* New York: Farrar, Straus & Giroux, 1997.

Brewer, John and Roy Porter (eds.), *Consumption and the World of Goods.* New York: Routledge, 1993.

Chaplin, Joyce, *An Anxious Pursuit: Agricultural Innovation and Modernity in the Lower South, 1730–1815.* Chapel Hill: University of North Carolina Press, 1993.

Conroy, David, *In Public Houses: Drink and the Revolution of Authority in Colonial Massachusetts.* Chapel Hill: University of North Carolina Press, 1995.

Klein, Rachel N., *Unification of a Slave State: The Rise of the Planter Class in the South Carolina Backcountry, 1760–1808.* Chapel Hill: University of North Carolina Press, 1990.

McKendrick, Neil, John Brewer, and J. H. Plumb, *The Birth of a Consumer Society: The Commercialization of Eighteenth-century England.* Bloomington: Indiana University Press, 1982.

Shields, David, *Civil Tongues and Polite Letters in British America.* Chapel Hill: University of North Carolina Press, 1997.

Steele, Ian K., *The English Atlantic, 1675–1740: An Exploration of Communication and Community.* New York: Oxford University Press, 1986.

Warner, Michael, *The Letters of the Republic: Publication and the Public Sphere in Eighteenth-century America.* Cambridge, MA: Harvard University Press, 1990.

8

Backcountry Worlds

Introduction

Article

Colin Calloway, "New Worlds for All: Indian America by 1775," prologue to *The American Revolution in Indian Country: Crisis and Diversity in Native American Communities* (New York: Cambridge University Press, 1995), pp. 1–25.

Documents

1 Charles Woodmason, *The Carolina Backcountry on the Eve of the Revolution: The Journal and Other Writings of Charles Woodmason, Anglican Itinerant,* ed. Richard J. Hooker (Chapel Hill: University of North Carolina Press, 1953), pp. 5–26 (excerpts).

2 John Killbuck, *On Behalf of the Ohio Delawares, Munsies and Mohicans, to the Governors of Pennsylvania, Maryland, and Virginia, December 4, 1771,* in K. G. Davies (ed.), *Documents of the American Revolution* (Shannon and Dublin: Irish University Press, 1972–81), vol. 3, pp. 254–5. [Source given: Public Records Office, Kew, England, Colonial Office Records, Series 5: America and West Indies, 5/90, fo. 5.]

3 David Jones, *A Journal of Two Visits made to Some Nations of Indians on the West Side of the River Ohio, in the Years 1772 and 1773* (Burlington: Isaac Collins, 1774 [repr., New York: Arno Press, 1971]), pp. 51–90 (excerpts).

Further Reading

Introduction

By the end of the colonial period, as Colin Calloway reminds us, new worlds had been created for all the inhabitants of eastern North America. The backcountry, where points of contact between Indians and colonists were most numerous, was often the crucible in which they were forged. Here European traders became prominent figures in Indian communities, encouraging Indian men to pursue beaver pelts and deerskins with such alacrity that they hunted both animal populations almost to extinction in some areas. European settlers in the backcountry likewise learned from Indian economic practices. They relied upon corn as their most important food crop, they learned to hunt in the Indian manner, and they adopted Indian modes of dress. In the backcountry, too, violent contact between Indians and Europeans was most prevalent and most destructive. During periods of warfare, Indians and colonists alike found their homes periodically devastated by vicious surprise attacks that spared no one. Earlier historians, like Frederick Jackson Turner, saw the frontier as an encounter between advanced and primitive civilizations, in which the Indians were inexorably displaced by European-descended peoples. Calloway describes a more complex and ambiguous process, in which the backcountry served as a meeting ground for cultures that interacted with, and decisively affected, one another over the course of many years. Consider Calloway's essay in relation to the essay by Virginia DeJohn Anderson that opened this volume. What conditions and attitudes changed in the intervening century? How did the identities and interests of colonists and Indians shift as a result of those changes? What role did violence play in cross-cultural exchanges?

One observer of backcountry settlements in the late colonial period was Charles Woodmason, an Anglican minister who served in the Carolina backcountry from 1766 to 1768 (document 1). As a cultivated gentleman, Woodmason hoped to find like-minded parishioners during his travels. Instead, he found the colonists to be rude, immoral, and ignorant, while the communities he visited lacked the most basic institutional supports of civilized life. What does Woodmason say about the origins and background of backcountry settlers? What does he believe to be lacking in their communities? How do you think the backcountry settlers themselves might respond to Woodmason's criticisms?

Backcountry settlements like those Woodmason describes competed with Indian communities for territory. Between the Seven Years' War, which ended in 1763, and the Revolution, which began in 1775, trans-Appalachian settlement expanded dramatically and became a source of grave concern to many Indian leaders. John Killbuck, a Delaware headman living in the Ohio Valley, addressed this issue straightforwardly in a speech to representatives of

Pennsylvania, Maryland, and Virginia (document 2). He predicted that, unless the colonies could restrain their backcountry settlers more effectively, war would ensue – a claim that proved to be prophetic, since the American Revolution unleashed a violent competition for western lands that eventually opened the Ohio Valley to settlement by United States citizens. How does Killbuck view the English colonists? What is he asking the colonial governments to do?

The final document follows a Baptist minister named David Jones as he traveled down the Ohio River in 1772 and 1773 (document 3). Jones hoped to begin a mission among the Shawnee Indians living in and around the town of Chillicothe, which stood near the point where the Scioto River meets the Ohio. His journal offers a remarkable view of the far backcountry on the eve of the American Revolution. All of the Indian towns he visited had a substantial number of European residents, he paid cash for all kinds of goods and services, and the Indians he met were a diverse and fascinating lot. How did they react to Jones? What accounts for the wide variations in their treatment of him? Jones also encountered many colonists. What attracted them to Indian country, and what roles did they play in their communities? Why were so many colonial traders accepted in the Shawnee towns, while Jones was regarded with such suspicion?

New Worlds for All: Indian America by 1775

Colin Calloway

In the summer of 1775, as news of the opening conflicts in the American Revolution spread west, a young Englishman recently arrived from Derbyshire in search of good land traveled to the "Indian country" of the Ohio Valley. Nicholas Cresswell went with a party that consisted of two Englishmen, two Irishmen, a Welshman, two Dutchmen, two Virginians, two Marylanders, a Swede, an African, and a mulatto. On August 27, Cresswell visited a mission town of Moravian Delawares at Wal-hack-tap-poke or Schönbrunn, a settlement of sixty log houses covered with clapboards, arranged along neatly laid-out streets, and a meeting house with a bell and glass windows. The parson preached through an interpreter, the Indian congregation sang hymns in Delaware, and the service was conducted with "the greatest regularity, order, and decorum, I ever saw in any place of Worship in my life." Four days later, Cresswell was at the Delaware town of Coshocton, where he participated in an Indian dance. The beating of drums, the gourd rattles, the rattling of deer hooves on the knees and ankles of the male dancers, and the jingling of the women's bells struck Cresswell's ears as "the most unharmonious concert that human idea can possibly conceive," and the sight of an "Indian Conjuror" in a mask and bear skin was "frightful enough to scare the Devil."[1]

Indian America by 1775 was a landscape of cultural polyphony, or more accurately perhaps, cultural cacophony, a country of mixed and mixing peoples. Cresswell's brief sojourn among the Delawares exposed him to some of Indian country's diversity and to its mixture of change and continuity. He saw Indians who wore European clothes but retained traditional loincloths and nose rings. He noted that they had learned to curse from Europeans, observed that white traders cheated them blind whenever they could, lamented the destructive effects of alcohol, and learned that smallpox had "made terrible havoc." He traveled with Indian girls who served as guides during the day and bedfellows at night. He witnessed Indian orators in council, and became something of an ethnographic observer. He had "been taught to look upon these beings with contempt," but instead developed "a great regard for the Indians" and felt "a most sensible regret in parting from them." Three months in a changing Indian world changed a visiting Englishman.[2]

The next year, a New Jersey captain in Iroquois country was struck, as Cresswell had been among the Delawares, by the contrast between the quiet and orderly church services of the Oneidas, and the noise, drumming, and chanting of Seneca, Cayuga, and Onondaga ceremonies. Many Oneidas by this time were Presbyterians, although traditional beliefs and rituals survived intact. Some people were literate in both English and Iroquoian. Some Oneida children attended school, many Oneidas were skilled carpenters and farmers, and trade with Europeans was a major economic activity.[3]

Other Indian communities throughout the eastern woodlands displayed similar blends of old and new. Single-family log cabins had replaced, or coexisted with, traditional wigwams and communal longhouses. At the mission village of Lorette on the Saint Lawrence, for example, the Huron Indians "built all their houses after the French fashion." In New England, Indian families who still lived in wigwams likely had their share of European-manufactured household goods, and even European-style furniture.[4] The palisaded villages of the seventeenth century had often given way to more open and dispersed settlements in which kin groups settled near their fields and livestock rather than around the village council house. Indian towns sometimes comprised clusters of small hamlets; sometimes they were large multiethnic trading centers.

Indian America had always experienced changes, of course, but their tempo and impact increased dramatically after the arrival of European and African people, producing what James Merrell has aptly described as a "new world" for Native Americans. "It is strange what revolution has happened among them in less than two hundred years," remarked Hector De Crèvecoeur. At first contact, America was what John Winthrop called a land "full of Indians." By the end of the colonial period, the Indians of the eastern woodlands numbered perhaps 150,000 people in a world teeming with immigrants. Most who survived did so by adjusting in some measure to Europeans and their ways.[5]

Adjusting to Indian country and Indian people also created a new world for the newcomers. Like the rest of colonial America, Indian country was an arena in which a "kaleidoscope of human encounters" generated a web of cultural exchanges as Indians, Africans, and Europeans made what T. H. Breen has called "creative adaptations" to new places and new peoples.[6] Those Indians, Africans, and Europeans were not representatives of monolithic groups, but individuals of different ethnicity, geography, gender, and status. "Indians" were Abenakis, Delawares, Senecas, and Cherokees; "Africans" were Ibos, Ashantis, and Yorubas; "Europeans" were Swedes, Germans, Scots, Irish, and English – and Englishmen from London were very different than Englishmen from Cornwall or Yorkshire.

Mohawks shared their villages with individuals from other tribes, and their valley home with people of Dutch, German, Scottish, Irish, and English descent. Delawares lived alongside Swedes and Finns before Germans, Scotch-Irish and Welsh settled their lands. Franco-Indian communities and individuals persisted long after the collapse of New France. Catholic Indians often spoke French and bore French names, wearing crucifixes as well. Cosmopolitan French communities that embraced both Indians and blacks dotted the landscape from the Saint Lawrence to the mouth of the Mississippi. Non-Indians lived and trespassed in Indian country, with or without the Indians' consent. Scotch-Irish borderers competed with Cherokee and Shawnee hunters in the latter's traditional hunting territories; Cherokee and Shawnee villages were home to Scots and Irish Indian agents; adopted white captives took their place in the kinship network of Indian societies. Runaway slaves added an African strand to the fabric of south eastern Indian communities. People who intruded on Indian country often pursued their own independence from eastern authorities and rendered ineffective much of colonial and early national Indian policy.

Indian people likewise participated in shaping colonial and revolutionary American society. They served in colonial armies as soldiers and scouts, traveled to colonial capitals as ambassadors, attended colonial colleges as students, walked the streets of colonial towns as visitors, came to settlements as peddlers, and worked as slaves, servants, interpreters, guides, laborers, carpenters, whalers, and sailors. The proximity and interconnectedness of Indian and colonial communities throughout large areas of North America gave the backcountry warfare of the Revolution a face-to-face nature that heightened its bitterness.

The "changes in the land" described by William Cronon in colonial New England were replicated with variations on other frontiers in the wake of European contact. Ecosystems, like cultures, experience perpetual change, and Indian people had been clearing and cultivating fields for hundreds of years before Europeans arrived. But the colonists, and in the South their African slaves, introduced new plants, new techniques of forestry, new agricultural practices, and domesticated livestock, which generated far-reaching changes in the physical world Indian people inhabited. Indians in Maryland had complained to the General Assembly in the seventeenth century that the colonists' cows ate their corn. "Your hogs & Cattle injure Us," they said. "We Can fly no farther let us know where to live & how to be secured for the future from the Hogs & Cattle." Later generations of Indian people incorporated cows and pigs into their economies. Old World grazing animals not only contributed to deforestation; they also brought new grasses like Kentucky bluegrass. English colonists in the south found Indians cultivating peach trees, introduced by Spaniards and diffused northward along native trade routes, as if they were indigenous to the region. Charles Woodmason noted that the Carolina backcountry had begun to "wear a new face" by the 1760s as colonists carved farms and fields out of the forest.[7]

For thousands of Indian people, the new world that Europeans created was also a graveyard. European and African people brought with them lethal diseases common in the Old World but unknown in America. Smallpox, plague, measles, influenza, pneumonia, tuberculosis, diphtheria, yellow fever, and a host of new diseases took hold in Indian America and produced one of human history's greatest biological catastrophes. Whole communities perished. Others lost 50 percent, 75 percent, or 90 percent of their population. Recurrent epidemics of the same or different diseases prevented population recovery. European travelers in Indian country saw abandoned villages and met stunned survivors. The new world of death even produced changes in burial practices. Not all Native American populations dropped at the same rate in the wake of European invasion; in the lower Mississippi Valley, among the Creeks, and in some areas of the Great Lakes, Indian populations were actually on the rise in the eighteenth century, in part because they absorbed refugees from other areas. Nevertheless, European invaders confronted Indian people whose capacity to resist often had been seriously eroded before they laid eyes on the enemy. British Indian superintendent Sir William Johnson had the Mohawks inoculated against smallpox, but "contagious Distempers" continued to thin Iroquois numbers.[8] Most Europeans simply accepted the slaughter; but on at least one occasion the British actively promoted it. When two Delawares came into Fort Pitt for talks during Pontiac's War in 1763, "we gave them two Blankets and an Handkerchief out of the Smallpox Hospital," wrote William Trent in his journal. "I hope it will have the desired effect." It did.[9]

The new world that emerged in the wake of European contact was also one of unprecedented violence. Social disruption created random individual violence; warfare reached new levels of intensity. Indians fought each other for access to European guns, then turned the guns on their enemies with deadly effect. Increasingly dependent upon European allies for the goods and guns vital to survival in a dangerous new world, they found it difficult if not impossible to avoid becoming involved in the wars for empire waged in North America. George Morgan, American Indian agent at Fort Pitt, knew that Indian neutrality in the Revolution was unlikely: "They have long been taught by contending Nations to be bought & sold."[10] Intertribal warfare escalated and, again, Europeans sometimes worked to curtail it, sometimes actively encouraged it as part of a "divide and conquer" strategy.[11]

Endemic warfare disrupted normal patterns of life. Communities that diverted their manpower into war felt the repercussions in lost sons and husbands, in reduced economic productivity and increased dependence on allies, in disrupted ceremonial calendars and neglected rituals, and in diplomatic chaos and political upheaval. War became normal, and the warrior culture that was ingrained in many societies as they battled their Indian and European enemies created a stereotype of Indians as warlike, which in European eyes justified treating them as "savages." In some societies, the influence of women declined as Europeans dealt exclusively with males as the hunters and warriors; in others, women's traditional roles escaped relatively undisturbed and provided a much-needed measure of stability.

In a world of escalating violence, war chiefs rose in status as civil chiefs lost influence. Richard White has painstakingly reconstructed the attempts of French and Algonkian people living in the Great Lakes region in the late seventeenth century to create a "middle ground" of common understanding and accommodation in a world of upheaval. Chiefs struggled to maintain peace, knowing that the alternative to coexistence and mutual dependency was a bloodbath. First the French, then the British, learned that success in this middle-ground world required mediation, moderation, and generosity, not force and coercion. But the Franco-Indian alliance unraveled as the Ohio Valley, once a haven between empires, became an imperial battleground, and chiefs found it increasingly difficult to control their warriors.[12]

Warriors now made commitments that undermined the consensus politics that traditionally guarded against rash decisions. Seneca warriors who traveled to see Sir William Johnson in the spring of 1762 explained that their sachems had not made the trip because the roads were very bad, but informed the superintendent, "We, are in fact the People of Consequence for Managing Affairs, our Sachims being generally a parcell of Old People who say Much, but who Mean or Act very little, So that we have both the power & Ability to settle Matters."[13] New leaders emerged as villages and bands coalesced in the reshuffling of population that European contact generated. Opportunists sometimes generated political fragmentation of their own: "We have been unhappy in loosing our old Chiefs who Conducted our affairs," said Pitchibaon, a Potawatomi chief in 1773; "we who are appointed in their place are no more listened to, every one sets up for Chief and make Towns and Villages apart."[14]

Chiefs who lacked traditional sanction often assumed influential roles as intermediaries and brokers with European colonists; older village chiefs found that these same roles offered new sources of authority. As traditional bases of power weakened, European agents and traders cultivated client chiefs, giving them medals and gifts to buy and bolster their support. Chiefs always had acted as redistribution agents, maintaining influence not by accumulating wealth but by giving it away, thereby earning respect and creating reciprocal obligations. The gifts client chiefs gave now came from European backers and represented their sole source of influence; without allies to supply them they often fell from power. By the eve of the Revolution, British Indian superintendent John Stuart was virtually appointing chiefs among the Choctaws, where traditional patterns and functions of leadership had collapsed amid a European scramble for allies within the nation. He handed out medals to Choctaw and Chickasaw chiefs at the Mobile congress in 1765; at the same congress in 1772 he convened the Choctaws to fill vacancies in the ranks of Britain's client chiefs created by war and old age:

> The competition and anxiety of the candidates for medals and commissions was as great as can be imagined and equalled the struggles of the most aspiring and ambitious for honours and preferment in great states. I took every step to be informed of characters and filled the vacancies with the most worthy and likely to answer the purposes of maintaining order and the attachment of this nation to the British interest.

Such interference further undermined traditional leadership structures: two years later Stuart was complaining that chiefs lacked the influence to control their young men.[15] The inroads of alcohol also deafened young men to the wisdom of their elders, and sachems lamented their inability to control their warriors in this new world of chaos and opportunity. Challenges to traditional authority and declining political deference were not unique to colonial white society in the years before the Revolution.

The pressures unleashed by European invasion threw the jigsaw map of Indian America into the air, and Indian people tried to rearrange the falling pieces into some kind of coherent world. Ancient communities collapsed; new, multiethnic communities grew up out of the ruins of shattered societies. New villages grew up around French missions on the banks of the Saint Lawrence as Abenakis and other people from New England pulled back from the northward-pushing English frontier. Iroquois towns seemed to absorb all comers. Shawnees, Delawares, and Senecas who turned their backs on colonial society and resettled the upper Ohio Valley early in the eighteenth century acquired new identities as little-known "Ohio Indians." In the Great Lakes region, the Ohio and Susquehanna valleys, and the South Carolina Piedmont, remnant groups, their old identities often all but lost to history, amalgamated. Europeans identified the new polyglot societies as "tribes." By the time William Bartram traveled through the South on the eve of the Revolution, the loose Creek Confederacy consisted of "many tribes, or remnants of conquered nations, united."[16] Indian country was a world of villages, bands, and clans, but European pressures and the need to deal with distant capitals demanded increasingly unified responses at a time when traditional structures often were in flux.

The localism of Indian politics did not confine Indian people to local activity. On the contrary, Indian communities throughout the eastern woodlands became more closely interconnected. By the middle of the eighteenth century, eastern Indian horizons had widened considerably from the world of small villages and narrow loyalties that had occupied their attention a century before. Competition between European powers for Indian allegiance, and between Indian nations for European trade, dominated Indian politics and foreign policies throughout most of the eighteenth century. Indian nations aligned and realigned themselves with European allies, played rival nations against each other to ensure their neutrality and survival while retaining a flow of trade goods, and divided into factions. "To preserve the Ballance between us & the French is the great ruling Principle of the Modern Indian Politics," wrote Peter Wraxall.[17] Indian warriors and diplomats, following an extensive network of trails and water courses, traveled, talked, and fought on a semicontinental scale. Iroquois diplomacy ranged from the Great Lakes to Quebec; Cherokee towns hosted ambassadors from other nations. Henry Hamilton, the British governor of Detroit early in the Revolution, sketched an

Indian whose name he forgot but whom he remembered as "one of those characters, always to be found among the Indians – He travels from Village to Village, being provided with news."[18] A multitribal conference that assembled on the Scioto plains in southern Ohio in 1770 to discuss united defense of Indian lands brought together "the Chiefs of the most powerfull Nations on the continent."[19] The cross-tribal nature of Indian communities and Indian actions would become even more apparent during the Revolution.

Most Indian communities were economically dependent upon Europeans to some degree by 1775. The rate and extent of dependency varied, but Cherokees in the mountains of the interior were no more willing or able to do without European trade goods than were coastal groups surrounded by European settlers. A Cherokee headman named Skiagunsta told the governor of South Carolina in 1753 that his people could not survive without the English: "The Cloaths we wear, we cannot make ourselves, they are made to us. We use their Ammunition with which we kill Dear [sic]. We cannot make our Guns, they are made to us. Every necessary Thing in Life we must have from the white People."[20] Skiagunsta probably exaggerated for his audience – Indian peoples in New England, the Ohio Valley, and the Southeast had learned to overcome total dependence on Europeans by repairing and maintaining their own firearms and metal tools – but the language of abject poverty and dependence was common in Indian speeches up through the Revolution. Captain Ouma of the Choctaws said his people were as "helpless as the Beasts in the woods," without British goods; Handsome Fellow of the Oakfuskie Creeks acknowledged in 1777 that "we have been used so long to wrap up our Children as soon as they are born in Goods procured of the white People that we cannot do without it."[21] Dependency rendered Indian people vulnerable to abuse: Choctaws at the Mobile congress in the winter of 1771–2 complained graphically that traders shortchanged them so often that the flaps of cloth provided as loin cloths "dont cover our secret parts, and we are in danger of being deprived of our manhood by every hungry dog that approaches."[22]

As Indian peoples became tied into the trade networks of western Europe, they also became participants in a consumer revolution that brought the products of industrializing Europe to frontier America. A "pan-Indian trade culture" emerged in many areas of the country.[23] When William Tapp or Taptico, last werowance of the Wicocomoco Indians of Chesapeake Bay, died, he left behind English clothing, a house furnished with tables, chairs, and chests, four feather beds, and "a parcell of Olde Books."[24] By the time of the Revolution, according to one observer, the Fort Hunter Mohawks lived "much better than most of the Mohawk River farmers." Oneida Indians cooked in metal kettles and frying pans, ate with spoons from pewter plates at meals illuminated by candlesticks, sipped out of teacups filled from teapots, served beverages from punch bowls, combed their hair with ivory combs while looking in glass mirrors, wore white flannel breeches, used silk handkerchiefs, and lived in "a very large framed house [with a] chimney at each end [and] painted windows."[25] Overhill Cherokees used combs, mirrors, scissors, pewter spoons, and a variety of metal tools and jewelry. White Eyes of the Delawares and Oconostota of the Cherokees both wore eyeglasses. European trade goods were so pervasive in eastern Indian communities before the Revolution that archaeological deposits often reveal little distinction between Indian and non-Indian sites. Native Americans, like their backcountry colonial neighbors, had been drawn into a larger Atlantic economy that shaped their tastes, their lives, and ultimately their landscape. For many Indian peoples, the most pressing question posed by the outbreak of the Revolution was not who should govern in America but who would supply the trade goods on which they had come to depend. For many of their colonial neighbors, the material wealth to be found in Indian communities by 1775 provided an economic incentive for going on campaigns into Indian country.

The fur and deerskin trades not only introduced new commodities to Indian America; they also introduced alien systems of value and meaning. New economic incentives undermined old spiritual relationships between hunters and their prey. Indian hunters and European traders combined to deplete deer and beaver populations; native and European economies intersected. In areas and eras of shrinking animal populations, consumption outstripped production, and Indians who had become commercial hunters often became debtor-hunters. Traders and their alcohol brought death and disruption to Indian communities, as village chiefs and colonial officials realized. From Maine to the Mississippi and throughout the century, Indian spokesmen complained about abuses by traders and the alcohol they peddled in Indian society. Christian Penobscots said "it hurts our souls." "You may find graves upon graves along the Lake," an Iroquois leader lamented to Albany officials in 1730, "all which misfortunes are occasioned by Selling Rum to our Brethren." In 1738 the Shawnees staved in all the kegs of rum in their villages and sent word to all French, British, and Indian traders that they would destroy any rum they brought. A chief from the Hudson River apologized to the Mohawks in 1756 for his inexperience in council proceedings, explaining "the Rum we get from the English hath drowned the Memory of all antient Customs & the Method of treating on public affairs." A Choctaw chief said rum "pours upon our nation Like a great Sea from Mobille and from all the Plantations and Settlements round about"; another admitted that "When the Clattering of the Packhorse Bells are heard at a Distance our Town is Immediately deserted young and old run out to meet them Joyfully crying Rum Rum; they get Drunk, Distraction Mischief Confusion and Disorder are the Consequences and this the Ruin of our Nation." Another Choctaw said "he had lost above a thousand people by excessive drinking in little more than 18 months." A British agent in the Choctaw towns in 1777 saw "nothing but Rum Drinking and Women Crying over the Dead Bodies of their relations who have died by Rum." By the time of the Revolution, according to Richard White, the Choctaws, "quite simply, hunted for liquor," and chiefs were powerless to halt the social chaos that resulted. In Cherokee society, too, drunkenness increased the aggressiveness of warriors and served as a way of challenging traditional leaders who could not keep peace in the villages.[26] Colonial officials lamented alcohol's effects but recognized its usefulness in destabilizing Indian communities.

The forces of change challenged people's spiritual lives. Missionaries from different countries and denominations entered Indian country to compete for a harvest of Indian souls. They promoted social revolution and produced factions in Indian communities. The divisions became further complicated after the Great Awakening in the colonies in the 1730s and 1740s severed ties with a single established church. In the 1760s, a Seneca warrior named Onoquadeahla told Presbyterian missionary Samuel Kirkland in no uncertain terms that his presence "would be distructive to the nation, & finally over throw all the traditions & usages of their Forefathers & that there would not be a warior remaining in their nation in the course of a few years." Another Seneca named Isaac, "painted black and red on each side of his face," took a shot at Kirkland.[27] Indian peoples confronted Christian invaders with movements of spiritual revitalization and cultural resistance such as those led by Neolin, the Delaware Prophet, and the Munsee Wingenund in the 1760s. Others embraced Christian messages in Indian ways. Many of the Indians who fought in the Revolution were Christians.

Everywhere, though, there was continuity in the midst of change. Indians who donned European clothes often retained traditional hairstyles, slit ears, and facial tattoos. New trade goods were fashioned into traditional motifs or endowed with traditional meanings. Traditional lithic and ceramic technologies declined, but basket making and wood carving survived and even were stimulated by European demand. Some Indians continued to prefer birch-bark containers to metal pots for maple sugaring. Moccasins and canoes were unmatched by European substitutes for travel along forest paths and lakes. People still found guidance in dreams and believed in the efficacy of spirits, ceremonies and omens, though missionaries urged them to look to the Bible for direction. Ancient rituals continued to renew the world and maintain harmony; participation in those rituals helped define community identity in a world where so much else was in flux. Old ways made strong crutches as people ventured down new paths.

The forces of contact, cultural exchange, transformation, and dependency operated along two-way streets. As Indian people traded for European cloth, guns, and alcohol, Europeans adopted Indian-style clothing, canoes, and foods. As Indian people adopted domesticated livestock, European colonists adopted Native American corn culture and hunting practices. British commander-in-chief, General Thomas Gage, realized on the eve of the Revolution that the intrusions of backcountry colonists onto Indian lands was due, in large measure, to the fact that they lived Indian-style, by hunting.[28] Indian and colonial economies affected each other and became interdependent. European traders needed Indian hunters and customers; European and colonial armies needed Indian scouts and allies, and, in time, adopted Indian methods of waging war; European missionaries needed Indian neophytes; colonial whaling industries employed local native laborers, settlers relied on Indian neighbors for their knowledge of the use of wild plants, and native herbal cures sometimes proved effective where European medicine failed; colonial schools even needed Indian students to help secure funding. In some areas of New England, Indians not only worked in the colonial economy but also lived with white families; in some areas of the South they worked alongside Africans as plantation slave laborers.

As old Turnerian notions of the frontier as a line of advancing settlement diminish, we can better understand the persistence and presence of Indian people in colonial cities, and better appreciate the tapestry of colonial life. Not only did Indian diplomats regularly visit colonial capitals from Quebec to New Orleans, but Indians living in the neighborhood of emerging towns actively participated in the urban economy. They sold food, plants, baskets, and firewood in market squares, and earned wages as day laborers, servants, and dockworkers. As traditional economies were disrupted and the fur and deerskin trades declined, many Indian people resorted to "a cycle of itinerant economic activities." Some actually moved closer to colonial towns, relying on the urban economy in hard times of readjustment. They learned new skills as bricklayers, coopers, wheelwrights, blacksmiths, and seamstresses, and they adopted traditional skills to meet new demands, as wood carvers, potters, and basket makers.[29]

Throughout Indian country, Europeans lived in and around Indian communities. Traders who went into Indian country to do business often found that they were most successful if they married into the kinship networks of Indian societies. Like other colonists who lived with Indians, many found themselves living as Indians. Rev. David Jones found 20 whites living at the Shawnee town of Chillicothe in the winter of 1772–3; as many as 300 English and Scots were living among the Creeks by the beginning of the Revolution. Scotsman Alexander Cameron married a Cherokee woman and lived with the Overhill Cherokees so long that he "had almost become one of themselves" by the time of the Revolution.[30]

Many other captives, traders, Indian agents, and even occasional missionaries underwent similar "conversion" to Indian ways. Like many of his Jesuit colleagues, Sebastian Rasles, missionary to the Abenakis at Norridgewock in Maine in the early eighteenth century, spent most of his adult life in Indian country. He spoke the Abenakis' language and shared their homes and hopes, food and fears, even as he sought to convert them. "As for what concerns me personally," Rasles told his brother, "I assure you that I see, that I hear, that I speak, only as a savage."[31]

"White Indians" often aroused fear and contempt in colonial society, but found a place in Indian country and exercised considerable influence as culture brokers. James Dean, who served as an American interpreter during the Revolution, spent his boyhood among the Oneidas and learned to speak their language without a trace of an accent. Simon Girty, captured as a boy by Senecas in 1755, made his home in Indian country and built a career as culture broker and interpreter that gave him far-reaching influence in Indian country during and after the Revolution.

Intermarriage between Indians and Europeans, and between Indians and Africans, produced "new peoples" of mixed ancestry. Most were incorporated into Indian communities, but many suffered psychological stress as racial conflicts increased. Some lived with racism in colonial communities; some developed separate communities and formed an ethnic identity of their own. Interaction between different peoples produced new languages in these new worlds. Refugee communities sometimes produced a babel of different dialects. Trade jargons emerged. Indians adopted Spanish, English, Gaelic, Dutch, French, and African words; Europeans incorporated Algonkian, Iroquoian, and Muskhogean terms into their vocabulary. In the 1750s, at Stockbridge, Massachusetts, where an Indian blew a conch shell every Sabbath to call the faithful to worship, the missionary's son heard so much more Mahican than English spoken that he frequently found himself thinking in the Indians' language. Traveling in New York in 1776, Joseph Bloomfield, then a captain in the Third New Jersey Regiment and later governor of New Jersey, heard spoken on a daily basis English, High Dutch, Low Dutch, French, Mohawk, Oneida, Seneca, Cayuga, Onondaga, and Tuscarora.

Even where whites did not live with Indians, the influence of Indian country and the evidence of cultural exchange was strong. In the Delaware Valley, Finns and Swedes lived closely with Indian neighbors, acquiring from them corn (and the knowledge of how to plant, cultivate, and prepare it), gourds, pumpkins, squash, turkeys, furs and skins, sassafras tea, bayberry candles, and maple syrup. "They adopted wholesale the Delawares' knowledge of edible and medicinal wild plants," and spoke a Delaware-derived pidgin. Intermarriage was common and Indian children were reported living in Swedish homes on the Schuylkill before the end of the seventeenth century. Long before Scotch-Irish and Welsh people came to dominate the midland backwoods population, Finns and Swedes set the pattern of trade, tolerance, and mutual acculturation "that was essential to the piecing together of a successful woodland pioneer culture." Later arrivals noted that the Swedes and their Indian neighbors were "like one people."[32] Things were not too different elsewhere. Ranger Robert Rogers recalled that growing up in a frontier town in New Hampshire in the early part of the century, he "could hardly avoid" gaining some knowledge of Indian ways and languages.[33]

Colonists from Europe, where hunting was a gentleman's sport, learned from Indians how to hunt for a living. Colonial hunters who operated in Indian country pulled on Indian leggings, breechclouts, and moccasins, dressed their long hair with bear grease, and sometimes donned war paint. Anglican preacher Charles Woodmason denounced settlers on the Carolina backcountry as being "hardly one degree removed" from their Indian neighbors. General Thomas Gage reckoned backcountry settlers on the Ohio River "differ little from the Indians in their manner of life." Missionary David McClure said that backcountry Virginians were "generally white Savages, and subsist by hunting, and live like the Indians." Whereas Indians in Canada took to wearing jackets and waistcoats like their French neighbors, Frenchmen traveling in Indian country "generally dressed like the natives," exchanging their trousers for leggings and loincloths. Young men in backcountry Virginia were proud of their "Indian-like dress," and even wore leggings and breechclouts to church, which apparently sparked the interest of young women in the congregation. When George Rogers Clark and his Virginians arrived at Kaskaskia in 1778, they were dressed Indian style, "in hunting shirt and breech cloth." Their appearance surprised the Spanish governor of Saint Louis but was not unusual for men accustomed to life in Indian country.[34] In the Mohawk Valley in the 1760s, Peter Warren Johnson met Europeans who tattooed their faces and chests like their Indian neighbors, "which is done by pricking the Skin with Pins, till the Blood comes, & then applying Gunpowder to it, which will remain for ever." French fur traders in Canada likewise tattooed their bodies.[35] Cultural boundaries between Indians and Europeans, and between Indians and Africans (as between Indians and other Indians), were often fuzzy and porous.

The mixing of peoples and cultures did not erase differences or eradicate conflict. Surveying the inventory of things colonists borrowed from Indians, James Axtell reminds us that "Their goal was not to become Indian, nor did their selective and piecemeal adaptations of native techniques and technology make them so."[36] The same can be said of Indians who borrowed from European culture: they did not intend to, nor did they, become Europeans. In fact, conflict between Indian and European cultures was increasing steadily by the eve of the Revolution, as growing pressure on Indian lands eroded previous patterns of coexistence.

As the eighteenth century wore on, Indian people and Indian cultures were being engulfed by an ocean of European and African people. The powerful Six Nations, renowned warriors and past masters of the art of playing European rivals against each other, had long been "sinking into irrelevance in a region more and more dominated by Euro-Americans."[37] As Indian numbers dwindled, immigration and natural increase sent America's non-Indian population skyward. The population of British North America doubled every twenty-five years and increased 400 percent between 1700 and 1750. The population of North Carolina shot from 45,000 in 1750 to 275,000 in 1775. Five thousand Scots migrated to North Carolina alone in the decade before the Revolution. By 1775 as many as fifty thousand whites lived west of the Appalachians.

The newcomers included Pennsylvania Germans and American-born Virginians, but increasingly in the eighteenth century the Europeans-turning-Americans on the frontier came from the Celtic fringes of the British Isles, propelled by failed rebellion, a decaying clan system, agrarian transformation and sheep enclosures, high rents, poverty, and famine. After their kinsmen and their dreams of a Jacobite restoration died in the sleet at Culloden, many Highland Scots came to America as soldiers, the only profession that permitted them to wear a tartan and gave steady employment in bleak times. Others joined victims of wrenching economic changes from the Lowlands, the north England borders, Ireland, and Wales, migrating to America in such numbers that authorities in Britain worried the exodus would empty Scotland of its people. Accustomed to lives of hardship and cultures of violence, Scotch-Irish and North Country immigrants brought their clan rivalries, blood feuds, and Old Testament sense of justice to the American frontier, where, said Quaker James Logan, they made "hard neighbors to the Indians." Colonial authorities steered Scotch-Irish immigrants toward the frontier, knowing they would provide effective defense against Indian attacks. Alternatively, they made excellent shock troops for the invasion of Indian lands.[38]

Land, of course, was the main source of contention between Indian people and their new neighbors. In the seventeenth century, although some colonial governments passed laws to protect Indian lands, others used deeds to legitimize the acquisition of Indian lands by trickery, coercion, and corruption – what Francis Jennings refers to as "the deed game." Many Indians learned the terms and implications of selling land to Europeans, struck the best deals they could in the circumstances, and endeavored to slow the rate of land loss, but they could not halt the pressure.[39] The problem increased in intensity throughout the eighteenth century. Long before the Revolution, Indians found themselves sucked into the practice of selling off lands to satisfy debts accumulated in trade with their colonial neighbors. Creek Indians called their Georgian neighbors "Ecunnaunuxulgee" – "people greedily grasping after the lands of the red people."[40]

The British victory in the Seven Years' War opened Indian country to a flood of settlement that the Royal Proclamation of 1763 and other official measures barely even checked. In the wake of their victory, British ministers in Whitehall tried to implement a program that would provide security for their colonies by maintaining garrisons in the West, establishing an Indian reserve, and regulating an equitable trade with the Indians. Their efforts to finance the program by such measures as the Stamp Act contributed to the challenge to British imperial authority that culminated in the Revolution.

The irony of British policy in the years between the Seven Years' War and the Revolution was that "although it aspired to control Indians, it foundered on the British government's inability to control its subjects." The victorious British at first rode roughshod over the traditions of the middle ground, but Pontiac's War in 1763 taught them a bitter lesson, and they worked to reconstruct the social and diplomatic arrangements they had thought they could do without. Even as they did so, however, the old middle ground was rapidly giving way to a world of violence as Anglo-American settlers swarmed into Indian country.[41]

A younger generation of colonists in the midst of an economic recession found that there were too many sons and not enough land in their home communities. The abundance of frontier land, combined with the scarcity of land at home, undermined fathers' traditional authority over their sons, and over daughters for whom they could no longer ensure a place in the world. British policymakers were no more able to control frustrated and ambitious young settlers than were those settlers' own fathers. In 1772, the acting governor of Georgia, James Habersham, took measures to remove from Indian lands "a parcel of stragling north-ward People" who threatened to frustrate the orderly transfer of those lands to the crown.[42] However, few colonists were willing to acquiesce in royal attempts to keep them from western lands. Scotch-Irish settlers who had emigrated to escape English domination paid little heed to an English proclamation in their new world. Veterans of the "French and Indian wars" were not about to be deprived of the fruits of their hard-won victory. British policies that tried to regulate the frontier often only aggravated the tensions, alienating backcountry settlers and ensuring that many of them would throw in their lot with the rebels once the Revolution began. Although settlers could ignore the proclamation, land speculators could not, and it helped push into rebellion Virginia gentry with western lands to sell.

New boundaries negotiated in the North at the Treaty of Fort Stanwix in 1768, and in the South at Augusta and Hard Labor in 1768 and 1770, did little or nothing to stem the tide. The Treaty of Fort Stanwix in particular infuriated Shawnees and others who felt the Six Nations had sold their lands out from under them: In the fall of 1770, Indian trader, agent, and land speculator George Croghan reported, "Last year, I am sure, there were between four and five thousand [new settlers] and all this spring and summer the roads have been lined with wagons moving to the Ohio."[43] Settlers and land speculators opened up new frontiers everywhere. Daniel Boone founded Boonesborough in April 1775, "opened a land office, disposed of over half a million acres in a few weeks, founded three more settlements, and convened a legislature before the year was out."[44] By the eve of the Revolution, Kentucky constituted a wedge of colonial settlement thrust into the heart of Indian America. The new settlements not only threatened Indian hunting territories but divided northern and southern tribes, disrupting old networks of trade and communication. Most of the settlers coming to Kentucky came from North Carolina, which was itself being settled from Pennsylvania, West Virginia, and Scotland.

Such constant movement, settlement, and resettlement alarmed Indian people struggling to hold onto their lands. Anglo-American history for generations has portrayed pioneers as settlers, Indians as nomads. But Indian people in the eastern woodlands, who lived in settled communities reliant upon a mixed subsistence economy that almost always included agriculture, must surely have regarded Scotch-Irish and Anglo-American invaders as the true nomads of colonial America. Others did: after the Revolution, Spanish officials regarded American backwoodsmen on Florida's northern frontier as "nomadic like Arabs and . . . distinguished from savages only in their color, language, and the superiority of their depraved cunning and untrustworthiness."[45]

By the eve of the Revolution, Indian people from Quebec and Maine to Georgia and the Floridas were complaining in vain to colonial authorities about trespasses on their land, and about schemes to get it. Indians from the seven New England "praying towns" were "reduced to such small pittances of land, that they could no longer remain there," and moved to New York to take up land granted to them by the Oneidas in 1774.[46] Delawares, Munsees, and Mahicans warned the governors of Pennsylvania, Maryland, and Virginia in December 1771 that the flood of settlers across the mountains was likely to produce disaster: "Unless you can fall upon some method of governing your people who live between the Great Mountains and the Ohio River and who are now very numerous, it will be out of the Indians power to govern their young men, for we assure you that the black clouds begin to gather fast in this country."[47]

"I know of nothing so likely to interrupt and disturb our tranquility with the Indians," reported John Stuart, "as the incessant attempts to defraud them of their land by clandestine purchase." The British authorities recognized the justice of the Indians' complaints and identified the roots of the problem, but could do little about it.[48] Frontier people came to believe that the British government and its agents favored Indians and the Indian trade over settlers; John Stuart's efforts to extend imperial control into the Indian country generated rumors that he was planning to use Indians against the colonists. By 1775 the southern backcountry was ready to explode. When the Revolution broke out, American patriots called it a war for liberty. Most Indian people knew, and the British reminded those who didn't, that it was also a continuation of the struggle about Indian land and who was to get it. Violence was always close to the surface in Indian–white relations. Indians and whites alike had long struggled to avert it, but by the eve of the Revolution, murder and revenge, not mediation and accommodation, typified relations. As Richard White sees it, the common world "yielded to a frontier over which people crossed only to shed blood."[49] Young warriors defied the authority of older chiefs by killing frontiersmen, who themselves ignored distant governments, killing Indians and occupying their lands.

In 1774, American frontiersmen lured a party of Mingo Indians into their camp, got them drunk, and then killed and scalped them, mutilating the pregnant sister of a Mingo chief known as Logan. The act was the most brutal in a spate of killings along the Ohio that spring. Despite Delaware efforts to avert it, and amid considerable diplomatic scrambling in Indian country, open war exploded between Virginia and the Mingoes and Shawnees. Lord Dunmore's War was both the latest in a series of escalating frontier conflicts and a precursor of the one to come.

Anglo-Americans were not the only people experiencing times to try men's souls by 1775. In Indian country, too, people wrestled with challenges to traditional sources of authority, felt the repercussions of religious ferment, struggled to deal with demographic changes, felt squeezed by economic strangleholds, resented growing threats to their liberty, and worried about the kind of world their children would inherit. Indian people had had plenty of experience of colonialism, and they had already fought their share of anticolonial wars. Choosing the winning side in the new war that broke out in 1775 was crucial but, as in past wars, victory was hardly a realistic goal. The best Indian people could hope for was damage control, but they could not know the extent of the damage the Revolution would cause to the worlds they and their colonial neighbors had created.

Most of North America was still Indian country in 1775. Indian people still dominated most of the continent and walked the streets of colonial towns. Much of colonial life involved Indians; much of colonial war, diplomacy, and commerce revolved around them. Writing to fellow revolutionary John Adams in 1812, Thomas Jefferson recalled that in Williamsburg before the Revolution, Indians "were in the habit of coming often, and in great numbers to the seat of our government, where I was much with them."[50] The Revolution that erupted in 1775 was bound to affect and involve Indians; but it also ushered in a new era and a new society from which they were to be increasingly excluded. The interethnic societies and cultural mixings that characterized much of Indian America by 1775 had been a long time in the making. The Revolution did not terminate them overnight, but did produce a new government and society increasingly committed to the notion that Indian country east of the Mississippi should cease to exist.

At the beginning of May 1775, before news of Lexington and Concord reached him, Major Arent Schuyler De Peyster, commanding officer at the remote British outpost at Michilimackinac, sat down to pen a report to General Thomas Gage. It had been an unusually mild winter on the Great Lakes, he wrote. "To use the Indian Phrase, the World seems to have had a great shove to the Southward."[51] There would be no more mild winters for De Peyster or his Indian neighbors for many years. In fact, their world never would be quite the same again.

Notes

1   *The Journal of Nicholas Cresswell, 1774–1777* (New York: Dial, 1924), 87, 106, 109.
2   *Journal of Nicholas Cresswell*, 49–50, 105–6, 108, 113, 118–19, 120–2.

3 Mark E. Lender and James Kirby Martin, eds., *Citizen Soldier: The Revolutionary War Journal of Joseph Bloomfield* (Newark: New Jersey Historical Society, 1992), 90–1.

4 Adolph B. Benson, ed., *Peter Kalm's Travels in North America*, 2 vols. (New York: Wilson-Erickson, 1937), 2: 462.

5 James H. Merrell, *The Indians' New World: Catawbas and Their Neighbors from European Contact through the Era of Removal* (Chapel Hill: University of North Carolina Press, 1989); J. Hector St. John De Crèvecoeur, *Letters from an American Farmer* (New York: Dutton, 1957), 102–3.

6 T. H. Breen, "Creative Adaptations: Peoples and Cultures," in Jack P. Greene and J. R. Pole, eds., *Colonial British America: Essays in the New History of the Early Modern Era* (Baltimore: Johns Hopkins University Press, 1984), 195–232.

7 William Cronon, *Changes in the Land: Indians, Colonists, and the Ecology of New England* (New York: Hill and Wang, 1983); Timothy Silver, *A New Face on the Countryside: Indians, Colonists, and Slaves in South Atlantic Forests, 1500–1800* (Cambridge, England: Cambridge University Press, 1990); *Archives of Maryland* 2 (1884), 15.

8 Milton W. Hamilton, ed., "Guy Johnson's Opinions on the American Indian," *Pennsylvania Magazine of History and Biography* 77 (1953), 326.

9 "Journal of William Trent," in John W. Harpster, ed., *Pen Pictures of Early Western Pennsylvania* (University of Pittsburgh Press, 1938), 103–4.

10 Carnegie Library, Pittsburgh, George Morgan Letterbook, 2: 2.

11 E.g., Thomas Gage to John Stuart, January 27, 1764, Clements Library, Gage Papers.

12 Richard White, *The Middle Ground: Indians, Empires, and Republics in the Great Lakes Region, 1650–1815* (Cambridge: Cambridge University Press, 1991).

13 James Sullivan et al., eds., *The Papers of Sir William Johnson*, 15 vols. (Albany: SUNY Press, 1921–65), 3: 698.

14 *Johnson Papers*, 8: 888.

15 Dunbar Rowland, ed., *Mississippi Provincial Archives, 1763–1766: English Dominion*, vol. I (Nashville: Brandon Printing Co., 1911): 229, 254; K. G. Davies, ed., *Documents of the American Revolution, 1770–1783* (Colonial Office Series), 21 vols. (Shannon: Irish University Press, 1972–82), 5: 37; 7: 102; 8: 110 (hereafter *DAR*); "Papers Relating to Congress with Choctaw and Chickasaw Indians," *Publications of the Mississippi Historical Society* 5 (1925), 158.

16 William Bartram, "Observations on the Creek and Cherokee Indians, 1789," *Transactions of the American Ethnological Society* 3, pt. I (1853), 12.

17 C. H. McIlwain, ed., *Peter Wraxall's Abridgment of the New York Indian Records* (Cambridge, MA: Harvard University Press, 1915), 219.

18 Henry Hamilton, "Drawings of North American Scenes and North American Indians, 1769–1778," Harvard University, Houghton Library, pf. MS Eng. 509.2.

19 E. B. O'Callaghan and Berthold Fernow, eds., *Documents Relative to the Colonial History of the State of New York*, 15 vols. (Albany: Weed, Parsons, 1853–87), 8: 281 (hereafter *NYCD*).

20 William L. McDowell, Jr., ed., *Colonial Records of South Carolina: Documents relating to Indian Affairs, Vol. I (1750–1754)* (Columbia: South Carolina Archives Department, 1958), 453.

21 "Papers Relating to Congress with Choctaw and Chickasaw Indians," 150; Talk from the Handsome Fellow of the Oakfuskeys, June 18, 1777, North Carolina State Archives, Raleigh: Treasurer's and Comptroller's Records, *Indian Affairs and Lands* (box I), Cherokee Nation, 1739–91.

22 "Proceedings of a Congress held by John Stuart with the Chickasaw and Choctaw Nation," December 31, 1771, enclosed in Stuart to Gage, May 23, 1772, Clements Library, Gage Papers, vol. 137, item 14: 5; "Papers Relating to Congress with Choctaw and Chickasaw Indians," 148.

23 George Irving Quimby, *Indian Culture and European Trade Goods: Archaeology of the Historic Period in the Western Great Lakes Region* (Madison: University of Wisconsin Press, 1966).

24 Stephen R. Potter, *Commoners, Tribute, and Chiefs: The Development of Algonquian Culture in the Potomac Valley* (Charlottesville: University Press of Virginia, 1993), 224–5.

25 William Campbell, ed., *Annals of Tryon County* (New York: Dodd, 1924), 130. On the material culture of the Oneidas see Massachusetts Historical Society, Boston: Timothy Pickering Papers, reel 62: 157–74.

26 Mass. Archives 29: 535; Charles Hanna, *The Wilderness Trail*, 2 vols. (New York: Putnam, 1911), 1: 309; 2: 307; Penobscots, see Colin G. Calloway, ed., *Dawnland Encounters: Indians and Europeans in Northern New England* (Hanover, NH: University Press of New England, 1991), 202; for the Iroquois, see Daniel K. Richter, *The Ordeal of the Longhouse: The Peoples of the Iroquois League in the Era of European Colonization* (Chapel Hill: University of North Carolina Press, 1992), 263–8, quote at 266; for the Shawnees, see Donald H. Kent, ed., *Pennsylvania Indian Treaties, 1737–1756*, in Alden T. Vaughan, gen. ed., *Early American Indian Documents: Laws and Treaties* (Frederick, MD: University Publications of America, 1984), 2: 5–6; for the Hudson River, see *Johnson Papers*, 7: 348; 9: 464; for the Choctaws, see "Papers Relating to Congress with Choctaw and Chickasaw Indians," 148–51; *DAR*, 8: 127; 13: 81; 14: 113; C.O. 5/78: 126, 128, 130; Richard White, *The Roots of Dependency: Subsistence, Environment, and Social Change among the Choctaws, Pawnees, and Navajos* (Lincoln: University of Nebraska Press, 1983), 74–5, 85; for the Cherokees, see Tom Hatley, *The Dividing Paths: Cherokees and South Carolinians through the Era of the Revolution* (New York: Oxford University Press, 1993), 48–51. Peter C. Mancall, "'The Bewitching Tyranny of Custom': The Social Costs of Indian Drinking in Colonial America," *American Indian Culture and Research Journal* 17 (1993), 15–42.

27 Walter Pilkington, ed., *The Journals of Samuel Kirkland* (Clinton, NY: Hamilton College, 1980), 38.

28 Public Records Office, Kew, England, Colonial Office Records, Series 5: America and West Indies (hereafter C.O.) 5/90: 87.

29 J. Leitch Wright, Jr., *The Only Land They Knew* (New York: Free Press, 1981), 154, 166.

30   *DAR*, vol. 12: 194; *Colonial Records of North Carolina*, 10: 767; C.O. 5/82: 114; Clements Library, Gage Papers, 137, item 8.

31   Reuben G. Thwaites, ed., *The Jesuit Relations and Allied Documents*, 73 vols. (Cleveland, Ohio: Burrows, 1896–1901), 67: 85–97, 143–5.

32   Terry G. Jordan and Matti Kaups, *The American Backwoods Frontier: An Ethnic and Ecological Interpretation* (Baltimore: Johns Hopkins University Press, 1987), 87–92.

33   *Journals of Major Robert Rogers* (London, 1765), vi–vii.

34   Richard J. Hooker, ed., *The Carolina Backcountry on the Eve of the Revolution: The Journal and Other Writings of Charles Woodmason, Anglican Itinerary* (Chapel Hill: University of North Carolina Press, 1953), 61; C.O. 5/90: 87 (Gage); McClure quoted in White, *Middle Ground*, 341; Benson, ed., *Kalm's Travels in North America*, 2: 462, 560; David Hackett Fischer, *Albion's Seed: Four British Folkways in America* (New York: Oxford University Press, 1989), 681; Lawrence Kinnaird, ed., "Clark–Leyba Papers," *American Historical Review* 41 (1935–6), 95, 97.

35   *Johnson Papers*, vol. 13: 194.

36   James Axtell, *The European and the Indian: Essays in the Ethnohistory of Colonial America* (New York: Oxford University Press, 1981), 302.

37   Richter, *Ordeal of the Longhouse*, ch. 11, quote at 271.

38   Logan quoted in Maldwyn A. Jones, "The Scotch-Irish in America," in Bernard Bailyn and Philip Morgan, eds., *Strangers within the Realm: Cultural Margins of the First British Empire* (Chapel Hill: University of North Carolina Press, 1991), 297.

39   Francis Jennings, *The Invasion of America: Indians, Colonialism, and the Cant of Conquest* (New York: Norton, 1976), 128–45.

40   Michael D. Green, *The Politics of Indian Removal: Creek Government and Society in Crisis* (Lincoln: University of Nebraska Press, 1982), 26.

41   White, *Middle Ground* 344.

42   "The Letters of James Habersham, 1756–1775," *Collections of the Georgia Historical Society* 6 (1904), 199.

43   Quoted in Thomas P. Slaughter, *The Whiskey Rebellion: Frontier Epilogue to the American Revolution* (New York: Oxford University Press, 1986), 65–6.

44   Bernard Bailyn, *Faces of Revolution: Personalities and Themes in the Struggle for American Independence* (New York: Knopf, 1990), 172.

45   Quoted in David J. Weber, *The Spanish Frontier in North America* (New Haven: Yale University Press, 1993), 272.

46   Hamilton College Library, Brothertown Records, 1774–1804; *American Archives*, 4th series, 2: 1047.

47   *DAR*, 3: 254–5.

48   *DAR*, 5: 202–4; 9: 90; Clarence Edwin Carter, ed., *The Correspondence of General Gage*, 2 vols. (New Haven, CT: Yale University Press, 1931–3), I: 334–6.

49   White, *Middle Ground*, 456.

50   Lester Cappon, ed., *The Adams–Jefferson Letters*, 2 vols. (Chapel Hill: University of North Carolina Press, 1959), 2: 307.

51   De Peyster to Gage, May 5, 1775, Clements Library, Gage Papers, vol. 128.

The Carolina Backcountry on the Eve of the Revolution: The Journal and Other Writings of Charles Woodmason, Anglican Itinerant (1766–8)

Charles Woodmason

September 12th [1766] Sett off from Charlestown to enter on my Mission – Wet to the Skin in several claps of Thunder – and greatly fatigu'd thro' Horses failing during this hot Weather.

Sunday 14th Officiated at St Marks Church 80 Miles from Town – 70 in Congregation – which is double the Number in Common—80 [miles][1]
    The Roads hot and Sandy – and Weather excessive Sultry.

16th Arriv'd at Pine Tree Hill and Centre of my Distric. This Week employ'd in riding the Environs and baptizing.—50 [miles]; 40 [miles]

Sunday 21st Officiated in the Presbyterian Meeting House to about 200 Hearers, Cheifly Presbyterians. Offer'd to give Sermon twice on ev'ry Sunday. Rejected.
    Beside this Meeting House, there is another of Quakers with a large Congregation – But they have neither Pastor or Teacher or Speaker at Either.
    The People around, of abandon'd Morals, and profligate Principles – Rude – Ignorant – Void of Manners, Education or Good Breeding – No genteel or Polite Person among them – save Mr. Kershaw an English Merchant settled here. The people are of all Sects and Denominations – A mix'd Medley from all Countries and the Off Scouring of America. Baptized 20 Children this Week and rode about 40 Miles Miles Brought over 220.

September 28 Officiated in the Meeting House – Promoted a Petition to the General Assembly to have a Chapel built, which ev'ry one of ev'ry Class and Sect sign'd. About 150 persons present at Service.
    Received Great Civilities from Mr. Samuel Wyly, an eminent Quaker in the Neighbourhood – who kindly rode about with me to make me known to the People.
    Not a House to be hir'd – Nor even a single Room on all this River to be rented, fit to put my Head or Goods in – The People all new Settlers,

extremely poor – Live in Logg Cabbins like Hogs – and their Living and Behaviour as rude or more so than the Savages. Extremely embarrassed how to subsist. Took up my Quarters in a Tavern – and exposed to the Rudeness of the Mobb. People continually drunk.

The Country being very Sickly, Mr. Kershaw would not permit me to move abroad much as this Week. Married a Couple – for the 1st Time – Woman very bigg.—20 [miles]

My English Servant Man whom I brought over, taken with the Fever. Excessive hot Weather for the Season.

October 5th The Season very dry – and people in Great distress for want of Provisions – Greatly relieved by the Kindness of Mr. Kershaw, who open'd all his Stores to them.

Offer'd to take 20 Boys and educate them Gratis would they fit up a Room for a School, which they promis'd to do.

About 100 People this day at Service – Offer'd to catchecise their Children in the Afternoon, but none brought – Do not find but one religious person among this Great Multitude.

The Weather comes more moderate. But my Horse quite worn down for want of Grass.—25 [miles]

October 8th Received a Subpena from C. T. [Charles Town] to attend Court to give Evidence in a Suit at Law; Went down the Country. Preached at the High Hills of Santee. Met here with some serious Christians But the Generality very loose, dissolute, Idle People – Without either Religion or Goodness – The same may be said of the whole Body of the People in these Back Parts.—[total] miles 305

Received at St Marks by Col Richardson – a Worthy sensible Gentleman and Pious Christian – Once more in a Christian family.—50 [miles] . . .

Sunday [December] 28 Officiated as usual at Pine Tree. Congregation about 80 people Tho' they are so populous around, that 500 might attend if they would.

January 1, 1767 Gave them a Sermon suited to the Day – and set off to accompany the Cheif Justice in his Return – The Tavern Keeper (who is a Rich fellow, and Who has made an Estate by encouraging Vice and Idleness) affronted at my Discourse against Immorality as if aim'd against Him – He cryed out like Demetrius that the Craft was in Danger – And (but behind our Backs) abus'd both my Self and Cheif Justice, vowing Vengeance on both.

Jan. 3) Took leave of my Hon'd Friend – and on Jan. 4.) assembled the People at the High Hills, and gave them Service.—25 [miles]

Had a large Congregation – but according to Custom, one half of them got drunk before they went home.

Next Day cross'd the River (Wateree) into the Fork to baptize several Children – A Shocking Passage. Obliged to cut the Way thro' the Swamp for 4 Miles, thro' Canes, and impenetrable Woods – Had my Cloaths torn to Pieces – After meeting some Religious People return'd back the same Way: and went down to St Marks Church w[h]ere I officiated on Sunday Jan. 11. and then returned back to Pine Tree Hill.—25 [miles]; 75 [miles]

Jan. 18) Officiated as usual at Pine Tree – and received an Invitation from the people on Pedee River to visit them – With Man and Horse to carry me, where (after many Difficulties, – much fatigue, and suffering Hunger, Cold, and no Bed to lye on, but only the Ground) I arrived the 22d—80 [miles]; 1300 [total miles]

Sunday January 25, 1767 A Congregation at the Cheraws of above 500 People. Baptiz'd about 60 Children – Quite jaded out – standing and speaking 6 Hours together and nothing to refresh me, but Water – and their Provisions I could not touch – All the Cookery of these People being exceeding filthy, and most execrable.

Next Day, I returned and preached the 27th in my Way back at Lynch's Creek to a great Multitude of People assembled together, being the 1st Episcopal Minister they had seen since their being in the province – They complain'd of being eaten up by Itinerant Teachers, Preachers, and Imposters from New England and Pensylvania – Baptists, New Lights, Presbyterians, Independants, and an hundred other Sects – So that one day You might hear this System of Doctrine – the next day another – next day another, retrograde to both – Thus by the Variety of Taylors who would pretend to know the best fashion in which Christs Coat is to be worn none will put it on – And among the Various Plans of Religion, they are at Loss which to adapt, and consequently are without any Religion at all. They came to Sermon with Itching Ears only, not with any Disposition of Heart, or Sentiment of Mind – Assemble out of Curiosity, not Devotion, and seem so pleas'd with their native Ignorance, as to be offended at any Attempts to rouse them out of it.—40 [miles]

I was almost tir'd in baptizing of Children – and laid my Self down for the Night frozen with the Cold – without the least Refreshment – No Eggs, Butter, Flour, Milk, or anything, but fat rusty Bacon, and fair Water, with Indian Corn Bread, Viands I had never before seen or tasted.—1340 [total miles]

I set off next day for Pine Tree, glad to be once more under the Roof of the good Samaritan, Mr. Kershaw, who poured Wine and Oil into my

Wounds, and would have prevented my moving from him for a Space:
But I was obliged to travel upwards – having engaged my Self for next
Sunday at the Settlement of Irish Presbyterians called the Waxaws,
among whome were several Church People.—40 [miles]

This is a very fruitful fine Spot, thro' which the dividing Line between
North and South Carolina runs – The Heads of P. D. [Peedee] River,
Lynch's Creek, and many other Creeks take their Rise in this Quarter –
so that a finer Body of Land is no where to be seen – But it is occupied
by a Sett of the most lowest vilest Crew breathing – Scotch Irish Presbyterians from the North of Ireland – They have built a Meeting House
and have a Pastor, a Scots Man among them – A good Sort of Man –
He once was of the Church of England, and solicited for Orders, but
was refus'd – whereon he went to Pensylvania, and got ordained by
the Presbytery there, who allow him a Stipend to preach to these
People, who (in his Breast) he heartily contemns – They will not suffer
him to use the Lords Prayer. He wants to introduce Watts' Psalms in
place of the barbarous Scotch Version – but they will not admit it – His
Congregation is very large – This Tract of Land being most surprisingly
thick settled beyond any Spot in England of its Extent – Seldom less
than 9, 10, 1200 People assemble of a Sunday – They never heard
an Episcopal Minister, or the Common Prayer, and were very curious
– The Church people among them are thinly scatter'd but they had a
numerous Progeny for Baptism – rather chusing they should grow up to
Maturity without Baptism than they should receive it by the hands of
Sectaries – So in Compliance with their Request to visit them, I appointed Sunday the 31st to go up to them – and the Presbyterian
Minister was to come down to this Meeting House in my Absence.—
1380 [total miles]

He came down on the Friday. I stay'd till Saturday till I moved – when
there arose such a Storm of Wind, Rain, Hail and Storm, as I think I
hardly ever before saw. I could not stir out of the House, and was obliged
to keep close Quarters.

But above, it was Fair Weather, and more than a thousand people
assembled to attend my coming – and returned greatly vex'd and dis-
apointed – Whereon I sent them Word, I would attend them very
soon.

Accordingly I wrote them (and enclosed advertisements) that I would
be with them (if Health and Weather permitted) the last Sunday in
February.

Mean time went down to the High Hills where I officiated and
baptiz'd on Sunday the 7th. Next day at St Marks – giving the people
Sermons and Lectures, in various Places, and at different Houses as I
went along – For I found it here, the same as at Lynch's Creek and the

Cheraws – Wherever you went to a House to marry or baptize, a Multitude would assemble, and desire a Discourse; which I was more ready alway to give, than they to ask.

At all these Places I've been at, I read the King's Proclamation against Vice and Immorality, which has had very good Effects. For thro' want of Ministers to marry and thro' the licentiousness of the People, many hundreds live in Concubinage – swopping their Wives as Cattel, and living in a State of Nature, more irregularly and unchastely than the Indians – I therefore made Public Notice ev'ry where be given, that whoever did not attend to be legally married, I would prosecute them at the Sessions – and that all who had liv'd in a State of Concubinage on application to me, I would marry Gratis – Numbers accepted of my Offer, and were married, and then I baptiz'd their Children – Several who were Episcopal, and who had been married by Itinerant Dissenting Ministers desir'd to be re-married by the Liturgy, as judging such their former Marriage invalid.—[total] Miles 1380

As there are no Clergy in North Carolina, the Magistrates are there permitted to Marry – and many of this Province travel over there for to be join'd – Several Couple married by them apply'd likewise to be re-married, as judging such their former Marriage temporary only.

From St Marks I returned to Pine Tree Hill, where my Good Samaritan had finish'd off two upper Rooms in a House belonging to an Old Widow Dutch Woman – And about this Time the Waggons with my Goods and Library came from C. T. the Carriage of which cost me Seven Guineas.—50 [miles] . . .

In Consequence of an Appointment and Invitation, went over the River to Rocky Mount, w[h]ere was kindly received by the younger Mr. Kershaw.—10 [miles]

Rocky Mount is an Hill on the West Side Wateree River, about 20 Miles below the Province Line. It is very elevated, and a fine Situation. The Land is good, and plowed to the Summit, bringing Wheat Rye Indian Corn and all kind of Grain and Fruit Trees – This is [a] most delightful healthy part of this Country – No Bogs, Marshes, Swamps, Fogs, Insects to annoy you. Its but newly settled. But the People are already crowded together as thick as in England.

On the 31 of March (Sunday) I gave Service to about 400 people among whom a great Number of Baptists and Presbyterians. I had here a good Clerk, and excellent Singing. The Women sing as well or better than the Girls at the Magdalene Chapel, London – They all came from Virginia and Pensylvania – Not an English person or Carolinian among them – I baptiz'd 4 Children and promised to visit them Monthly. . . .

July 2. Returned from Rocky Mount – 3d Gave Sermon at Beaver Creek and Baptiz'd several Negroes and Mullatoos. Married several Couple on the Proclamation – 5th Gave Service at Pine Tree and 12th at Rafting Creek – the 19th at Lynch's Creek – where received an Invitation to preach to a Congregation on Granny Quarter Creek, which I attended next Day, and found about 100 people assembled together – More rude ignorant, and void of things, than any Circle hitherto among. Not a Bible or Prayer Book – Not the least Rudiments of Religion, Learning, Manners or Knowledge (save of Vice) among them.—65 [miles]; 60 [miles]

Such a Pack I never met with – Neither English, Scots Irish, or Carolinian by Birth – Neither of one Church or other or of any denomination by Profession, not having (like some of the Lynchs Creek people) ever seen a Minister – heard or read a Chapter in the Scriptures, or heard a Sermon in their days.—15 [miles] ...

I forgot to set down that in the last Excursion from Lynchs Creek to the Cheraws, my Horse fail'd and was obliged to stay in the Woods, in the Night when he got from me and I got lost – wandering a Day and Night in the Wilderness, not knowing where I was, famished, and without any Sustenance.

Thus You have the Travels of a Minister in the Wild Woods of America – Destitute often of the very Necessaries of Life – Sometimes starved – Often famished – Exposed to the burning Sun and scorching Sands – Obliged to fight his Way thro' Banditti, profligates, Reprobates, and the lowest vilest Scum of Mankind on the one hand, and of the numerous Sectaries pregnant in these Countries, on the other – With few Friends, and fewer Assistants – and surmounting Difficulties, and braving Dangers, that ev'ry Clergyman that ever entered this Province shrinked even at the thoughts off – Which none, not even the meanest of the Scotch Clergy that have been sent here, would undertake, and for which he subjected himself to the Laughter of Fools and Ridicule of the Licentiousness [sic] for undertaking.

Number of Persons married this Year about	40	Couple
Children baptized about	760	782
Adults	10	that took a
Negroes and Mullatoes	12	Register off.

Beside many others, whose Names were not given in, or attended too.

No other Clergyman of the Church of England from the Sea to the Mountains, on the North Side of Santee River to the Province Line. Number of Miles rode this year (All perform'd by one Horse) 3185. May say, full four thousand Miles. ...

Note

1   Woodmason's manuscript journal included notes in the margin that recorded
    the number of miles he had traveled on each of his trips. In addition, he
    sometimes made a record of the total number of miles he had traveled since
    the beginning of his journeys. These numbers appear in the text as [miles]
    when they record only the length of his most recent journey, and as [total
    miles] when they refer to the cumulative miles traveled since the time he
    began to keep the journal.

On Behalf of the Ohio Delawares, Munsies, and Mohicans, to the Governors of Pennsylvania, Maryland, and Virginia (December 4, 1771)

John Killbuck

[4 December]

Brethren, in former times our forefathers and yours lived in great friendship together and often met to strengthen the chain of their friendship. As your people grew numerous we made room for them and came over the Great Mountains to Ohio. And some time ago when you were at war with the French your soldiers came into this country, drove the French away and built forts. Soon after a number of your people came over the Great Mountains and settled on our lands. We complained of their encroachments into our country, and, brethren, you either could not or would not remove them. As we did not choose to have any disputes with our brethren, the English, we agreed to make a line and the Six Nations at Fort Stanwix three years ago sold the King all the lands on the east side of the Ohio down to the Cherokee River, which lands were the property of our confederacy, and gave a deed to Sir William Johnson as he desired. Since that time great numbers more of your people have come over the Great Mountains and settled throughout this country. And we are sorry to tell you that several quarrels have happened between your people and ours, in which people have been killed on both sides, and that we now see the nations round us and your people ready to embroil in a quarrel, which gives our nation great concern, as we on our parts want to live in friendship with you, as you have always told us you have laws to govern your people by (but we do not see that you have). Therefore, brethren, unless you can fall upon some method of governing your people who live between the Great Mountains and the Ohio River and who are now very numerous, it will be out of the Indians' power to govern their young men, for we assure you the black clouds begin to gather fast in this country. And if something is not soon done those clouds will deprive us of seeing the sun. We desire you to give the greatest attention to what we now tell you as it comes from our hearts and a desire we have to live in peace and friendship with our brethren the English. And therefore it grieves us to see some of the nations about us and your people ready to strike each other. We find your people are very fond of our rich land. We see them quarrelling every day about land and burning one another's houses. So that we do not know how soon they may come over the River Ohio and drive us from our villages, nor do we see you brethren take any care to stop them. It's now several years since we have met together in council, which all nations are surprised and concerned at. What is the reason you kindled a fire at Ohio for us to meet you (which we did and talked friendly together) that you have let your fire go out for some years past? This makes all nations jealous about us as we also frequently hear of our brethren the English meeting with Cherokees and with the Six Nations to strengthen their friendship, which gives us cause to think you are forming some bad designs against us who lives between the Ohio and Lakes. I have now told you everything that is in my heart and desire you will write what I have said and send it to the Great King. A belt. Killbuck, speaker.

A Journal of Two Visits made to Some Nations of Indians on the West Side of the River Ohio, in the Years 1772 and 1773

David Jones

... *Tuesday 12*, having taken breakfast with Mr. Butlar and Mr. Nailar, set out for Pickaweeke in company with my Indian friend, whose name is *Cutteway*, his wife and some others. It may be well thought that my journey was solitary, for three words of the Shawannee language were not known by me, and as little English by my fellow-traveller; so that we could converse none by the way. The day being cold induced us to ride fast, so that about two o'clock we came to the town. About one mile from the town my Indian friend cast off, and hid part of his load, and leaving the women behind, made signs for me to ride on with him. Perhaps the reason of his conduct was, lest we should be molested by drunken Indians; for when they are intoxicated, their abuses are not confined to white people, but they will even rob Indians. Drawing near the town, many thoughts arose about the event, for to me it was not known that there was one white man in town; but all anxiety was removed by seeing Mr. Joseph Nicholas, a former acquaintance when at Fort Pitt. With kindness he received and entertained me with such refreshments as the situation afforded. While we were refreshing ourselves Mr. John Irwine came in, and invited me home with him. Mr. Irwine's chief habitation is a small town, situated W. N. W. of Pickaweeke about three miles. By the English it is called Blue Jackets Town, an Indian of that name residing there. Before this is described, it is proper to take notice of Pickaweeke – it is situated south of a brook that, east of the town, empties into Deer Creek. It takes its name from a nation of Indians called Picks, some of them being the first settlers – the word signifies "the place of the Picks." Now it consists of about one hundred souls, being a mixture of Shawannees and other nations, so that it is called a Shawannee town. It is the most remarkable town for robbers and villains, yet it pretends to have its chief men, who are indeed very scoundrels guilty of theft and robbery without any apology or redress. Some of these took four or five mares from Mr. McMechen on Ohio, nor was there any prospect of redress. Leaving this, went with Mr. Irwine to his habitation. This town is situated east of Deer Creek, and north of a large plain. This creek is clear and beautiful, appearing useful for mills and healthful for the inhabitants. The buildings here are logs, their number about twelve. This is a peaceable town, and in it lives *Kishshinottisthee*, who is called a king, and is one of the head men of this nation. The English of his name is *Hardman*.

Wednesday 13, Mr. Irwine invited the king and some of his friends to take breakfast with me, having previously informed him that I was no trader, but was a good man, whose employment among white people was to speak of GOD and heavenly matters, and came with that view to see my brothers the Indians. None of this nation ever saw a minister, except a chance one at some fort; so that they have little prepossessions only what are natural. When the king met me, it was with all appearance of friendship, and respectfully gave me the right-hand of fellowship, with some kind of obeisance. His friends that came with him he ordered to do the same. When breakfast was ready, which consisted of fat buffalo, beavers tails and chocolate – in a solemn manner, acknowledged the goodness of GOD, desiring Mr. Irwine to acquaint him with the design of my proceeding, and he said the king approved well of it. In our conference at breakfast, he desired to know my business among them, seeing that I was no trader – told him that I could not give a full answer, being a stranger to their language, and not yet having got a good interpreter to speak for me, but expected one, and then he should fully know my business. At present told him only a few things, because Mr. Irwine could not interpret only in common affairs, not having long traded in this nation. – Kishshinottisthee is indeed a man of good sense, and by all that appeared was my hearty friend. He was desirous that I should instruct them into the knowledge of GOD, but he was only one, and there were many against me, especially at *Chillicaathee*. During my present stay, visited the king in his own dwelling, and was always received kindly, treating me with hickory nuts, which is part of their food, being much superior to any of that kind in our eastern world. He is neither distinguished in apparel or house, that being one of the least in town, being about fourteen feet by twelve. He may be said to possess some degree of hospitality – being much indisposed one day, the king's wife came with what was thought might suit a weak stomach as a present to me; the dish consisted of pumkins which had been dried, but were now boiled, and with it some bears oil to eat with the pumkin. As it was a demonstration of benevolence, tho' my appetite was poor, yet I eat a little. About this time it snowed near six inches deep, and for some days it felt near as cold as winter in Philadelphia, though it is thought to be about two degrees south, so that cold weather in common is not long. Before removal from this town captain McKee, in company with major Smallman arrived. Mr. McKee is now agent for this department of Indians, and as his influence might be great, acquainted him with my design. He appeared to be pleased, promising to do what was in his power to make my journey prosperous. The Indians having told me, that my old interpreter David Owens was down Ohio below the falls towards the Waabash river, therefore inquired of Mr. McKee for an interpreter – he recommended one whose name is Caesar, who was a foreigner, and, as he said, understood something about religion, and therefore would be best for an interpreter on that subject – but was so unhappy as never to see him. We parted expecting to see each other at Chillicaathee. It was with reluctance this town was left, before an opportunity was obtained to instruct the Indians; but being destitute of an interpreter, concluded to move to the chief town.

Friday 22, in company with Mr. Irwine, set out for Chillicaathee, and arrived there in the afternoon. Here Mr. Irwine kept an assortment of goods, and for that purpose rented an house from an Indian whose name is *Waappee Monneeto*, in English, often called the White Devil, but the word Monneeto is not of any certain signification. Went to see Mr. Moses Henry a gunsmith and trader from Lancaster. This gentleman has lived for some years in this town, and is lawfully married to a white woman, who was captivated so young that she speaks the language as well as any Indian. She is a daughter of major Collins, formerly an inhabitant of the south branch of Potomack, but now lives near the Little Canhawa on Ohio. Mr. Henry lives in a comfortable manner, having plenty of good beef, pork, milk, &c. His generosity to me was singular, and equal to my highest wishes. Soon after my arrival, dieted altogether with Mr. Henry; but slept on my blankets at Mr. Irwine's. By living on such victuals as formerly used, soon recovered my health, in a comfortable degree. Chillicaathee is the chief town of the Shawannee Indians – it is situated north of a large plain adjacent to a branch of Paint Creek. This plain is their corn-field, which supplies great part of their town. Their houses are made of logs, nor is there any more regularity observed in this particular than in their morals, for any man erects his house as fancy directs. North of this town are to be seen the remains of an old fortification, the area of which may be fifteen acres. It lies near four square, and appears to have had gates at each corner, and in the middle likewise. From the west middle gate, went a circular entrench-ment including about ten acres, which seems designed to defend on all quarters. This circle included a spring. Mr. Irwine told that another exactly in this form is to be seen on the river Siota, the banks of which remain so high as to intercept sight of men on horseback. 'Tis evident to all travellers that this country has been inhabited formerly by a martial race of mankind enjoying the use of iron, for such entrenchments, as appear in various places, could not have been made otherwise: but of this part of antiquity we shall remain ignorant.

Saturday 23, in company with Mr. Irwine, went to see captain McKee, who lives three miles about west and by north from Chillicaathee in a small town called *Wockachaalli*, which signifies Crooked Nose's Place. Here the captain's Indian relatives live, and some others. This seems only a new town, not having as yet much ground cleared. 'Tis situated east of a creek, which I suppose to be a branch of Paint Creek. Some of the Indians of this town have a large number of the best horses in the nation; nor are they worse supplied with cattle, so that they chiefly live by stock. Captain McKee was very courteous, and still promised well. – Returned the same evening to Chillicaathee. The day following, being Lord's day, remained at Mr. Henry's reading *Sherlock* on revealed reli-gion, which is a good book on that subject, and may be profitable to the reader: but if the author could have visited the Indians, he might have saved many arguments, and perhaps been more fully convinced, that without revelation there would have been little, or rather no religion among mankind. It is granted, that the apostle speaks of the Gentiles which have not the law, yet do *by nature* the things contained in the law, &c. 'Tis true that *nature may* direct to some parts of the second table of the law, which includes our duty to *man*; but it is far from being evident, that it directs to the first table, which includes our *duty more immediately to God*; nay, the scripture sayeth in this point, "that there is none that understandeth, there is none that seeketh after God" [Romans 3: 11]. Had a deeper sensation of this truth, when amongst the Indians, than is common with us. In this town were near twenty white people, some at least of them were disposed to hear the gospel, but dare not preach without leave from the Indians; for tho' when among us they are lambs, found them *lions* at home. To be debarred from preaching on the Lord's day was very grievous, and made the day seem very long; nay, it seemed impracticable to attempt social prayer, for not a minute was certain to be free from the insults of rude heathens. How great is the mercy to enjoy opportunities of worshipping God without fear! yet alas! how many are insensible of it! and under all advantages, remain *real heathens* in practice; "how shall we escape if we neglect so great salvation?"...

February 1, an Indian lately returned named *Othaawaapeelethee*, in English the Yellow Hawk, came with some others to Mr. Henry's to converse with me. This Indian is one of their chiefs, and esteems himself as a great speaker and very wise: and this may be justly said of him, that he is saucy enough. On this occasion Mr. John Gibson a trader, was my interpreter, being a man both of sense and learning. After common formalities were past, he told me that he wanted to know my business among them; for he understood that I was no trader. First, informed him from whence I came, and that my chief business was to instruct them from GOD, for his mind was revealed to us, &c. – That I had a great desire for many years to see my brothers the Indians – now wanted to talk with them, and was in hopes that he would allow me an opportunity. He replied that he thought something of that nature was my business. Then he proceeded to make a long *speech*, not with a very pleasant countenance, nor the most agreeable tone of voice, and replied to this effect, viz. "When GOD, who at first made us all, prescribed our way of living, he allowed white people to live one way, and Indians another way; and as he was one of the chiefs of this town, he did not desire to hear me on the subject of religion, for he was resolved not to believe what might be said, nor pay any regard to it. And he believed it would be the mind of the other Indians." His thoughts were only natural, and seemed to have no other conceptions of my instructions, than as referring to the common affairs of life, consisting in living *like* white folks.

He said that they had lived a long time as they now do, and liked it very well, and he and his people would live as they had done. This Indian seemed like some among us, who consider religion only as state policy. And without doubt there is enough of such religion in the world, even under the name of the CHRISTIAN; but this affects not the nature of the religion of the Son of GOD, whose *kingdom* is not of this world, but is purely *spiritual*, which does not promise its avouchers *livings* and WORLDLY preferments; but what is infinitely greater, it assures all that truly embrace it, that tho' in this world they may have tribulations, yet in that which is to come, they shall inherit *eternal* life. HOW often do we find it true, that the natural man receiveth not the things of the spirit of GOD. This Indian supposed that I would learn them to read, and said it would look very foolish for a man to have a book before him learning to read when old. In reply I said, that suppose GOD gave us the right way of living at first, that if any of us got wrong, it would be kind in the other to say, brother, you have missed your way, this is the road you should follow. Adding that he did not know what I would say before he heard me; that he could not tell but what he might like it. And if he would give liberty, if I did not speak good, he might tell me, and I would say no more. He replied that it did not signify to make any trial, for let me say what I would, he was resolved not to believe me. Indians can bear no contradiction, therefore by this time his savage soul began to be raised. Finding that no good could be done by saying any thing more, for it was only making bad worse; therefore as the weather was cold, and had no horse, begged liberty to stay in town till I could remove. This was granted with coldness.

He said, may be some other nation might receive me, and I might go to them. From this time prepared for my journey, only waiting for good weather. . . .

Thursday 11, set out for a small town called Conner's, a man of that name residing there.

Our course was near northeast – the distance was less than the preceding day's journey, so that we arrived to town some time before sunset. Travelled this day over a good country, only wanting inhabitants. This town is situated near no creek, a good spring supplying them with water – the land about it is level and good, the timber being chiefly blackoak, indicates it will produce good wheat, if a trial was made. Mr. Conner, who is a white man, a native of Maryland, told me that he intended to sow wheat in the fall following, and was resolved to proceed to farming at all events. 'Tis probable that he will be as good as his word, for he is a man that seems not to fear GOD, and it is likely that he will not regard man. His connections will favour his attempts, for according to their way, he and the chief Indian of this town are married to two sisters. These women were captives, and it is likely from childhood, for they have the very actions of Indians, and speak broken English. It seemed strange to me to see the captives have the exact gestures of Indians. Might we not infer from hence, that if Indians were educated as we are, they would be like us? This town consists of Shawannees and Delawares; and some of them dwell in pretty good log houses well shingled with nails. Mr. Conner keeps a sort of a tavern, and has moderate accommodations, and though he is not what he should be, yet he was kind to me.

Friday 12, here we parted with some of our company, whose absence was very agreeable, and in company with Mr. Duncan, set out for New-Comer's Town, which is the chief town of the Delawares. Had gone but a few miles till we came to the Little Shawannee Woman's Town. This is situated on the west side of Muskingum, and chiefly consists of Shawannees. Here we crossed the river in a canoe, our horses swimming by its side. The country began to be hilly, interspersed with some barren plains. We passed Captain White Eye's Town, but this noted Indian was down Ohio, perhaps with my old interpreter, so that I could not have the satisfaction of seeing him this time, but I saw him several times the first visit. He was the only Indian I met with in all my travels, that seemed to have a design of accomplishing something future. He told me that he intended to be religious, and have his children educated. He saw that their way of living would not answer much longer – game grew scarce – they could not much longer pretend to live by hunting, but must farm, &c. – But said, he could not attend to matters of religion now, for he intended to make a great *hunt* down Ohio, and take the skins himself to Philadelphia. I was informed that he accomplished this, and went round by the gulf of Florida to Philadelphia. On this occasion, could not but think of that text of scripture, which says, "one went to his farm and another to his merchandise." And it may be said, the Indian went to his hunting. This was the case last year, and perhaps something as important may employ the next year, and so the life of man is spent, few remembring that ONE THING is *needful*.

Further Reading

Calloway, Colin, *New Worlds for All: Indians, Europeans, and the Remaking of Early America*. Baltimore: Johns Hopkins University Press, 1997.

Cayton, Andrew R. L. and Fredrika J. Teute (eds.), *Contact Points: American Frontiers from the Mohawk Valley to the Mississippi, 1750–1830*. Chapel Hill: University of North Carolina Press, 1998.

Dowd, Gregory Evans, *A Spirited Resistance: The North American Indian Struggle for Unity, 1745–1815*. Baltimore: Johns Hopkins University Press, 1992.

Hatley, Tom, *The Dividing Paths: Cherokees and South Carolinians through the Era of Revolution*. New York: Oxford University Press, 1993.

Hinderaker, Eric, *Elusive Empires: Constructing Colonialism in the Ohio Valley, 1673–1800*. New York: Cambridge University Press, 1997.

Mancall, Peter C., *Deadly Medicine: Indians and Alcohol in Early America*. Ithaca: Cornell University Press, 1995.

Merrell, James, *The Indians' New World: Catawbas and Their Neighbors from European Contact through the Era of Removal*. New York: W. W. Norton, 1989.

Merrell, James, *Into the American Woods: Negotiators on the Pennsylvania Frontier*. New York: W. W. Norton, 1999.

Perdue, Theda, *Cherokee Women: Gender and Culture Change, 1700–1835*. Lincoln: University of Nebraska Press, 1998.

Saunt, Claudio, *A New Order of Things: Property, Power, and the Transformation of the Creek Indians, 1733–1816*. New York: Cambridge University Press, 1999.

White, Richard, *The Middle Ground: Indians, Empires, and Republics in the Great Lakes Region, 1650–1815*. New York: Cambridge University Press, 1991.

Index

Page numbers in italics denote illustrations

task system
  and low country slaves   163, 173
taste
  and gentility   300, 315, 316
Taylor, Edward   51, 52–3
thunder and lightning   48–9
Tillett, Ruth
  petition against Zachareah
    Jordan   99, 139–40
Tillotson, John   245
tobacco cultivation   98–9, 167, *168*,
    172, 173
Tunxis Indians   14
Turner, Frederick Jackson   198,
    336
Turner, William   43–4

Uncas (Mohegan saschem)   13

Virginia colony   2, 98, 210
Virginia Gazette   243
Virginia Slave Codes   99, 130–9
Voiture, Vincent   308

Walsh, Lorena   253
Wampanoagm Indians   21–3
Wardwell, Samuel   65
Warren, Mercy Otis   309–10
Washington, George   285–6, 288,
    316
  'Rules of Civility'   279, 280, 311
Washington, Martha   277
Water, Joseph   113
Wedgewood, Josiah   243, 254
Weekly History   244–5, 249
Wentworth, Benning   204
Wesley, John   240, 243, 252, 257
West India Company   148, 149
Weston, Thomas   58
wheat cultivation   172
Wheelwright, John   62
White, Richard   341, 346, 353
Whitefield, George   236, 237–61
  advance publicity and use of print to
    promote work   238–9, 240
  and advertising   241, 249

appropriation of commercial
    techniques to publicize
    revivals   237, 238
on commerce and religion   257
creative pricing schemes for
    publications   248–9
dissemination of journals through
    various media forms   247–8
and fund-raising   251
and Georgia orphan house
    (Bethesda)   255, 256, 259
influence on and encouragement of
    evangelical entrepreneurs   259
inspiration and influences in
    appropriating commercial means
    to promote revivals   252–3
and letter-writing network   247,
    258
marketing and merchandising
    techniques   248–9, 251, 255,
    258, 260
opposition to   249, 250, 260–1
press coverage and role of colonial
    newspapers in promoting
    239–41, 242–4
and printed sermons and
    journals   245–7
publications   259–60
relations with businessmen   258
relationship with Franklin   239,
    244, 245, 248, 249, 250
sensitivity to readers as
    consumers   245
serialization of sermons and
    journals   248
support of by merchants   257
testimonials and
    endorsements   250–1
use of mercantile imagery and
    commercial language   257–8
view of by Nathan Cole   236, 264–6
view of by Charles Chauncy
    267–9
wealth and possessions   251, 256
and *Weekly History*   244–5, 249
and world of commerce   255–6